John Allen Giles

Hebrew and Christian Records

Vol. 1 (Hebrew Records)

John Allen Giles

Hebrew and Christian Records
Vol. 1 (Hebrew Records)

ISBN/EAN: 9783337166427

Printed in Europe, USA, Canada, Australia, Japan

Cover: Foto ©ninafisch / pixelio.de

More available books at **www.hansebooks.com**

HEBREW AND CHRISTIAN RECORDS;

AN HISTORICAL ENQUIRY CONCERNING THE AGE AND AUTHORSHIP OF THE OLD AND NEW TESTAMENTS;

BY THE
REV. DR GILES,
RECTOR OF SUTTON, SURREY, AND FORMERLY FELLOW OF CORPUS CHRISTI COLLEGE, OXFORD.

NOW FIRST PUBLISHED COMPLETE.

VOL. I.—HEBREW RECORDS.

LONDON:
TRÜBNER & CO., LUDGATE HILL.
1877.

PREFACE.

THE works contained in these volumes, and now first published complete, were written nearly thirty years ago. A portion only—not quite half—was then printed, and withdrawn from circulation very soon after it issued from the press. The cause which led to this, and the results which followed, have probably been forgotten, or at all events, being now wholly unconnected with the subject, need not to be remembered.

Such questions as those which form the subject of these volumes, were less familiar then than they now are, and were indeed, if I may use the words of one of the most eminent clergymen and writers* of our times, "regarded as difficulties and as dangerous to religion, chiefly, I am persuaded, through the mistaken fear with which the advocates of religion regard them. As things now are, a man cannot prosecute a critical inquiry, as to the date and authors of the books of Scripture, without the fear of having his Christian faith impeached, should his conclusions, in any instance, be at variance with the common opinion." It is satisfactory to know that, since those words were written, there is less disposition to treat unfairly any attempt which is honestly and modestly made to extend the boundaries of Truth, and this

---

* Dr Arnold's Sermons, vol. iii, Appendix.

fact has perhaps had its weight in causing me to publish the whole of these works complete, as the result of thoughts which have occupied my mind since the earliest period to which memory goes back.

But the chief encouragement to publish these works complete has been the judgement which more than one writer has expressed in favour of the views which I have advocated, and of the moderation with which they have been stated. On such points as these the opinion quoted below, of the most eminent historian* that this country has produced during the last fifty years, cannot fail to be as satisfactory to the reader as it is flattering to myself. At a time also when so many interesting inquiries have arisen with regard to the origin and interpretation of our sacred books, " the adjustment of science and theology needs more than ever to be properly balanced." Our main preservative against all forms, both of superstition on the one hand and unbelief on the other, " is to be found in maintaining the truth and

---

* "Mr Grote lent me Dr Giles's Christian Records, which he recommended as one of the best hand-books concerning early Christianity and the Canon of the New Testament. He did not always agree with the author, but liked the way in which, besides many judicious criticisms, the *ipsissima verba* of the various authorities, both Pagan and Christian, are given within a short space." Letter from Babbage to Tollemache, in Macmillan's Magazine for April, 1873.

An anonymous correspondent, apparently the editor himself, of the Morning Advertiser (July 26, 1856) wrote as follows: "Dr Giles, it appears, is an advocate of the progressive principle, being of opinion that the revealed law is designed for man in every stage of society and state of improvement. In his *Christian Records*, he has made admirable use of the profound historical knowledge for which he is distinguished throughout Europe and America, and his researches have enabled him to do more for the truth of the New Testament against Infidels, Deists, and other antagonists, than all the preceding writers taken together. For example, certain discrepancies in the Gospels have hitherto furnished the strongest arguments against Christianity employed by Deists; and these arguments were never satisfactorily answered, by accounting for the disagreements in a natural and probable manner, before the appearance of Dr Giles's Christian Records, in which he shows himself a zealous defender of the Church of England."

authority of History, and the inestimable value of the historic spirit."* But it is above all important that the facts of history should be thoroughly sifted, for no history has ever yet appeared which can be taken without such examination in all its details. That this observation applies to the Old Testament as well as the New must be acknowledged by all who are competent to pass an unbiassed opinion on the subject. The whole of Christendom yields to the authority of the Bible, "not only because it is the most sacred of sacred oracles, but because it is the greatest of all great books."

It is the evidence of moral and intellectual greatness, as Dean Stanley justly says, which makes the Bible, even from a purely mental point of view, so invaluable an instrument in popular education, and may enable us to regard with indifference those difficulties and controversies upon matters of detail and the letter, which cannot touch the true "supernatural" element—that inner spiritual life which remains when criticism has done its best and its worst. "The early chapters of Genesis contain many things at which the man of science stumbles; but none will question their unapproachable sublimity. The Book of Isaiah furnishes endless matter for the critic; but the more fastidious he is, the more freely will he acknowledge its magnificence of thought and diction. The authorship of the four Gospels may be defended, attacked, and analyzed interminably; but the whole world bows down before the grandeur of the eight Beatitudes, and the Parable of the Prodigal Son, and the Farewell Discourses, and the story of Gethsemane and Calvary."

It is unnecessary to say more of the books which formed the canon of the Jews, and which enter largely, though in a lower degree, into that of all Christians: for it has been

---

* Gladstone.

fully admitted that these books are amenable to be tested in all the various modes which learning and science can suggest. It is then evident that the present works have reference chiefly to the latter and more valuable half of the Canonical Scriptures. For the Christian religion not only sets forth a peculiar morality little insisted upon, though not wholly unknown, among the ancient nations of the world, but propounds also a variety of speculative or scholastic doctrines, scarcely intelligible to the people—or even to a large number of their teachers—as the principles upon which it professes to base its moral code; and it recites a series of historical facts, on which both the moral and doctrinal codes are founded. The points of inquiry, then, to all who would study Christianity with minuteness, are three; 1. Its moral or practical character; 2. Its doctrines or speculative aspect; and, 3. Its historical evidence.

It is right to state, lest the general appearance of the present work should lead to a misconception of its nature, that it has nothing to do with the first and second points here referred to. It is only with the historical facts of Christianity in the second volume, as with the historical facts of Judaism in the first, that the present work is concerned, and even this field of inquiry has been narrowed within limits which give the work a specific character, not to be misunderstood, except by those who wilfully pervert or carelessly misinterpret the plain and obvious meaning of what they read.

My object has been to show in the first volume that the whole of the Old Testament, as it now appears, both style of language and order of events, is due, not to the first establishment of the Hebrews in Canaan fifteen hundred years before Christ, but to the re-establishment of the nation five hundred years before our era: and in the second volume that the historical books of the New Testament were not in their present form before the year 150 after Christ, but were then put forth, with the other books, to form the Christian Canon which we now have. The proofs of this assertion are to be found in the work itself, which, however large, is so concisely written, that even a summary of the arguments would occupy half of one volume. Those, therefore, who wish to know the grounds on which so important a conclusion is founded, must obtain the object they are in search of by a patient perusal of the work. Those who are persuaded beforehand that such a conclusion cannot be proved by any arguments whatever, will do well to close the book at once; for their reluctance to give up cherished opinions cannot be greater than my own unwillingness to induce them to do so. It will, on the other hand, be a great relief, in reading the Scriptures, to get rid of awkward difficulties in the shape of contradictions that cannot be reconciled, imperfections that would greatly detract from compositions that all might allow to have had a human origin, and erroneous principles of morality that would have hardly found a place in the most incomplete systems of the philosophers of Greece and Rome.

For many centuries after the Christian era the apostolic authorship of the four Gospels was taken for granted; no one was heard either to impugn or to defend it. The objections of the ancient philosophers, Celsus, Porphyry, and others, were drowned in the tide of orthodox resentment, which flowed in a thousand channels, or were consumed in the fire to which their writings were consigned; and when ancient literature was overwhelmed by the irruption of the barbarians, there was no one left to question the articles of faith which the Church put forth as her landmarks, whilst the low ebb of scholarship even in the Church itself was such that, if any one had been able to attack, it is certain that no one would have been qualified to defend the received opinion, which ascribed their authorship to the Apostles. The revival of learning in the fifteenth century witnessed also as its result a disposition to examine more carefully the nature of those books which were the sole depositories of Christian doctrines. A few faint signs of life were occasionally given by the spirit of free inquiry, to show that the idea of private judgement was not yet abandoned and might some day be revived. Still there was a natural unwillingness in the minds of men to encourage a train of argument by which their most important interests were thought to be endangered. But the cause of free inquiry still progressed, and the spread of critical intelligence has at last prevailed against those who still look upon the four Gospels as the undoubted writings of Matthew, Mark, Luke, and John. The most orthodox defenders of their faith are obliged to modify the terms in which the authenticity and genuineness of the four Gospels are expressed. There remains little to encounter but the reluctance which is felt to abandon what has hitherto been held by almost the whole Christian world as sacred as the cause of truth itself. But this reluctance is unreasonable, and cannot be maintained. There is now no longer the power even if there be the wish to prevent free inquiry into every question which it is possible to raise on this or any other subject. It cannot be said that the latitude which is now given to individual opinion has been met by apathy on the part of the intelligent public, for all classes show the greatest anxiety to know more on a subject about which they now see that they have taken too much for granted, under the false impression that they knew all that was to be known.

Neither can it be said that practical morality has suffered in the present day from the less respect shown to dogmas resting upon no demonstration or pretence of demonstration, but hitherto accepted on implicit faith in the authority of the Church. Practical morality, which is irrespective of modes of faith, is justly considered, in the present day, as the great object to which our religious feelings should be directed; and it will be best attained by availing ourselves, successively, of the fresh knowledge and new aids to devotion which the course of nature daily unfolds to us, not by slumbering at our posts, as if we had already completed the investigation and reached the end of truth. If the volumes here published shall promote the feeling that our duties are not stationary, but onward, I shall be pleased to think that my labours have not been in vain. If the conclusions which I have arrived at are thought to be not logically drawn from the premises which are laid down as their basis, it will be the part of those who hold a different view of the matter, not to censure what may displease them, but to refute what may be wrong; if any one shall be found to admit the truth of my conclusions, but to question the utility of making them public, such an objection seems not worthy of a reply. Lastly, if any one shall complain that the rules of ordinary criticism have here been applied to the New Testament, in the same way as to any other book, I reply that in every other path of life the richest commodities are all meted by the same standard of weight or measure as the meanest; and that, if those principles of literary discrimination, which have been taught, and are still taught to thousands in our universities at so great a public cost, are to be warped or modified before they can be applied to what concerns us most, it is time that the public should know how weak are the bulwarks which they have erected, at so great an outlay, between error and truth; and how futile are the studies on which the wealth of the nation and the energies of its most valued youth are now employed and wasted.

J. A. G.

Sutton Rectory,
    July, 1877.

TABLE OF CONTENTS.

CHAPTER I.

INTRODUCTION 17

CHAPTER II.

Chronology of the books which form the Hebrew Canon of the Old Testament—The Apocrypha . . 19

CHAPTER III.

That the books of the Old Testament are not thirty-nine in number, but seventeen only . . . 25

CHAPTER IV.

That the five books of Moses, with the books of Joshua, Judges, Ruth, I Samuel, II Samuel, I Kings and II Kings are closely connected, and form a continuous narrative 28

CHAPTER V.

That the Old Testament is compiled from more ancient works 33

§ 1. Interruptions in the narrative, 33—§ 2. Repetitions, 35—§ 3. Earlier writings are quoted by the authors of the Old Testament, 38—§ 4. Different names given to the Almighty, 41.

CHAPTER VI.

Chronological summary of Jewish History . . 43

Table I. From the Creation to the Flood, 45—Table II. From the Flood to the Call of Abraham, 46—Chronological outline from the invasion of the kingdom to the Captivity, 49.

CHAPTER VII.

First appearance of the Bible in Europe—Josephus—Sketch of his Life and Works . . . 52

CHAPTER VIII.

Of the Septuagint translation of the Old Testament—The Targums 58

CHAPTER IX.

Value of Contemporary History 61

CHAPTER X.

Of the reputed authors of the several books in the Old Testament 64

CHAPTER XI.

The claims of Moses to the authorship of the Pentateuch investigated: first, from Tradition or Universal Consent 71

CHAPTER XII.

Examination of the Internal Evidence which the Pentateuch is said to furnish for the belief that it was written in its present form by Moses . . . 97

CHAPTER XIII.

The case of the Samaritan Pentateuch examined . 103

CHAPTER XIV.

That Moses is not the author of the Pentateuch, proved from internal evidence 108

§ 1. The Two Tables of Stone seem to have supplied the place of the Book of the Law, 108—§ 2. Manner in which Moses is mentioned in the Pentateuch, 111— 3. A book more ancient than the Pentateuch mentioned by the writer of the Pentateuch, 113—§ 4. Anachronism concerning the enmity of the Egyptians towards shepherds, 114—§ 5. Anachronism that Moses should record his own death, 116—§ 6. Anachronism in names, especially of places, mentioned in the Pentateuch, 118: Hebron, 119; Dan, 120; Succoth, 121; Eshcol, 122; Bethlehem, 122; Bethel, 123; Beersheba, 123; Hormah, 124; Gilead, 125; Land of Hebrews, 125; Beer, 127—§ 7. Allusion to events that are known to have happened after the death of Moses, 128. The expulsion of the Canaanites, 128. Allusion to the kings of Israel, 130. The ceasing of the Manna, 132. The sinew that was not eaten, 132—§ 8. The Pentateuch betrays a more advanced state of knowledge than prevailed in the time of Moses, 133—§ 9. Variation in the name given to the priest of Midian, father-in-law of Moses, and to Joshua, 139—§ 10. Argument derived from the use of the expression "unto this day," 141—§ 11. Allusion to the want of a regular government, 143.

CHAPTER XV.

Book of Joshua examined: anachronisms and other internal evidence, showing that it was written in a later age 144

CHAPTER XVI.

The Book of Judges similarly examined . . 154

CHAPTER XVII.

The Book of Ruth examined . . . 158

CHAPTER XVIII.

First Book of Samuel examined. . . 159

CHAPTER XIX.

Second Book of Samuel examined . . . 163

CHAPTER XX.

The two Books of Kings examined 165

CHAPTER XXI.

The two Books of Chronicles examined . . . 168

CHAPTER XXII.

The Books of Ezra, Nehemiah, and the Apocryphal Books of Esdras examined 171

CHAPTER XXIII.

The Prophets 180

CHAPTER XXIV.

The Khetubim or Hagiographa 191

CHAPTER XXV.

The historical books of the Khetubim or Hagiographa, namely, Ruth, Chronicles, Ezra, and Nehemiah . 194

CHAPTER XXVI.

The poetical writings of the Hagiographa, namely, the Psalms, Proverbs, Ecclesiastes, Song of Solomon, Lamentations 197

§ 1. The Psalms, 197—§ 2. The Proverbs, 201—§ 3. Ecclesiastes, 203—§ 4. The Canticles or Song of Solomon, 205—§ 5. The Lamentations, 209.

CHAPTER XXVII.

Works of moral and historical fiction in the Hagiographa, namely, Job, Esther, and Daniel . . 210

§ 1. The Book of Job, 210—§ 2. The Book of Esther, 216—§ 3. The Book of Daniel, 222.

CHAPTER XXVIII.

Further discrepancies, anachronisms, errors, laws and

customs neglected or forgotten in the books of the Old Testament generally, showing that they are not contemporary records, but compiled later than the Babylonish Captivity 228

§ 1. Close connection of the narrative from Genesis to the Second Book of Kings. The Prophets and the Psalms similarly classified, 229—§ 2. Inconsistencies concerning Abraham and Sarah, 231—§ 3. Inaccuracies concerning Jacob's children, 233—§ 4. Different accounts of the length of time which the Israelites sojourned in Egypt, 235—§ 5. The expression, 'on this side Jordan,' 'beyond Jordan,' examined, 240—§ 6. Ordinance of the scape-goat, 246—§ 7. Circumcision, 249—§ 8. The Sabbath, 252—§ 9. The two versions of the Ten Commandments, 258—§ 10. Inconsistency between Samuel's picture of a king and that ascribed to Deuteronomy, chapter xvii, 260—§ 11. Discrepancies in the history of David and Saul, 261—§ 12. Error in the number of Solomon's officers, 264—§ 13. Error in the number of talents brought from Ophir, 265—§ 14. Concerning the situation of Tarshish, 265—§ 15. Excessive accounts of the population of the Holy Land, 266—§ 16. The law of Moses not observed by the Israelites, and especially by King Solomon, 267—§ 17. The Captivity and Assyria are actually mentioned in the early books of the Old Testament, 268—§ 18. Allusion in Genesis to the Babylonish mode of building, 270—§ 19. Silence concerning the mode in which the Book of the Law was preserved during the Captivity, 271.

CHAPTER XXIX.

Pre-historic records—Allegorical readings of early Israelitish history—Philo the Jew—Shishak or Sesostris—Pharaoh Nechoh—Details of the Babylonish Captivity—Assyrian kings, Pul, Tiglath-pileser, Shalmanezer, and Esarhaddon—Nebuchadnezzar, king of Babylon 275

CHAPTER XXX.

Slavery among the tribes of Syria and Palestine—The

Babylonian Captivity growing out of political motives—Its limited nature as to slavery . . 290

CHAPTER XXXI.

References to facts of which no records have been preserved 296

§ 1. The Call of Abraham, 298—§ 2. Bedan—§ 3. The appointment of a captain to lead the Israelites back to Egypt, 300—§ 4. Sprinkling the book—§ 5. The contest between Michael and the Devil, 301—§ 6. The magicians, Jannes and Jambres, 302—§ 7. Concerning Moses, 303.

CHAPTER XXXII.

Grammatical Subtleties are a proof of a later age . 305

CHAPTER XXXIII.

That the Israelites spoke Egyptian in Egypt, and afterwards acquired the Canaanitish or Hebrew language by a long residence in Canaan . . . 309

CHAPTER XXXIV.

That the Chaldee language was the result of a late gradual change, and finally of the Roman Conquest of Judæa, and not of the Babylonish Captivity . 329

CHAPTER XXXV.

That the Chaldee paraphrases called Targums, together with the vowel-points and accents are later than the time of Christ 336

CHAPTER XXXVI.

That the Jewish nation spoke Hebrew as late as the time of Christ, proved from the New Testament . 341

CHAPTER XXXVII.

Successive changes in the religion of the Hebrews resulting from their contact with foreign nations . 350

CHAPTER XXXVIII.

On the art of writing—Its gradual improvement through five stages: 1. Mexican picture-writing; 2. Egyptian hieroglyphics; 3. Chinese word-writing; 4. Hebrew syllabic or consonantal writing; 5. Alphabetic writing 367

§ 1. Mexican picture-writing, 372—§ 2. Hieroglyphics, 373—§ 3. Word-writing, 375—§ 4. Syllabic or consonantal writing in use among the Hebrews, 378—§ 5. Alphabetical writing as used by the Greeks and other ancient and modern nations, 380.

CHAPTER XXXIX.

Alphabetic writing unknown to the Egyptians, and consequently to Moses 380

§ 1. Positive testimony of ancient authors to a peculiar character of writing among the Egyptians, 384—§ 2. Absence of all mention of phonetic or alphabetic legends in the writings of the ancients, 390—§ 3. Present appearance of the Egyptian monuments and various opinions about them, 391—§ 4. Sameness of the written but difference of the spoken language in the various parts of ancient Egypt, 394—§ 5. The introduction of the Greek alphabet into the Coptic or later Egyptian language shows that there was no previous Egyptian alphabet, 396.

CHAPTER XL.

Marks of hieroglyphics in the Bible . . . 399

§ 1. Holiness to the Lord, 399—§ 2. Urim and Thummim, 401—§ 3. Mene, mene, tekel, upharsin, 401.

CHAPTER XLI.

Style of the Old Testament the same throughout, because all written or compiled at the same time—Chaldaisms in the early parts of the Bible, though not so many as in the later books—Reason of this—Chaldee and Hebrew very similar . . . 403

CHAPTER XLII.

Alphabet of Cadmus—Phœnician origin of letters—Conclusion 410

HEBREW RECORDS.

CHAPTER I.

INTRODUCTION.

THE belief in a Supreme Being has been found to exist in almost every nation of the world. Travellers have, indeed, discovered a few tribes of savages, who seemed entirely unconscious of the existence of a God, or of any power superior to the ordinary law of nature. These exceptions, therefore, do not interfere with the course of our present argument, which, being addressed to those who are living in a civilized country, and not to ignorant savages, may assume as a fact an opinion so generally and almost universally entertained. Religion, which regulates the conduct of men in their relation towards the Deity, is a term naturally varying according to the modes of belief prevalent in different countries. Experience also has shown that, even among the same people, an exact identity of religious belief cannot long exist. This has been the case, even among the four principal religions, which, from their having been reduced to writing and promulgated to the world in a set canonical form, would, we might suppose, have saved the people who professed them, from this breach of unity. Yet we find that Jews, Christians, Brahmins, and Mahometans are equally divided into sects, which disagree severally among themselves as much as they are at variance generally with each other. The most remarkable feature in this universal spirit of variance, is the fact that, whilst all the sects which belong to the same faith, differ in their application of it, as widely as the imagination can conceive; they all appeal to the same religious books or scriptures, as favouring their own individual views, and authorizing their own particular practice. If this be true, it becomes not only important, but an absolute duty, to examine with the most scrupulous minuteness that standard, which, though in such general use among mankind, is perpetually producing a want of uniformity, in what so intimately concerns all of us, both as a society and as individuals, namely *truth*, about our everlasting interests, and *moral practice*, as it regards our comfort and social happiness in this present life.

As I have before remarked, there are four* principal religions, still prevalent among the civilized inhabitants of the earth: these are; 1. The Brahminical, 2. the Mahometan, 3. the Christian, and 4. the Jewish. Of the three first it is sufficient to observe that the Brahminical—by which term, I mean the religion of the Hindoos—is so revolting to common sense, that it would be an useless labour to discuss its tenets, or to balance its excellencies and its defects, among Europeans; the Mahometan is evidently the work of an enthusiast, making use of human fanaticism as his tool; and the Christian, though based on the noblest object, that of ameliorating and renovating the human race, must be considered an offshoot from its parent, the religion of the Jews; for Christianity and Judaism are inseparably united; neither can exist without the other; or, at least, they can only abstractedly exist as separate religions; but in an historical point of view they are indivisible: they must maintain their ground or fall together; for, though the practical precepts of Christianity may be taught without the slightest reference to the Jews, or to the Old Testament, yet the doctrinal parts of the Christian scheme, and all that gives to it the character of a Divine revelation, become destitute of meaning, until they are explained by the antecedents of the Jewish scriptures, concerning the temptation of Eve, the fall of Adam, and his ejection from Paradise.

* Bhuddism will perhaps hereafter be added as a fifth principal religion, when a larger intercourse with China shall have made us better acquainted with its doctrines. I am informed by an able Chinese scholar that the writings of Confucius are in some parts remarkably similar to our Gospels, and a learned friend has often suggested to me that our Lord's struggle against the Pharisees seemed to him similar to that of the Bhuddists against the Brahmins in India.

It seems, therefore, that the Old Testament is a volume of the highest value to Christians, because its contents are essential to the existence of our own creed, of which the older religion of the Jews is, in fact, the precursor. To this must be added that the moral precepts which it contains rest on Divine authority, which so far from being set aside at the opening of the New Dispensation, has continued to sanction the union of the two systems, and to blend them together as the base and groundwork of our present Christianity. The book of the Old Testament is therefore made the subject of this volume, in which it is proposed to inquire into the historical value of the several books of the Old Testament, their authors, the time when they were written, the harmony, as well as discrepancies, which exist between them, besides many other points which will incidentally arise, and may be useful in determining the historical character of these scriptures, and their value as evidences, concerning those accounts of the early history of the world which are generally received among mankind, on *their* authority alone.

CHAPTER II.

CHRONOLOGY OF THE BOOKS WHICH FORM THE HEBREW CANON OF THE OLD TESTAMENT—THE APOCRYPHA.

THE Old Testament, according to the English Bible, consists of thirty-nine books, written mostly in the Hebrew, but partly in a different language, called *Chaldee*, besides Apocryphal books, which exist in Greek or Latin only, and for that reason principally, have been considered by some classes of Christians to possess less authority than the former, whilst by others they have been excluded from the Bible altogether. The names of these books are as follows:—

Genesis	Joshua	I Kings
Exodus	Judges	II Kings
Leviticus	Ruth	I Chronicles
Numbers	I Samuel	II Chronicles
Deuteronomy	II Samuel	Ezra

Nehemiah	Jeremiah	Jonah
Esther	Lamentations	Micah
Job	Ezekiel	Nahum
Psalms	Daniel	Habakkuk
Proverbs	Hosea	Zephaniah
Ecclesiastes	Joel	Haggai
Song of Solomon	Amos	Zechariah
Isaiah	Obadiah	Malachi.

Names of the Apocryphal books.

I Esdras	Wisdom	Story of Susanna
II Esdras	Ecclesiasticus	Bel and the Dragon
Tobit	Baruch, containing the Epistle of Jeremiah	Prayer of Manasseh
Judith		I Maccabees
The conclusion of Esther	Song of the Three Children	II Maccabees.

It may be mentioned, as a minor fact, but still of some importance to our present subject, that these books are not always placed in the same order; the Greek translation, called the Septuagint, and the Latin, called the Vulgate, differ in their arrangement from the Hebrew and English Bibles and from one another. Neither do they agree wholly in their contents: for the Hebrew Bible excludes all those books which in England are called Apocryphal; whilst the Vulgate or Latin Version admits only Tobit, Judith, Wisdom of Solomon, Ecclesiasticus, Baruch, with the First and Second books of Maccabees. The Greek Bible admits the first book of Esdras, Tobit, Judith, Ecclesiasticus, Baruch, and the two books of Maccabees, to which is added a third book of Maccabees, not to be found in either the Hebrew, Latin, or English Bible: and two other books, a fourth and a fifth, pass under the name of Maccabees, though not found generally either in the Greek or Latin versions.

Let us now briefly review the contents of these books one after another, principally for chronological purposes; and as we shall hereafter have occasion to refer to this subject, such a summary will save the reader from the necessity of consulting the books themselves, except on important points, in the argument, which will presently be unfolded.

1. GENESIS.—This book relates the history of the world from the creation to the time of Abraham, who is thought to have lived nineteen hundred years before Christ; after

which it takes up the history of the Israelitish people only, and brings it down to the death and burial of Joseph, which are supposed to have happened about the year before Christ 1635.

2. EXODUS.—The book of Exodus continues the narrative, begun in Genesis, to the delivery of the law from God to Moses, about the year 1490 before Christ.

3. LEVITICUS.—The contents of this book are limited almost wholly to legislative enactments. A few historical facts, connected with the principal subject of the book, such as the ordination of Aaron and his sons, are mentioned incidentally; the period occupied by these events is supposed not greatly to exceed one month.

4. NUMBERS.—The book of Numbers comprehends the space of thirty-nine years, being, in fact, the whole period of the Israelitish wanderings in the wilderness from the year 1490 to 1451 before Christ. From the absence of chronological data it is impossible to ascertain the exact time of the events which happened in the interval between the Exodus of the Israelites from Canaan, and their entry into the promised land.

5. DEUTERONOMY.—The time occupied by the events mentioned in Deuteronomy is limited to one year at the utmost, the year 1451 before Christ, in which the Israelites, having wandered forty years in the desert, at length prepare to invade the land of Canaan. The last events related in this book are, the death of Moses and the succession of Joshua as leader of the Israelitish people.

6. JOSHUA.—The book of Joshua comprehends a period of about twenty-five years, from B.C. 1451 to 1425, during which the able captain, from whom the book takes its name, subdued the Canaanitish nations and divided their territories among his followers.

7. JUDGES.—The chronology of the book of Judges is more uncertain than that of the preceding: it comprehends, probably, about the space of three hundred and ten years, i.e. from B.C. 1425 to 1115; but the want of chronological connection between the events which it relates renders it impossible to arrive at any more accurate conclusion.

8. RUTH.—This book gives us an account of the fortunes

of Ruth and her family, during a space of ten years, immediately preceding the time at which the book of Judges ends.

9, 10.—THE BOOKS OF SAMUEL.—The first of these books records the history of Samuel, who judged Israel immediately before the election of a king, together with the reign of King Saul, a period as is supposed of about 115 years, from B.C. 1170 to 1055.

The second book of Samuel comprises the reign of David, which lasted forty years, from B.C. 1055 to 1015.

11, 12.—THE TWO BOOKS OF KINGS.—The narrative is continued from B.C. 1016, the year of David's death, in the first of these books, down to the death of Jehoshaphat, in 889; and, in the second book of Kings, from the year last named, to the thirty-seventh year of the captivity of Jehoiachin king of Judah, coinciding with the 562nd year before Christ.

13, 14.—THE TWO BOOKS OF CHRONICLES.—The first book of Chronicles contains a series of genealogical tables, followed by a variety of events that happened in the reign of David, which is stated to have lasted forty years, from B.C. 1055 to 1015. The second book of Chronicles contains the whole Jewish history from the accession of Solomon in B.C. 1015 to the decree of Cyrus in 536. Many of the facts which it relates are mentioned in the books of Kings, but others are introduced, some of which are not in harmony with those recorded in Kings, and several passages occur which are identical in language with others found in the Prophets and elsewhere.

15. EZRA.—The book of Ezra comprehends the space of eighty years from the decree of Cyrus to the year B.C. 456.

16. NEHEMIAH.—This book takes up the history ten years after the conclusion of Ezra, i.e. in 446, and brings it down to about the year B.C. 434.

17. ESTHER.—This book comprises the history of only twelve years from B.C. 521 to 1509. A book, purporting to be the concluding portion of Esther, is found in the Apocrypha.

18. JOB.—The chronology of this book is altogether unknown; and it partakes of a didactic, if not a poetic, rather than of an historic character.

19. PSALMS. — 20. PROVERBS. — 21. ECCLESIASTES. — 22.

SOLOMON'S SONG.—These four books contain few direct historical allusions: they are supposed to have been mostly written by David and his son Solomon; i.e. between the years 1056 and 975 before Christ; though some are of a later date, as for instance the 137th Psalm, which was certainly written after or during the Babylonish Captivity.

23 to 39. THE SEVENTEEN PROPHETICAL BOOKS.—The seventeen prophetical books contain many historical facts, though they are not of a strictly historical nature. They are not arranged chronologically in our Bibles, but as they will be cited in this work for historical purposes only, it will be useful to place them in the order of time, as follows:

Jonah is said to have written between	856	—	784 B.C.
Amos (in the reign of Uzziah)	810	—	785
Hosea (Uzziah, Jotham, Ahaz, Hezekiah)	810	—	725
Isaiah (Uzziah, Jotham, Ahaz, Hezekiah)	810	—	698
Joel (Uzziah, Jotham, Ahaz, Hezekiah, Manasseh)	810	—	650
Micah (Jotham, Ahaz, Hezekiah)	758	—	699
Nahum (Hezekiah)	720	—	698
Zephaniah (Josiah)	640	—	602
Jeremiah (Josiah, Jehoahaz, Jehoiachin, Zedekiah)	628	—	586
Habakkuk (Jehoahaz, Jehoiakin)	612	—	598
Daniel (during the Captivity)	606	—	534
Obadiah (Zedekiah)	588	—	583
Ezekiel (Jehoiachin, Zedekiah)	595	—	536
Haggai (during the Captivity)	520	—	518
Zechariah (during the Captivity)	520	—	517
Malachi (during the Captivity)	436	—	397

The books which follow next are classed under the general name of Apocrypha.

1. The *First Book of Esdras* is found in the Greek language only, and first occurs in the Alexandrian MS. of the Septuagint, where it is placed before the canonical book of Ezra; it relates events which happened before, during, and after the Babylonish captivity.

2. The *Second Book of Esdras* existed in a Latin text only,

the age of which is unknown; some versions in Arabic, and other Eastern languages have been found. We shall see hereafter that it contains one notice which bears forcibly upon our present subject, and for which some original authority must at some time or other have existed.

3. The *Book of Tobit* is in various languages, and may have been written a hundred years before or a hundred years after the Christian era; it is a dull narrative of the life of one Tobit, and contains miracles more fit for the Arabian Nights than for the Christian Scriptures.

4. The *Book of Judith*, in Greek, relates the defeat of the Assyrians by the Jews, but labours under so many difficulties, that some critics have described it as a fiction rather than a real history.

5. The remaining chapters of the *Book of Esther* are found in Greek and Latin early in the Christian era; their origin is wholly unknown.

6. The *Wisdom of Solomon* is found in the Greek of an early date; like the rest of these books, its author is wholly unknown.

7. The *Wisdom of Jesus, the son of Sirach*, or *Ecclesiasticus*, was written possibly two hundred years before the Christian era, and is found now in the Greek translation only.

8. The *Book of Baruch*; 9. The *Song of the Three Children*; 10. The *History of Susanna*; 11. *Bel and the Dragon*; and 12. The *Prayer of Manasseh*, are all found in a Greek text only; their origin is obscure, and their value the smallest that can be assigned.

13. The *Books of Maccabees*, however, are of a very different character. Two only appear in our English Bibles; but two others are found in some copies of the Septuagint. They occur now only in the Greek, but, as Jerome saw one of them in Chaldee, they possibly all were written in that or some similar dialect. A fifth book, in Latin only, is given in Walton's Polyglott Bible, and all the five have been edited in the English translation by the Rev. Dr. Cotton, and printed at the University Press, 8vo., Oxford, 1832.

The foregoing works have been often described as semi-canonical, and except the last three books of Maccabees, have been admitted as a sort of Appendix, useful for "example of life and instruction of manners," to the canonical Scriptures in our English Bible. But a work of more literary importance, although still less useful as regards its contents, is the book of Enoch, in Ethiopic, discovered in modern times, and printed in an English translation by Archbishop Lawrence in 1838, at the Oxford University Press. It is believed to have been current among the Jews before the Christian era, and to be the work spoken of in verse 14 of the Epistle by St Jude.

Besides the preceding, numberless other writings, most of which are in these days unworthy of more than a passing notice, were widely circulated among both Jews and Christians in the early days of our era. The learned Fabricius, in his *Codex Pseudepigraphus* of the Old Testament (Hamb. 1722), notices no less than three hundred and twenty such documents which once were in existence, but now, with a few exceptions, have either perished or are unknown.

CHAPTER III.

THAT THE BOOKS OF THE OLD TESTAMENT ARE NOT THIRTY-NINE IN NUMBER, BUT SEVENTEEN ONLY.

ALTHOUGH the Old Testament is divided into thirty-nine parts or books, yet we must not understand that it contains so many separate works, unconnected in their subjects, or written by so many different authors. In the Hebrew Bible are twenty-two books only, which is also the number of letters in the Hebrew alphabet. These twenty-two books were divided into three classes; the first class consisted of five, namely, Genesis, Exodus, Leviticus, Numbers, and Deuteronomy, which they called the Law; the second class consisted of thirteen, namely, Joshua, Judges and Ruth, in one book; the two books of Samuel, of Kings, and of Chronicles respectively, in single books; Ezra and Nehemiah in one book; Esther; Job; Isaiah; the two books of Jeremiah in one; Ezekiel; Daniel; and the twelve minor prophets in one book; these thirteen were called the Prophets: the third class consisted of the four remaining books, namely, Psalms, Proverbs, Ecclesiastes, and the Song of Solomon, which were called by the Jews Chetubim, and by the Greeks Hagiographa; this class was also called the Psalms, from the name of the first book in it.

We must not, however, conclude that there are even twenty-two separate works in the Hebrew Bible; but rather that this division* was adopted for the convenience of reference, which would naturally be required in the case of so bulky a volume as the Hebrew Scriptures.

The connection between the number of these books, and the number of letters in the Hebrew alphabet, demands to be noticed. We are not informed to what origin this fact is to be referred; but the Jews have always been fond of allegory and similitude: hence we may suspect that the coincidence was not undesigned, but that it was contrived at the time when the Masoretic notes and points were invented, and when the Jewish doctors took so much pains to count the words and even letters contained in their Sacred Books. This subject will be noticed more fully in a future chapter.

Some of these twenty-two books are to be considered as portions of the same work rather than separate works; for, although Genesis, Exodus, Leviticus, Numbers, and Deuteronomy stood as separate books in the private copies used by the Jews in the time of Josephus, they were written in one continued work, and still remain in that form, in the public copies read in the Jewish synagogues. These five books are now generally known by the name of the Pentateuch. As the public copies read in the synagogues are undoubtedly more likely, than the private copies, to retain the original form of these writings, we may consider the number of books to be reduced to seventeen by the union of the first five, namely, Genesis, Exodus, Leviticus, Numbers, Deuteronomy, into one.

But there is an ambiguity in the use of the word book, which must be carefully guarded against. Sometimes it

---

* "It is not known when this division took place, but probably it was first adopted in the Septuagint version, as the titles prefixed are of Greek derivation. The beginnings of Exodus, Leviticus, Numbers, and Deuteronomy, are very abrupt, and plainly show that these books were formerly joined to Genesis."—TOMLINE'S *Elements of Christian Theology*, vol. i, p. 3.

means a whole work, whether divided into parts or not; sometimes it means a separate volume, and it has also a third meaning, that of part or division of a work, in which sense it is analogous to chapter, canto, part, &c., which are terms used arbitrarily by writers to denote the separate divisions of the same work.

Looking at the contents of the second or Prophetical class into which the Hebrew Scriptures were divided, we may inquire why the books of Joshua, Judges, Samuel, and others, which certainly are Historical and not Prophetical, at least in our acceptation of the word, are included in the same class with Isaiah, Jeremiah, and the rest, whom we now, more appropriately, as might be thought, designate as Prophets. The answer to this question is suggested by the meaning which the Jews ascribed to the word Prophet, by which term they designated a teacher or poet, and not merely one who foretold future events. In this sense, Joshua and the Judges were called Prophets with no less propriety than Daniel, Jeremiah or Isaiah. That the Pentateuch was kept apart from that which follows it in the Hebrew Canon, arose partly from the higher honour which was due to their great law-giver, and partly from the fact that the whole of the Jewish Law was contained in those five books, which consequently were often designated simply as the Law, whereas the following books were merely histories of the lives of the teachers who successively ruled Israel after the death of Moses.

The third class, into which the Jews divided the books of the Old Testament, Hagiographa or Chetubim, contained neither law nor history, but moral and didactic writings, with exhortations addressed to the people, that they should continue steadfast in the service and worship of their God.

It appears, then, that the Hebrew Scriptures, according to the copies which were publicly used in the synagogues, were divided into seventeen books only, though in all the versions which have been made of them, whether into Greek, Latin or any of the modern languages of Europe, the number of books has been increased to more than the double of this amount. In all such cases, subdivision is the work of a later age, and never coeval with the original work. In the case of the Old Testament, the moderns have abandoned the ancient division of the whole volume into three classes, as unnecessary; and have, for the sake of convenience, adopted the more simple arrangement into books, the number of which, by minute subdivision, they have raised from twenty-two to thirty-nine and upwards.

CHAPTER IV.

THAT THE FIVE BOOKS OF MOSES, WITH THE BOOKS OF JOSHUA, JUDGES, RUTH, I SAMUEL, II SAMUEL, I KINGS AND II KINGS, ARE CLOSELY CONNECTED, AND FORM A CONTINUOUS NARRATIVE.

IF we examine the early part of the Old Testament attentively, we shall find strong marks of connection between many of the seventeen books, which stand separate in the public Jewish copies. As the books of Genesis, Exodus, Leviticus, Numbers and Deuteronomy are admitted to have formed but one book in the Hebrew Canon, it is unnecessary to apply the present argument to them: but it is remarkable that the succeeding books, Joshua, Judges, Ruth, Samuel, and Kings, are all as closely in continuation the one of the other, as the five books before mentioned. The book of Joshua is also in immediate continuation of Deuteronomy; and, in short, so close is the connexion of all the early part of the Old Testament, from Genesis to the end of the Second Book of Kings, that if it was all printed without division in one continuous narrative, it would be impossible for the most sagacious critic to restore it to the form which it now bears.

As this is an assertion of fact which can only be proved by adducing all the instances, it is necessary to extract the beginnings and endings of each book in succession from the close of Deuteronomy to the end of the Second Book of Kings. The reason why this examination is less applicable to the books of Chronicles, Ezra, and the others, will be evident hereafter.

The book of Deuteronomy ends with these words:

And there arose not a prophet since in Israel like unto Moses, whom the Lord knew face to face: in all the signs and the wonders, which the Lord sent him to do in the land of Egypt to Pharaoh, and to all his servants and to all his land; and in all that mighty hand, and in all the great terror which Moses showed in the sight of all Israel.

The book of Joshua, which follows Deuteronomy, takes up the narrative exactly at the point where the preceding book terminates, in the following manner:

Now, after the death of Moses, the servant of the Lord, it came to pass that the Lord spake unto Joshua, the son of Nun, Moses's minister, saying, "Moses, my servant, is dead, &c."

Our quotation from the end of Joshua must be more extended, in order to show more clearly that it bears a similar relation to the book of Judges, which is the next in order.

And it came to pass, after these things, that Joshua the son of Nun, the servant of the Lord, died, *being* an hundred and ten years old. And they buried him in the border of his inheritance in Timnath-Serah, which *is* in Mount Ephraim, on the north side of the hill of Gaash. And Israel served the Lord all the days of Joshua, and all the days of the elders that over-lived Joshua, and which had known all the works of the Lord, that he had done for Israel.

And the bones of Joseph, which the children of Israel brought up out of Egypt, buried they in Shechem, in a parcel of ground which Jacob bought of the sons of Hamor the father of Shechem for an hundred pieces of silver: and it became the inheritance of the children of Joseph.

And Eleazar the son of Aaron died, and they buried him in a hill *that pertained* to Phineas his son, which was given him in Mount Ephraim.

Consistent with this extract is the beginning of the book of Judges, which opens thus:

Now after the death of Joshua it came to pass that the children of Israel asked the Lord, saying, "Who shall go up for us against the Canaanites first, to fight against them?"

After Judges comes the book of Ruth, which is very short, and gives us an account of her adventure and subsequent marriage with Boaz, it opens as follows:

Now it came to pass in the days when the Judges ruled, that there was a famine in the land.

If it be asserted that these words form a very appropriate exordium to a separate work or book, I refer the reader back to the nineteenth chapter of Judges, which he will find commences in a similar manner:

And it came to pass in those days, when there was no king in Israel, that there was a certain Levite sojourning on the side of Mount Ephraim, &c.

The history of this Levite forms the subject of the last three chapters of Judges, and is as much distinct from the rest of that work as the book of Ruth. The history of the Levite and the history of Ruth, are, in fact, a sort of episode to "Judges;" both of them contain prominent events which happened in Israel "whilst the Judges ruled," and "whilst there was no king," which evidently are synonymous expressions.

Equally applicable to our argument are the books of Samuel and Kings, as will appear from the following extracts.

The first book of Samuel opens with the history of Samuel, the last of the Judges:

Now there was a certain man of Ramathaim-zophim, of Mount Ephraim, &c.

It may be said to follow in chronological order, and to bear quite as close a connection with the book of Judges as the history of Ruth, or that of the Levite which is admitted to form part of the book of Judges. It concludes with the death of Saul:

And when the inhabitants of Jabesh-Gilead heard of that which the Philistines had done to Saul; all the valiant men arose and went all night and took the body of Saul and the bodies of his two sons from the wall of Bethshan, and came to Jabesh, and burnt them there: and they took their bones, and buried them under a tree at Jabesh, and fasted seven days.

The opening of the second book of Samuel is in the closest harmony with the preceding:

Now it came to pass after the death of Saul, when David was returned from the slaughter of the Amalekites, and David had abode two days in Ziklag, it came even to pass on the third day, that, behold, a man came out of the camp from Saul with his clothes rent, and earth upon his head, &c.

The book concludes with the words:

David built there an altar unto the Lord, and offered burnt-offerings and peace-offerings: so the Lord was intreated for the land, and the plague was stayed from Israel.

This is generally believed to have happened in the latter part of David's life. Accordingly, we find the first book of Kings confirms that opinion, and takes up the history where the preceding book had left it:

Now king David was old *and* stricken in years, and they covered him with clothes, but he gat no heat.

The book concludes with the reign of Ahaziah, thus:

Ahaziah the son of Ahab began to reign over Israel in Samaria the seventeenth year of Jehoshaphat king of Judah, and reigned two years over Israel: and he did evil in the sight of the Lord, and walked in the way of his father, and in the way of his mother, and in the way of Jeroboam the son of Nebat, who made Israel to sin: for he served Baal, and worshipped him, and provoked to anger the Lord God of Israel, according to all that his father had done.

But all the events of Ahaziah's reign are found in the second book of Kings, the beginning of which follows so closely after the extract just made, that it is difficult to conceive the two books of Kings in any other light than as a continued history; and it comprehends, as we have seen in the last chapter, a space of about five hundred and forty years. The opening of the second book of Kings is as follows:

Then Moab rebelled against Israel after the death of Ahab. And Ahaziah fell down through a lattice in his upper-chamber that *was* in Samaria, and was sick, &c.

Thus all the writings of the Old Testament from Genesis to the two books of Kings form an uninterrupted narrative of events, which are described as having happened, first to the world at large from the Creation down to about 1900 years before Christ, and afterwards to the family and posterity of Abraham down to about the 600th year before the same era, when the tribes of Israel were torn by violence from the paternal land of Canaan, and carried to Babylon, where they remained in captivity until the first year of the reign of Cyrus king of Persia.

As no evidence remains to prove that the separate divisions, entitled Genesis, Joshua, Judges, &c., are any more than consecutive parts of the same work, we are justified in viewing them in this light until good grounds shall be adduced for disconnecting them.*

Next in order to the books of Kings succeed the Chronicles, which certainly do not form a sequel, nor yet, strictly speaking, a supplement to the books of Kings; for they comprise the same period of history often in the very same words, and record many particulars omitted in the books which precede. The beginning of Chronicles is remarkably abrupt, but its connection with the end of Kings is not more incoherent than is the relation which its own internal parts bear to one another. It may be suggested as probable that the compilers of the Bible, seeing these books to be composed of unconnected fragments, or perhaps having them only as separate fragments, treating on subjects which were already woven into the continuous history, which they had already put together, added them as a sort of appendix, that the information which they contained might not be altogether lost, although in some parts inconsistent with the collateral narrative.

They contain so many allusions to the Babylonish Captivity, that they must undoubtedly have been written after that event. They are admitted by all the commentators to have been written, perhaps, by Ezra, after the Babylonish Captivity, whereas most of the preceding books are said to have been written, before the destruction of the Hebrew Commonwealth.

The remaining books, which complete the volume of the Old Testament, do not at present require to be noticed: they will supply us in a future chapter with numerous argu-

---

* An illustration of this subject may be drawn from the case of Herodotus, who wrote a history of the wars between the Greeks and Persians, in nine books. These *books* bear, each the name of one of the nine Muses, Clio, Melpomene, &c., and no one has ever disputed their unity, the identity of their author, or the continuity of their subject.

ments serving to support the theory that the whole volume must be received as the production of that period of Jewish history which extends from the re-building of Jerusalem to the beginning of the Christian era.

CHAPTER V.

THAT THE OLD TESTAMENT IS COMPILED FROM MORE ANCIENT WORKS.

If the reasons produced in the last chapter are sufficient to establish the belief that the several books of the Old Testament are but different sections of the same work, and form a continuous narrative; so, also, are there other equally strong reasons for believing that the Old Testament is a compilation, and not an original work. These reasons are all deduced from the books themselves, and may be classed as follows.

§ 1. *Interruptions in the narrative.*

The narrative of the Old Testament, though historically continuous from the end of one book to the beginning of the next, is, in other places, interrupted by the insertion of separate and complete histories, which are even distinguished by such appropriate titles as, in any other volume of antiquity, would be acknowledged to point out the beginning of detached compositions. Thus, at Genesis ii, 3, is concluded the account of the creation of the world with the words: "And God blessed the seventh day and sanctified it; because that in it he had rested from all his work, which God created and made."

Then follows another brief history of the creation, the garden of Eden, and the fall of man, with an exordium which intimates a distinct and independent composition. "These are the generations of the heaven and of the earth, when they were created, &c." GEN. ii, 4.

This second narrative ends with Chapter the Third. The Fifth Chapter begins with an appropriate title, which more particularly indicates a distinct and independent composition: "This is the book of the generations of Adam. In the day that God created man, in the likeness of God made he him."

The history of the creation of man is here again briefly recited, as an introduction to a separate book, which is complete in its kind; it begins from the creation and concludes with the birth of the sons of Noah. It might be regarded by many as a transcript from an authentic genealogical table or pedigree, which had been regularly kept in the family of the patriarch.

We have afterwards—"These are the generations of Noah,"—"These are the generations of the sons of Noah, &c."

The reflections, which flow from these observations, are obvious. Those which follow are taken from the Celtic Researches, the author of which has entered deeply into several subjects that will occur to our notice in the course of this volume.

These things I cannot but consider as internal proofs, that Moses has not only alluded to writings which existed before his own time, but has actually given us transcripts of some of the compositions of the primitive ages: and that the book of Genesis, like other historical parts of the Scriptures, consists in a great measure of compilations from more early documents. May not these several books, which recapitulate the same events, and the matter of which has not been wholly forgotten by the heathens, be regarded as so many primitive records, adding mutual strength to each other, and reflecting mutual light, in the same manner as the books of Kings and Chronicles, and the narratives of the four evangelists?

If we duly consider the matter contained in the book of Genesis, I think we shall be led to conclude that much of it must necessarily have been collected from prior documents. For example (Gen. xxii, 20) Abraham receives information respecting the family of his brother Nahor. No reason is given why it was told Abraham: nor does anything immediately follow, as a consequence of such information. But as the account related to Abraham's family, we are left to conclude, that he recorded it; and, *upon his authority*, Moses preserves the record. He gives it not as a subject of revelation, nor as the result of his enquiry amongst the descendants of Nahor, nor yet does he content himself with registering the simple fact, but he tells us *what had been told Abraham at such a time.* At a distance of 400 years, he transcribes the names of Nahor's eight sons in due order, with some particular circumstances respecting them, *as it had been told Abraham*, and therefore, as it must have been recorded in some memorials in Abraham's family. Moses must have possessed a very exact detail of the transactions of Abraham's time. Hence the circumstantial account of the expedition of the four kings, of that patriarch's treaties with the princes of the land in which he sojourned, of his sacrifices, and of the promises he received, and the allusion (Ex. xii) to the *year*, the *month*, and the *very day* on which he began his peregrinations.

In confirmation of the opinion advanced above, it may be observed, that history furnishes no instance of an exact chronology having been preserved, for a series of ages, by any people who were totally illiterate. Relative dates, and the enumeration of months and days, would soon become unmanageable in oral tradition: and the precise length of men's lives, and their age at the birth of their children, are circumstances not likely to have been the subject of immediate revelation to Moses. Yet his history of the primitive world preserves an unbroken chain of chronology, from the creation.—DAVIES's *Celtic Researches*, p. 40.

§ 2. *Repetitions.*

In the several portions of which each book of the Old Testament consists, the same events are recapitulated, to the same general effect, and sometimes with the addition of fresh matter. The earliest instance of this is in the history of the creation which is related over again three several times, yet putting the subject each time in a somewhat different light. The instances of similar repetition are so numerous that, if duplicates were rejected, the Pentateuch would not occupy more than half of its present compass. It is sufficient to name two or three notable instances which are the most difficult to be explained, except on the supposition that there once were earlier records, and, perhaps, fragments, out of which our present books were compiled.

The first which I shall adduce is the repetition of many parts of the Jewish Law, and in particular the ten commandments, which are first given in the twentieth chapter of Exodus, and in such a manner that their insertion furnishes an example of a *break* in the recital, as well as of a repetition. The nineteenth chapter of Exodus ends with these words: "So Moses went down unto the people and spake unto them."

He went down, as we learn from the preceding verses, to caution the people not to come too near. There is nothing said of his going up again: but the next words to these, which are certainly the words that God spoke to him, are: "And God spake all these words, saying I am the Lord thy God, &c."

The narrative is here plainly broken, and must be re-united by inserting an account of Moses going up again into the Mount: if, indeed, the narrative is continuous at all.

The ten commandments are again enumerated in the fifth chapter of Deuteronomy from the mouth of Moses, and prefaced by the admonitions of the lawgiver not to forget those commandments and the other parts of the covenant which God had given them. It cannot be supposed that Moses wrote them twice, though he may have recited them many times to the people, neither would a later historian have written them twice in an original historical work; but in a collection of narratives taken from earlier documents, it is plain that, to preserve the original words as far as possible, many such repetitions would be unavoidable.

The whole of II Kings xviii, 13, to xx, 19, is the same as Isaiah, xxxvi, 1, to the end of the thirty-ninth chapter: the two passages contain the history of Hezekiah's alarm at the approach of Sennacherib, and God's vengeance on the Assyrian army. As it is impossible to say which of the claimants for these chapters is the real author, it is best to ascribe them to some third unknown author, from whom both have copied them.

The next instance of repetition is still more striking, because we fall into an inevitable dilemma, in endeavouring to explain it. The 36th chapter of Genesis contains a separate and complete account of the genealogy of Esau, entirely disconnected with what goes before, and with what follows. In the 31st verse of this chapter we find the heading or title: "And these are the kings that reigned in the land of Edom, before there reigned any king over the children of Israel."

This verse and the twelve which follow, occur almost verbatim in the First Book of Chronicles, i, **43**; and this circumstance involves us in a double dilemma. Either the two documents were copied, the one from the other, or both were copied from a common original. It will not, I presume, be readily allowed that the author of Genesis copied these thirteen verses from Chronicles; though even this argument has been put forward: neither can I admit that the author of Chronicles, supposed to be Ezra, would copy from Genesis, because Ezra is supposed to have written Chronicles as supplementary to preceding books, and not as copies from them; he is said also by some to have revised and amended all of the Old Testament for public use; and it is the design of this work to show that he re-wrote, from ancient documents and other sources, the greater part of the Old Testament, and more particularly the Pentateuch and the Historical Books, at a time when the Jewish nation had risen from its downfall under the auspices of the Persian kings, and was again asserting its nationality on the scene of its former greatness.

The same observations apply also to other chapters of Chronicles, which need not now be noticed. It remains, therefore, to suppose that the two identical accounts were drawn from some common source. Original authors seldom abound in repetitions; two independent authors never use the same words to any great extent; but compilers, out of respect to early and valuable records, retain them in their first shape.

The thirty-first chapter of the First Book of Samuel, consisting of thirteen verses only, is verbatim the same as the first twelve verses of I Chronicles, chap. x. The position of this tenth chapter of Chronicles is remarkable: it follows the preceding nine chapters of genealogies, without any preface whatever, leaving us to the only admissible hypothesis, that the writer of it copied two prior documents, leaving each to tell its own story. If Ezra wrote this, he either could not have revised or written the preceding and earlier Scriptures, or he did not publish both as an uniform work, or he published them professedly as a collection of separate documents and not as an homogeneous work. If Ezra revised or wrote the other books of Scripture, assigning them to earlier names, and then copying whole chapters from them, published these to the world as his own in the books of Chronicles, he was guilty of a plagiarism, which would be aggravated, not palliated, by the sacred nature of the subject. It would also be not only an useless, but a pernicious labour, to increase the size of the Scriptures without adding to the value of their contents.

Comparing the argument of the last chapter with that of the present, I lay the stress of my observations upon this fact—that the division into books, Genesis, Exodus, Leviticus, &c., is arbitrary, and does not coincide with the real division, which shows itself in numerous places, by the abrupt change of subject, by repetitions, and such like indications. In other words, where there is a continuity of subject, our present headings or titles make breaks, and where there is no continuity, the narrative is made to run on without interruption. This is plainly the process of a compiler, or artist, who, having united his materials together, cuts them into different lengths for the convenience of use.

§ 3. *Earlier writings are quoted by the authors of the Old Testament.*

In the twenty-first chapter of Numbers, at verse 14, we find these words:

"Wherefore it is said in *the book of the wars of the Lord*, What he did in the Red Sea, and in the brooks of Arnon, and at the stream of the brooks that goeth down to the dwelling of Ar, and lieth upon the border of Moab."

The note to this passage in the Bible, edited by Doyly and Mant, is as follows:

Some ancient record of those countries, to which Moses refers: or, more probably, the following account of the wars of the Israelites, given in the sacred history by Moses and other inspired writers.—PYLE, DR. WELLS.

We shall have occasion to recur to these verses hereafter: at present I adduce them to show that the writer or writers of the Old Testament actually quoted earlier writings.

In the tenth chapter of Joshua is the account of Joshua's commanding the sun to stand still; at verse 13 we read:

"And the sun stood still, and the moon stayed, until the people had avenged themselves upon their enemies. Is not this written in the *book of Jasher?* So the sun stood still in the midst of heaven, and hasted not to go down about a whole day."

The book of Jasher is again mentioned in II Samuel, i, 17, 18:

"And David lamented with this lamentation over Saul and over Jonathan his son. Also he bade them teach the children of Judah the use of the bow: behold, it is written in the *book of Jasher.*"

In the First Book of Kings, xi, 41, we read:

And the rest of the acts of Solomon, and all that he did, and his wisdom, are they not written in the *book of the Acts of Solomon?*

The note attached to this passage is taken from Bishop Patrick:

The kings of Israel were accustomed to maintain some wise persons who committed to writing all that passed in their reign. Perhaps this practice was begun by Solomon; for we read not of any book of the acts of David. Out of these annals, the sacred writer of this book took what he thought most useful, and omitted the rest, which he did not judge so necessary and instructive.

Bishop Patrick, when he wrote this, must have forgotten the following extract from I Chron. xxix, 29, where the Acts of David are said to have been recorded in the same manner as those of his predecessors:

Now the acts of David the King, first and last, behold, they are written in the *book of Samuel the seer*, and in the *book of Nathan the prophet*, and in the *book of Gad the seer*.

The Chronicles of King David are also referred to in I Chron. xxvii, 24, and were probably the same book as the "Acts:"

Joab the son of Zeruiah began to number, but he finished not, because there fell wrath for it against Israel; neither was the number put in the account of *the chronicles of king David*.

The second book of Chronicles, ix, 29, takes notice of the Acts of Solomon, and names three writers who recorded them:

Now the rest of the acts of Solomon, first and last, are they not written in the *book of Nathan the prophet*, and in the *prophesy of Ahijah the Shilonite*, and in the *visions of Iddo the seer* against Jeroboam the son of Nebat.

In numerous other passages of Chronicles, we find writers of Acts mentioned:

II Chron. xii, 15. Now the acts of Rehoboam, first and last, are they not written in the *book of Shemaiah the prophet* and of *Iddo the seer* concerning genealogies?

—xiii, 22. And the rest of the acts of Abijah, and his ways, and his sayings, are written in the *story of the prophet Iddo*.

—xx, 34. Now the rest of the acts of Jehoshaphat, first and last, behold, they are written in the *book of Jehu* the son of Hanani, who is mentioned in the book of the Kings of Israel.

II Chron. xxvi, 22. Now the rest of the acts of Uzziah, first and last, did *Isaiah the prophet*, the son of Amoz, write.

—xxix, 30. Moreover Hezekiah the king and the princes commanded the Levites to sing praises unto the Lord with the words of *David*, and of *Asaph the seer*.

—xxxii, 32. Now the rest of the acts of Hezekiah, and his goodness, behold they are written in the *vision of Isaiah the prophet*, the son of Amoz, and in the *book of the kings of Judah and Israel*.

—xxxv, 25. And Jeremiah lamented for Josiah, and all the singing men and the singing women spake of Josiah in their lamentations to this day, and made them an ordinance in Israel: and, behold, they are written in the *Lamentations*.

Besides these various books, the authors of which are named, we have the "Chronicles of the Kings of Israel and Judah" referred to more than thirty times at least. Of the manner in which they are mentioned, the following is an example:

I Kings, xiv, 19. And the rest of the acts of Jeroboam, how he warred, and how he reigned, behold they are written in the *book of the chronicles of the kings of Israel*.

The book of the "Chronicles of the Kings of Israel" is mentioned altogether in nineteen places:—I Kings, xiv, 19: xv, 31: xvi, 5. 14. 20. 27: xxii, 39. II Kings, i, 18: x, 34: xiii, 3. 12: xiv, 15. 28: xv, 11. 15. 21. 26. 31.

The book of the "Chronicles of the Kings of Judah" is similarly mentioned in I Kings, xiv, 29: xv, 7. 23: xxii, 45: II Kings, viii, 23: xii, 19: xiv, 18: xv, 6. 36: xvi, 19: xx, 20: xxi, 25: xxiii, 28.

These quotations are found in our present books of Kings; and in the Chronicles are quoted, in a similar manner, "the book of the kings of Judah," and "the book of the kings of Israel,"—or, unitedly, "the book of the kings of Judah and Israel,"—they are mentioned in II Chronicles xvi, 11: xx, 34: xxv, 26: xxvii, 7: xxviii, 26: xxxii, 32: xxxiii, 18: xxxv, 27: xxxvi, 8.

In some of these places the subject admits the supposition that our existing books of Kings are referred to; but it also admits of the same view which has been taken above, namely, that earlier writings are quoted.

§ 4. *Different names given to the Almighty.*

An argument in favour of the theory that the Pentateuch is a compilation from earlier records has been founded on the variation of name given to the Supreme Being.

In the first chapter of Genesis, to the fourth verse of the second chapter, he is called Elohim, " the Gods," which occurs thirty-five times, and he is there called by no other name. But in the rest of Chapter ii, and in Chapter iii, (except by the serpent, who also calls him Elohim) he is otherwise named Jehovah Elohim, which we translate the " Lord God," and this name occurs twenty times. The use of these terms as here described, is a peculiarity which could not well have happened, in the original and entire composition of one age, one country, and one man. For however the mysterious meaning of the terms themselves may be discriminated, yet Elohim in the first chapter, and Jehovah Elohim, in the second and third, are evidently used in a synonymous sense, and precisely the same operations are ascribed to them.

For this reason many critics have come to the reasonable conclusion that our present text has been formed out of two separate traditions or histories, in each of which one or the other of those names was used to denote the Almighty in describing the creation of the world. As this notion has been abundantly discussed in several works of great repute, and indeed has necessarily found a place in almost every work which treats of the Bible and its contents, it is needless here to add more than a few remarks on the subject. The early chapters of the Bible, in which the name Elohim appears, mixed with others, where Jehovah is the name of God, will be found to contain a continuous narrative of the Creation; to which the Jehovistic parts, as they have been termed, present in one respect a parallel, and in another a contrast. In one of these we may infer that woman was created as well as man—" male and female created he them." (Gen. i, 27,)— whereas in the corresponding part of the other narrative, man alone is the created being, and, when a deep sleep had fallen upon Adam, the Almighty Creator took from his side " one of his ribs, and closed up the flesh thereof," and from this rib " made he a woman, and brought her to the man " (ii, 22). In a similar manner all the earlier part of the Bible shows marks of two traditions blended into a continuous narrative, some of which have Jehovah, others Elohim, and others again a combination of the two, Jehovah Elohim, to designate the Almighty. The last of these epithets, that which is combined out of the other two, at length prevailed over them, and the Jews, adopting the general name Elohim, although of plural number, from the inhabitants of the Promised Land, among whom they settled, and who appropriately used a plural name for the multitude of gods whom they worshipped, added to it the name of Jehovah, whom they especially adored, and whom we still worship under the name of the "Lord God," in contradistinction to all the deities of heathen nations.

But several other appellations also, as Adonai and Shaddai, are found in various parts of the Old Testament, and all designate the Supreme Being, with equal propriety. They appear to be independent of one another, and neither by metaphor, etymology or periphrasis, can be reduced to one origin, as Deity and Divinity from Deus in Latin, the Supreme Being, and other similar expressions, which are found in all the modern languages. The name Adonai, adopted without doubt from one of the Canaanitish nations, may be identified with Adonis, who appears at an early period in the Phœnician, the Grecian, and afterwards the Roman Mythology. The name seems to have been retained much later, and even perhaps by Christians; for we find in the learned work of Fabricius, (i, 22,) a psalm, absurdly ascribed to Adam, in which the five sections begin each with these words:

| Adonai Domine Deus meus, secundum magnam misericordiam tuam miserere mei! | My Lord Adonai, pity me according to thy great mercy. |

The name Jehovah also, or rather the combination of Hebrew letters, which we pronounce Jehovah, but which is variously written by ancient authors IAO, IEVO, &c., is clearly identified with Jove, whose worship was introduced at an early date among the Etruscans, and Eli (related to Elohim) is identical with Ali, or Allah, the name of God over a large part of Arabia, and other Mahometan countries, where the Arabic tongue wholly or in part prevails.

CHAPTER VI.

CHRONOLOGICAL SUMMARY OF JEWISH HISTORY.

The Hebrew Scriptures contain the most ancient accounts now existing of the world and of the human race. On this head they are often described as presenting a remarkable and pleasing contrast to the early histories of the Greeks, the Romans, and all other ancient nations that we are now acquainted with. In these last we trace with difficulty a few obscure facts preserved to us by the poets, who transmitted with all the embellishments of poetry and fable, what they had received from oral tradition. I do not speak of those stupendous monuments which cover the plains of Arabia, Asia, and the East, or of our own remains at Stonehenge, Avebury, and elsewhere. These, if we could read them, would probably tell us of events as ancient as those which are recorded in the Pentateuch; but the comparison which we are instituting, concerns written records only, in which particular the Jews claim precedence over all other nations. For the Hebrew scriptures give us a minute and even dramatic description of events which precede by many centuries all other historical records or traditions.

Notwithstanding this distinction, the chronology of the events related in the Bible stands as much in need of elucidation as that of the Grecian histories. Both are based upon the probable duration of human life, and on a system of genealogies, which, though tolerably accurate on the whole, is liable to many an error in its component parts.

Although the remarks which I shall here make upon Bible Chronology may afford little interest to those who confine themselves to the practical lessons which this book will teach, yet this work would be incomplete, in the estimation of critical readers, if I were wholly to pass over the subject of which we are now speaking. To all zealous inquirers after truth, the data on which the period of history contained in the Old Testament has been fixed from the year 4004 to the year 400 before Christ, cannot but furnish the most lively and enduring interest. Yet with *all* the questions that are connected with this ample subject we cannot occupy ourselves,—partly for want of space, but more from inability to throw light upon the subject. The points more particularly alluded to are: 1. The extraordinary duration of human life recorded in the history of the early patriarchs; and 2. The allegorical character ascribed by some writers, as Philo the Jew, among the ancients, and many others, even Churchmen in modern times, to the accounts of the Creation, the Fall of Man, his consequent expulsion from Paradise, the Deluge, and many other events, which are related in the book of Genesis, but have no counterpart in any events that have happened in the world since that time. If these histories are allegorical, and were written as such, to convey, by a series of types, lessons of morality and practical religion to a rude race, from whom the truths of Science, and the true lights of God's physical universe were hopelessly shut out; such an opinion respecting those extraordinary features which are impressed upon the first chapters of our Bible would render it a superfluous task to arrange the chronology of events, when their moral character, and not their reality, is all that concerned the people, to whom they were first addressed.

Whatever may be the truth on these exciting topics, whilst we might show, on the one hand, the inutility, in a practical point of view, of attempting to confirm the literal interpretation, we should equally abstain from treating too roughly the received system of chronology for that part of our Bible which treats of the patriarchs who lived before the flood. It is also a fortunate circumstance for those who are moderate and cautious in handling a book of such importance to Christians, that the principal difficulty arising from conflicting authorities is confined almost wholly to those who came immediately after or before the flood: but does not so much affect the historic period of Jewish history from the Exode to the extinction of the monarchy.

In speaking of the authorities for the chronology of the Bible, we use a plural term to designate what, on examination, will turn out to be a singular idea. The only sources from which our knowledge of the Jewish history is derived, are: 1. The Hebrew Bible. 2. The Septuagint; and 3. Josephus's Antiquities of the Jews. But these three, apparently distinct, are, however, one and the same witness.

The Septuagint translation of the Bible was taken from the Hebrew text; and it seems that Josephus had little other source of information for his history than the Hebrew Bible itself. And yet the chronology of these three authorities, as we now have them, varies in the dates more than a thousand years, the one from the other. It is impossible to explain this in any other way than by supposing that the texts of these writers have been altered. It is difficult to conceive that unintentional errors have crept in, to such an amount, by the carelessness of scribes; for the errors are all based upon a system which shews intention—not, certainly, neglect. We find that, for the antediluvian period, the variation between the Hebrew Bible and the Septuagint is 606 years; whilst that between the Hebrew text and Josephus is 600 years. If we consult the Samaritan copies of the Bible, the subject becomes still more perplexing, for their antediluvian chronology falls short of the Hebrew text by 349 years; and Julius Africanus and Theophilus, two early Christian chronologers, have arrived at results which differ from all the former.

Subjoined is a scheme of the six systems of antediluvian chronology, from which the reader will see how hopeless is the possibility of ever arriving at the truth. The first column, in each case, denotes the age of the patriarch before the birth of his son: the second column indicates the residue of his life.

TABLE I. FROM THE CREATION TO THE FLOOD.

	Hebrew.		Septuag.		Samar.		Joseph.		Theoph.		Afric.	
1 Adam	130	800	230	700	130	800	230	700	230	700	230	700
2 Seth	105	807	205	707	105	807	205	707	205	707	205	707
3 Enos	90	815	190	715	90	817	190	715	190	715	190	715
4 Cainan	70	840	170	740	70	840	170	740	170	740	170	740
5 Mahalaleel	65	830	165	730	65	830	165	730	165	730	165	730
6 Jared	162	800	162	800	62	785	162	800	162	800	162	800
7 Enoch	65	300	165	200	65	300	165	200	165	200	165	200
8 Methuselah	187	782	187	782	67	653	187	782	167	802	187	782
9 Lamech	182	595	188	565	53	600	182	595	188	589	188	589
10 Noah	600		600		600		600		600		600	
TOTAL BEFORE THE FLOOD	1656		2262		1307		2256		2242		2262	

The sum total of the ten generations in the first column of each system, gives the length of time between the Creation and the Flood. The duration of the Flood, a year and ten days, from the 600th year of Noah, the 17th day of the 2nd month, to the 27th day of the 2nd month in the following year, is supposed to be compressed into an historical point, namely the end of Noah's 600th year, and the beginning of his 601st year, in order to prevent the year of the Flood from being reckoned twice.

TABLE II.—FROM THE FLOOD TO THE CALL OF ABRAHAM.

		Hebrew.	Septuag.	S-mar.	Joseph.	Theoph.	Afric.
11	Shem	2 500	2 500	2 500	12		
12	Arphaxad	35 403	135 330	135 303	135 303	135 303	135 303
13	Salah	30 403	130 330	130 303	130 303	130 303	130 303
14	Heber	34 430	134 270	134 270	134 330	134 330	134 339
15	Peleg	30 209	130 209	130 109	130 109	130 109	130 109
16	Reu	32 207	132 207	132 107	130 107	130 107	130 107
17	Serug	30 200	130 200	130 100	132 100	130 100	130 100
18	Nahor	29 119	79 120	79 69	120 69	75 73	79 69
19	Terah	70 135	70 135	70 135	70 135	70 135	70 135
20	Abraham	75	75	75	75	75	75
	TOTAL OF SECOND PERIOD	367	1017	1017	1068	1011	1015

At Chapter xi, 10, Shem is said to have begotten Arphaxad two years after the Flood. This may perhaps be reckoned from the time when the Flood began: they were one year and ten days in the ark.

In Chapter v, 32, we read, "Noah was 500 years old: and Noah begat Shem." Again, in Chapter vii, 6, Noah was 600 years old at the time of the flood: from this it follows that Shem must then have been 100 years old; but in Chapter xi, 10, it is stated that Shem was 100 years old when he begat Arphaxad, which was two years after the Flood. There is here evidently an error, however slight, on one side or the other, and this will at once show to the intelligent reader the utter impossibility of making a correct chronology for this period, when the only data are at variance.

From the Call of Abraham to the Exode are reckoned 430 years, on data equally at variance with one another, as in the two former periods.

The principal difficulty which we have here to contend with is the statement made to Abraham, that his seed should be oppressed in a foreign land four hundred and thirty years. But elsewhere (Genesis xv, 13, 16, and Acts vii, 6,) the number is four hundred only, perhaps in round numbers, the writer not caring to be exact. An ordinary reader would suppose that this period was to begin at the time when the second Pharoah, who "knew not Joseph," *did* oppress the Israelites. But, as only two generations intervene between

Moses and Levi, one of Jacob's sons, and as the days of patriarchal longevity were long gone by, it is impossible to reckon 430 years between the actual bondage and the Exode. A more minute examination of this subject will be given in a future chapter.

The Exode of the Israelites, under Moses, according to the system of chronology usually adopted, took place in the year 1491 before Christ. Forty years were spent in the Arabian deserts; but the few events, which there took place, are briefly described, and it is difficult to arrange them in order as they happened.

The year 1451, then, is our next date of importance, being the year in which Joshua led the Israelites into the Promised Land. From this point to the election of King Saul, which was the beginning of the Jewish monarchy, the chronology is still more vague and uncertain than in the preceding periods; and all the systems vary both in its general duration and in the length of its several parts. The order of events is not accurately pointed out in Joshua, Judges, or the books of Samuel, and it is only possible to arrive at an approximative result by adding together the different sum totals of years occupied by the different events. Thus the following particulars are all that can be gathered from the books themselves:

Government of Joshua and the elders—*uncertain*	
Servitude under the Mesopotamians	8
Government of Othniel	40
Servitude to Moab	18
Government of Ehud	80
Servitude to the Philistines—*uncertain*	
Government of Shamgar—*uncertain*	
Servitude to the Canaanites	20
Government of Deborah and Barak	40
Servitude to Midian	7
Government of Gideon	40
Abimelech made king	3
Government of Tola	23
Government of Jair	22
Servitude to the Ammonites	18
Government of Jephthah	6
— — Ibzan	7
— — Elon	10

Government of Abdon	8
Servitude to the Philistines and Government of Samson	40
Government of Eli	40
Interval—*uncertain*	
Government of Samuel	20
Total of the Judges until the election of King Saul besides four uncertain intervals	450

From the various breaks which occur in the foregoing table, it is impossible to arrive at the exact length of time during which the Judges ruled Israel. The same circumstance therefore leaves it uncertain in what year before the Christian era King Saul began to reign. But as it is desirable to fix on *some* date, as near as can be found to the right one, chronologers have generally agreed to assume the year B.C. 1095, as that from which the beginning of Saul's reign is to be counted. But two difficulties here attend us: 1. Whether the early part of Saul's reign was not coincident with the last years of Samuel's judgeship; and 2. It is unknown how long Saul reigned. St Paul, indeed, tells us, in the passage before quoted, that Saul reigned 40 years, and in this statement we are compelled to acquiesce, because we have no better data to guide us. The reigns of David and Solomon, also, are reckoned each at 40 years—a coincidence which tells strongly in favour of its traditional character, for no authentic history can furnish an instance of three successive kings reigning so long, and each the same number of years.

We now arrive at the next epoch in Jewish history, the dismemberment of the monarchy into the two smaller kingdoms of Judah and Israel.

	Date at Saul's accession—			B.C. 1095
40	years, the reign of	Saul ended		1055
40	—	—	David ended	1015
40	—	—	Solomon ended and the kingdom divided	975
120	Total.			

From this point down to the time of the Captivity, there is still much difficulty in arriving at exact dates, and there are several inaccuracies which can now only be remedied by conjecture; as, for instance, we read in II Kings i, 17, that

Jehoram, son of Ahab, king of Israel, and brother of Ahaziah Ahab's son, began to reign in the 2nd year of Jehoram, son of Jehoshaphat, king of Judah, whereas we read in the same book of Kings iii, 1, that he began to reign in the 18th year of Jehoshaphat, father of the same Jehoram, king of Judah. Such discrepancies as these require no comment. They are unavoidable in the case of a nation whose existence had been broken up and held in abeyance seventy years, whilst their cities were sacked, their treasures torn from them, and their wives and daughters led away to sit down and weep by the waters of Babylon, when they remembered that they were daughters of Sion, and had once been so happy! What records could survive so great a national desolation? It is wonderful that any history of preceding events should have been preserved at all; but that a work like the Book of the Old Testament should have been compiled out of the relics of ancient Hebrew records, and be free from the blemishes which we are now pointing out, is a fact which has no parallel in the history of any other nation.

CHRONOLOGICAL OUTLINE FROM THE DIVISION OF THE KINGDOM TO THE CAPTIVITY.

B.C.	KINGS OF JUDAH.	KINGS OF ISRAEL.
975	Rehoboam, 1st year	Jeroboam, 1st year
958	Abijam, 1st year	— 18th year
955	Asa, 1st year	— 20th year
954	—	Nabad, 1st year
953	— 3rd year	Baasha, 1st year
930	— 26th year	Elah, 1st year
929	— 27th year	Zimri reigned 7 days
925	— 31st year	Omri, 1st year
918	— 38th year	Ahab, 1st year
914	Jehoshaphat, 1st year	— 4th year
897	— 17th year	Ahaziah, 1st year
896	— 18th year	Jehoram, 1st year
892	Jehoram, 1st year	— 5th year
885	Ahaziah, One year	— 12th year.

We get this concurrence of dates from II Kings, viii, 25; but in the next chapter, ix, 29, we read that Ahaziah became king of Judah in the 11th year of Jehoram, king of Israel.

884	Athaliah, 1st year	Jehu, 1st year
878	Jehoash, or Joash, 1st year	— 7th year

856 Jehoash, or Joash, 23rd year.		Jehoahaz, 1st year.
841 — 37th year		Joash, 1st year
839 Amaziah, 1st year		— 2nd year
825 — 15th year		Jeroboam 11 years.

In II Kings, xiv, 21, we read that Amaziah was slain, and that his son Azariah was made king in his stead; that Jeroboam II became king of Israel at the same time, and reigned forty-one years. But in chapter xv, 1, we read that Azariah began to reign in the 27th year of Jeroboam II, and reigned fifty-two years. This discrepancy is explained by the supposition that the 27th year may mean really the 16th year of Jeroboam II, for that during the ten preceding years he may have reigned jointly with his father. But this explanation is wholly unsupported, and the chronology from this point is so obscure that it may suffice for the purpose of reference to add the names only of the succeeding kings, together with the dates which are generally assigned to them in our ordinary tables of chronology.

810 Azariah or Uzziah, 1st year.

773	—	33rd year.	Zachariah, one year
772	—	39th year.	Shallum—Menahem, 1st year
770	—		Pul imposes a tribute on Menahem
761	—	50th year.	Pekahiah, 1st year
759	—	52nd year.	Pekah, 1st year
758 Jotham			
742 Ahaz, 1st year			
740 —			FIRST CAPTIVITY by Tiglath-pileser
729 — 12th year			Hoshea
726 Hezekiah, 1st year			— 3rd year
721			— 9th year
698 Manasseh, 1st year			SECOND CAPTIVITY of Israel by Shalmaneser, king of Assyria
678 —			THIRD CAPTIVITY by Esarhaddon.
643 Amon, 1st year			
641 Josiah, 1st year			
610 Jehoahaz—Jehoiakim, 1st year.			

606 FIRST CAPTIVITY.
   Jekoiachim supposed to be otherwise called Jeconiah and Coniah—SECOND CAPTIVITY.
599 Mattaniah or Zedekiah, 1st year.
588 THIRD CAPTIVITY, by Nebuchadnezzar.
536 Date of the edict of Cyrus, authorizing the Jews to return into their own country.
515 The Temple is finished and dedicated in the sixth year of Darius, king of Persia.
457 Ezra goes down from Babylon to Jerusalem in the seventh year of Artaxerxes, king of Persia.
445 Nehemiah goes to Jerusalem in the twentieth year of Artaxerxes.

From there having been three different invasions of Judah, and three of Israel, at all of which large numbers of captives were carried away to Babylon, it is doubtful which of these is to be taken as the beginning of the seventy years spoken of by the prophets. If the first of the six in 740 is fixed on it is evident that the seventy years will be extended to more than 200; the return of the Jews took place in the first year of Cyrus king of Persia, which is generally calculated to fall in B.C. 536. If, however, the last and final captivity of Judah alone (Israel having long since disappeared from the scene), in 606, is taken, we shall then have an exact period of 70 years, if, at least, it is certain that Cyrus began to reign in 536. But this, also, is doubtful; nay, it is hardly possible to fix the first year of Cyrus's reign to 536, without supposing that, what was considered as his first year in Persia, was not his first year in Media, and that this date was reckoned in a third and different manner at Babylon. But, even if we could clearly arrive at the seventy years as dating from 606, yet there is still a difficulty to surmount; for the kingdom of Judah did not cease until 588 —only 52 years before the first year of Cyrus; and the Jewish people still inhabited, and no doubt tilled the land up to that year. The land, therefore, did not rest from tillage and did not then begin to "recover her sabbaths," as announced by the prophets. But this is understood to have been the object of its lying waste, that the people might be punished just as many years as the Sabbatical years, which had been neglected, should amount to in number. It results therefore that the "seventy years" must not be measured too accurately. We must understand the term to denote a long period, approaching near to seventy, but without any minute specification of its duration.

It is unnecessary to protract this sketch of Bible Chronology any further; because we have brought it down to the reign of Cyrus the Persian, in whose first year the Jews returned to their own land and in process of time rebuilt their famous temple. It is the opinion of many, but no doubt an erroneous opinion, that the historic period of the existence of this remarkable people begins at this point, for there is no evidence that we still possess any original records earlier than this date—our existing books seem to be a compilation made from scattered original documents collected and edited by Ezra and his successors.

One object of this work is to show that the whole subject of Bible Chronology is hopelessly obscure, which hardly would be so if we had accounts of each event recorded by contemporary writers; and that those who compiled our present books, although they have done their best, have failed to recover what the ruthless Babylonian, sent down upon them by Providence like a wolf on the fold, had utterly and irretrievably destroyed,

CHAPTER VII.

FIRST APPEARANCE OF THE BIBLE IN EUROPE.—JOSEPHUS.—
SKETCH OF HIS LIFE AND WORKS.

In the year 71 of the Christian Era Vespasian and his son Titus, with all the pride and pomp of Imperial power, led up to the Roman Capitol the triumphal procession which indicated the downfall of the Jewish nation. We learn from

Josephus* that, "last of the spoils" which were then, with coarse and unfeeling pride, exhibited to the Roman populace, "was brought the *Law of the Jews*." Another passage from the autobiography of the same writer tells us that amongst other gifts received from the Emperor were the "Sacred Books," which he chose above all the captive treasures as most likely to console him for the utter destruction of his people. The principal work of Josephus is his "Antiquities of the Jews," wherein he closely copies the Bible narrative, and, as he always quotes his authority under the name of the "Sacred Books," and intimates that his intentions are to inform the heathen world more fully about the history of his countrymen, it is not an unreasonable supposition that the Book of the Old Testament was, until then, generally unknown to the Greeks and Romans in Europe. The term *sacred* was applied by the ancients to those books which were kept apart from the public, and known only to the initiated or privileged classes. It is not, indeed, to be denied that at Antioch, Babylon, and Alexandria, where there were large colonies of Jews speaking the Greek tongue, the knowledge of the Jewish sacred volume could scarcely be kept from many strangers with whom the Jewish residents were in daily communication. Moreover, the fact of there having been at least one Greek translation—the Septuagint—current in the countries round Judea, at or soon after, if not long before, the time of Christ, precludes us from supposing that the whole Bible was confined to the priestly class. But, when we find from a passage in the poet Juvenal that, even fifty years after the time of Josephus, the Book of Moses is termed the *secret* or *mysterious* volume, we cannot believe that a work so interesting would have remained so little known, unless it were the set design of the priests to keep the knowledge of it to themselves. Such a mode of acting has been found in all countries, ages, and religions; nearly fifteen hundred years passed away before the still more beautiful volume of the New Testament became known to the world at large, and even now it is kept as much as possible, by the priests of the largest section

---

* De Bello Judaico, vii. v. 5. Josephus alone of ancient writers gives us a full account of the Roman Conquest of Judæa. It is much easier to acquiesce in the authenticity of this author's works than to guess by any stretch of the imagination who else could have written them.

of Christians, from the knowledge of the laity. Nor can it be said that when the Jewish Scriptures fell into the hands of Josephus, they were then free from every hindrance which might impede their circulation. For Josephus, proud of his position at the Roman Court, and ambitious of the honours due to authorship on a new subject, would be little eager to put forward an ancient book, the fame of which might eclipse his own. Nor would he, moreover, be willing to produce as his authority an authentic narrative from which his own history of the Jews deviated so signally. It is therefore highly probable that the *Book of the Law*, and indeed the whole Hebrew Bible did not gain much publicity in the heathen world by having been consigned by Titus to the care of the Jewish writer Josephus. We may also believe that his own writings were designed quite as much for Jews, speaking the Greek tongue, of whom there were great numbers in the large Grecian cities of Egypt and Asia, as for the heathen world.

A short account of this writer and his work will be interesting, and may be useful in our examination of the New Testament in the second volume of this work.

Joseph, the son of Mathias, a Jewish priest, was born at Jerusalem in the year of our Lord 37, about six years after Christ's crucifixion. His name Josephus, by which he is usually called, is merely the Latin form of the Hebrew original, and his prænomen, Flavius, was adopted by him late in life in honour of the Flavian family, of which Vespasian, and after him Titus, was the head. The family of Josephus was ancient and distinguished, tracing its origin to the first of the twenty-four old priestly courses, and his mother was lineally descended from the Asmonean princes. Whilst still a child he was remarkable for his wit and understanding; at the age of fourteen he was so fond of letters, that the chief priests meeting at his father's house used to put to him difficult questions about the Jewish law. When he was sixteen years old, he resolved to learn the doctrines and opinions of the three chief sects of the Jews—the Pharisees, the Sadducees, and the Essenes: in order that, by a minute inquiry into the tenets of their philosophy, he might determine which he should himself follow. Having heard that one Banus, an Essene, was living the life of a hermit in the desert, making his raiment from the trees, his food from the fruits of the earth, bathing in cold water at all seasons of the year, and using every kind of mortification to increase his sanctity, Josephus became ambitious of imitating so holy an example, and accordingly joined him in his cell. But when he had spent three years of pain and penance in the wilderness his zeal was tamed, and at the age of nineteen he again entered the busy world, leaving his companion and teacher to aim alone at the rewards of his solitary philosophy. He now joined the Pharisees, in whose doctrines he found plenty of that worldliness which, after all, does less harm to the progress of mankind than the harsh, self-denying asceticism of the Essenes.

In the twenty-ninth year of his age Josephus undertook a voyage to Rome, to make interest in favour of some priests who had been sent thither by Felix to answer some unimportant charge. On this voyage he was shipwrecked, and in great danger of being drowned. Eighty of those who were on board saved their lives by swimming, and were picked up by a ship from Cyrene. On his arrival at Puteoli, the usual landing-place at that time, Josephus made acquaintance with Aliturus, an actor, who was of Jewish birth, and in high credit with the Empress Poppæa. By his intervention Josephus obtained the release of the prisoners, as well as valuable presents from Poppæa, and returned to Judæa. During all this time he had studied carefully and successfully the Greek language, which few of his countrymen could write, and still fewer pronounce correctly. On his return he found his countrymen disposed to revolt against the power of Rome, and after vainly endeavouring to oppose them he joined their cause, and held various commands in their armies. At Jotapata, a small town of Galilee, he showed his military skill by maintaining a siege of forty-seven days against Vespasian and Titus. When the town was at last taken, forty thousand men were put to death, whilst only twelve hundred became prisoners. Josephus, with forty others, saved his life in a cave; all his companions but one killed themselves, to escape falling into the hands of the Romans, but Josephus and that survivor gave themselves up to the Roman general Vespasian, whose favour he soon gained by foretelling that he would one day become master of the Roman Empire. He went with the Romans to besiege Jerusalem, and urged his countrymen to submit to their superior power, but the Jews would not listen to one whom they looked upon as a traitor, and the Roman soldiers also were far from holding him in the same light as he was held by their commanders. As a reward for his adherence to the Roman cause, he was allowed to save more than 200 of his own kinsmen and friends from the lot of slavery, and received a large grant of land from the Emperor. But he lived afterwards mostly at Rome, where he stood in high favour with all the three princes of the Flavian family. He married first a Jewess of Cæsarea, but divorced her, and took to wife a lady of Alexandria, who bore him three sons, one only of whom—Hyrcanus—lived to be a man. Josephus then divorced this wife also, and married a Cretan woman of Jewish birth, of high rank and great wealth.

Whilst living at Rome, Josephus turned his attention to literature, and wrote first a "History of the Jewish War" in the Hebrew tongue, for the use of his own countrymen dispersed throughout the East. He afterwards translated the work into Greek, and in the fifth century it was translated into Latin by Rufinus of Aquileia, or by Cassiodorus. [See Muratori, *Antiq. Ital.*, 3,929.] It was not until A.D. 93 that he published his great work on the "Antiquities of the Jews," in twenty books. This work, following in general the Bible narrative, contains the history of the chosen people from the Creation down to the reign of Nero, when the thread of events is taken up by the "History of the Jewish War," before published, so that the two together give us an unbroken history of the Jews from the creation of the world to the destruction of Jerusalem. The end which Josephus proposed to himself in his longer work was to make his countrymen better known to the Greeks and Romans, and to remove the contempt in which they were generally held by those superior nations. "The Antiquities of the Jews" gives us facts not found in the Bible, and it quotes Eastern writers of whom we otherwise know nothing; but it differs from the Bible in its system of chronology, and also in the remarkable fact that it mostly ignores those miraculous circumstances with which, according to the Bible, all the leading events of Jewish history are clothed. Josephus allows himself the liberty of adding to the recital of an event circumstances which change its entire nature; in every part of the work he represents his countrymen in a point of view likely to conciliate the respect of the Romans; and these are reasons for thinking that the original Hebrew volume of the Old Testament would be withheld by Josephus as much as possible from the knowledge of the heathen public, lest the remarkable divergency between that and his own work should bring discredit on the character of his nation or on the truthfulness of his own delineation of it. Nor is it needful, in order to substantiate this opinion, to show that Josephus has wholly set aside the peculiar tenets of the Jews. He has ignored the most striking of their miracles; but he has not ignored their Monotheism, and he would not thereby offend the prejudices of philosophers and all the educated classes, for no one above the condition of an artizan or a peasant any longer believed in the plurality of gods whose statues adorned the Pantheon in the reigns of the Cæsars. The doubt or disbelief which was falling upon Jupiter, Juno, and Hercules, though it might not promote the worship of Christ and of the Trinity, would undoubtedly stop short of denying the existence of a God. We read in many passages of heathen writers the name of God used in the singular number, and showing that polytheism was going out of fashion, not by a gradual diminution of the number, but by a rejection of the principle of a plurality as contrasted with the simple belief of the one God who made and upholds all things by his supreme power. This is, in fact, the ground which Josephus takes in his works, though the nature of the case would lead him to deviate unwittingly from uniformly and in every instance following the line of argument which he had at first marked out. Keeping these things in mind, we may observe that the "Antiquities of the Jews" is a very interesting work—both to compare with the Old Testament and as affording a faithful picture of Jewish manners in the time of the historian himself—whilst it fills up a void in Jewish history during the four centuries which passed between the writings of Malachi and the beginning of the Christian era.

Besides the two works just named, Josephus wrote an "Answer to Apion," a celebrated grammarian of Egypt who had given currency to many ancient fictions of Egyptian tradition about the Jews and also his own "Life." In the former work we must acquiesce in the statements of Josephus; for the work of his adversary is no longer extant; but we may lament its loss the less from some information about Apion gleaned from other writers. Pliny in one passage of his Natural History refers him to a class of magicians, and in another quotes his authority for the existence of a lake in Sicily where nothing sinks, but everything thrown into it floats upon the surface. The same Apion is also named by Aulus Gellius in his amusing work "Noctes Atticæ," as author of a History of all the wonders that have been witnessed in Egypt, apparently from the earliest times. It is to be regretted that Time has not spared us this work; for we might have found in it some notice of facts connected with Jewish history, and might have seen how far Josephus, who extenuated the Jews' miracles, in addressing a people superior to his own, may have resented similar conduct in Apion, who addressed the Egyptians, a nation more on a par with the Hebrews in arts and general civilization.

In his "Life," also, Josephus writes against a literary adversary, Justus of Tiberias, who like himself, had published a "History of the War," written with much elegance in the Greek language.

CHAPTER VIII.

OF THE SEPTUAGINT TRANSLATION OF THE OLD TESTAMENT —THE TARGUMS.

THE Hebrew Scriptures have been often translated into foreign languages; but no version of them seems to have been made earlier than the beginning of the Christian era, into any other language than the Greek, and of the four Greek versions, namely that by Aquila, Theodotion, Symmachus, and the Seventy, the last, said to have been made by that number of translators at the command of Ptolemy king of Egypt, and hence called the Septuagint, is the only one still in existence. There are indeed some fragments of six other versions, and notices of them in the works of ancient writers, and it is a curious circumstance connected with this subject, that the text of the book of Daniel according to Theodotion had up to the present century been inserted among the other books of the Septuagint version, instead of the real text of the book of Daniel, properly belonging to that version. The author of the Introduction to the critical study of the Scriptures (ii, 175) tells us that this rejection of the real book of Daniel arose from the very erroneous translations which it contained, and that Theodotion's version was substituted in its place. However that may be, things remained in this state, until the year A.D. 1722, when the real Daniel according to the Septuagint, supposed for several centuries to have been lost, was published in a folio volume at Rome, and since that time has often been reprinted, both separately and also in parallel columns with the Daniel of Theodotion, in the later editions of the Septuagint.

The other three Greek versions, whose authors we know, were all made at no earlier period than the middle of the second century, when the Jews having been dispersed, after the destruction of their city, into various countries, were less able to read and perhaps less able to procure, the Bible in their own language. The narrative of Josephus to which reference has before been made at page 53 of this volume, would indicate that copies of the Hebrew text, even if more than one was saved, were exceedingly rare; and his countrymen, although they were not likely, as imagined by certain modern writers, to have spoken Greek previously as their native tongue, were not unlikely to acquire it, when they found themselves dispersed among the various nations, in which it was spoken. To this cause, and to the rise of Christianity, which naturally would comprise a large majority of Grecian converts, may be assigned the appearance of so many Greek versions of the Old Scriptures, as noticed and corrected by the Christian Father Origen at the end of the Second Century of our era.

To the decay of the Hebrew language may also be ascribed the Targums which made their appearance about that time.

The earliest of these Targums, i.e. paraphrases, in what is called the Chaldee dialect, made for the use of the Jews themselves, when they no longer were able thoroughly to understand the older Hebrew dialect, was written by Onkelos, who is indeed supposed by Professor Eichhorn to have been contemporary with Christ, though Baur, Jahn, and others with much greater reason place him with others in the second century after the Christian era. For our present purpose therefore, which is to ascertain, on credible evidence, the real date and origin of the Hebrew Bible, all these Targums or paraphrases may be set aside: for no one supposes that the Bible is of a date as recent as the Christian era: although it may fairly be said that, if the paraphrases which were meant to facilitate the understanding of the Hebrew were only written after the Christian era and the destruction of the Hebrew nation, the original text itself must have remained in circulation and still been read by the people up to the date of that great national calamity.

There remains therefore the Septuagint translation, which is generally understood to have been made about 280 years before Christ; and this, if true, is a sufficient proof that the Hebrew Bible, from which, however, it varies in many places and of which it is here and there a very inaccurate translation, was at that time extant and well known. A brief notice of the Septuagint will here suffice.

When Alexander the Great died at Babylon in the year 323 before Christ, his empire was broken up into its component parts. Ptolemy Soter, son of Lagus, became King of Egypt, and in 312 added to his territories Jerusalem and the Holy Land, which continued for a hundred years to be governed by him and his descendants. A vast number of Jews were carried into Egypt, where they settled, and learned the Greek language, which was generally spoken at Alexandria, a Grecian city. Ptolemy and his descendants were great patrons of learning, and there is no reason to doubt the assertion of Josephus and Philo Judæus, that the Greek translation of the Hebrew Bible was made, wholly or in part, in the reign, if not by the command of his son, Ptolemy Philadelphus. With the critical questions that may arise concerning the dialect, grammatical forms, and peculiar idiom to be found in that translation, we have nothing to do at present: nor need we here speak of the miraculous interference of Providence to aid the translators, or of the successful issue of their work; for these facts may be found recorded in the work of Josephus and in any modern work which professes to take cognizance of Biblical inquiries. The existence of the Septuagint translation made from the Hebrew Bible at that time, leads to the inference that the Hebrew itself was then extant, or else to the less probable conclusion, which nevertheless has found its advocates, that the Hebrew text is a version and the Greek Septuagint an original.

CHAPTER IX.

VALUE OF CONTEMPORARY HISTORY.

It has been said that the authority of historical writings depends entirely on its being known who is their author. This, however, is not universally true; for many historical accounts, mostly fragments, and short treatises, are now in existence, the names of whose authors have perished, whilst the accounts themselves, being known by the antiquity of the MSS. where they are found, or by other means, to be contemporary with the events, are of the greatest historical value. We shall, therefore, speak more correctly if we say that an historical record is *more likely* to contain the truth when we know not only who wrote it, but that its author had a good opportunity of ascertaining the truth of the facts which he relates. It is indeed not absolutely necessary that both these conditions should exist together; it is sufficient that an historical record can be traced back to the very time when the facts which it relates are said to have occurred; in this case it becomes what is called Contemporary History, which is always considered more valuable than any other, though, to give it a place among first-class historical documents, it is still necessary that we should know where or how the writer gained his information, and if possible, we should know who that writer was. This will be evident from a few examples.

The campaigns of Julius Cæsar in Britain are related to us by the pen of that general himself, whose writings contain the only authentic records remaining of the events which happened to the Roman army which invaded this island. But several of the later Roman writers have recounted the same events, and their narratives, if Cæsar's Commentaries had perished, would have given us the only account of Cæsar's invasion and its consequences. In reading their histories, we should naturally have asked the question where they obtained their information, seeing that they wrote, some two hundred, some three hundred, and others even four hundred years after the events which they relate.

One more illustration may suffice. The Roman historian, Livy, wrote in the reign of Augustus: he recounts the actions of Romulus the first Roman king with the greatest minuteness, and he not only does not tell us where he obtained his information, but he even laments that all the early records of Rome were destroyed, when that city was burnt by the Gauls. For this reason the early part of Livy's history is deservedly looked upon with suspicion and unbelief.

As an instance of the credit which is always given to a history known to have been composed at the very time when the events which it records are said to have occurred, we may adduce the valuable history of the Peloponnesian war by Thucydides, who commanded an Athenian fleet during that war; and the Retreat of the Ten Thousand by Xenophon, to whose military talents mainly was due the success with which that retreat was conducted.*

It is evident that the memory of an event, no matter what may have been its magnitude, must entirely perish from the earth, if all those who lived at the time should die before the account of that event has been taken down in writing, or has otherwise been delivered to posterity, by monuments, coins, statues, and such other devices as the ingenuity of man has contrived. This remark does not, of course, apply to physical phænomena, such as the inunda-

* In our own times may be quoted the History of Napoleon's campaign in Russia by the Count de Segur, who served in that remarkable war, and whose narrative is regarded with the greatest respect, as a work of undoubted truth and authenticity.

tion of the rivers, the falling of avalanches, the disruptions of mountains, earthquakes, &c., all of which leave the most conspicuous memorials in the ruin which they create, and the debris which remain behind them. It is true, also, that the works of mankind may also, in their remains, convey to future ages an idea of what they once were: thus the works of Roman art are still turned up by the plough throughout the whole of Western Europe, confirming, beyond a doubt, the truth of what we read concerning that mighty people, and verifying the prediction of the poet,

> The time shall one day come when in that soil,
> The ploughman, as he ploughs the earth with toil,
> Shall turn up helmets eaten out with rust,
> And gaze at mighty bones buried beneath the dust.*

But these imperishable records of the past cannot communicate to us the varied movements of man's avarice, pride, or ambition: they cannot trace the minute distinctions which separate the nations of the world: all the busy vicissitudes that form the life and soul of that magnificent science, which we call written history, can not be wholly handed down to posterity, though they can be usefully illustrated, by the ruins which time makes of man's works, after their authors have perished. To perpetuate the acts, the inventions, and the wisdom of our species, no other instrument can be used but the pen of the writer; and numberless other appliances are needful to give effect to the agency of the pen itself. Sculpture seems to have supplied the place of writing till a very late epoch in the history of mankind. Afterwards, when the arts were somewhat advanced, wooden tablets, leather, leaves of trees, vellum, and parchment were found serviceable to supply the place of stone, and it is a reasonable belief that the invention of these last materials in conjunction with the use of an alphabet, dates from a period not much further back than the seventh century before the Christian era.

It will be granted, then, that our estimate of an historical work must depend on the means which the writer has

---

* Scilicet et tempus veniet, quum finibus illis
Agricola, incurvo terram molitus aratro,
Exesa inveniet scabra rubigine pila,
Grandiaque effossis mirabitur ossa sepulcris.
VIRG. *Ge.* i, 493.

enjoyed of ascertaining the truth of the facts which he records; supposing always that he has honestly employed his materials. If we apply this remark to the Old Testament, it becomes necessary to inquire who are the authors of the several books, or, if we cannot ascertain who actually wrote them, whether it can be satisfactorily shown that the authors, whoever they were, had a good opportunity of knowing that they wrote nothing but the truth.

CHAPTER X.

OF THE REPUTED AUTHORS OF THE SEVERAL BOOKS IN THE OLD TESTAMENT.

In the introduction prefixed to Genesis, in the first volume of D'Oyly and Mant's edition of the Bible, I find the following passage:

The first five books of the Bible, commonly called the Pentateuch, were composed by Moses, as the concurrent testimonies of all ages declare; and, as hath ever been firmly believed by the Jews, with whom the fact continues to this day to be one of the thirteen articles of their creed. The word "Pentateuch" is of Greek original; being compounded of two words, signifying *five*, and *book* or *volume*. It was probably first prefixed to the Greek version of the "Septuagint" or seventy translators; to denote Genesis, Exodus, Leviticus, Numbers and Deuteronomy: all of which had been written by the hand of Moses in Hebrew, probably in the order in which they now stand, though not distributed by their author into books, but forming one continued work.

The same editors give us compiled from Dr. Gray and Bishop Tomline, the following remarks concerning the reputed author of the book of Joshua:

The book of Joshua continues the sacred history from the death of Moses to the deaths of Joshua and Eleazar, a space of about thirty years. It contains an account of the conquest and division of the land of Canaan, the renewal of the covenant with the Israelites, and the death of Joshua. There are two passages in this book which show that it was written by a person who lived at the time when the events happened. In the first verse of chap. v, the author speaks of himself as being one of those who passed into Canaan, by using the expression, "Until *we* were passed over." And in the 25th verse of the following chapter, it appears that the book was written when Rahab was alive : for it is said of her, "she dwelleth in Israel unto this day." There is not a perfect agreement among the learned, respecting the author of this book ; but by far the most general opinion is, that it was written by Joshua himself. The five verses, giving an account of the death of Joshua, were added by one of his successors, probably by Phinehas or Samuel.

As I shall hereafter enter more fully into the internal evidence which the book of Joshua furnishes, it is unnecessary to say more in this place concerning the two passages, which are here quoted as a proof that the work is of a contemporary character. The extract is made at present, as showing the opinion generally received concerning the origin of the book of Joshua and its author.

Of the book of Judges, the same commentators remark :

This book has been variously attributed to Samuel, to Phinehas, to Hezekiah, to Ezekiel, and also to Ezra, who is supposed by some to have collected it from the memoirs, which the several judges respectively furnished of their own government. It seems, however, most probable, that Samuel was the author ; who, being a prophet or seer, and described in the book of Chronicles as an historian, may reasonably be supposed, as he was the last of the judges, to have written this part of the Jewish history, since the inspired writers alone were permitted to describe those relations, in which were interwoven the instructions and judgments of the Lord. That it was certainly written before the reign of David is proved from the following passage, i, 21, "The Jebusites dwell with the children of Benjamin unto this day :" for it is certain, II Samuel v, 6, that the Jebusites were driven out of the city early in the reign of David.

The assumed fact of David's expulsion of the Jebusites will be hereafter noticed.

Of the book of Ruth a similar statement is made.

The book of Ruth is so called from the name of the person, a native of Moab, whose history it contains. It may be considered as a supplement to the book of Judges, to which it was joined in the Hebrew canon, and the latter part of which it greatly resembles, being a detached story belonging to the same period. Ruth had a son called Obed, who was the grandfather of David ; which circumstance probably occasioned her history to be written, as the genealogy of David, from Pharez the son of Judah, from whom the Messiah was to spring, is here given; and some commentators have thought the descent of our Saviour from Ruth, a Gentile woman, to be an intimation of the comprehensive nature of the Christian dispensation. We are nowhere informed when Ruth lived, but, as king David was her great-grandson, we may place her history about 1250 years before Christ. This book was certainly written after the birth of David, chap. iv, 22, and probably by the prophet Samuel, though some have attributed it to Hezekiah, and others to Ezra. The subject of it is of so private a nature, that at the time of its being written, the generality of people might not have thought it worth recording.

Of the first book of Samuel :

The Hebrews suppose that Samuel wrote the twenty-four first chapters of the first book, and that the rest were added by the prophets Gad and Nathan. This opinion is founded on these words in the first book of Chronicles, chap. xxix, 29, "Now the acts of David the king, first and last, behold, they are written in the book of Samuel the seer, and in the book of Nathan the prophet, and in the book of Gad the seer:" and it is approved by many writers of considerable authority. We may therefore assent to this general opinion, that Samuel was the author of at least the greater part of the first book, and that he probably composed it towards the latter end of his life.

Nothing is said by the commentators above-mentioned concerning the author of the second book of Samuel, but in Bishop Tomline's Elements of Christian Theology, vol. i, page 87, we find the following passage :

The second book of Samuel continues the history of David, after the death of Saul, through a space of 40 years. It was probably written, as was just now observed, by Gad and Nathan, but it is impossible to assign to them their respective parts.

The same writer, as quoted by the editors of the Bible before-mentioned, speaks of the two books of Kings in the following manner :

The two books of Kings formed only one in the Hebrew canon. They cannot be positively ascribed to any particular author : some have ascribed them to Jeremiah, some to Isaiah ; and some, again, with more probability, suppose them to have been compiled by Ezra, from the records which were regularly kept, both in Jerusalem and Samaria, of all public transactions. These records appear to have been made by the contemporary prophets, and frequently derived their names from the kings whose history they contain. They are mentioned in many parts of Scripture; thus, in the first book of Kings, we read of the book of the Acts of Solomon, which is supposed to have been written by Nathan, Abijah and Iddo. We elsewhere read that Shemaiah the prophet and Iddo the seer, wrote the acts of Rehoboam; that Jehu wrote the acts of Jehoshaphat, and Isaiah those of Uzziah and Hezekiah. We may therefore conclude, that from these public records, and other authentic documents, were composed the two books of Kings; and the uniformity of their style favours the opinion of their being put into their present shape by the same person.

The two books of Chronicles are prefaced in the same edition of the Bible as follows:

The two books of Chronicles formed but one in the Hebrew canon which was called the book of Diaries or Journals. In the Septuagint version they were called, the books of "things omitted," and they were first named the books of Chronicles by St Jerome. They are supposed to be designed as a kind of supplement to the preceding books of Scripture, to supply such important particulars as had been omitted, because inconsistent with the plan of former books. They are generally, and with much probability, attributed to Ezra, whose book which bears his name is written with a similar style of expression, and appears to be a continuation of them. Ezra may have compiled these books, by the assistance of Haggai and Nehemiah, from historical records, and the accounts of contemporary prophets.

The book of Ezra "derives its name from Ezra the author of it;" according to those same commentaries, and Nehemiah is introduced as follows:

The book of Nehemiah, being subjoined in the Hebrew canon to that of Ezra as a continuation of his history, was often considered as his work: and in the Latin and Greek Bibles it is called the second book of Ezra; but it undoubtedly was written by Nehemiah, for he professes himself the author of it in the beginning, and uniformly speaks in the first person.

The book of Esther:

The author of the book is not certainly known. Some of the Fathers suppose it to have been written by Ezra; others contend that it was composed by Joachim, high-priest of the Jews, and grandson of Josedech. The Talmudists attribute it to the joint labours of the great synagogue, which succeeded Ezra in the superintendence of the canon of Scripture. The 20th verse of the 9th chapter of the book has led others to believe that Mordecai was the author; but what is there related to have been written by him, seems only to refer to the circular letter which he distributed. There are, lastly, other writers who maintain that the book was the production of Esther's and Mordecai's united industry; and probably they may have communicated an account of events so interesting to the whole nation, to the great synagogue at Jerusalem, some of the members of which may with great reason be supposed to have digested the information thus received into its present form. We have, however, no sufficient evidence to determine, nor is it, perhaps, of much importance to ascertain precisely, who was the author: but that the book contains a genuine and faithful description of what did actually happen, is certain, not only from its admission into the canon, but also from the institution of the feast of Purim, which from its first establishment has been regularly observed as an annual solemnity, on the 14th and 15th of the month Adar, in commemoration of the great deliverance which Esther, by her interest, had procured; and which is even now celebrated among the Jews with many peculiar ceremonies, and with rejoicings even to intoxication. This festival was called Purim, or the feast of lots, (PUR in the Persian language signifying a *lot*), from the events mentioned in chap. iii, 7; ix, 24.

The book of Job also is described as an autobiography, and the critical reader cannot fail to be amused at the frankness with which the commentator founds this opinion not on any argument that might support it, but on the advantages which it would furnish to those who maintain its authenticity.

It appears probable that Job himself was the writer of his own story . . . . If we allow Job himself to have been the writer of the book, there will be evidently two advantages hereby gained to it: as first, that all objections to the historical truth of it will vanish at once, &c., &c.

Psalms:

The book of Psalms, that is, the book of Hymns of Praises of the Lord, contains the productions of different writers. These productions are called however the Psalms of David, because a great part of them were composed by him. Some of them were perhaps penned before and some after, the time of David; but all of them by persons under the influence of the Holy Ghost, since all were judged worthy to be inserted into the canon of Sacred Writ. Ezra probably collected them into one book, and placed them in the order which they now preserve.

Proverbs:

The Proverbs, as we are informed at the beginning, and in other parts of the book, were written, for the most part, by Solomon, the son of David ; a man, as the Sacred Writings assure us, peculiarly endued with Divine wisdom. Whatever ideas of his superior understanding we may be led to form by the particulars recorded of his judgment and attainments, we shall find them amply justified on perusing the works which remain, and give testimony of his abilities. This enlightened monarch, being desirous of employing the wisdom which he had received to the advantage of mankind, produced several works for their inspection. Of these, however, three only were admitted into the canon of Sacred Writ by Ezra ; the others being either not designed for religious instruction, or so mutilated by time and accident, as to have been judged imperfect. The Book of Proverbs, that of Ecclesiastes, and that of the Song of Solomon, are all that remain of the writings of him, who is related to have spoken "three thousand proverbs," whose "songs were a thousand and five," and who "spake of trees from the cedar that is in Lebanon, even unto the hyssop that springeth out of the wall," who "spake also of beasts, and of fowl, and of creeping things, and of fishes." If, however, many valuable compositions of Solomon have perished, we have reason to be grateful for what still remains. Of his Proverbs and Songs the most excellent have been providentially preserved ; and, as we possess his doctrinal and moral works, we have no right to murmur at the loss of his physical and philosophical productions.

But it is not contended that King Solomon was the author of *all* the Proverbs contained in this book: for

The Proverbs which are included between the twenty-fifth and thirtieth chapters, and which constitute the fourth part, are supposed to have been selected from a much greater number by the "men of Hezekiah ;" that is, by the prophets whom he employed to restore the service and the writings of the Church, as Eliakim, and Joah and Shebna, and probably Hosea, Micah, and even Isaiah, who all flourished in the reign of that monarch, and doubtlessly co-operated with his endeavours to re-establish true religion among the Jews. These Proverbs, indeed, appear to have been selected by some collectors after the time of Solomon, as they repeat some which he had previously introduced in the former part of the book. The fifth part contains the prudent admonitions which Agur the son of Jakeh delivered to his pupils Ithiel and Ucal : these are included in the 30th chapter. It contains, also, the precepts which the mother of Lemuel delivered to her son, as described in the 31st chapter. Concerning these persons, whose works are annexed to those of Solomon, commentators have entertained various opinions.

The original words which describe Agur as the author of the thirtieth chapter, might be differently translated; but admitting the present construction as most natural and just, we may observe, that the generality of the Fathers and ancient commentators have supposed that, under the name of Agur, Solomon describes himself, though no satisfactory reason can be assigned for his assuming this name. Others, upon very insufficient grounds, conjecture that Agur and Lemuel were interlocutors with Solomon. The book has no appearance of dialogue, nor is there any interchange of person: it is more probable that though the book was designed principally to contain the sayings of Solomon, others might be added by the "men of Hezekiah:" and Agur might have been an inspired writer, whose moral and proverbial sentences (for such is the import of the word Massa, rendered prophesy) were joined with those of the Wise Man, because of the conformity of their matter. So likewise the dignity of the book is not affected, if we suppose the last chapter to have been written by a different hand, and admit the mother of Lemuel to have been a Jewish woman, married to some neighbouring prince; or Abijah, the daughter of the high-priest Zechariah, and mother of king Hezekiah; since in any case it must be considered as the production of an inspired writer, or it would not have been received into the canon of Scripture. But it was perhaps meant that by Lemuel we should understand Solomon; for the name which signifies one belonging to God, might have been given unto him as descriptive of his character, since to Solomon God had expressly declared that he would be a father.

Ecclesiastes:

The book of Ecclesiastes is called in Hebrew "*Coheleth*," a word which signifies one who speaks in public; and which indeed is properly translated by the Greek word Ecclesiastes, or the Preacher. It is unquestionably the production of Solomon, who for the great excellency of his instructions is emphatically styled, "the Preacher:" for the writer of it styles himself, "the son of David, king of Jerusalem," chap. i, 1; he describes too his wisdom, his riches, his writings, and his works in a manner which is applicable only to Solomon; and by all tradition, Jewish and Christian, the book is attributed to him. It is said by the Jews to have been written by him, upon his awakening to repentance, after he had been seduced, in the decline of life, to idolatry and sin; and if this be true, it affords valuable proofs of the sincerity with which he regretted his departure from righteousness.

Song of Solomon:

This book was written by Solomon, to whom it is expressly ascribed by the Hebrew title. It is almost universally allowed to have been a marriage-song of that monarch, composed on the celebration of his nuptials with a very beautiful woman, called "the "Shulamite," the daughter, as has been supposed, of Pharaoh, and the favourite and distinguished wife of Solomon.

The Prophetical books of the Old Testament:

It is universally acknowledged, that the remaining books of the Old Testament, namely the sixteen prophetical books, and the Lamentations of Jeremiah, were written by the persons whose names they bear. The prophets profess themselves to be the respective authors of these books: and internal testimony is confirmed both by Jewish and Christian tradition.

In these extracts we have the view which is generally entertained by the English reader, not based upon any investigation of facts, but taken for granted without examition and growing through a long period of time, like many other opinions which have got possession of the popular belief, but which shrink into their due proportions when the light of criticism is applied.

CHAPTER XI.

THE CLAIMS OF MOSES TO THE AUTHORSHIP OF THE PENTATEUCH INVESTIGATED: FIRST, FROM TRADITION OR UNIVERSAL CONSENT.

It is admitted by all who have examined this subject, that the earliest accounts and traditions of all nations are either wholly fabulous, or are so intermingled with fable that it is difficult, if not impossible, to distinguish the true from the false. Of our own island we know almost nothing before the invasion of Cæsar: and France, Spain, Germany, with all the rest of northern Europe, are enveloped in equal obscurity until the second century before the Christian æra. Rome herself, the conqueror and mistress of the civilized world, has nothing to tell us, which merits our belief until the third century before Christ: all the accounts of the four hundred and fifty years preceding the Punic wars, are of so legendary a character that they convey no clear facts to the judgment, however they may furnish material for poetry to the imagination. Greece, also, the parent of European literature, becomes lost in darkness, anterior to the Trojan war; and even that celebrated campaign of Europe against Asia, has been so adorned by the poets, that beyond the simple fact of its having happened, we cannot rely on any of the details which have come down to us. With the exception of Homer alone, who was a poet and lived nine hundred years before Christ, we possess no literary works, except fragments and a few songs, earlier than the History of Herodotus written about five hundred years only before the Christian era. But from what we know of Grecian letters, it is admitted by all that they owed their origin to Phœnicia, from whence civilization and learning are said to have been brought into Europe by the Phœnician Cadmus about fourteen hundred years before Christ. Yet of the written records of Phœnicia it may with truth be said that hardly a particle survives, beyond what has been preserved in the Grecian writers, Herodotus, Diodorus, and others.

In harmony with this view is the fact that all the histories which we possess, to whatever nation they belong, become less credible in proportion to their antiquity; not that the writers have invented the facts which they relate, but that those facts, having come down to them by oral tradition only, have been so altered in the transmission from one mouth to another, that it becomes difficult to discern their first and original character. We may form some idea of this process, if we compare two separate narratives of the same fact happening in our own times. It is rarely that such accounts tally, even in the features of that which they describe. It may, even, be doubted whether a single isolated event, witnessed by two different persons, would convey exactly the same idea to the minds of both: but when the two come to relate what they have seen, to a third person, we can hardly expect that the descriptions will coincide in every respect with the original or with one another. What then will be likely to happen in the case of events which occurred three thousand years ago, and which have been handed down for a long time by no other than the uncertain mouth of tradition? We cannot be wrong in exacting the most scrupulous proof of a narrative which rests on such a basis: for though we may believe that the author who first wrote it, has faithfully told us what he heard from others, yet the picture, having been taken, not from the original, but from the last of a long succession of pictures, each copied from the other, we can no longer depend upon the likeness; for, whilst it has lost some of its features by the treacherous inexactitude of one painter, it has probably gained others which the glowing imagination of a second has added, until at last it assumes an appearance wholly different from that which the prototype presented. To those who are conversant with the discrepancies, on the one hand, and the obscurity, on the other, which all Ancient History presents, the value of a Contemporary Writer becomes more and more apparent, and intermediate narratives, based upon tradition alone, sink proportionably in estimation.

But these remarks apply with much greater force to Eastern than to European History; and for a reason which Mr Clinton has stated with much justice and perspicuity in his Fasti Hellenici, volume II, page 373, of the third edition.

In the great monarchies of Asia, Oriental history has seldom been faithfully delivered by the Orientals themselves. In the ancient times, before the Greek kingdoms of Asia diffused knowledge and information, it is not likely that history would be undertaken by private individuals. The habits of the people, and the form of their governments, precluded all free inquiry and any impartial investigation of the truth. The written histories of past transactions would be contained in the archives of the state; and these royal records, drawn up under the direction of the reigning despot, would deliver just such a representation of fact as the government of the day thought fit to give; just so much of the truth as it suited their purpose to communicate. Of the authority of such materials for history we may judge, by comparing the account which has been transmitted to us from Ctesias of the rise of the Medes and the fall of Nineveh, with the very different account which Herodotus has left of the same transactions: the one utterly at variance with any thing possible, convicted of absurdity in every circumstance by the plain evidence of Scripture, the other confirmed by the same authority in all the particulars both of facts and dates. And yet Ctesias drew his narrative from royal archives; and, in this part of his subject at least, had no temptation to wilful falsehood.

It becomes necessary, therefore, to investigate the grounds upon which the Jews have claimed for the authors of their scriptural books the character of contemporary writers, and, that we may enter clearly into such an inquiry, it seems best to proceed through the several divisions of the Old Testament, beginning with the Five Books of the Pentateuch, said to have been written by Moses, who died about the year B.C. 1451, just before the Israelites entered the land of Canaan.

The ascription of the authorship of the Pentateuch to Moses the Hebrew legislator, seems to rest upon the following arguments.

1. Those books have always been supposed to have been written by Moses; or, in other words, *Universal Tradition* asserts that Moses was the writer. 2. It is said, on the authority of the books themselves, especially of Deuteronomy, xxi, 26, where Moses is described as saying, " *Take this book* of the law, and put it in the side of the ark of the covenant of the Lord your God, that it may be there for a witness against them".. that these books, i.e. the Pentateuch, written by the hand of Moses, were placed by him, not long before his death, in the tabernacle, under the custody of the priests, where they were preserved, either in the original autograph, or in an authentic copy, for many hundred years and so have descended to posterity.

This is the argument to which the name of INTERNAL EVIDENCE has been affixed: and, in confirmation of this direct kind, have been cited certain texts of an indirect nature, implying that the same books were certainly written by somebody who was situated like Moses. Thus, Deuteronomy, i, 1, "on this side Jordan" is quoted to prove that the books must have been written in the wilderness, and therefore, by Moses; but I shall show in a future chapter of this work, that in this and other passages, the Hebrew word has been wrongly so translated.

The first of these arguments is a question of fact, and

must be determined, like all other facts, by positive evidence alone.

Tradition originally implied oral transmission, as opposed to written testimony, and was in use before the art of writing was known; but when we consider the great obscurity and even the glaring absurdities in which all History, previous to the introduction of letters, is involved we cannot, I think, admit the validity of a tradition which mounts back through the period of fourteen hundred and fifty years, the interval between the death of Moses and the Christian era. But it seems difficult to say what is the meaning of the expression that tradition has always named Moses as the author of the Pentateuch. Our examination is not of the books of Moses alone, but of the Hebrew Scriptures or Old Testament in its totality, of which I hold the Pentateuch to be merely a division or section, and not a separate work. Taken in this light, coupled with the fact that all the tradition is derived from the books themselves, surely such tradition cannot prove the antiquity of that book. For besides the tradition derived from the Old Testament, there is none other for a space of thirteen hundred years after the time of Moses. In other words, no other book exists which mentions the Old Testament until thirteen hundred years from the time of Moses. But let us waive this point, and hear what so-called tradition, has to say. As the tongues which were the successive vehicles of this tradition, are now all silent, we can have no other mode of determining what they said, than by referring to what has come down to us in a written form: for tradition is a being of a very unsubstantial character, and soon expires, unless its words are perpetuated by being copied before their meaning evaporates: like the Common Law of England, and the unwritten laws of states in general, which, though termed *unwritten*, were nevertheless, at a very early period, taken down in writing and so lost their original form, for assuredly no other process would have preserved the knowledge of them to posterity.

In the case of a simple fact like that which we are now considering, namely that Moses was the author of the Pentateuch; it does not appear how tradition can be an effective ground for such a belief; for, if the first person who originated the assertion, could produce no proof of what he said, it is unimportant whether it has been repeated ten or ten thousand times, or whether one year or a thousand have since elapsed. We must therefore qualify the argument of tradition, and consider it to mean that in all ages since the time of Moses the Pentateuch has been admitted to have been written by his hand. To establish such an assertion, it becomes necessary to show that a series of writers, beginning in the time of Moses or at least in the next generation, have ascribed to him the authorship of the book in question.

In support, then, of the claims of Moses, certain passages are quoted from the Book of Joshua, which continues the Jewish History after the death of Moses; and it is thought that these passages allude to the Pentateuch, such as we now have it, proving thereby that this book was then in existence. Thus in Joshua, i, 7, 8, we read the following exhortation addressed by the Lord to Joshua:

Only be thou strong and very courageous: that thou mayest observe to do according to all the law, which Moses my servant commanded thee: turn not from it to the right hand or to the left, that thou mayest prosper whithersoever thou goest. This BOOK OF THE LAW shall not depart out of thy mouth; but thou shalt meditate therein day and night, that thou mayest observe to do according to all that is written therein: for then thou shalt make thy way prosperous, and then thou shalt have good success.

Again, at Joshua, xxiii, 6, we read:

Be ye therefore very courageous to keep and do all that is written in the book of the law of Moses, that ye turn not aside therefrom to the right hand or to the left.

In another passage of the same book, viii, 34, we are told that Joshua, the successor of Moses,

read all the words of 'the law, the blessings and cursings, according to all that is written in the book of the law; there was not a word of all that Moses commanded, which Joshua read not before all the congregation of Israel.

From which passage, according to Bishop Tomline, as we read in his Elements of Christian Theology, vol. i, p. 35, "it is evident, that the Book of the Law, or *Pentateuch*, existed in the time of Joshua, the successor of Moses." But this inference is certainly more than is warranted by the premises. It may be readily admitted as an inference from the passage above quoted, that the Book of the Law existed in the time of Joshua, but that the Book of the Law was the Pentateuch that now exists, does not appear so clearly from the words of Joshua. In drawing this distinction, I would impress upon the reader's mind the necessity of his not confounding the authorship of a book with the truth of its contents. A book may be a true history, and yet not the production of the author to whom it is ascribed. Further, it may contain the sentiments, laws, and deeds, of an eminent man, without having been written by him. Thus the Pentateuch may contain, and I doubt not does contain, the substance of all that Moses ever wrote, and is a correct account, as far as human things admit, of what Moses did and taught, but it does not follow from the words of Joshua above quoted, that the Book of the Law there mentioned is the very book which we now possess, called the Pentateuch, and subdivided into the five books called Genesis, Exodus, Leviticus, Numbers, and Deuteronomy.

An objection might indeed lie, as before observed, in conducting an inquiry like the present, which will extend to all the books of the Hebrew Canon, against receiving the testimony of Joshua at all; for we know the Hebrew Canon, in no other form than as an undivided work, and the continuity of its contents, together with the sequence observed between each part of it and that immediately preceding, as shown in a former chapter, seems to favour the idea that it was compiled in one continuous narrative. If so, the testimony of its various parts is the testimony of that man only, who compiled it, and in a chain of chronological evidence forms one link only, and not a series of links. It might therefore be argued that no evidence of fact from one part of it should be admitted in support of another, at least in such a question as that which now lies before us, namely that of the concurrent testimony of ages; for it would be necessary, first, to prove that Joshua wrote the book which passes under his name, or at all events that the book of Joshua was written in the age immediately succeeding that of Moses. If the book of Joshua was not written till some hundreds of years later, its testimony cannot be taken as contemporary or nearly contemporary testimony to the authorship of the books of Moses. But the weakness of the first link in the chain of universal consent is sufficiently apparent without breaking the chain altogether. I am content, at present, to rest my objection to the testimony of Joshua on the fact that the Book of the Law which he quotes is not proved to be the same as our Pentateuch: and I think that it can be satisfactorily proved to have been a different book from that which we now possess.

In the meantime, even if we admit the statement in Joshua to prove that in his time there was a certain book called the Book of the Law: yet from this point the continuity of the witnesses is entirely broken. We certainly read in JUDGES, i, 20, "And they gave Hebron unto Caleb as Moses said: and he expelled thence the three sons of Anak." But this language is too vague to fix the identity of the Book of the Law with our Pentateuch; it does not necessarily imply that Moses wrote any book at all: and we in vain search through the rest of Judges, as also Ruth and the two books of Samuel for a continuation of the testimony —not the most remote trace is to be found of the Book of the Law or its author.

If it be conceded that these four last-mentioned books were written about the time of David's death, which happened in the year B.C. 1015,—for this is the point at which the history contained in them terminates,—and if it appears that these books, the only surviving records of those five hundred years, make no mention either of the Book of the Law, or of Moses its author, it necessarily results that the chain of testimony is interrupted, and that we cannot, on the strength of it, prove the Pentateuch to be the Book of the Law, written by Moses.

But the whole drift and force of our argument will be made more clear by adducing whatever testimony can be found in the remaining Hebrew writers and others, after which we may take a general view of the information which they give us.

As the Second Book of Samuel could not have been written before the reign of David, because it records the events of his old age, and some of the Psalms were written by David; the author of these Psalms, namely David himself, must be a little earlier in point of time than the author of the Second Book of Samuel: but neither does David, in the Psalms, nor his son Solomon, in the Books of Proverbs, Ecclesiastes and Canticles, make the most remote allusion to the Book of the Law, so that they furnish no link by which we may re-unite the broken chain of universal consent. It is true that David, in the Psalms, mentions Moses. The following are all the passages in which his name occurs.

Ps. lxxvii, 20. Thou leddest thy people like a flock by the hand of Moses and Aaron.

Ps. xcix, 6. Moses and Aaron among his priests, and Samuel among them that call upon his name.

Ps cv, 26. He sent Moses his servant, and Aaron whom he had chosen.

Ps. cvi, 16. They envied Moses also in the camp, and Aaron the saint of the Lord.

Ps. cvi, 23. Therefore he said that he would destroy them, had not Moses his chosen stood before him in the breach, to turn away his wrath, lest he should destroy them.

Ps. cvi, 32. They angered him also at the waters of strife, so that it went ill with Moses for their sakes.

The facts alluded to in these verses are certainly found in our Pentateuch; but many books exist, containing histories of the same facts without ever having been thought to be the same books. In fact we have seen above, in chapter v of this work, that the writer of the Pentateuch quotes other books, about the same transactions which himself records.

The author of the books of Proverbs, Ecclesiastes and Canticles, who is generally considered to be King Solomon, makes no mention either of the Book of the Law or of Moses its author.

This observation brings us down to the year B.C. 1055, when Solomon began to reign over Israel, but with the exception of the poetical books, Psalms, Proverbs, Ecclesiastes and Canticles, generally ascribed to Solomon and his father David, we have no written records of any kind for nearly three hundred years until the time of Jonah, who is supposed to be the earliest of the Prophets. But the Book of Jonah makes no mention of either Moses or of the Law, and none of the earlier * prophets have the most remote allusion to the

---

* There are a few slight allusions to the Book of the Law in the prophets, who are admitted to have written after the Captivity; the principal of these is in Daniel ix, 11.

subject, except Jeremiah and Malachi, in whose books of prophecies we find the following passages:

The word that came to Jeremiah from the Lord, saying, Hear ye the words of this covenant, and speak unto the men of Judah, and to the inhabitants of Jerusalem; and say thou unto them, Thus sayeth the Lord God of Israel; Cursed be the man that obeyeth not the words of this covenant, which I commanded your fathers in the day that I brought them forth out of the land of Egypt. JEREM. xi, 1—4.

Then said the Lord unto me, Though Moses and Samuel stood before me, yet my mind could not be toward this people. JEREM. xv, 1.

Remember ye the law of Moses my servant, which I commanded unto him in Horeb for all Israel, with the statutes and judgments. MALACHI, iv, 4.

These words, however, give us no assistance in identifying the writings of Moses with the Pentateuch which we now have: and no other testimony can be found until we come to about the thirty-seventh year of Jehoiachin king of Judah, which is the year 562 before Christ. As this is the last year mentioned in the books of Kings, it is clear that the writer of them could not have lived[*] before that time. Concurrent with the two Books of Kings are those of Chronicles, which are supposed to have been written by Ezra[†] after the Jewish captivity, about 500 years before the Christian era.

But between the time of Joshua—whose testimony to the existence of a Book of the Law has been admitted, on the supposition that he wrote the book which passes by his name —and the year 562 before Christ, when the author of the

---

[*] That the Books of Kings were written after the Babylonish Captivity, is admitted by all the Commentators, take, for instance, the following passage from Bishop Tomline's "Elements of Christian Theology," vol. i., p. 25.—"It seems probable, therefore, that the Books of Kings and Chronicles do not contain a complete compilation of the entire works of each contemporary prophet, but are rather an abridgement of their several labours, and of other authentic public writings, digested by Ezra after the Captivity, with an intention to display the sacred history under one point of view, and hence it is that they contain some expressions, which evidently result from contemporary description, and others which as clearly argue them to have been composed long after the occurrences which they relate."

[†] The Book of Ezra is, in fact, no more than a continuation of the Second Book of Chronicles; singularly enough the last two verses of Chronicles are the first two of Ezra, and there is no break in the narrative.

Books of Kings lived, there is an interval of nearly 900 years; and, it will be borne in mind, as far as we have yet proceeded, that no mention has been made by any intermediate writer of the Book of the Law, much less has any expression been discovered, by which it can be shown that the Book of the Law, which they had then, and the Pentateuch, which we have now, are one and the same book.

Let us, however, now see in what manner the writers of the Books of Kings and Chronicles speak of the Book of the Law or of Moses, in the course of their narratives, wherein they relate the transactions of the two Jewish kingdoms from the time of David and Solomon down to the reign of Jehoiachin, and from that time, as recorded in Chronicles alone, to the end of the Babylonish Captivity.

The first passages in chronological order occur in Chronicles: David alludes both to the Law, and to the ark of the covenant, but not to the Book of the Law. He says to his son Solomon:

Only the Lord give thee wisdom and understanding, and give thee charge concerning Israel, that thou mayest keep the law of the Lord thy God. Then shalt thou prosper, if thou takest heed to fulfil the statutes and judgments which the Lord charged Moses with concerning Israel. I CHRON. xxii, 12—13.

He addresses the princes of Israel in these words:

Now set your heart and your soul to seek the Lord your God; arise therefore, and build ye the sanctuary of the Lord God, to bring the ark of the covenant of the Lord, and the holy vessels of God, into the house that is to be built to the name of the Lord. I CHRON. xxii, 19.

In the First Book of Kings, viii, 53, occurs the following passage in the thanksgiving to the Lord which the writer puts into the mouth of King Solomon:

For thou didst separate them from among all the people of the earth to be thine inheritance, as thou spakest by the hand of *Moses* thy servant, when thou broughtest our fathers out of Egypt, O Lord God.

Also, in verse 56 of the same chapter:

Blessed be the Lord that hath given rest unto his people Israel, according to all that he promised! there hath not failed one word of all his good promise, which he promised by the hand of *Moses* his servant.

I Kings, ii, 3, David cautions Solomon his son:

And keep the charge of the Lord thy God, to walk in his ways, to keep his statutes, and his commandments, and his judgments, and his testimonies, as it is written in the *law of Moses*, that thou mayest prosper in all that thou doest, and whithersoever thou turnest thyself.

II Kings, xiv, 6. But the children of the murderers he [Amaziah] slew not; according unto that which is written in the *book of the law* of Moses, wherein the Lord commanded, saying, The fathers shall not be put to death for the children, nor the children be put to death for the fathers; but every man shall be put to death for his own sin.

The corresponding account, in II Chronicles, xxv, 4, is almost in the same words:

But he slew not their children, but did as it is written in *the law* in the *book of Moses*, where the Lord commanded, saying, The fathers shall not die for the children, neither shall the children die for the fathers, but every man shall die for his own sin.

The name of Moses is mentioned in II Chron. xxiv, 6, under the reign of Joash, but not the Book of the Law;

And the king called for Jehoiada the chief, and said unto him, Why hast thou not required of the Levites to bring in out of Judah and out of Jerusalem the collection, *according to the commandment* of Moses the servant of the Lord, and of the congregation of Israel, for the tabernacle of witness?

In the reign of Hezekiah, a solemn festival was held in Jerusalem, and the Law of Moses is mentioned by the writer of II Chronicles, xxx, 15—16:

Then they killed the passover on the fourteenth day of the second month: and the priests and Levites were ashamed, and sanctified themselves, and brought in the burnt-offerings into the house of the Lord. And they stood in their place after their manner, according to the law of Moses the man of God: the priests sprinkled the blood, which they received of the hand of the Levites.

In the corresponding chapters of the Book of Kings, we find no notice of this festival, or of the Law of Moses.

These texts require no comment: they contain mere notices of the Book of the Law, in connection with festivals and other events which took place in the reigns of the different kings of Israel and Judah. But the reader must continually be reminded that the histories in which these notices occur were not written or compiled until after the Babylonish captivity, and consequently they furnish the testimony of that man only, who compiled them, at the distance of nine hundred years from the time of Moses. His words, moreover, do not indicate that the Book of the Law, as it then existed, was the same as our Pentateuch, but only that there was at that time in existence a Book of the Law which passed under the name of Moses.

There are, however, some remarkable passages in the books of Chronicles and of Kings, which have not been noticed, because they are of a very different character from the foregoing, for they seem to prove that the Book of the Law was nothing more or less than the two tables of stone which God delivered to Moses on Mount Sinai. The first passage is as follows:

And all the elders of Israel came, and the priests took up the ark. And they brought up the ark of the Lord, and the tabernacle of the congregation, and all the holy vessels that were in the tabernacle, even those did the priests and the Levites bring up.

And king Solomon and all the congregation of Israel, that were assembled unto him, were with him before the ark, sacrificing sheep and oxen, that could not be told nor numbered for multitude.

And the priests brought in the ark of the covenant of the Lord unto his place, into the oracle of the house, to the most holy place, even under the wings of the cherubims. For the cherubims spread forth their two wings over the place of the ark, and the cherubims covered the ark and the staves thereof above. And they drew out the staves, that the ends of the staves were seen out in the holy place before the oracle, and they were not seen without: and there they are unto this day. *There was nothing in the ark save the two tables of stone*, which Moses put there at Horeb, when the Lord made a covenant with the children of Israel, when they came out of the land of Egypt. I KINGS, viii. 3—9.

These words form part of the narrative concerning the building of the Temple and the arrangement of the sacred utensils and other furniture with which it was stored.

Among the things that Solomon placed in it, was the ark of the covenant, which had formerly been kept in the Tabernacle before the Temple was built.

It was in the side of this very ark of the covenant that Moses commanded the Book of the Law to be placed, as appears from Deuteronomy, xxxi, 26; and yet, when Solomon caused the ark of the covenant to be removed to the Temple, it is expressly stated in the passage just quoted that there was then "*nothing in the ark save the two tables of stone*, which Moses put there at Horeb, when the Lord made a covenant with the children of Israel, when they came out of the land of Egypt." How then is this discrepancy to be explained? If Moses put both the two tables of stone and the Book of the Law into the ark, and only the former were still there in the time of Solomon, it is manifest that the Book of the Law must have been removed in the interval; probably, it may be said, by the Philistines, when they carried away the ark among the spoils of the defeated Israelites. If this be so, when was the Book of the Law restored? If it was never restored, how did the Israelites obtain the copy which we shall hereafter notice as having been carried round Judah by the order of king Jehoshaphat, and afterwards discovered in the Temple in the reign of king Josiah? It may, also, be asked, why the Philistines did not carry away the two tables of stone also; for these were still safe in the time of Solomon.

To these perplexing questions a simple answer may be given, which will solve the whole difficulty. The two tables of stone were the Book of the Law given by Moses, and besides them was no other: as I shall endeavour to prove more plainly in a future chapter. At present we will return to the point from which we have digressed, and proceed to show that the writer of the Books of Kings makes no mention of the Book of the Law, which will enable us to identify it with the existing Pentateuch, but rather that his words exclude the possibility of such a book having then existed.

It has been observed that there are certain passages connected with the notice of the Book of the Law, which bear upon our present argument. The first has been already produced, the second is as follows: Solomon is still supposed to be speaking:

And the Lord hath performed his word that he spake, and I am risen up in the room of David my father, and sit on the throne of Israel, as the Lord promised, and have built an house for the name of the Lord God of Israel. And I have set there a place for the ark, wherein is the covenant of the Lord, which he made with our fathers, when he brought them out of the land of Egypt. I KINGS, viii, 20—21.

This is an important passage: for it corroborates in every respect the explanation which has been given of the former passage: in the one we read that the two tables of stone were in the ark; in the other it is said that the covenant of the Lord was therein. The two tables of stone were, therefore, the same thing as the covenant; the ark is from them called the ark of the covenant; it is also called the ark of the testimony. The Book of the Law also is called the Book of the Testimony: and the whole matter becomes plain and intelligible; stone, and perhaps sometimes wood, were in those early days, the only material used to write upon, and so the Lord gave two tables of stone containing a summary of his commandments, to be the basis of the Jewish constitution and the foundation of their morals and government. As a fitting receptacle for these heirlooms of the nation, an *arca*, ark, coffer, or chest, was constructed, and this chest was called the ark of the covenant, because it contained the two tables aforesaid, and nothing besides them. If the Pentateuch had been in existence, it would have made the two tables of stone no longer necessary: they would have been a cumbersome and useless load.

If, however, it should be argued that Solomon *may* have placed the Book of the Law in the Temple, distinct from the ark of the covenant, I would ask where is the notice of this fact? It is impossible to prove a negative in any other way than by showing that there is no proof of such a thing having taken place. But, if Solomon placed the Book of the Law in the Temple, so valuable a treasure might surely have been worth mentioning among the lamps, censers, and other furniture, which were then placed there. In the First Book of Kings, vii, 51, we read:

So was ended all the work that king Solomon made for the house of the Lord. And Solomon brought in the things which David his father had dedicated; even the silver, and the gold, and the vessels, did he put among the treasures of the house of the Lord.

The passage in the Second Book of Chronicles (iv, 19—23) which corresponds to this is still more full and explicit.

And Solomon made all the vessels that were for the house of God, the golden altar also, and the tables whereon the show-bread was set: moreover, the candlesticks with their lamps, that they should burn after the manner before the oracle, of pure gold: And the flowers, and the lamps, and the tongs, made he of gold, and that perfect gold; and the snuffers, and the basons, and the spoons, and the censers of pure gold: and the entry of the house, the inner doors thereof for the most holy place, and the doors of the house of the temple, were of gold.

But the Book of the Law, it seems, was not brought in and placed in the Temple; at least, there is no record of its having been so placed. It is more merciful towards the judgment of the wise Solomon to conclude that it was not in existence, than that, being in existence, this imperishable record was less esteemed than the silver and gold, and the lamps and the tongs, with which the perishable fabric of the Temple was embellished.

About seventy years after the death of Solomon, Jehoshaphat was reigning over the kingdom of Judah. His prudent measures for reforming and instructing his subjects are related in II CHRONICLES, xvii, 7—9:

Also in the third year of his reign he [Jehoshaphat] sent to his princes, even to Benhail, and to Obadiah, and to Zechariah, and to Nethaneel, and to Michaiah, to teach in the cities of Judah. And with them he sent Levites, even Shemaiah, and Nethaniah, and Zebadiah, and Asahel, and Shemiramoth, and Jehonathan, and Adonijah, and Tobijah, and Tob-adonijah, Levites; and with them Elishama and Jehoram, priests. And they taught in Judah, and had the Book of the Law of the Lord with them, and went about throughout all the cities of Judah, and taught the people.

The emissaries of the king, it is here stated, *had the Book of the Law.* Was there then only one copy of this book, and that the original which had been given by the hand of Moses? It would appear from this verse (which however has no corresponding notice in the Books of Kings), that there was no other copy of the Book of the Law, or the teachers who went through the country would not have been under the necessity of carrying it with them. Here too, if we suppose, as has been before repeatedly observed that the Book of the Law was nothing more than the two tables of stone, all difficulties vanish; and the history is reduced to harmony with our antecedent notions respecting those primitive times, when writing consisted rather in monuments and inscriptions upon stone than in the more refined usage of books and alphabets, which, I purpose, in a future chapter, to show, had not then been invented. Meanwhile let us examine the last passages in the Books of Kings and Chronicles, which mention the Book of the Law the subject of our present inquiry.

The occasion on which the subject is revived is curious, and has given rise to much discussion. The writer of the Second Book of Kings describes it as follows:

It came to pass in the eighteenth year of King Josiah, that the king sent Shaphan the son of Azaliah, the son of Meshullam, the scribe, to the house of the Lord, saying, " Go up to Hilkiah the high-priest, that he may sum the silver which is brought into the house of the Lord which the keepers of the door have gathered of the people: and let them deliver it into the hand of the doers of the work, that have the oversight of the house of the Lord: and let them give it to the doers of the work which is in the house of the Lord, to repair the breaches of the house, unto carpenters, and builders and masons, and to buy timber and hewn stone to repair the house." Howbeit there was no reckoning made with them of the money that was delivered into their hand, because they dealt faithfully.

And Hilkiah the high priest said unto Shaphan the scribe, " I have found the BOOK OF THE LAW in the house of the Lord:" and Hilkiah gave the book to Shaphan, and he read it. And Shaphan the scribe came to the king and brought the king word again and said, " Thy servants have gathered the money that was found in the house, and have delivered it into the hand of them that do the work, that have the oversight of the house of the Lord." And Shaphan the scribe showed the king, saying "Hilkiah the priest hath delivered me a book." And Shaphan read it before the king, and it came to pass, when the king had heard the words of the Book of the Law, that he rent his clothes: and the king commanded Hilkiah the priest, and Ahikam the son of Shaphan, and Achbor the son of Michaiah, and Shaphan the scribe, and Asahiah a servant of the king's, saying, " Go ye, inquire of the Lord for me, and for the people, and for all Judah, concerning the words of this book that is found: for great is the wrath of the Lord that is kindled against us, because our fathers have not hearkened unto the words of this book, to do according unto all that which is written concerning us," II KINGS, xxii, 3—13.

In the next chapter (xxiii, 1) is an account of the passover which was held by Josiah, in consequence of this discovery of the Book of the Law. The narrative opens with these words:

And the king sent, and they gathered unto him all the elders of Judah and of Jerusalem. And the king went up into the house of the Lord, and all the men of Judah and all the inhabitants of Jerusalem with him, and the priests, and the prophets, and all the people, both small and great; and he read in their ears all the words of the Book of the Covenant which was found in the house of the Lord. And the king stood by a pillar, and made a covenant before the Lord, to walk after the Lord and to keep his commandments and his testimonies and his statutes with all their heart and all their soul, to perform the words of this covenant that were written in this book. And all the people stood to the covenant.

The whole of this narrative is confirmed by the writer of the second book of Chronicles (xxxiv, 14) with the addition that the Book of the Law then found was *given by Moses*, or, according to the marginal translation, *by the hand of Moses*.

The passover, also, is described in a similar manner, and almost in the very same words, and the book that had just been found, is said to have been the model by which the ceremonies were regulated.

II Chron. xxxv, 11, 12. And they killed the passover and the priests sprinkled the blood from their hands, and the Levites flayed them. And they removed the burnt offerings, that they might give according to the divisions of the families of the people, to offer unto the Lord, as it is written in the Book of Moses.

These, then, are all the notices which we find in the books of Chronicles and Kings, concerning the Book of the Law, given by the hand of Moses for the use of the Israelitish people. They may be analyzed as follows.

In all those verses where no historical fact is related concerning the very volume itself, i.e. where there is merely a quotation from it, as in the words, "as it is written in the Law of Moses," we can derive no evidence whatever, concerning the nature of the book: because the writer of the history, living after the Babylonish captivity, and having the Book of the Law before him, may be supposed to have himself inserted these verses for the benefit of his readers. But from the relation of the events which happened in the reign of Jehoshaphat and Josiah, connected with the silence observed concerning any Book of the Law at all in the reign of Solomon, we are led, I think, to believe that the Book of the Law was only the tables of stone delivered by God to Moses on Mount Sinai. The facts are briefly these. In the reign of Solomon we have positive evidence that the two tables of stone were still preserved, but not the Book of the Law. In the reign of Jehoshaphat, 70 years later, the law is carried round the country for the general edification of the people; and in the reign of Josiah, more than two hundred years after Jehoshaphat, it is found and revived. If these historical facts are correctly related, I cannot conceive any other inference to be drawn from them than that the Book of the Law and the two tables of stone were the same, and that besides them there was no other.

But whatever curious inquiries may be based upon these facts, whether the Book of the Law was different or not from the tables of stone, it is almost certain that there was but one copy in existence during the whole duration of the Israelitish kingdoms, and nothing has yet been adduced to prove that it was the same book, which we now call the Pentateuch. Indeed the writer who records these facts, living after the Babylonish captivity, can give us evidence only for the opinions which prevailed in his own age, and furnishes no link to re-unite the chain of tradition which has been broken for 900 years since the time of Joshua. What a long period—nine hundred years! Nations have arisen and passed away: revolutions upon revolutions have been made and again forgotten; empires have been formed and perished in half that time: languages have changed so totally that if those who lived at the two extremities of such a space could be brought together, they could neither converse with one another, nor have two ideas in common. Scarcely have eight hundred years elapsed since the Norman Conquest, and yet what changes have happened even in the comparatively stable and civilized monarchy of England. What then must be the case with the nation of the Israelites, a fugitive and half-barbarous people, escaped out of Egypt, governed first by a sort of theocratic chieftains called Judges, then a monarchy, and finally divided into hostile kingdoms;

and during the whole nine hundred years rent in pieces by intestine convulsions, such as never before or since distracted so small a community.

And, what strengthens this argument tenfold, is the fact that this long period of nine hundred years lies wholly in the regions of obscurity and not of civilization; it ends before civilization and learning had begun. In every country of the world, few records have been preserved, except the works of Homer and Hesiod, as early as even the end of this period of nine hundred years. It may with reason be doubted whether the Pentateuch or any other volume copied by the pen and of equal size, could be preserved entire and in its original state under such circumstances. But this is not my present argument; I only contend that the silence of nine hundred years altogether refutes the argument of that Universal Consent on which is based the belief that the Book of the Law, or the Book of Moses, is the same as the Pentateuch which we now have.

Let us, however, hear what Dr Kennicott, the commentator on the Hebrew Bible, says concerning the Book of the Law found in the Temple in the eighteenth year of King Josiah.

The law, after being so long concealed, would be unknown to very many of the Jews; and thus the solemn reading of it by Josiah would awaken his own and the people's earnest attention. The copy produced was probably the original, * written by Moses, which would excite still greater veneration. The distance of time was not such as to make it incredible that the copy now found was that written by Moses himself: for there was certainly not a greater interval from the death of Moses to the death of Josiah than 950 years; and we have manuscripts existing among us at the present day of greater age than this.

* The following passage from Milman's "History of the Jews," vol. i, p. 316, shows that the able author of that work also considered the Book of the Law, found by Hilkiah, to have been the original copy delivered by Moses, or, at least, he seems to take it for granted according to the opinion which generally prevailed.

"Josiah surpassed even his most religious predecessors, Asa, Jehoshaphat, Azariah, or Hezekiah, in zeal for the reformation of the national religion. His first care was to repair the temple. While the work was proceeding, the king and the whole nation heard with the utmost exultation that Hilkiah, the high-priest, had discovered the original copy of the Law. But so little were its real contents known, that on its first reading, the king was struck with terror at its awful denunciations. The book was read in public; Josiah and all the nation renewed the solemn covenant with their God."

It is true, as the writer of this passage remarks, that we have manuscripts which are more than 950 years old. Perhaps in all the British islands there are twenty manuscripts as old as the eighth and ninth centuries after Christ: but I do not allow this comparison to be a fair one. Four hundred years ago the art of printing was invented, and from that time manuscripts began to be less used: they have consequently been preserved as curiosities, and are no longer liable to be worn out by frequent use; add to which that there were several hundred convents in the British isles as early as eleven centuries ago, inhabited by thousands of men who had little else to do but copy manuscripts. The whole of the last thousand years has also been marked by the revival and growth of literature, however slow; the modern nations of Europe have, even during that long period, been gradually consolidating themselves after the disruption of the Roman empire, and the taste for learning such as it was, in every country of Europe, produced mutual encouragement and emulation in copying the classical, theological and other manuscripts which still remained. Yet even under these circumstances it is certain that manuscripts were exceedingly scarce and dear; many valuable and interesting works have been lost to mankind from the difficulty and expense of copying them, and from the same cause have doubtless arisen the many interpolations and various readings which are found in the greater number of ancient writers. Few readers would ever see more than one copy of a work, and thus it would be insuperably difficult in most cases to collate them. One example of this scarcity will suffice.

The Italian historian Tiraboschi speaks of a letter written by Pope Paul I to King Pepin, (A.D. 757) in which he tells him that he has sent as many books as he could get together. We might expect here to see an ample catalogue of books, a present worthy of the pope who sent, and of the king of France, to whom they were presented. But how meagre is the catalogue of these books: we find only about seven or eight volumes, under the following names: *Antiphonale et Responsale, Grammatica Aristotelis, Dionysii Areopagitæ Libri, Geometria, Orthographia, Grammatica omnes Græco eloquio scriptores,* "all of them writers in the Greek speech."

We cannot say whether manuscripts were so rare as this among the more polished nations of Greece and Rome, yet even among them, judging from the fact that all the existing remains of Latin literature would hardly extend to an hundred octavo volumes, it is probable that books were more rare than is usually supposed; and it is on the remarkable scarcity of books during the middle ages that the learned Hardouin bases his supposition that the greater number of writings attributed to the ancients were only forgeries of modern times. This theory however goes too far; modern forgers would have found themselves unequal to the task of producing the noble writings of the ancients, and it is safer to conclude that the imperfections of our editions of ancient authors arise from the scarcity of copies which remain.

Let us now revert to the case of the Israelites. Here everything is widely different from that of the Greeks and Romans, and even from the middle ages of the European nations. All the history of Israel during the first half of the nine hundred years is described in the Book of Judges, and it gives us a most extraordinary picture of barbarous tribes, engaged in nothing but seditions and intestine wars. In reading that history, we cannot find the briefest interval, between the tales of blood, for learning or the polite arts: books seem to have been utterly unknown, and even the Book of the Law, for which the Jews in more recent times have shown such reverence, is not even once mentioned, either by David, Solomon, or any of the early Jewish writers during the whole space of nine hundred years from the time of Joshua to the end of the Babylonish captivity, five hundred years only before the Christian era.

Let us notice the back-ground of this picture. Ezra the scribe was a ready writer conversant with the law of God. Nehemiah, also, was an able and learned teacher of the Jews, *after the Babylonish captivity:* and in all the writings, which they are generally admitted to have composed, the Book of the Law is mentioned, as becomes so valuable a treasure. This will be evident from the ensuing extracts taken from the books which pass under the names of Ezra and Nehemiah.

EZRA, iii, 2. Then stood up Joshua the son of Jozadak, and his brethren the priests, and Zerubbabel the son of Shealtiel and his brethren, and builded the altar of the God of Israel, to offer burnt offerings thereon, as it is written in the law of Moses the man of God.

vii, 6. This Ezra went up from Babylon; and he was a ready scribe in the law of Moses, which the Lord God of Israel had given: and the king granted him all his request, according to the hand of the Lord his God upon him.

NEHEMIAH, i, 7. We have dealt very corruptly against thee, and have not kept the commandments, nor the statutes, nor the judgements, which thou commandedst thy servant Moses.

viii, 1—3. And all the people gathered themselves together as one man into the street that was before the water-gate; and they spake unto Ezra the scribe to bring the Book of the Law of Moses which the Lord had commanded to Israel. And Ezra the priest brought the law before the congregation both of men and women, and all that could hear with understanding, upon the first day of the seventh month. And he read therein before the street that was before the water-gate from the morning until mid-day, before the men and the women, and those that could understand: and the ears of all the people were attentive unto the Book of the Law.

viii, 7. Also Jeshua and Bani, and Sherebiah, Jamin, Akkub, Shabbethai, Hodijah, Maaseiah, Kelita, Azariah, Jozabad, Hanan, Pelaiah, and the Levites, caused the people to understand the law, and the people stood in their place. So they read in the Book in the Law of God distinctly, and gave the sense, and caused them to understand the reading......

And they found written in the law which the Lord had commanded by Moses, that the children of Israel should dwell in booths in the feast of the seventh month: and that they should publish and proclaim in all their cities, and in Jerusalem, saying, "Go forth unto the mount and fetch olive-branches, and pine-branches, and myrtle-branches, and palm-branches, and branches of thick trees, to make booths, as it is written." So the people went forth, and brought them, and made themselves booths, every one upon the roof of his house, and in their courts, and in the courts of the house of God, and in the street of the water-gate and in the street of the gate of Ephraim. And all the congregation of them that were come again out of the Captivity made booths, and sat under the booths: for since the days of Joshua the son of Nun unto that day had not the children of Israel done so: and there was very great gladness. Also day by day from the first unto the last day, he read in the Book of the Law of God. And they kept the feast seven days; and on the eighth day was a solemn assembly, according unto the manner.

From the Jewish writers we must now turn to the Greeks and Romans, among whom literature had hardly begun to make its appearance, at the very time that the canon of the Jewish Scriptures is said to have been brought to its termination. Malachi, the last of the prophets, wrote the short book which bears his name about the year B. C. 400. No Grecian writer, however, has mentioned the Israelites or their sacred books until long after that period. Even the conquests of Alexander did not open any communication with the Jews during his lifetime. It is in the reign of the Ptolemies kings of Egypt, that the two nations are first brought into connection. The Bible was then, about the year B.C. 280, as we have seen in a previous chapter, translated into Greek for the use of the Jews who lived in Alexandria, and were better acquainted with the Greek than the Hebrew language. This is sufficient to account for the appearance of a Greek translation of the Bible at so early a date as the beginning of the third century before Christ: but the Hebrews have wished us to believe that the execution of that laborious work is due principally to the admiration which King Ptolemy felt towards the sublime truths contained in their sacred books. It is impossible at this distance of time, to determine how far these motives operated, for not a particle of evidence has come down to us; neither has any Grecian nor Roman writer made the most remote allusion to Moses or his writings, and few of them have even mentioned the name of the Iraelitish people, until about the time of the Christian era, when Herod the Great was made king of Judæa, and kept up a constant correspondence with his friend Augustus and the court of Rome.

One of the most intimate friends of Herod was Nicolaus of Damascus, a peripatetic philosopher, poet, and historian, of considerable eminence. Of his extensive works nothing except fragments has survived: but extracts from his writings have been preserved by Josephus, in one of which reference is made to Moses the lawgiver of the Jews, and his writings. I subjoin the whole extract in an English translation:

All those who have written the barbarian (i.e. profane) histories, mention this deluge and the chest [ark] : one of them is Berosus the Chaldæan : in relating about the deluge he proceeds thus :—" It is said that there is still remaining a portion of the vessel in Armenia, at the mountain of the Corduæans, and that people take off and carry away with them some of the bitumen : and men use what is carried away principally as things to avert evil."

Hieronymus, who compiled the archæology of Phœnicia, and Mnaseas, and several others, mention these things. Nicolaus of Damascus, also, in his 96th book speaks of them thus : " There is above the Minyad a great mountain, in Armenia, called Baris, to which it is said that many fled in the time of the deluge and were saved, and that one of them, floating in a chest, came to land at its top, and that fragments of its timbers were long preserved. This may be the man whom Moses also the lawgiver of the Jews mentioned."—Jos. *Ant. Jud.* i, 3.

Contemporary with Nicolaus was Alexander Polyhistor, also quoted by Josephus.

What I have said is confirmed by Alexander Polyhistor, whose words are these :—" It is said by Cleodemus the prophet, who is also called Malchas, and who wrote about the Jews, in the same way as Moses their law-giver has recorded, that Abraham had many children by Keturah."—Jos. *Ant. Jud.* i, 15.

These extracts may suffice as specimens of the notice which profane writers have taken of the Jewish Scriptures. To those which I have here given might be added a few lines from Diodorus Siculus and others, but as none of them lived earlier than about the beginning of the Christian era, their evidence has nothing to do with our present subject, which is to show, not that the Old Testament did not exist before the Christian era, but that it was compiled since the termination of the Babylonish Captivity.

After the beginning of the Christian era, we have many notices both of Moses and of the Pentateuch, or at least of a book, which at that time existed and which professed to have Moses for its author. Strabo and Galen among the Greeks, Justin, Pliny and Tacitus among the Latins, besides many other writers whose testimony it is unnecessary to adduce,* make frequent allusion to Moses, but none to the books

---

* The testimonies of all these writers have been fully given in my work, *Heathen Records to the Jewish Scripture History.* London, 8vo., 1856.

which are ascribed to him, until a later period still. It was to be expected that the introduction of Christianity into Europe would bring with it a knowledge of the Hebrew Scriptures, on which Christianity is based as on a foundation stone. It was also to be anticipated that all later writers who should mention the Pentateuch would speak of it as the Book of Moses, because for a long time previous to the Christian era the Jews themselves considered the Pentateuch to be the original work as it came from the hand of Moses. It is not essential to our argument to follow the chain of evidence which later writers furnish, because it cannot be denied that the Pentateuch existed long before this latter half of the chain of evidence commences. I have endeavoured to show, not that the chain of universal consent is broken after it reaches the period of the Christian era, but that it cannot be traced during the fifteen hundred years which elapsed before the Christian era, and after the death of Moses. It may be useful now, in order to make this the more forcible, to sum up the present argument by recapitulating the several notices of Moses and the book in question, which occur in the Hebrew Bible between the death of Moses and the last of the sacred writers.

1. It has been admitted that *a Book of the Law* is twice named in the Book of Joshua, which is said to have been written in the next generation after Moses. I have reserved the right to show hereafter that the book of Joshua was not written until several hundred years after the date usually ascribed to it. 2. The second link in the chain is found in the author of the Books of Kings and Chronicles which were written about the time of the Babylonish captivity: i.e. 900 years after the death of Moses.

These are the only two Jewish writers who mention the Book of the Law at all for the long period of nine hundred years, and probably much longer.

But the argument derived from this fact, must be reduced to still narrower dimensions; for the authors of Kings and Chronicles describe facts, which prove, to a demonstration, that the Pentateuch which we now have is not the Book of the Law, as given by Moses. They tell us that when Solomon conveyed the ark of the covenant, in which the Book of the Law was kept, into the temple, there was nothing in it but the two tables of stone which had been given by God to Moses. These tables, therefore, were the Book of the Law, and no other Book of the Law is mentioned as having existed at that time. They tell us, secondly, that in the time of Josiah the Book of the Law was found by the priests whilst they were cleansing and purifying the Temple. If any other book were the subject of these observations, it would be contended that the authorship of it belonged to that period of time when it was described as having been found in the Temple by the priests in the reign of Josiah, or even to a later, but certainly not to an earlier period.

But there are reasons, to be hereafter stated, why this inference is not admissible in the present instance. It may rather be conjectured that the two tables are what was found in the reign of Josiah, or perhaps some other records, which may have lain undiscovered in the Temple for many years: but still not the Pentateuch, in the form which it now bears. With these observations I shall conclude the examination of the witnesses who are supposed to furnish universal consent for the belief that the Pentateuch is the original work of Moses.

CHAPTER XII.

EXAMINATION OF THE INTERNAL EVIDENCE WHICH THE PENTATEUCH IS SAID TO FURNISH FOR THE BELIEF THAT IT WAS WRITTEN, IN ITS PRESENT FORM, BY MOSES.

HAVING, in the preceding chapter, examined the argument of Tradition or Universal Consent, which is adduced as a basis for the belief that the Pentateuch was written by Moses, let us now proceed to investigate the second argument which has been brought forward in the same cause, namely, that of the *Internal Evidence* which the Pentateuch itself furnishes.

This part of our subject labours under an antecedent difficulty, resulting from our imperfect knowledge of the language in which the books of the Old Testament are written, and the comparatively few persons who possess even a superficial acquaintance with it. It is necessary to take many interpretations of individual passages upon trust, aided only by such occasional verification as may result from comparing the testimony which men of different opinions will supply.

An illustration of my meaning on this point is furnished by a passage which I shall transcribe from a work of Bishop Tomline:

It is sometimes asserted that there is a sameness of language and style in the different books of the Old Testament, which is not compatible with the different ages usually assigned to them, and thence an inference is drawn unfavourable to the authenticity of these books, and particularly to that of the Pentateuch.

To this objection we may answer that it is founded upon an untrue assertion; those who are best acquainted with the original writings of the Old Testament agree, that there is a marked difference in the style and language of its several authors; and one learned man in particular concludes from that difference, "that it is certain the five books, which are ascribed to Moses, were not written in the time of David, the Psalms of David in the age of Josiah, nor the Prophecies of Isaiah in the time of Malachi."—*Elem. of Christian Theology*, vol. i, p. 74.

Contradictory assertions, unsupported by evidence, or only supported by evidence which nine-tenths of mankind are unable to verify, never elicit truth, and must be discarded from an inquiry, which has truth alone for its object. Setting aside, therefore, for the present, the style of the language in which the Pentateuch is written, let us inquire what historical or other evidence it furnishes, by which we may determine to what age this venerable literary monument owes its origin.

It has been inferred from certain passages in the five books, commonly called the Pentateuch, that Moses was the writer of them. On this head we will hear the argument as it is stated by the Bishop above-named:

Moses frequently [Ex. xvii, 14, xxiv, 4: Numb. xxxiii, 2.] speaks of himself as directed by God to write the commands which he received from him, and to record the events which occurred during his ministry; and at the end of Deuteronomy he expressly says, "And Moses wrote this law, and delivered it unto the priests, the sons of Levi, which bare the ark of the covenant of the Lord, and unto all the elders of Israel" [Deut. xxxi, 9]; and afterwards, in the same chapter, he says still more fully; "And it came to pass, when Moses had made an end of writing the words of this law in a book, until they were finished, that Moses commanded the Levites, which bear the ark of the covenant of the Lord, saying, 'Take this Book of the Law, and put it in the side * of the ark of the covenant of the Lord your God, that it may be there for a witness against thee.'"—*Vol. i, p.* 34.

Bishop Tomline, by a remarkable boldness of interpretation, makes the following comment on this passage:

It appears from Deuteronomy [xxxi, 26] that the Book of the Law, *that is the whole Pentateuch, written by the hand of Moses*, was by his command deposited in the tabernacle, not long before his death.

But surely these passages, so far from proving that Moses was the author of the Pentateuch, are, on the contrary, the most convincing argument that Moses was not the writer.

Can a man truly write, that when the book which he is writing was finished, he gave it to another man with orders to deposit it in any specified place? The act of writing the book must have preceded the completion of it, and its completion must have preceded the command: the record of this command, being late in time, must have come from another person; i.e. the Pentateuch, which records that Moses wrote the Book of the Law, and then gave it to the priests with a command where it should be kept, must be the work, not of Moses, but of some other writer.

The loose mode of interpretation generally applied to such passages as that which we have just quoted, results from the readiness with which most men acquiesce in what is proposed to them, rather than take the trouble of examining for themselves. For this reason also the title "Book of Moses," which means no more than the "History of Moses" or the "Mosaic History," is generally considered to mean the "Book written by Moses," notwithstanding that the

---

* The expression "in the side of the ark," seems to mean no more than "within or inside the ark." A similar phrase occurs in Jonah (i, 5): "But Jonah was gone down into the sides of the ship."

whole tenor of the history shows that Moses could not have been its author.

I have suggested in a previous page of this work, that Moses wrote no other Book of the Law than the two tables of stone: it is not, however, incumbent on me to prove the truth of this negative assertion, but from those who assert that Moses wrote a Book of the Law, and that the Pentateuch now existing is that book, the most convincing proof may with justice be demanded.

Up to the point then at which we are now arrived has been shown, not only the weakness of the commonly received arguments for identifying the Pentateuch with the Book of the Law, namely Universal Consent and Internal Evidence, but that these very arguments tend rather to destroy the identity of the two. For in tracing back the chain of consent, we find that during the nine hundred years of Jewish History which precede the Babylonish captivity, we have no mention made of the Book of the Law at all. As regards the Internal Evidence then, it is equally clear that the very expressions, on which most stress has been laid, could not have been written, if written by Moses, until after the book in which they occur was completed; which is an absurdity, involving a manifest contradiction of terms.

I conclude this chapter with annexing the principal passages (if not all) of the Pentateuch in which mention is made of the Book of the Law, or the tables of stone, or of Moses having written any book at all.

Exod. xvii, 13—14. And Joshua discomfited Amalek and his people with the edge of the sword. And the Lord said unto Moses, Write this for a memorial in a book, and rehearse it in the ears of Joshua: for I will utterly put out the remembrance of Amalek from under heaven.

—— xxiv, 4. And Moses wrote all the words of the Lord and rose up early in the morning, and builded an altar under the hill, and twelve pillars, according to the twelve tribes of Israel. And he sent young men of the children of Israel, which offered burnt offerings, and sacrificed peace-offerings of oxen unto the Lord. And Moses took half of the blood, and put it in basons, and half of the blood he sprinkled on the altar. And he took the book of the covenant and read in the audience of the people: and they said "All that the Lord hath said will we do, and be obedient." And

Moses took the blood, and sprinkled it on the people, and said, "Behold the blood of the covenant, which the Lord hath made with you concerning all these words."

Then went up Moses, and Aaron, Nadab and Abihu, and seventy of the elders of Israel: and they saw the God of Israel: and there was under his feet as it were a paved work of sapphire stone, and as it were the body of heaven in his clearness. And upon the nobles of the children of Israel he laid not his hand: also they saw God, and did eat and drink. And the Lord said unto Moses, "Come up to me into the mount, and be there: and I will give thee tables of stone, and a law, and commandments which I have written, that thou mayest teach them." And Moses rose up, and his minister Joshua: and Moses went up into the mount of God.

—— xxv, 16. And thou shalt put into the ark the testimony which I shall give thee.

—— xxxi, 18. And he [God] gave unto Moses, when he had made an end of communing with him upon Mount Sinai, two tables of testimony, tables of stone written with the finger of God.

—— xxxii, 15. And Moses turned, and went down from the mount, and the two tables of the testimony were in his hand: the tables were written on both their sides; on the one side and on the other were they written. And the tables were the work of God, and the writing was the writing of God graven upon the tables.

—— xxxiv, 1. And the Lord said unto Moses, "Hew thee two tables of stone like unto the first: and I will write upon these tables the words that were in the first tables, which thou brakest, &c."

—— xxxiv, 4. And he [Moses?] hewed two tables of stone like unto the first, and Moses rose up early in the morning, and went up unto Mount Sinai, as the Lord had commanded him, and took in his hand the two tables of stone.

—— xxxiv, 27—29. And the Lord said unto Moses, "Write thou these words: for after the tenor of these words I have made a covenant with thee and with Israel." And he was there with the Lord forty days and forty nights: he did neither eat bread, nor drink water. And he wrote upon the tables the words of the covenant, the ten commandments. And it came to pass, when Moses came down from mount Sinai with the two tables of testimony in Moses' hand, &c.

—— xl, 20, 21. And he took and put the testimony into the ark, and set the staves on the ark, and put the mercy-seat above upon the ark: and he brought the ark into the tabernacle, and set up the veil of the covering, and covered the ark of the testimony; as the Lord commanded Moses.

NUMBERS, xxxiii, 1, 2. These are the journeys of the children of Israel which went forth out of the land of Egypt with their armies under the hand of Moses and Aaron. And Moses wrote their goings out according to their journeys by the commandment of the Lord; and these are their journeys according to their goings out.

DEUT. iv, 13. And he declared unto you his covenant, which he commanded you to perform, even ten commandments; and he wrote them upon two tables of stone.

—— v, 22. These words the Lord spake unto all your assembly in the mount, out of the midst of the fire, of the cloud, and of the thick darkness, with a great voice: and he added no more. And he wrote them in two tables of stone and delivered them unto me.

—— ix, 10, &c. And the Lord delivered unto me two tables of stone written with the finger of God; and on them was written according to all the words, which the Lord spake with you in the mount, out of the midst of the fire, in the day of the assembly. And it came to pass at the end of forty days and forty nights, that the Lord gave me the two tables of stone, even the tables of the covenant.

—— x, 1. At that time the Lord said unto me, "Hew thee two tables of stone like unto the first, and come up unto me into the mount, and make thee an ark of wood. And I will write on the tables the words that were in the first tables which thou brakest, and thou shalt put them in the ark." And I made an ark of shittim wood, and hewed two tables of stone like unto the first, and went up into the mount, having the two tables in mine hand. And he wrote on the tables, according to the first writing, the ten commandments, which the Lord spake unto you in the mount out of the midst of the fire in the days of the assembly: and the Lord gave them unto me. And I turned myself, and came down from the mount, and put the tables in the ark which I had made; and there they be, as the Lord commanded me.

—— xxvii, 8. And thou shalt write upon the stones all the words of this law very plainly.

—— xxviii, 58. If thou wilt not observe to do all the words of this law that are written in this book, that thou mayest fear this glorious and fearful name THE LORD THY GOD, &c.

——xxxi, 9—13. And Moses wrote this law, and delivered it unto the priests the sons of Levi, which bare the ark of the covenant of the Lord, and unto all the elders of Israel. And Moses commanded them, saying, "At the end of every seven years, in the solemnity of the year of release, in the feast of tabernacles, when all Israel is come to appear before the Lord thy God in the place which he shall choose, thou shalt read this law before all Israel in their hearing. Gather the people together, men and women and children, and thy stranger that is within thy gates, that they may hear, and that they may learn, and fear the Lord your God, and observe to do all the words of this law," &c.

—— xxxi, 19. [MOSES SPEAKS] "Now therefore write ye this song for you and teach it the children of Israel: put it in their mouths, that this song may be a witness for me against the children of Israel," &c.

—— xxxi, 22—26. Moses therefore wrote this song the same day, and taught it the children of Israel. And he gave Joshua the son of Nun a charge, and said, "Be strong and of a good courage: for thou shalt bring the children of Israel into the land which I sware unto them : and I will be with thee."

And it came to pass, when Moses had made an end of writing the words of this law in a book until they were finished, that Moses commanded the Levites, which bare the ark of the covenant of the Lord, saying, "Take this Book of the Law, and put it in the side of the ark of the covenant of the Lord your God, that it may be there for a witness against thee."

CHAPTER XIII.

THE CASE OF THE SAMARITAN PENTATEUCH EXAMINED.

As an argument for the belief that Moses was the author of the five books has been drawn from the existence of the Samaritan Pentateuch, it is necessary to take some notice of the book which passes under this name; although there is one significant fact connected with it which would seem to disqualify it from being adduced as an evidence upon the subject at all. It is little more than 200 years ago that the Samaritan Pentateuch first became known in Europe and there is not the slightest information to be found in any ancient author concerning the character in which it is written: whilst the language is the same as the Hebrew, with no other variation than such as is generally found in different editions of the same work. All that we know about the Samaritan Pentateuch may be told in few words. There had always been an opinion prevalent among the learned, that the Samaritans, who were bitter enemies to the Jews, might possess a copy of the Bible, differing possibly in some particulars from the received Hebrew text. This notion may perhaps be traced to Origen, who collated such copies of the Pentateuch as he found among the Samaritans for his great work on the Old Testament. Many hundred years, however, elapsed, and nothing was discovered to support the current opinion. At last, in very modern times, a copy of the Pentateuch, written in letters differing from the Hebrew letters but in the same language, was brought into Europe. This copy was unfortunately very imperfect, but Archbishop Usher afterwards procured six other copies of the same book. The fact of its being in substance and in language the same as the Hebrew Bible seemed to confirm the authority of the latter volume, but of the fact that it is written in a different sort of letter an ingenious solution has been propounded. It was suggested that this particular copy of the Pentateuch had been preserved, in the old Hebrew character, by the obscure people who remained in Samaria, when the others and more distinguished of their countrymen were carried captive to Babylon. It is said that the Jews, during the captivity, lost the knowledge of the old Hebrew language, and their teachers, who read the Hebrew Scriptures to them in their synagogues, were obliged to interpret the meaning by using a Chaldee paraphrase. To bear out this explanation it is necessary to suppose, also, that the Jews transferred their scriptures from the old Hebrew character, which, according to this theory, was the same as the Samaritan, into the present Hebrew character, which is generally understood to be the Chaldee, as used at Babylon, where it was adopted by the Jews. In confirmation of this theory it is observed that the character found in the Samaritan Pentateuch is very similar to the inscriptions occurring on ancient Israelitish coins. Many learned divines have acquiesced in this solution of a fact, which is certainly curious, and seemed at first to present a philological difficulty.

But before this explanation of the case concerning the Samaritan Pentateuch can be received, it is necessary to show, 1. that the book is a genuine remnant of antiquity, 2. that the coins to which it bears a resemblance are also genuine and ancient.

The first of these requirements is rendered necessary on account of the very short time that the book has been known to scholars in Europe: and the second is equally important; because the resemblance between the letters of the Samaritan Pentateuch and those found on the coins is the only circumstance which gives the slightest support to the theory suggested, or which at all exempts it from being considered as a mere conjecture. It is well known how skilful are the Orientals in imitating what appears to be eagerly sought after by Europeans; and perhaps no imposition is more easily practised than copying a book out of one character into another, the language still remaining unaltered. Coins, it is notorious, are often fabricated, and this fact would make it necessary to test the genuineness of all those which might be brought forward to decide the question now under consideration.

As regards the question, who was the author of the Pentateuch, the Samaritan copy furnishes no argument either affirmative or negative, for the claims of Moses. If we admit the explanation, above given, to be true, the only inference which could be drawn from it is that the Pentateuch was in existence before the Babylonish captivity, i.e. about the year 600 before Christ, but it does not touch the long period of 900 years between Moses and the beginning of the Babylonish captivity. The Pentateuch might be as old as 600 years before Christ, and yet not as old as 1500 years before the same era.

But two grave objections lie against the arguments adduced to support the explanation above-mentioned of the existence of the Samaritan Pentateuch.

1. Why did the Jews transcribe their copies of the Bible out of the old letters used by their fathers into the new letters used by the Chaldees their enemies? Was it because, during the captivity, they had lost the use of the Hebrew

tongue? Yet they would not be more able to read the Bible when written in Chaldee than in the old Hebrew letters. We do not find that Greek words become more intelligible to those who do not know the Greek language, by being written with the Roman alphabet, than when they are written in their own character. The Hebrew doctors, Ezra and the others, would be likely to understand the Bible, even if written in the old character; and the common people would have no occasion to read it at all.

It is not found, in the history of other nations, that such changes take place suddenly, or in consequence of any particular event. Changes of style in writing are made gradually, and are continually being made,—it is impossible that the handwriting of a nation can either remain stationary or be completed suddenly: it flows on like the course of time, imperceptible in its course, but wonderful in its result. If we could trace the progress of man through all the variations to which he is subject, we should find, in all cases, a continuity of thought, though, judging from the appearance of distant points only in our history, we are apt to regard as heterogeneous, varieties of the same species acting under the same natural laws.

2. The argument drawn from coins may be summarily disposed of, and in refuting it I shall adduce the evidence of one who is well acquainted with the Hebrew language and literature, and author of a learned and valuable Hebrew Grammar,* Mr Stuart, associate professor of sacred literature in the institution at Andover. His words are these:

The present *square* form of the Hebrew letters, is not the most ancient one; as is evident from inscriptions on Hebrew *coins, stamped in the time of the Maccabees,* which have characters such as are designated in alphabet No III, [*alluding to his table of alphabets in which No III gives the Samaritan letters*]. The present square letter is evidently derived from the Aramæan forms of letters, and probably originated some time *after* the birth of Christ. This, Kopp has recently shown, in a satisfactory manner, in his *Bilder und Schriften der Vorzeit,* II, pp. 95 seq., particularly pp. 156 seq.†

* Grammar of the Hebrew Language, &c. Fourth Edition, reprinted with the concurrence of the author, 8vo., Oxford, D. A. Talboys, 1831.

† A learned work on the subject of Jewish Coins, is MADDEN's *History of the Jewish Coinage,* 8vo, London, 1864. The author successfully maintains that the earliest Jewish coins were struck by Simon Maccabæus about 140 years before Christ.

This extract throws a clear light upon the subject before us. The present Hebrew letters are, it seems, later than the Christian era, whilst on the other hand the coins which have been adduced to prove the antiquity of the Samaritan Pentateuch, were struck long after the Babylonish captivity. The same process of inference therefore goes to prove; first that the Samaritan letters are not necessarily as old as the period of the Captivity, but only as the time of the Maccabees, and secondly, that the Jews did not change the form of their letters in consequence of their slavery in Babylon, but in a much later age, namely after the beginning of the Christian era.

The Samaritan Pentateuch, therefore, can furnish no aid towards our present inquiry, which is to ascertain who was the author of the book : or if it bears at all upon the question, it rather furnishes a testimony unfavourable to the claims of Moses. For if the book had been written by Moses in its present form, it is probable that the Israelitish people would never have consented to its being transferred into another character.

In conclusion, I will propose an easy and natural solution for the case of the Samaritan Pentateuch. It is known that the hand-writing of all nations gradually changes with time. No two generations write exactly alike; and if we take the writings of the same people at two different periods removed to the distance of two or three centuries apart, the diversity will be so great that the two specimens may be supposed to belong to different countries and to different languages. The Samaritans are known to have borne a national enmity towards the Jews; there was no intercourse between the two nations. Together with their manners and habits, their handwriting also would naturally vary: it seems therefore in no way remarkable that their Bibles, as they appeared in the seventeenth century after Christ, should be written in a different character from those of the Jews, who also have adopted different modes of writing, partly through time alone, and partly in consequence of their dispersion into foreign countries. The reader will find in the Appendix an extract about the Samaritan Pentateuch, which furnishes good reason for believing that the Samaritans received their sacred books from the Jews themselves in the time of

Manasseh, and long after the return of the latter from their captivity in Babylon.

―――――

CHAPTER XIV.

THAT MOSES IS NOT THE AUTHOR OF THE PENTATEUCH, PROVED—1, FROM INTERNAL EVIDENCE.

THUS far then have we examined the grounds upon which it is generally believed that Moses is the author of those five books which form the beginning of the Hebrew Scriptures or Old Testament, as they are termed by Christians, in contradistinction to their own books, which they call the New Testament.

It remains to produce more positive testimony to the same end, and in doing so I shall class the various arguments under two heads also: 1, The Internal Evidence furnished by the books themselves that Moses is not their author; and 2, External Evidence, obtained from various sources, leading to the same conclusion.

The Internal Evidence, which will now have to be considered, shall be also classified under different sections, as tending to make the subject more clear, and to give greater force to the general principles of criticism on which the inferences, which I would draw, are founded.

§ 1. *The two tables of stone seem to have supplied the place of a Book of the Law.*

That the Hebrew legislator should deliver to his countrymen TWO TABLES OF STONE, on which the principal heads of their law were engraved, is consistent with all the information which History supplies concerning those early times and the practice of other nations. But, if we suppose a book of such length and bulk as the Pentateuch to have been given at the same time to the Israelites, what becomes of the two tables of stone? where was the necessity that these also should be given? It was not that they might be set up as monuments visible to the whole people, or as exponents of the heads of the law, which the written books would develop more fully, for the two tables of stone were never set up at all, and could not have been set up in the wilderness, by a tribe of men, who were daily changing their abode. They were kept in the ark of the covenant, and there is no mention made of their ever being taken out; not even when the Temple of Solomon was built, when they might with propriety have been set up in some public place, if this had been the use for which they were originally designed. But no such use is hinted at by the writer, nor were they originally given by God for such a purpose; as is manifest from their size, for when Moses came down from the mount, he held the two tables in his hand, which he could not have done, if they were of the usual size of monuments made to be set up in public.

But the supposition that the two tables of stone were intended to be set up as monuments, is refuted by the fact that other stones were actually set up by Joshua, according to a command given by Moses, and that on them was inscribed a copy of the Law of Moses. The original injunction of Moses is found in Deuteronomy, xxvii, 1—8.

And Moses with the elders of Israel commanded the people saying, "Keep all the commandments which I command you this day. And it shall be on the day when ye shall pass over Jordan unto the land which the Lord thy God giveth thee, that thou shalt set thee up great stones, and plaster them with plaster: and thou shalt write upon them all the words of this Law, when thou art passed over, that thou mayest go in unto the land which the Lord thy God giveth thee, a land that floweth with milk and honey; as the Lord God of thy Fathers hath promised thee. Therefore it shall be, when ye be gone over Jordan, that ye shall set up these stones, which I command you this day, in mount Ebal, and thou shalt plaster them with plaster. And there shalt thou build an altar unto the Lord thy God, an altar of stones : thou shalt not lift up any iron tool upon them. Thou shalt build the altar of the Lord thy God of whole stones : and thou shalt offer burnt offerings thereon unto the Lord thy God : and thou shalt offer peace offerings, and shalt eat there, and rejoice before the Lord thy God. And thou shalt write upon the stones all the words of this Law very plainly."

The fulfilment of the command is related in Joshua, viii, 30—32:

Then Joshua built an altar unto the Lord God of Israel in mount Ebal, as Moses the servant of the Lord commanded the children of Israel, as it is written in the Book of the Law of Moses, an altar of whole stones, over which no man hath lift up any iron: and they offered thereon burnt offerings unto the Lord, and sacrificed peace-offerings. And he wrote there upon the stones a copy of the Law of Moses, which he wrote in the presence of the children of Israel. And all Israel, and their elders, and officers, and their judges, stood on this side the ark and on that side before the priests the Levites, which bare the ark of the covenant of the Lord, as well the stranger, as he that was born among them; half of them over against mount Gerizim, and half of them over against Mount Ebal; as Moses the servant of the Lord had commanded before, that they should bless the people of Israel. And afterwards he read all the words of the Law, the blessings and cursings, according to all that is written in the Book of the Law. There was not a word of all that Moses commanded, which Joshua read not before all the congregation of Israel, with the women, and the little ones, and the strangers that were conversant among them.

This narrative is remarkable, for it commemorates a public solemnity, held for no other purpose than that the Laws of Moses might be exhibited to the sight and impressed on the minds of the Jewish people. The writer also tells us that it was held in accordance with the Book of Moses, and yet he does not tell us that the Book of Moses was produced on that occasion, though we are led to suppose that it was in existence. Yet something is then done which seems to prove, by implication, that there was no such book at all at that time. Joshua is said to have engraved on certain stones a copy of the Law of Moses, and afterwards to have read all the words of the Law, and the concluding paragraph relates that "there was not a word of all that Moses commanded, which Joshua read not before all the congregation of Israel." Must we then suppose that the whole of the Pentateuch was inscribed on those stones by Joshua! what could be the use of inscribing the historical parts of the Pentateuch on those stones, or reading them afterwards to the people, if the object was simply to admonish them that they should observe the Law of Moses? It is more probable that an inscription, much shorter than the whole of the Pentateuch, was carved upon those stones, and, as no mention is made of any book at all on the same occasion, we have a negative proof that no such book was in existence at that time.

The delivery of the two tables renders it unlikely that any other writing was bequeathed by Moses to the Israelitish people, particularly as the age in which Moses lived precedes by many centuries the times in which books, as far as we know of them, can be proved to have been written.

§ 2. *Manner in which Moses is mentioned in the Pentateuch.*

If, however, notwithstanding this antecedent improbability, it should yet be contended that Moses certainly wrote a book called the Book of the Law, it may be shown that the Pentateuch, at all events, is not that book, as must be evident to every one who will dispassionately consider the manner in which the Pentateuch is written. This is a consideration which involves no question of grammatical idiom or style, which can be intelligble to the Hebrew student only—I reserve that for a separate chapter—but is easy of comprehension to the most ordinary intellect. My meaning may be illustrated in this manner. If we read in a book the account of certain transactions in which a particular man is concerned, and his name always occurs in the third person, it is a natural inference that this man did not write the book, in which he is so described. This general principle is, no doubt, to be taken with some limitation; for it is well known that some persons have, from modesty or some other motive, introduced their own names in the third person into the narrative of events in which they have acted a prominent part. Thus Thucydides, the celebrated historian of the Peloponnesian War, prefaces his work with these words;

Thucydides, of Athens, has [here] written * the war between the Peloponnesians and Athenians, how they fought one against the other.

This mode of introducing his work, however, does not prevent the author from speaking, elsewhere, in the first person, as for instance in the forty-eighth chapter of the second book of his history, where he describes the plague at Athens:

* This is the strict meaning of the aorist tense in Greek, as may be seen in a phrase which occurs in the dialogues of the Tragedians, Καλῶς ἰλίξας thou hast said well; or, as we might express it, Thou sayest well!

But I will tell both of what nature it was, and will point out such details from which any one judging might best be able from foresight, if ever it should come again, not to be ignorant about it, having both myself had the disease and myself seen others who had it.

It is clear, from this passage, that Thucydides was the author of the book which bears his name; and the mode of speaking in the third person, with which the history commenced, is compensated by other direct expressions, and does not detract from his claims to be regarded as the author of the book. Indeed, the former sentence may be considered as equivalent to a modern title page, "The History of the Peloponnesian war, &c., by Thucydides."

It is also observable that writers, speaking of themselves in the third person, use a sort of reserve in all such self-descriptions. The admirable historian just mentioned alludes to himself in two or three passages (ii, 48; iv, 105; v, 26) only of his immortal work, and with the utmost modesty and taste, though he held an important command as admiral in the war which he describes, and received the honour of ostracism from his democratic countrymen. But when we recur to the Hebrew Pentateuch, these two indications of authorship altogether fail us. Moses is invariably described in the third person, and, as three-fourths of the book concern him most intimately, it is impossible to conceive that the book could have been written by him.

This then is the second objection which Internal Evidence furnishes against Moses being the author of the Pentateuch, namely the manner in which as the author of that book he would be made to speak of himself. There is not a single passage in which can be found the most distant hint that Moses himself was its author. On the contrary the whole tenor of the book exhibits Moses as described by another person living in a later age, and some passages may be found which, if supposed to have been written by Moses, would attribute to him a vain-glorious character, which is highly inconsistent with his known virtues, but would be appropriate from the pen of a later writer, who wished to exalt and panegyrize the great law-giver to whom their nation owed its political existence. The following passages are instances of panegyric on Moses, which would much detract from our opinion of his modesty, if we could suppose them to have proceeded from his own pen :

Exod. xi, 3. And the Lord gave the people favour in the sight of the Ægyptians. Moreover the man Moses was very great in the land of Ægypt, in the sight of Pharaoh's servants, and in the sight of the people.

Numbers, xii, 3—8. Now the man Moses was very meek, above all the men which were upon the face of the earth. And the Lord spake &c. .... "My servant Moses is not so, who is faithful in all mine house. With him will I speak mouth to mouth, even apparently, and not in dark speeches; and the similitude of the Lord shall he behold; wherefore then were ye not afraid to speak against my servant Moses?"

Deuter. xxxiii, 1. And this is the blessing, wherewith Moses the man of God blessed the children of Israel before his death. And he said, "The Lord came from Sinai, and rose up from Seir unto them; he shined forth from mount Paran, and he came with ten thousands of saints: from his right hand went a fiery law for them. Yea, he loved the people; all his saints are in thy hand: and they sat down at thy feet; every one shall receive of thy words." Moses commanded us a law, even the inheritance of the congregation of Jacob. And he was king in Jeshurun, when the heads of the people and the tribes of Israel were gathered together.

To these passages may be added another, which seems to belong to the same class, and furnishes a singular mode of expression if we suppose it to come from Moses speaking of himself and his brother.

Exod. vi, 26. 27. These are that Aaron and Moses, to whom the Lord said, "Bring out the children of Israel from the land of Egypt according to their armies." These are they which spake to Pharaoh king of Egypt, to bring out the children of Israel from Egypt: these are that Moses and Aaron.

§ 3. *A book more ancient than the Pentateuch quoted by the writer of the Pentateuch.*

The writer of the Pentateuch quotes a more ancient work, "The Book of the Wars of the Lord," which yet had for its subject the same events that are related in the Pentateuch. This appears from the following passage in Numbers.

Numbers, xxi, 11. And they journeyed from Oboth, and pitched at Ije-abarim, in the wilderness which is before Moab toward the sunrising. From thence they removed, and pitched in the valley of Zared. From thence they removed, and pitched on the other side of Arnon, which is in the wilderness that cometh out of the coasts of the Amorites: for Arnon is the border of Moab, between Moab and the Amorites. Wherefore it is said in the Book of the Wars of the Lord, " What he did in the Red Sea, and in the brooks of Arnon."

We might infer also from the language of Genesis (v, 1), that there was a book entitled "The Book of the Generations of Adam," which the compiler of the Pentateuch had embodied wholly in his own work. Numerous other works also appear in the history of the Israelites after their entrance into the promised land. We shall have to notice them hereafter at the proper place.

§ 4. *Anachronism concerning the enmity of the Egyptians towards shepherds.*

In Genesis, xlvi, 34, it is said as a reason for the Israelites being placed in the land of Goshen, that "every shepherd is an abomination to the Egyptians." But it appears from every other part of the history of Joseph and Pharaoh, that there was no such enmity between them. This is also the opinion of Dr Shuckford; whose account of the matter is as follows:

There is indeed one passage in Genesis, which seems to intimate that there was that religious hatred, which the Egyptians were afterwards charged with, paid to creatures even in the days of Joseph; for we are informed that he put his brethren upon telling Pharaoh their profession, in order to have them placed in the land of Goshen, for, or because, " Every shepherd is an abomination to the Egyptians, Gen. xlvi, 34." I must freely acknowledge, that I cannot satisfy myself about the meaning of this passage; I cannot see that shepherds were really at this time an abomination to the Egyptians; for Pharaoh himself had his shepherds, and when he ordered Joseph to place his brethren in the land of Goshen, he was so far from disapproving of their employment, that he ordered him, if he knew of any men of activity amongst them, that he should make them rulers over his cattle; nay the Egyptians were at this time shepherds themselves, as well as the Israelites, for we are told, when their money failed, they brought their cattle of all sorts unto Joseph, to exchange them for corn, and among the rest, their flocks of the same kind with those which the Israelites were to tell

Pharaoh that it was their profession to take care of, as will appear to any one that will consult the Hebrew text in the places referred to. Either therefore we must take the expression that every shepherd was an abomination to the Egyptians, to mean no more than that they thought meanly of the employment, that it was a lazy, idle, and unactive profession, as Pharaoh seemed to question, whether there were any men of activity amongst them, when he heard what their trade was; or, if we take the words to signify a religious aversion to them, which does indeed seem to be the true meaning of the expression from the use made of it in other places of Scripture, then I do not see how it is reconcilable with Pharaoh's inclination to employ them himself, or with the Egyptians being many of them at this time of the same profession themselves, which the heathen writers agree with Moses in supposing them to be. [Diod. Siculus, Book i.]

The learned have observed that there are several interpolations in the books of the Scriptures, which were not the words of the Sacred Writers. Some persons, affecting to show their learning, when they read over the ancient MSS., would sometimes put a short remark in the margin, which they thought might give a reason for, or clear the meaning of some expression in the text against which they placed it, or to which they adjoined it; and from hence it happened now and then, that the transcribers from manuscripts so remarked upon, did, through mistake, take a marginal note or remark into the text, imagining it to be a part of it. Whether Moses might not end his period in this place with the words *that ye may dwell in the land of Goshen;* and whether what follows, *for every shepherd is an abomination to the Egyptians,* may not have been added to the text this way, is entirely submitted to the judgment of the learned. CONNECTION, Book V, vol. i, p. 341.

The learned writer of this extract is more correct in his statement of the difficulty than in its solution. It is a principle in criticism to consider a book as free from interpolation, until it is proved that interpolations have certainly been made. The charge of interpolation is brought against the books of the Old Testament, for no other reason than to reduce them into harmony with the pre-conceived opinion that they were written by the authors to whom they are commonly ascribed. In the present instance there has been no interpolation. The compiler, relating the honours paid to the family of Jacob in Egypt, and endeavouring to harmonize them with the state of things in his own times, a thousand years later, when the Egyptians, by their religious absurdities, had been made to entertain an enmity towards shepherds, has given us a description which, in this particular, is inconsistent with itself. In short the Egyptians held shepherds in aversion in the fifth, but not in the fifteenth century before the Christian era.

§ 5. *Anachronism that Moses should record his own death.*

There are certain passages in the Pentateuch, neither few in number nor ambiguous in meaning, which prove that Moses was not the writer of that book, and that it could not have been written until several hundred years after his time; events are there mentioned which could not be recorded by Moses, because they did not happen during his life-time.

The most striking of these anachronisms occurs in the last chapter of Deuteronomy, where the death of Moses is related. The whole chapter must be transcribed, because it bears in it the most complete refutation of every expedient which has been had recourse to for solving the anomaly that an author should record his own death.

And Moses went up from the plains of Moab unto the mountain of Nebo, to the top of Pisgah, that is over against Jericho. And the Lord showed him all the land of Gilead, unto Dan, and all Naphtali, and the land of Ephraim, and Manasseh, and all the land of Judah, unto the utmost sea, and the south, and the plain of the valley of Jericho, the city of palm trees, unto Zoar. And the Lord said unto him, "This is the land which I sware unto Abraham, unto Isaac, and unto Jacob, saying, I will give it unto thy seed: I have caused thee to see it with thine eyes, but thou shalt not go over thither."

So Moses the servant of the Lord died there in the land of Moab, according to the word of the Lord. And He buried him in a valley in the land of Moab, over against Beth-peor: but no man knoweth of his sepulchre unto this day. And Moses was an hundred and twenty years old when he died: his eye was not dim, nor his natural force abated. And the children of Israel wept for Moses in the plains of Moab thirty days; so the days of weeping and mourning for Moses were ended.

And Joshua the son of Nun was full of the spirit of wisdom; for Moses had laid his hands upon him: and the children of Israel hearkened unto him, and did as the Lord commanded Moses. And there arose not a prophet since in Israel like unto Moses, whom the Lord knew face to face, in all the signs and the wonders, which the Lord sent him to do in the land of Egypt to Pharaoh, and to all his servants, and to all his land, and in all that mighty hand and in all the great terror which Moses showed in the sight of all Israel.

As it is impossible for a writer to relate his own death, those who maintain that the Pentateuch is the work of Moses, make an exception in favour of the last chapter. Dr Gray has the following remarks upon this subject:

> The account of the death and burial of Moses, and some other seemingly posthumous particulars described in this chapter, have been produced to prove, that it could not have been written by Moses: and in all probability these circumstances may have been inserted by Joshua, to complete the history of this illustrious prophet; or were afterwards added by Samuel, or some prophet who succeeded him. They were admitted by Ezra as authentic, and we have no reason to question the fidelity of the account.

This language is too authoritative. Truth, when questioned, comes out purer and brighter for the ordeal through which it has passed: whereas error is scorched and withered by the touch of criticism. The chapter before us is admitted by all not to have been written by Moses. Why then was it ever attached to the book of Moses without some strong mark to denote that it was only an appendix! It cannot be allowed that Joshua, Samuel, or Ezra could connive at such a deception; nor is it necessary to suppose that any one has practised deception in this matter. The Old Testament is no forgery: it is an authentic collection of histories, poems and other documents put together by Ezra and his successors during the four centuries that preceded the birth of Christ, and it contains the genuine records, as far as they could be recovered from a great national calamity, of the Law given by God to the Israelites, and therefore possessing divine authority both for the Jews themselves and those who trace back their religion to the same source.

There is a remarkable word found in the first book of Samuel, which was however written after Samuel's death, furnishing a peculiar kind of internal evidence that neither Joshua nor Samuel made this addition to the Pentateuch;

the word Nabi, rendered in English prophet, indicates an age later than that of Samuel.

He who is now called a Prophet was beforetime called a Seer (SAMUEL, ix, 9).

If, therefore, the thirty-fourth chapter of Deuteronomy had been written before or in the time of Samuel, Moses would have been designated as ראה *Roeh*, a Seer, and not as נביא *Nabi*, a Prophet. This exculpates both Joshua and Samuel from having added to the book of Moses without mark of such addition. There are also other indications in the same chapter that Joshua could not have written it, for he would hardly have written of himself that Joshua the son of Nun was "full of the spirit of wisdom": neither would he have said "there arose not a prophet *since* in Israel like unto Moses," for there was no other prophet to whom Moses could be compared except Joshua himself. The word *since* implies that many years had passed since the death of Moses, and that many prophets had arisen, none of whom could be placed in comparison with him who led them out of Egypt. Moreover, the words "no man knoweth of his sepulchre," i.e. the sepulchre of Moses, "unto this day" are another proof that the chapter was not added by Joshua, for they imply that a considerable space of time had elapsed, during which the sepulchre of Moses remained unknown. As Joshua died only twenty-five years after Moses, these words coming from his mouth would lose half their force, and would probably, also, convey an untruth, for we cannot believe that the great Hebrew legislator was buried clandestinely, or that Joshua, the next in command, and almost his equal, could be ignorant where his body was laid.

§ 6. *Anachronism in names, especially those of places, mentioned in the Pentateuch.*

Many names of places occur in the Pentateuch, which were not given to those places until long after the time of Moses. This proves either that the book was written after those places had received the names by which they were then known; or that some later writer has inserted into the original work of Moses the names by which those places were known in his own age. The latter supposition is wholly untenable: it would be an outrage upon the integrity of a book like the Bible, which derives its importance from its being an immaculate record. The number of such passages is so great, amounting to several hundreds altogether, that a large part of the whole must be cut off as not genuine, if such texts are interpolations. It would, moreover, be a positive infringement of that very Law which Moses delivered to the Israelites; for we find in Deuteronomy, (iv, 2) it is expressly forbidden to make any change whatever in the covenant which God gave through Moses.

DEUT. iv, 2. Ye shall not add unto the word which I command you, neither shall ye diminish aught from it, that ye may keep the commandments of the Lord your God, which I command you.

If it should be replied that the mere insertion of the name of a place into the historical part of the Pentateuch is not an infringement of the Law of Moses, such a reply is tantamount to an admission of the whole question.

The perfect Law of Moses is doubtless contained in the Pentateuch, but the terms "Pentateuch" and "Law of Moses" are not convertible terms. The Law of Moses was given fifteen hundred years before Christ, but the Pentateuch was compiled probably not more than four or five hundred years before Christ.

The passages where more modern names of places occur in the Pentateuch are these:

1. HEBRON.

GEN. xiii, 18. Then Abram removed his tent, and came and dwelt in the plain of Mamre, which is in Hebron, and built there an altar unto the Lord.

Instead of the words the "plain of Mamre," we find in the Samaritan Pentateuch the "oak of Mamre," and this reading is supported by the Hebrew according to the Latin interpretation given in Walton's Polyglot Bible, whereas "plain of Mamre" rests on the authority of the Septuagint and the Targum of Onkelos. As all the interpreters read "in Hebron," we may deem the better reading to be "oak of Mamre": for it is evident, although an oak may be in a city, a plain can only be in its neighbourhood.

GEN. xxiii, 2. And Sarah died in Kirjath-arba; the same is

Hebron in the land of Canaan : and Abraham came to mourn for Sarah, and to weep for her.

—xxiii, 19. And after this, Abraham buried Sarah his wife in the cave of the field of Machpelah before Mamre; the same is Hebron in the land of Canaan.

— xxxv, 27. And Jacob came unto Isaac his father unto Mamre, unto the city of Arbah, which is Hebron, where Abraham and Isaac sojourned.

— xlix, 30. In the cave that is in the field of Machpelah, which is before Mamre, in the land of Canaan, &c.

It appears from some of these passages that the city of Hebron, which was also called Mamre, formerly bore the name of Kirjath-arba, i.e. the city of Arba. A question therefore arises, as to the time when the name Kirjath-arba was exchanged for that of Hebron. We in vain search the Pentateuch for an answer to this question, but in the Book of Joshua the difficulty is cleared up.

Joshua, xiv, 6—15. Caleb, the son of Jephunneh the Kenezite, said unto him [Joshua] "..........give me this mountain, whereof the Lord spake in that day; for thou heardest in that day how the Anakims were there, and that the cities were great and fenced : if so be the Lord will be with me, then I shall be able to drive them out, as the Lord said." And Joshua blessed him, and gave unto Caleb the son of Jephunneh Hebron for an inheritance. Hebron therefore became the inheritance of Caleb the son of Jephunneh the Kenezite unto this day, because that he wholly followed the Lord God of Israel. And the name of Hebron before was Kirjath-arba; which Arba was a great man among the Anakims. And the land had rest from war.

If the name of Hebron was not given to the city formerly called Kirjath-arba, until after it was taken from the Anakims by Caleb the son of Jephunneh, it follows that the Pentateuch, in which the name 'Hebron' occurs several times, could not have been written until after the time when that town was taken by Caleb the son of Jephunneh.

2. DAN.

Gen. xiv, 14. And when Abram heard that his brother was taken captive, he armed his trained servants, born in his own house, three hundred and eighteen, and pursued them unto Dan.

In the time of Abraham, and even in the time of Moses, there was no place called Dan : there was a city called Laish, which afterwards was captured by a marauding expedition of the Israelites and received the name of Dan. Bishop Patrick, in the Family Bible, gives the following note upon this passage:

—*pursued them unto Dan.*] As far as the place where one of the springs of Jordan breaks forth called Dan, as Josephus relates, where he speaks of this history.

The words of Josephus here follow:
Falling upon the Assyrians the fifth night near Dan—for so is one of the fountains of the Jordan called—&c.

We cannot doubt that in the time of Josephus the name Dan was well known to the Jews, whether applied to the tribe of Dan in the south of Palestine, to the little town formerly called Laish but afterwards Dan, or to the fountain of the Jordan, which seems to have been called Dan, because it was in the immediate neighbourhood of the town. This does not interfere with the question, whether the word Dan, as applied to these places, could have been in existence in the time of Moses. If it was not then known, as we have the best evidence to prove, we must infer that the Pentateuch was written or compiled after the name of Dan was given to the town of Laish: i.e. some time during or after the government of the Judges.

3. SUCCOTH.

GEN. xxxiii. 17. And Jacob journeyed to Succoth, and built him an house, and made booths for his cattle: therefore the name of the place is called Succoth.

Dr Wells, as quoted by the editors of the Bible, remarks on the name Succoth: "So the place was afterwards called: it is situated not far from Jordan to the East."

This is, of course, the natural and obvious meaning of the text. It is not stated that Jacob gave the name of Succoth to this place, and, as he soon after went down into Egypt, and none of his posterity ever came again into Canaan, until the time of Moses, it is almost certain that the place did not receive the name of Succoth until the Israelites were settled in the land, and gratified their natural vanity by finding out the places where their great ancestors Abraham, Isaac, and Jacob, had formerly resided, and naming the places in memory of the remarkable events which had happened at each of them.

4. ESHCOL.

NUMBERS, xiii, 23. And they came unto the brook of Eschol, and cut down from thence a branch with one cluster of grapes, and they bare it between two upon a staff: and they brought of the pomegranates and of the figs. The place was called the brook Eschol, because of the cluster of grapes which the children of Israel cut down from thence.

Bishop Patrick's note on this verse is sensible and appropriate :

The place was called the brook Eschol.] That is, when the Israelites got possession of the land, they called this brook, or valley, "Eschol," in memory of this bunch of grapes, for so Eshcol signifies.

But the book, which relates that the place was called Eshcol, cannot have been written until the act of naming had taken place.

5. BETHLEHEM.

GENESIS, xxxv, 19. And Rachel died and was buried in the way to Ephrath, which is Bethlehem.

This form of speech implies that the place once called Ephrath was better known in the time of the writer by the name of Bethlehem. This is natural and consistent if we consider it as coming from a later writer, but it is difficult to conceive *Moses* writing in such a manner. Neither he nor the people, for whom he wrote, had ever been in the promised land, and could not have understood such a description.

The names again occur in Genesis, xlviii, 7.

"And as for me,"—Jacob is speaking—"when I came from Padan, Rachel died by me in the land of Canaan in the way, when yet there was but a little way to come unto Ephrath: And I buried her there in the way of Ephrath;" the same is Bethlehem.

The concluding words 'the same is Bethlehem,' if not meant to explain the obsolete name Ephrath by one that was more intelligible, can have no meaning at all. It will be observed that many of these second names given to places in Palestine, are compounds of the word 'Beth.'* They

---

* This is the Hebrew word for house or abode, and this latter word, with its correlatives, bide, abide, &c., are evidently derived from some common

were mostly given to these places, after the Israelites expelled the original inhabitants and took possession of the country for themselves. An exception may be taken in the case of a few places whose names are said to have been changed by Abraham, Isaac or Jacob: of which there are several examples.

6. BETHEL.

In Genesis, xii, 8, we read the following passage concerning Abraham:

And he removed from thence unto a mountain on the east of Bethel, and pitched his tent, having Bethel on the west, and Hai on the east: and there he builded an altar unto the Lord, and called upon the name of the Lord.

It is an obvious comment to make on this verse that there was no such place as Bethel in the days of Abraham: for in Genesis, xxviii, 18, 19, we find that Jacob gave the name of Bethel, which means "the house of God," to the place before called Luz. The words are these:

And Jacob rose up early in the morning, and took the stone that he had put for his pillow, and set it up for a pillar, and poured oil upon the top of it. And he called the name of that place Bethel: but the name of that city was called Luz at the first.

The city was called Luz in the time of Joshua:

JOSHUA, xviii, 13. And the border went over from thence toward Luz, to the side of Luz, which is Bethel, south-ward: and the border descended to Atarothadar, near the hill that lieth on the south side of the nether Beth-horon.

7. BEERSHEBA.

In Genesis, xxi, 31, we read the origin of the name Beersheba; namely the oath or covenant made between Abraham and Abimelech: "Wherefore he called that place Beersheba: because there they sware both of them." The place had been already mentioned in the 14th verse of the same chapter: "She [Hagar] departed, and wandered in the wilderness of Beersheba."

---

root to which the Hebrew beth may be ascribed. The Hebrew word Kirjath, which occurs in several passages, allied to the Celtic caer and the Latin castrum, has the meaning of city, as appears in the case of Kirjatharba, elsewhere rendered in our Bibles the city of Arba. Such names should, if possible, be uniformly rendered into foreign languages.

But in Genesis, xxvi, 26—31, we find the same story of the oath, told of Isaac and Abimelech: with a variation concerning the name Beer-sheba:

vv. 32, 33. And it came to pass the same day, that Isaac's servants came, and told him concerning the well which they had digged, and said unto him, "We have found water." And he called it Sheba: therefore the name of the city is called Beer-sheba unto this day.

The comment given on this text is from Dr Wells: "Isaac renewed the well dug by his father at this place, where in later times a city was built." But the words of the text are, "Therefore the name of the city is called Beer-sheba unto this day;" therefore, i.e. because Isaac's servants had found water, and digged a well, and an oath was sworn between Isaac and Abimelech. The same story being told of Abraham first and afterwards of Isaac leaves us in doubt which of these is the true one. It is sufficient to remark that no city of Beersheba existed in the time of Moses: consequently the book in which it is mentioned could not have been written by Moses or any of his contemporaries.

8. HORMAH.

NUMBERS, xiv, 44. But they presumed to go up unto the hill-top: nevertheless the ark of the covenant of the Lord, and Moses, departed not out of the camp. Then the Amalekites came down, and the Canaanites which dwelt in that hill, and smote them, and discomfited them even unto Hormah.

— xxi, 1—3. And when king Arad the Canaanite, which dwelt in the south, heard tell that Israel came by the way of the spies; then he fought against Israel and took some of them prisoners. And Israel vowed a vow unto the Lord and said, If thou wilt indeed deliver this people into my hand, then I will utterly destroy their cities: and the Lord hearkened to the voice of Israel, and delivered up the Canaanites, and they utterly destroyed them and their cities, and he called the name of the place Hormah.

"This," according to Dr Shuckford, "was effected in the days of Joshua, (Jos. xii, 14,) or a little after his death. JUDGES, i, 17."

JOSHUA, xii, 7. And these are the kings of the country which Joshua and the children of Israel smote on this side Jordan on the west. . . . . . 14. The king of Hormah, one; &c.

JUDGES, i, 17. And Judah went with Simeon his brother, and they slew the Canaanites that inhabited Zephath, and utterly destroyed it. And the name of the city was called Hormah.

Yet Dr Shuckford did not perceive that the relation of events, which happened in the days of Joshua, could not be made by the pen of Moses. The second of the passages above quoted, namely the first three verses of Numbers xxi, describes the fulfilment of Israel's vow, not in a mere word or short sentence, such as others which the commentators explain by saying that they are interpolations. The present text is too full for us to suppose so: it is evidently an integral portion of the main narrative, and cannot be separated from it. The whole of this part of the history, therefore, is liable to the same observation which has been so often made, that it was written by some one who lived long after the time of Moses.

9. GILEAD.

When Jacob fled from Laban, he is said, in Genesis xxxi, 21, to have "set his face toward the mount Gilead:" "so called," according to Dr Wells, "by anticipation." But in verses 46, 47, 48, of the same chapter we read:

And Jacob said unto his brethren, "Gather stones:" and they took stones, and made an heap: and they did eat there upon the heap. And Laban called it Jegarsahadutha: but Jacob called it Galeed. And Laban said, "This heap is a witness between me and thee this day." Therefore was the name of it called Galeed.

The Hebrew word in these verses is the same, formed of the four consonants גלעד *Glyd*, but the vowel points are different, for which reason our English translation renders the word Galeed in the one case and Gilead in the other. But, whatever was the name of the place, whether it was called so by Jacob or by Abraham, the word might properly be used by Moses, who lived later than both of them. This instance then furnishes a contrast to the other passages, already cited, of which Moses could not have been the writer.

10. LAND OF THE HEBREWS.

In Genesis, xl, 15, Joseph in prison asks the chief butler of Pharaoh, when he shall be set free, to think of Joseph his fellow-prisoner and use his influence with the king to get him also released.

For indeed [says he] I was stolen away out of the *land of the Hebrews:* and here also I have done nothing that they should put me into the dungeon.

By the "land of the Hebrews" here is meant Palestine or Canaan, the land which the Hebrews did not occupy till two if not four hundred years afterwards: for the Israelites were not until then named Hebrews, and only then were so named by the natives of Canaan because they were foreigners and came from *over* or beyond the river.

Similar incongruities may be observed in the following passages, taken from the Book of Numbers.

NUMBERS, xxxii, 34—42. And the children of Gad built Dibon and Ataroth, and Aroer, and Atroth, Shophan, and Jaazer, and Jogbehah, and Beth-nimrah, and Bethharan, fenced cities: and folds for sheep.

And the children of Reuben built Heshbon, and Elealeh, and Kirjathaim, and Nebo, and Baal-meon, (their names being changed) and Shibmah: and gave other names unto the cities which they builded.

And the children of Machir the son of Manasseh went to Gilead, and took it, and dispossessed the Amorite which was in it. And Moses gave Gilead unto Machir* the son of Manasseh; and he dwelt therein.

And Jair the son of Manasseh went and took the small towns thereof, and called them Havoth-Jair.

And Nobah went and took Kenath, and the villages thereof, and called it Nobah, after his own name.

The foundation of all these towns, with the other events there related, could not have been effected in the two years which passed between the first invasion of Bashan by those tribes, and the death of Moses. The account of these things, therefore, must be considered as proceeding not from him, but some later writer, who describes not only the settling of those tribes which had obtained their allotments beyond Jordan, in the life-time of Moses, but also the erection of towns and cities, which occupied them many years.

---

* In Deuteronomy iii, 15, we read this in the first person coming directly from Moses:—" And I gave Gilead unto Machir!"

11. BEER.

The word Beersheba, *Well of Oath*, has been quoted in page 123 as a seventh instance of a place the name of which was given to it after the time of Moses. We have now to notice the simple word Beer 'Oath,' from which the name aforesaid has been confounded, and in doing so, it will be necessary to repeat the verse, Numbers, xxi, 14, where the Book of the Wars of the Lord is named as a work from which certain details there mentioned have been derived.

Wherefore it is said in the Book of the Wars of the Lord, "What he did in the Red Sea, and in the brooks of Arnon, and at the stream of the brooks that goeth down to the dwelling of Ar, and lieth upon the border of Moab." And from thence they went to Beer: that is the well whereof the Lord spake unto Moses, "Gather the people together, and I will give them water." Then Israel sang this song, "Spring up, O well; sing ye unto it: the princes digged the well, the nobles of the people digged it, by *the direction* of the lawgiver with their staves."

The name of the town Beer was no doubt taken from the neighbouring well: it is again mentioned in Judges, ix, 21; and in the Second Book of Samuel, xx, 14, we read of the Berites, the inhabitants of Beer, all of whom went out to join Joab in pursuing Sheba the son of Bichri.

The first verse of this extract is a fragment of poetry, recited out of the Book of the Wars of the Lord, and speaks of things which either had not happened before the time of Moses, or if they had happened, are nowhere mentioned in connection with the Israelitish people, and the poet who wrote those lines had more knowledge of the books of Arnon and of the geographical boundaries of Moab than could possibly have been possessed by Moses or any of his people. The whole passage however is very interesting, as containing three fragments of ancient poetry, quoted evidently by a writer of a later date, who delights, as those mostly do who chronicle the deeds of their early ancestors, in finding out the legends from which places existing in their own time have derived their names, and the scenes at which the deeds of their forefathers have been achieved.

Understood thus the verses extracted from Numbers might seem to need no further comment, nor would it generally be profitable or necessary to multiply illustrations of an argument which must of itself extend to some length and require many instances. I cannot however refrain from quoting an illustration of those verses from Dr Smith's Dictionary of the Bible, which may arrest the momentary attention, but certainly cannot tend to the edification of those who possess the average information of their time on the subject of Biblical criticism.

According to the tradition of the Talmudists—a tradition in part adopted by St Paul (1 Cor. x, 4)—this was one of the appearances, the last before the entrance on the Holy Land, of the water which had "followed" the people, from its first arrival at Rephidim, through their wanderings. The water—so the tradition appears to have run—was granted for the sake of Miriam, her merit being that, at the peril of her life, she had watched the ark in which lay the infant Moses. It followed the march over mountains and into valleys, encircling the entire camp, and furnishing water to every man at his own tent door. This it did till her death (Num. xx, 1), at which time it disappeared for a season, apparently rendering a special act necessary on each future occasion for its evocation. The striking of the rock at Kadesh (Num. xx, 10) was the first of these; the digging of the well at Beer by the staves of the princes, the second; Miriam's well at last found a home in a gulf or recess in the sea of Galilee, where at certain seasons its water flowed, and was resorted to for healing purposes (Targums Onkelos, and Ps. Jon. Num. xx, 1, xxi, 18, and also the quotations from the Talmud in Lightfoot on John, v, 4).

§ 7. *Allusion to events that are known to have happened after the death of Moses.*

Under this head will be placed certain passages which bear a sort of negative or indirect testimony to the argument which we are pursuing. Such are the following:

1. THE EXPULSION OF THE CANAANITES.

And Abram passed through the land unto the place of Sichem, unto the plain of Moreh. *And the Canaanite was then in the land.* GENESIS, xii, 6.

The observation, which concludes this passage, is unmeaning, if the Canaanites were still in the land when the book of Genesis was written. As the Canaanites were one of the nations against whom Joshua fought after Moses was dead, it is evident that Moses could not have written these words, but that they must be referred to an author who lived when the Canaanites had been exterminated. There is another passage in the Pentateuch, of similar import:

And there was a strife between the herdmen of Abram's cattle and the herdmen of Lot's cattle : *and the Canaanite and the Perizzite dwelled then in the land.* GENESIS, xiii, 7.

The inferential force of these passages, proving that they were written after the expulsion of those tribes from the Holy Land, has not escaped the notice of those who maintain the Pentateuch to be the work of Moses. The explanation, which Dr Graves gives of them, cannot be listened to for an instant.

It does not follow that the Canaanites had been expelled when this clause was written : it may mean no more than that the Canaanites were *even at that time* in the land, which God had promised to give the seed of Abram. The observation, in the former place, may have been intended to illustrate the faith of Abram, who did not hesitate to obey the command of God, by sojourning in this strange land, though even then inhabited by a powerful nation, totally unconnected with, if not averse to, him; a circumstance intimated by Abram's remonstrance to Lot, to avoid any enmity between them, "because they were brethren:" as if he had said, It would be extreme imprudence in us, who are brethren, who have no connexion or friendship but with each other, to allow any dissension to arise between us, surrounded as we are by strangers, indifferent or even averse to us, who might rejoice at our quarrel, and take advantage of it to our common mischief : "for the Canaanite and the Perizzite dwelled" even "*then* in the land." Another reason may be given why Moses noticed the circumstance of the Canaanite and the Perizzite having been then in the land, which he, immediately after the first notice of it, declares that God promised to the seed of Abram. The Israelites might thus be most clearly satisfied, that no change had taken place in the purpose of God to give them this land : when they were reminded, that at the very time this purpose was declared, the very same nation possessed the country who now occupied it.

This is puerile, and has nothing to do with the question : the introduction of the little word *even* into the text, without any authority derived from the original Hebrew, is unwarrantable. The expressions "And the Canaanite was then in the land," "And the Canaanite and the Perizzite dwelled then in the land," seem to have been introduced by the writer for no other purpose than to show that the land was at that time occupied by strangers, that Abraham and Lot were not its masters, and therefore were obliged to conduct themselves with more restraint than their descendants who drove out these people and had the land all to themselves. If the translators of our Bible understood the passages in the same sense as Dr Graves, why did they not adopt a less ambiguous mode of rendering it into English, by inserting the word *even*, or by placing the word *then* in such a manner that it might have the force of *even then?* To give it this meaning, they ought to have placed it the last word in the sentence; thus—"The Canaanite was in the land *then.*" But they have not given it this signification, neither have the translators of the Septuagint and the Vulgate understood the word *then* in that sense. The former translates the passages thus:

Οἱ δὲ Χαναναῖοι τότε κατῴκουν τὴν γῆν.—Gen. xii, 6.   But the Canaanites then inhabited the land.

Οἱ δὲ Χαναναῖοι καὶ οἱ Φερεζαῖοι τότε κατῴκουν τὴν γῆν.—Gen. xiii, 7.   But the Canaanites and the Perizzites then inhabited the land.

The Latin Vulgate, also, conveys the same signification:

Chananæus autem tunc erat in terra.—Gen. xii, 6.   But the Canaanite was then in the land.

Eo autem tempore Chananæus et Pherezæus habitabant in terra illa.—Gen. xiii, 7.   But at that time the Canaanite and Perizzite dwelt in that land.

2. ALLUSION TO THE KINGS OF ISRAEL.

The next passage which I shall adduce is still more decisive of the age in which the Pentateuch was written.

GENESIS, xxxvi, 30, 31. Duke Dishon, duke Ezer, duke Dishan; these are the dukes that came of Hori, among their dukes in the land of Seir. And these are the kings that reigned in the land of Edom, before there reigned any king over the children of Israel.

These words prove as plainly as words can express, that since that time there *had* been kings who reigned over Israel. Now the first king of Israel was Saul, who reigned 500 years after the death of Moses. Yet those who maintain that the Pentateuch is the work of Moses, have endeavoured to explain the passage by supposing that Moses himself was a sort of king over Israel. Thus in the Family

Bible is given in the following note upon the text now under consideration :

Before there reigned any king over the children of Israel.] Moses, having recently mentioned the promise of God to Jacob, that " kings should come out of his loins," observes it as remarkable, that Esau's posterity should have so many kings, and yet there was no king in Israel when he wrote this book. Moses might have written this by inspiration or he might well write it without a spirit of prophesy; and we might affirm, if necessary, that his meaning is, " All these were kings in Edom, *before his own time ;*" who was, in a certain sense, the first king in Israel, DEUT. xxxiii, 5 ; for he truly exercised royal authority over them, as Selden observes. BP PATRICK. See the note on Deut. xxxiii, 5.

To save the reader the trouble of referring to this note, it is here subjoined :

He was king in Jeshurun.] Many persons are called kings in Scripture, whom we should rather denominate *chiefs* or *leaders*. Such is the sense of the word in this passage. Moses was the *chief*, the *leader*, the *guide* of his people, fulfilling the duties of a 'king,' but he was not *king* in the same sense as David or Solomon was afterwards. This remark reconciles Gen. xxxvi, 31, ' These kings reigned in Edom, before there reigned any king over the children of Israel,' for Moses, though he was *king* in an inferior sense, yet did not *reign*, in the stronger sense, over the children of Israel, their constitution not being monarchical under him. *Calmet's Dictionary.* Moses was king ; that is, under God the supreme ruler and governor of Israel. *Bp Patrick, Dr Wells.* Moses was a prince or governor, he gave laws and ruled the people. *Bp Kidder.* Was appointed of God the leader and governor of the Israelites. *Pyle, Bishop Hall.*

These notes, so far from reconciling the two texts, actually contradict one another. Moses "was king," yet it was "in an inferior sense ;" he " was not king in the same sense as David or Solomon." This style of interpretation is highly censurable in historical criticism, and never has been allowed, where there was not a preconceived notion, or a particular theory to support. The truth, however, of the texts that have been quoted, lies upon the surface, and common sense will be found to be the best interpreter. The Pentateuch, which informs us that there had been up to that time no king in Israel, was not written until there actually *was* a king in Israel, and the words, *he was king in Jeshurun*, applied to Moses, have nothing to do with the matter :

they form part of a chapter describing the blessing of Moses, and are in a highly poetical or declamatory style, showing that 'king' must be interpreted not literally, but metaphorically, a *prince, leader* or *governor*, as it is rendered in that portion of the note which was written by Bishop Kidder, Pyle, and Bishop Hall.

3. THE CEASING OF THE MANNA.

And the children of Israel did eat manna forty years, until they came to a land inhabited; they did eat manna until they came unto the borders of the land of Canaan.

This passage might perhaps have passed unnoticed, even though Moses died at least one month before the forty years were expired, as we read in Deuteronomy, xxxiv, 8:

And the children of Israel wept for Moses in the plains of Moab thirty days, &c.

The expression, forty years, might be understood in round numbers, were it not for the fact that the manna had not ceased when Moses died. This we learn from Joshua, v, 12.

The manna ceased on the morrow after they had eaten of the old corn of the land; neither had the children of Israel manna any more; but they did eat of the fruit of the land of Canaan that year.

It appears, then, that an allusion is here made to an event, the ceasing of the manna, which is known not to have happened until after the death of Moses. The relation of its ceasing could not, therefore, have been written by Moses.

4. THE SINEW THAT WAS NOT EATEN.

The thigh of Jacob is said to have shrunk after his interview and wrestling with the angel. The account is found in Genesis, xxxii, 31, 32.

And as he passed over Penuel, the sun rose upon him, and he halted upon his thigh. Therefore the children of Israel eat not of the sinew which shrank, which is upon the hollow of the thigh, unto this day: because he touched the hollow of Jacob's thigh in the sinew that shrank.

This reference to a custom still existing among the Israelites seems decidedly to indicate a later date than that of Moses. No one has ventured to assert that the Mosaic law was observed by the Jews before it was instituted by Moses. Now the words of the passage before us seem to show that the Israelites had, for a very long time, abstained from eating the sinew which shrank. Moses being conscious that this custom was ordained by himself, could hardly have used such language, or have claimed such great antiquity as the words seem to indicate.

§ 8. *The Pentateuch betrays a more advanced state of knowledge than prevailed in the time of Moses.*

Many expressions, used in the Pentateuch, indicate a more advanced state of knowledge than was likely to exist among the Jews, when they were just escaped from Egyptian bondage. The writer introduces these expressions apparently for the purpose of leading his readers to comprehend his meaning by alluding to something well known among them.

This peculiarity is observable in numerous passages which here follow.

1. In the account of the four rivers which watered the garden of Eden, which runs thus:

The name of the first is Pison: that is it which compasseth the whole land of Havilah,* where there is gold: and the gold of that land is good; there is bdellium and the onyx-stone. And the name of the second river is Gihon: the same is it that compasseth the whole land of Ethiopia. And the name of the third river is Hiddekel: that is it which goeth toward the east of Assyria. And the fourth river is Euphrates. GENESIS, ii, 11—14.

The first three of these rivers were little known to the Israelites, even in the most civilized periods of their commonwealth: they therefore required to be more fully described; but of the well known Euphrates no description was necessary. Yet in the time of Moses it may be doubted

---

* The land of Havilah, mentioned in Genesis, and there described as encompassed, or enclosed rather, by the river Pison, has been assigned, by consent of the learned, as the first and chief settlement of the son of Cush, and identified with the province, on the Persian gulf, now denominated Hagar or Bahrein; a district anciently watered, as we gather from the concurrent testimonies of Pliny and the Portuguese traveller Texeira, by a branch of the Euphrates, which, diverging from the course of its other channels, ran southward, parallel with the gulf, and fell into it nearly opposite the Bahrein islands. A direct proof, unnoticed by preceding writers, that this region once bore the name of Havilah, is furnished by the fact that the principal of the Bahrein islands retain to this day the original name in that of Aval."—FORSTER, vol. ii, p. 40.

whether the Israelites were not in too ignorant and degraded a state, owing to their severe slavery in Egypt, to render the above distinction at all applicable. They probably knew less* of the Euphrates than of the Gihon, which is supposed to be another name of the Nile. For the Septuagint, translating Jeremiah, ii, 18, reads, 'the river Geon,' where the Hebrew and the English versions have the 'waters of Sihor' in connection with Egypt; and a Latin scholiast, supposed to be Germanicus, has the words the "Nile which is also thought to be the Gion," in his Scholia on the *Phœnomena* of the Greek poet Aratus.

2. In the description of the ark resting on Mount Ararat.

And the ark rested in the seventh month, on the seventh day of the month, upon the mountains of Ararat.

Now the mountains of Ararat are situated a long way to the north-east of the Holy land, and the Israelites, having never crossed the Jordan, but dwelling in the Arabian wilderness during all the life of Moses, would not be likely to know even where Mount Ararat was to be found. But in later times, when the Jews were in correspondence with foreign nations, such a description would be intelligible and appropriate.

3. The case is somewhat the same with Damascus, mentioned in GENESIS, xiv, 15.

And he divided himself against them, he and his servants, by night, and pursued them unto Hobah, which is on the left hand of Damascus.

Hobah and Damascus were equally unknown to the Israelites, when they first came out of Egypt: the situation of Hobah could not, therefore, be more clearly explained by reference to that of Damascus. The whole of Palestine lay between the Israelites and Syria, of which Damascus was the capital.

---

* The same observation has occurred to W. A. W [right]. author of the article "Eden," in Dr. Smith's "Dictionary of the Bible," whose work appeared many years after mine. But the inference which he draws from it is very dissimilar. He writes : " It is scarcely possible to imagine that the Gihon, or as some say the Pison, is the Nile ; for that must have been even more familiar to the Israelites than the Euphrates, and have stood as little in need of a definition." It would have needed none if they were just come from Egypt ; but if from Babylon, they would probably know very little about the Nile, and the fact that a definition has been given seems, therefore, to imply that they had lately come from Babylon.

4. A similar allusion, less applicable in the time of Moses than in an after-age, is found in GENESIS, ix, 18.

And the sons of Noah that went forth of the ark, were Shem, and Ham, and Japheth: and Ham is the father of Canaan.

But the Israelites knew nothing of the Canaanites until after the death of Moses, when they were conducted by Joshua over the Jordan, and came in contact with the Canaanites, Hivites, and other nations, who at that time occupied the land of promise. If, however, we suppose the Pentateuch to have been written in a later age, when the Canaanites were too well known to the Israelites by repeated wars, the allusion to them acquires a propriety which hardly belongs to it at a time, when these people were comparatively unknown.

5. A fifth instance of the same peculiarity is the manner in which those who sold Joseph into slavery are variously named, in one passage Ishmeelites, in another Midianites.

GENESIS, xxxvii, 25—28. And they [i.e. Joseph's brethren] sat down to eat bread: and they lifted up their eyes and looked, and, behold, a company of *Ishmeelites* came from Gilead with their camels bearing spicery and balm and myrrh, going to carry it down into Egypt.

And Judah said unto his brethren, " What profit is it if we slay our brother, and conceal his blood ? Come, and let us sell him to the *Ishmeelites*, and let not our hand be upon him; for he is our brother and our flesh." And his brethren were content.

Then there passed by *Midianites* merchantmen: and they drew and lifted up Joseph out of the pit, and sold Joseph to the Ishmeelites for twenty pieces of silver; and they brought Joseph into Egypt.

Here the merchants, to whom Joseph is sold, are twice called Ishmeelites, and once Midianites. Bishop Patrick explains the inconsistency in the following extraordinary manner:

Ishmeelites.] They are called below Midianites. These people were near neighbours to each other; and were joined together in one company or caravan, as it is now called. It is the custom, even to this day, in the East, for merchants and others to travel through the deserts in large companies, for fear of robbers or wild beasts.

If the passage, to which these comments are annexed,

occurred in one of the famous Greek or Latin historians, Livy, Thucydides, or any other, such a note would not be taken as sound criticism, because none of those able writers would be guilty of such an absurdity as applying two names, known to be distinct, to the same people, within the space of four lines. If some trivial tale contained the inconsistency, the mode of interpreting it, which Bishop Patrick applies to the passage before us, might be passed over without notice, but, even then, more from its being of no importance, than from its soundness or its propriety. When however we find this discrepancy in a work, which is really the most valuable book in the world, and by hundreds of millions has been thought to be divinely inspired, it is desirable that such an inconsistency or discrepancy should be cleared up. Why have none of the commentators remarked on the singular circumstance of their being Ishmaelitish merchants at all, in the time when Joseph was sold into Egypt? Ishmael was Jacob's uncle, being brother to Isaac, Jacob's father. The family of Ishmael could not have increased to such an extent in the time of which the history treats. The mention of Ishmaelites, in the text before us, indicates that the writer lived many generations later, when Ishmaelitish merchants were well known. Still less likely is it that there were Midianitish merchants in those days; for Midian was also one of the sons of Abraham, and as we may infer from GENESIS, xxv, 2, only fifty-four years younger than Isaac. At all events, the variation in the name of this tribe of merchantmen renders it impossible that Moses could have written the narrative, unless we suppose that, when he had it in his power to describe the matter accurately and definitely, he rather chose to relate it in such a manner as to puzzle all future ages as to its exact meaning. *

6. The Sidonians are also named, where we should not expect it.

DEUTERONOMY, iii, 9. Which Hermon the Sidonians call Sirion; and the Amorites call it Shenir.

But the Sidonians lived a long way off from the deserts of

† The writer of the article "Midian" in Dr Smith's excellent "Dictionary of the Bible" suggests that Midianites is equivalent to Arabs, and that the Ishmaelites were a tribe of Arabs. But this, whilst it is a weak conjecture about the names, does not help us to explain the anachronism at all.

Arabia, where Moses and the Israelites wandered, and were probably unknown to them. The passage was written by some one who not only knew the Sidonians and Amorites but was aware that his readers knew them also, and he mentions them for the purpose of rendering his narrative more intelligible.

7. Meribah is another similar instance of minute and needless description.

NUMBERS, xx, 13. *This is the water of Meribah; because the children of Israel strove with the Lord, and he was sanctified in them.*

This mode of specifying the place was less necessary in the time of Moses: but would be requisite if the account is to be referred to a period of time, a thousand years later than Moses; when the site of Meribah, however interesting, would otherwise have been unknown.

8. The same observation is applicable to Beer mentioned in NUMBERS, xxi, 16:

And from thence they went to Beer: that is the well whereof the Lord spake unto Moses, "Gather the people together, and I will give them water."

Both of these texts were written to teach the Israelites the great things which God had done for their ancestors under Moses.

9. Nor can any other remark be made concerning the way in which the town of Jericho is mentioned.

NUMBERS, xxii, 1. *And the children of Israel set forward, and pitched in the plains of Moab on this side Jordan by Jericho.*

Jericho was but a small town; and I should think unknown to the Israelites, before they crossed the Jordan.

10. The bedstead of Og is named as an object of antiquarian curiosity.

DEUTERONOMY, iii, 11. *For only Og king of Bashan remained of the remnant of giants; behold, his bedstead was a bedstead of iron: is it not in Rabbath of the children of Ammon? nine cubits was the length thereof, and five cubits the breadth of it, after the cubit of a man.*

Dr Pyle remarks on this passage:

It is probable, that either Og conveyed his iron bedstead with other furniture of his palace, into the country of the Ammonites, to prevent their falling into the hands of the Israelites: or else the Ammonites had taken it from him in some former conquest, and kept it as a monument of their victory.

Either of these cases would be probable, if it could be first proved that Moses wrote this verse, and that he knew of Og's bed being kept in Rabbath. But Rabbath was not taken by the Israelites until the time of David, as we read in II Sam. xii, 26. "And Joab fought against Rabbah of the children of Ammon, and took the royal city." It is therefore very unlikely that the Israelites knew anything about the bedstead of king Og until then. In the reign of David, five hundred years had passed since Og lived, and his bedstead had consequently then become an object of curiosity*: but it is hardly possible that Moses knew any thing about this bedstead of king Og, afterwards so famous.

11. We may perhaps refer to this head of argument certain passages, in which the Temple is obscurely prefigured.

The Song of Moses undoubtedly is based on some original composition which had been handed down to the later period of the Jewish nation. But its archaisms, though not wholly effaced, have been softened by the editor into harmony with the rest of the Bible. In this Song, at Exodus, xv, 13—17, we read:

Thou in thy mercy hast led forth the people which thou hast redeemed: thou hast guided them in thy strength unto thy holy habitation.........Thou shalt bring them in and plant them in the mountain of thine inheritance, in the place, O Lord, which thou hast made for thee to dwell in, in the Sanctuary, O Lord, which thy hands have established.

It is difficult to believe that the words "thy holy habitation"—"Sanctuary"—"place for thee to dwell in" do not point to the Temple of Jerusalem as already built when these words were written.

12. A similar anachronism occurs in the Book of Numbers, xxiv, 7: where in the prophesy of Balaam the name of Agag, king of Amalek, is mentioned—

---

* Like the great bed of Ware, which is still shown in that town, though only three hundred years old.

He [Israel] shall pour the water out of his buckets, and his seed shall be in many waters, and his king shall be higher than Agag, and his kingdom shall be exalted.

It has been faintly suggested that Agag may have been a name common to all the kings of Amalek, as Pharaoh was the common name of Egyptian kings. But there is not the slightest proof of this suggestion: we must therefore be content to believe that Agag was king of the Amalekites four hundred years after the time of Balaam, and was hewn in pieces by Samuel before the Lord in Gilgal.

13. The last instance I shall adduce is the distinctive manner in which the South country is mentioned. We read in GENESIS, xii, 9:

And Abram journeyed going on still toward the South.

It is true we need not infer that the writer intended to denote any particular place or tract of country which went by the specific name of the South. But in the next chapter it is impossible to interpret the same word as having any other than a special meaning.

And Abram went up out of Egypt, he and his wife and all that he had, and Lot with him, into the South.

A traveller coming out of Egypt, could hardly be said to go up into the South: the direction is wholly towards the North; and the obvious inference is that the South of Palestine is the country into which Abraham went; and the omission of the word, which would have fixed more clearly the meaning of this passage, can only be explained by supposing that the writer, living in Palestine, did not think it necessary to add words which every reader would be able to supply for himself.

§ 9. *Variation in the name given to the priest of Midian father-in-law of Moses, and to Joshua.*

It is not probable that Moses should designate his own father-in-law by three different names. Yet we find he is called in one passage Reuel, in a second Jethro, and Raguel in a third. The first passage is in Exodus, ii, 16—21.

Now the priest of Midian had seven daughters: and they came and drew water and filled the troughs to water their father's flock. And the shepherds came and drove them away: but Moses stood up and helped them, and watered their flock. And when they came to Reuel their father, he said "How is it that ye are come so soon to-day?" And they said "An Ægyptian delivered us out of the hand of the shepherds, and also drew water enough for us and watered the flock." And he said unto his daughters, "And where is he? why is it that ye have left the man? call him that he may eat bread." And Moses was content to dwell with the man: and he gave Moses Zipporah his daughter.

Here he is plainly called Reuel, but in the 18th chapter of the same book, verse 1, he is as evidently designated by the name Jethro.

When Jethro, the priest of Midian, Moses' father-in-law, heard of all that God had done for Moses and for Israel his people, and that the Lord had brought Israel of Egypt; then Jethro, Moses' father-in-law, took Zipporah, Moses' wife, after he had sent her back, &c.

In a third passage the same man is called Raguel, according to the text of our authorized version.

NUMBERS, x, 29. And Moses said unto Hobab, the son of Raguel the Midianite, Moses' father-in-law, "We are journeying unto the place," &c.

In the last of these passages the difference between Reuel and Raguel is to be ascribed to the fact that our version of the Bible was entrusted to different translators, who adopted each his own mode of rendering names, and took no precautions to avoid that want of uniformity which may now in several cases be observed. The names in the original are composed of the same Hebrew letters רעואל ROUAL, and should have been rendered by the same letters in English: but the variation which occurs in the other passage that has been cited admits of no explanation, although some commentators have vainly endeavoured to show that the son of Raguel, Hobab, who is named in Numbers, x, 29, was the father-in-law of Moses, and that Raguel consequently was not the father but grandfather of the Hebrew legislator.

History produces few instances, even in profane literature, of names thus confused; and few books can be mentioned in which the writer, describing a near relative of his own, has called him by two different appellations with no allusion to his identity or reason for his being so variously named. The interpretation which I put on this and other remarkable passages, simplifies the whole matter: the two different accounts have been taken from separate documents, and the Pentateuch, where they meet, is consequently a compilation, and not an original work.

A similar variation will be found between those passages of the Pentateuch where the name of Joshua occurs :

EXODUS, xxiv, 13. And Moses rose up, and his minister Joshua : and Moses went up into the mount of God.

NUMBERS, xiii, 16. These are the names of the men which Moses sent to spy out the land. And Moses called Oshea the son of Nun Jehoshua.

DEUTERONOMY, xxxii, 44. And Moses came and spake all the words of this song in the ears of the people, he and Hoshea the son of Nun.

Thus four forms of the name occur in our Bibles, but in the Hebrew, the Septuagint, and the Vulgate translations, there are only two, occasioned by the change of name recorded in Numbers, xiii, 16, which is denoted by Osee and Jehoshua in the English, by Αὐσὴ and Ἰησοῦς in the Greek, and by Osee and Josue in the Latin Vulgate translation.

§ 10. *Argument derived from the use of the expression " unto this day."*

There is a remarkable mode of expression, occurring in several parts of the Pentateuch, which excludes the possibility of Moses, or indeed of any one, having written it until long after the time of the events related in the order of the history: I mean the words "until this day," by which is of course meant the day or time when the author lived and wrote his history. As this expression occurs in some of the passages which have been already cited for other purposes, it is unnecessary to repeat them, but to refer to the places where they are given, and to cite at present the remaining passages of the Pentateuch, where the same expression is to be found. It must however be premised that in some of these the expression "unto this day," is appropriate as referring to the time of Moses himself, but in others, where the principal event belongs to the age of Moses, and the result, effect, or other posterior event is referred to a future age, we can only conclude that the writer, in whose life-time the posterior event happened, lived at a later period than the age of Moses.

1. The first place in which these words are found, is Genesis, xix, 37:

And the first-born [i.e. of the daughters of Lot] bare a son, and called his name Moab: the same is the father of the Moabites *unto this day*.

Here, no inference can be drawn to ascertain the age of the writer. The whole period of time, during which Moab existed as a nation, is equally applicable to the words 'unto this day.' If, however, it could be shown that the Moabites did not exist as a nation in the time of Moses, this passage would furnish the same proof which is drawn from others where the words occur, that Moses could not have been the writer. But as the Moabites were probably a tribe, even in the time of the Exodus, the words before us may have been written even by Moses himself.

2. In Genesis, xxii, 14, we read as follows:

And Abraham called the name of that place Jehovah-jireh: as it is said *to this day*, In the mount of the Lord it shall be seen.

This verse also, as far as concerns the words 'unto this day,' may have been written by Moses; but it is not equally obvious in what sense Moses could be made to say that his readers might still see the place Jehovah-jireh. He had never seen it himself, and probably knew nothing about it. Jehovah-jireh was in Canaan: and the Israelites had hitherto had no communication with the people of that country.

3. The third place, where we find the same words 'unto this day,' Gen. xxxii, 32, has been already cited at page 132. This instance, however, has no similarity to the two preceding. The custom of refraining from eating the sinew which shrank, is nowhere shown in the Bible to have existed before the time of Moses: it was he who instituted the custom, wherefore it would be highly inappropriate for *him* to advert to the length of time that the custom had lasted. It could by no possibility have lasted longer than a few years. A law-giver who alludes to a custom, of which he was himself the originator, says "Wherefore we still observe the custom *at* the present day," not "*until* this day." The word *until* denotes a prior date and a posterior date, "*from* the former *until* the latter," and in general implies a long

interval. Such an interval cannot be traced, if Moses wrote the words "until this day."

4. A fourth instance may be quoted, which occurs at Deuteronomy, iii, 14.

Jair the son of Manasseh took all the country of Argob unto the coasts of Geshuri and Maachathi, and called them after his own name Bashan-Havoth-Jair unto this day.

Equally impossible is it to look on these words as written by Moses; for we read in Numbers, xxxii, 41, that the exploits of Jair took place in the life-time and under the chief command of Moses himself.

§ 11. *Allusion to the want of a regular government.*

In the 12th chapter of Deuteronomy, we find a variety of admonitions about the manner in which the Israelites should conduct their various offerings and sacrifices, when they should come into the promised land. In verse 8, we read:

Ye shall not do after all the things that we do here this day, every man whatsoever is right in his own eyes.

This is the very expression which occurs so often in the Book of Judges, in reference to the time when there was no king in Israel. It is certainly curious that the same form of expression should occur in the text before us, and leads to the suspicion that it was written at the same time and by the same author who uses the same form of words elsewhere. The following note on Deuteronomy, xii, 8, is from Bishop Patrick:

Every man whatsoever is right in his own eyes.] This does not mean that there was no good order kept among them, or that they were at liberty to sacrifice where they pleased: but that in such an uncertain state, when they were removing from place to place, many took the liberty in those matters to do as they thought good.

This annotation, like too many similar ones found in our Commentaries, is grounded on the supposition that the words "every man doing what was right in his own eyes" can have two different meanings. There may, no doubt, be different *degrees* of force attached to the words: but, in *kind*, their meaning is invariable: they imply a great license, unrestrained by a settled and regular form of government; and this state of license certainly did not prevail in the time of Moses, whose punishments of crime were, in all cases, prompt and severe. I therefore refer the form of speech to a later day, even to those lawless times which followed the Babylonish Captivity.

CHAPTER XV.

BOOK OF JOSHUA EXAMINED—ANACHRONISMS AND OTHER INTERNAL EVIDENCE, SHOWING THAT IT WAS WRITTEN IN A LATER AGE.

THE Book of Joshua is generally understood to have been written by the great captain whose name it bears; and who succeeded Moses in the supreme command of the Israelitish people. In support of this opinion the same arguments are usually adduced which have been cited in the previous part of this work concerning the Books of Moses, GENERAL CONSENT and INTERNAL EVIDENCE. I use the expression *general* instead of universal consent, because, if the reader will turn back to page 65, where an account is given of the supposed author of this book, he will observe that " there is not a perfect agreement among the learned, respecting the author of this book." Even this modified form of expression loses much of its force, when we consider that no ancient author, either sacred or profane, before the Christian era, mentions the name of Joshua or gives the least hint that there was any book written by him at all. It is therefore unnecessary to waste time in refuting the argument of general consent, which means nothing more than a vague opinion, entertained by some but rejected by others, and only beginning to show itself fourteen hundred years after the death of Joshua.

But the second argument, of internal evidence, requires to be noticed, because it is put forward with more confidence, on the strength of two passages which occur in the book before us. The first of these is JOSHUA, v, 1 :

And it came to pass, when all the kings of the Amorites, which were on the side of Jordan westward, and all the kings of the

Canaanites which were by the sea, heard that the Lord had dried up the waters of Jordan from before the children of Israel, UNTIL WE WERE PASSED OVER, that their heart melted, neither was there spirit in them any more, because of the children of Israel.

Bishop Tomline remarks on this passage :

The use of the word " we " proves that this book was written by Joshua, or by some one else alive at the time.

This inference is obvious, and cannot be objected to, if it can be shown that the words of the text, *until* WE *were passed over*, are a correct translation of the corresponding words in the original Hebrew Bible. This, however, is not the case : the passage before us is one of the parts of the Bible which have been corrupted by time, and the error has arisen in the present instance from a confusion between the Hebrew words צברנו *Aberanoo* " we passed over " and צברם *Aberocm* "he caused them to pass over." These words are very similar, and though the common text of the Hebrew Bible now reads ABERANOO, which gives the sense of " we passed over," yet this was not the old reading of the passage, but ABEROOM " he [i.e. God] caused them to pass over," and among the various readings of the text ABEROOM actually is found. The Hebrew letter מ M has in some way or other been divided into the two letters ו and ב, N U, and it is not difficult to see how this has happened, without ascribing either carelessness or dishonesty to the copyist. The materials on which we write, whether paper, vellum, or parchment, are apt to imbibe grease from contact with the hand or with other things, and the two last materials have it frequently in their own nature. A slight vein of grease interrupting the pen would resolve the Hebrew letter M into two parts exactly corresponding with the letters N U, and the next copyist would thus perpetuate an error which, as has happened in the present instance, might run through many hundred years before it was detected. The translators of the Bible, not perceiving this error, and perhaps tempted to make a choice which would attach to the book the value of a contemporary record, have given the passage that interpretation which has misled so many critics, and on which is built so fallacious a theory.

That the error is such as I describe it, and consequently that the theory built upon it is fallacious, must inevitably result from the accuracy of our present statement, which becomes almost a matter of certainty from the concurrence of the Septuagint and Vulgate translations. In the former of these the words which are rendered in our own version "until we were passed over," are,

ἐν τῷ διαβαίνειν αὐτούς   in their passing over.

And the passage in the Latin Vulgate is in accordance:

donec transirent   until they passed over.

In the German translation of the Bible also the error has been corrected, and the proper reading of the word restored.

It appears, then, that the first passage which has been made the basis for the belief that the Book of Joshua is a contemporary writing, has been incorrectly translated in our common English Bibles, and consequently the opinion built upon it must fall to the ground.

The second passage which has been selected as proving that the Book of Joshua was written in or immediately after the time of Joshua, is found in Chapter vi, verse 25.

Joshua saved Rahab the harlot alive, and her father's household and all that she had; *and she dwelleth in Israel unto this day;* because she hid the messengers, which Joshua sent to spy out Jericho.

It is argued that if she was dwelling in Israel even unto this day, i.e. in the time of the writer, the book must have been written in the life-time of Rahab.

It may be replied to this that even if Rahab was alive when the Book of Joshua was written, the words 'even until this day' seem to imply that many years had elapsed, and that Rahab was consequently a very old woman. Joshua, also, must have been a long time dead; for he was more than eighty years old when the city of Jericho was taken.

But it is an error to infer that Rahab was alive when the passage before us was written. It means that her descendants were then still living among the Israelites, and not she herself. This is one of the most common forms of speech found in all the Jewish writings: Moab, Ammon, Israel, denote, not the individuals who bore those names, but the whole of their posterity. It is hardly necessary to give instances of this form of speech: one only may suffice. In the Book of Judges, i, 3, we read:

> Judah said unto Simeon his brother, "Come up with me into my lot, that we may fight against the Canaanites: and I likewise will go with thee into thy lot." So Simeon went with him.

As Judah and Simeon had been dead two, three, or perhaps even four hundred years, it is evident that it was their descendants, and not themselves, who made a covenant to assist one another in subjugating the Canaanites.

As no other passages have been quoted from the Book of Joshua to furnish Internal Evidence that it was written during or soon after the time of Joshua, we may at once proceed to enumerate the passages which furnish internal evidence that it certainly was *not* written until long after his time.

I shall briefly notice each passage by itself, following the order, not of a regular argument digested under separate heads, but of the chapter and verse where these passages occur.

CHAP. iv, 9. And Joshua set up twelve stones in the midst of Jordan, in the place where the feet of the priests which bare the ark of the covenant stood; *and they are there unto this day.*

If the stones had not been there a long time, the writer of the book would not have used such an expression. It would have been in no wise remarkable that the twelve stones or pillars should have stood forty or fifty years; but the writer means that they had stood five hundred, or perhaps a thousand years.

CHAP. iv, 14. On that day the Lord magnified Joshua in the sight of all Israel; and they feared him, as they feared Moses, all the days of his life.

Again, at chapter vi, verse 27,—we read:

> So the Lord was with Joshua; and his fame was noised throughout all the country.

If Joshua wrote this of himself, the words are a serious imputation of his modesty; if written by a contemporary, the information conveyed by them could hardly have been necessary; but if written by an historian in a later age, the passage becomes both natural and appropriate.

Chap. v, 3. And Joshua made him sharp knives and circumcised the children of Israel at the hill of the Foreskins.

Bishop Patrick observes on this verse:

Some understand the Hebrew words thus translated, Gibeah-haaraloth, to be the name by which the place where they were circumcised was afterwards called.

I have no doubt that the name was given to the place afterwards from the deed done there by Joshua: the expression evidently savours of a later age, to explain a local name of which the origin, by lapse of time, had been forgotten.

Chap. v, 9. And the Lord said unto Joshua, "This day have I rolled away the reproach of Egypt from off you." Wherefore the name of the place is called Gilgal unto this day.

Writers are not so particular in recording the reasons why places are named, whilst the fact is fresh in the memory of every one: and in the verse before us this mark of a later age is strengthened by the additional words *unto this day*.

Chap. vii, 26. And they raised over him [Achor] a great heap of stones unto this day. So the Lord turned from the fierceness of his anger. Wherefore the name of that place was called the valley of Achor unto this day.

Chap. viii, 28—29. And Joshua burnt Ai, and made it an heap for ever, even a desolation unto this day. And the king of Ai he hanged on a tree until eventide: and as soon as the sun was down Joshua commanded that they should take his carcase down from the tree, and cast it at the entering of the gate of the city, and raise thereon a great heap of stones, *that remaineth* unto this day.

The words *that remaineth* do not occur in the original Hebrew: they have been added by the translators to make the sense complete. The only inference which both these last quoted passages carry with them, concerning the age when they were written, is that it was a very long time after the death of Achor in the first text, and of the king of Ai in the second. A similar inference is deduced from the verse which follows:

Chap. ix, 27. And Joshua made them [the Gibeonites] that day hewers of wood and drawers of water for the congregation, and for the altar of the Lord, *even unto this day, in the place which he should choose*.

The "place which the Lord should choose" was finally

Jerusalem, and, if the words were written in the later period of the Israelitish government, the Lord had already chosen Jerusalem to be the site of his Temple and the place of his worship.

CHAP. x, 1. Now it came to pass, when Adonizedec king of Jerusalem had heard how Joshua had taken Ai, and had utterly destroyed it; &c.

This chapter is full of names that did not exist until many years afterwards, some more, some less. The first is Jerusalem, which was formerly called Jebusi and did not receive the name of Jerusalem until the reign of David, proving that the book, in which the word Jerusalem occurs, was not written until the reign of David, or that, if written before that time, it has since been interpolated. Of these two probabilities the former is the stronger: because we find it confirmed by the last verse of the same chapter:

CHAP. xv, 63. As for the Jebusites the inhabitants of Jerusalem the children of Judah could not drive them out: but the Jebusites dwell with the children of Judah at Jerusalem unto this day.

It has been asserted that these words can apply only to the few years which immediately followed the death of Joshua; for, say the Commentators, the Jebusites *were* then driven out, as we read the account in Judges, i, 7. 8. We shall find, on enquiry, that they were *not* then driven out; at least, it is not so stated, nor can any such meaning be inferred from the narrative there contained.

JUDGES, i, 7. 8. And Adonibezek said, "Threescore and ten kings, having their thumbs and their great toes cut off, gathered their meat under my table: as I have done, so God hath requited me." And they brought him to Jerusalem, and there he died.

Now the children of Judah had fought against Jerusalem, and had taken it, and smitten it with the edge of the sword, and set the city on fire.

The Jebusites, no doubt, fled out of the city, before it was set on fire, and the children of Judah then took possession; but a portion of it, the citadel, was certainly in their hands in the time of David, and the two nations seem to have lived together in the city and adjoining territory, at peace, during the whole time that the Judges bore rule. This will appear more fully from the quotations which will be given in the next chapter.

Bethhoron is next mentioned at verse 10, and was built by an Israelitish lady after the conquest, as we learn from I Chron. vii, 23, 24:

And when he [Ephraim] went in to his wife, she conceived, and bare a son, and he called his name Beriah, because it went evil with his house. And his daughter was Sherah, who built Beth-horon the nether, and the upper, and Uzzen-sherah.

The comparison of these texts involves an anachronism. Sherah was only the fourth in descent from Jacob—thus: Joseph, Ephraim, Beriah, Sherah. Whether the Israelites remained 430 years or only 215—for there is a great variation between the texts of Scripture on this subject—it is impossible that only one generation, Beriah, could have intervened between Ephraim, who was a child when Jacob went down into Egypt, and Sherah who built Bethhoron.

CHAP. x, 13, 14. And the sun stood still, and the moon stayed, until the people had avenged themselves upon their enemies. Is not this written in the book of Jasher? So the sun stood still in the midst of heaven, and hasted not to go down about a whole day. And there was no day like that before it or after it, that the Lord hearkened unto the voice of a man: for the Lord fought for Israel.

Here we obtain a fact that bears with great force upon our present argument. The writer of the book of Joshua quotes an earlier work, to which he refers his readers for a more full account of the miracle which he records, namely the arresting the sun and moon in their course that the Israelites might be avenged on their enemies. It is impossible to conceive that Joshua himself, who wrought that miracle, could have referred his readers to another book in which a better account of it was to be found. It is far more likely that a compiler, in a later age, finding this miraculous event well described in a book still popular in his time, called the Book of Jasher, should have referred his readers to that book, for further information.

But this is not the only observation elicited by the mention made of the Book of Jasher in this place. The same work is quoted in II SAMUEL, i, 17. 18:

And David lamented with this lamentation over Saul and over Jonathan his son. Also he bade them teach the children of Judah the use of the bow; behold it is written in the book of Jasher.

Here we learn that the Book of Jasher contains the narrative of king David teaching his subjects the use of archery in war. The Book of Jasher was therefore written in or after the reign of David: and the Book of Joshua, which quotes the Book of Jasher, must have been written later still.

Some writers, indeed, have endeavoured to show that the 'Book of Jasher,' Sepher Hayashur, as it might be written according to the Hebrew, was a collection of national poems, and others, that it was in part at least a chronicle of events, enlarged from time to time by successive writers, in the same way as the Mediæval Chronicles were continually augmented in many of the monasteries. But of this there is not a trace in any part of the Hebrew Scriptures, and the interval between Joshua and David's reign, about 500 years, full of wars and revolutions, forbids us to think that such an explanation can be accepted.

The burial-place of the five kings was marked out to posterity by a lasting monument, a heap of stones which Joshua caused to be placed over the cave where they were buried.

CHAP. x, 27. And it came to pass at the time of the going down of the sun, that Joshua commanded, and they took them down off the trees, and cast them into the cave wherein they had been hid, and laid great stones in the cave's mouth, which remain *unto this very day.*

CHAP. xiii, 13. Nevertheless the children of Israel expelled not the Geshurites nor the Maachathites: but the Geshurites and the Maachathites dwell among the Israelites until this day.

CHAP. xiv, 14. Hebron therefore became the inheritance of Caleb the son of Jephunneh the Kenezite *unto this day,* because that he wholly followed the Lord God of Israel. And the name of Hebron before was Kirjath-Arba; which Arba was a great man among the Anakims; and the land had rest from war. [See xv, 13—19.]

Every part of this verse shows a later writer and a later age. The city had lost its ancient name of Kirjath-arba, and was known by the name of Hebron: it had become the inheritance of Caleb, by which is implied that Caleb was dead and his descendants were in possession of it, *until this day,* i.e. for a great length of time. And this is further confirmed by the concluding words, " And the land had rest from war."

The war of the invasion was over, and the children of Israel had quiet possession of the country, when the Book of Joshua was written.

CHAP. xv, 8, 9, 10. And the border went up by the valley of the son of Hinnom unto the south side of the JEBUSITE; *the same is Jerusalem:* and the border went up to the top of the mountain that lieth before the valley of Hinnom westward, which is at the end of the valley of the giants northwards: and the border was drawn from the top of the hill unto the fountain of the water of Nephtoah, and went out to the cities of mount Ephron; and the border was drawn to BAALAH, *which is Kirjath-jearim:* and the border compassed from Baalah westward unto mount Seir, and passed along unto the side of mount JEARIM, *which is Chesalon,* on the north side, and went down to Beth-shemesh, and passed on to Timnah.

The observations made in CHAPTER xiii, concerning the anachronisms which occur in the names of places, apply in all their force to this passage; we have three distinct places here mentioned, each of them designated both by its ancient and modern appellation, Jebusi, Jerusalem—Baalah, Kirjath-jearim—mount Jearim, Chesalon.

CHAP. xvi, 10. And they [*the Ephraimites*] drave not out the Canaanites that dwelt in Gezer: but the Canaanites dwell among the Ephraimites unto this day, and serve under tribute.

CHAP. xvii, 12, 13. Yet the children of Manasseh could not drive out the inhabitants of those cities, but the Canaanites would dwell in the land. Yet it came to pass, when the children of Israel were waxen strong, that they put the Canaanites to tribute; but did not utterly drive them out.

Compare with this the account given in Judges, i, 28—29.

It came to pass, when Israel was strong, that they put the Canaanites to tribute, and did not utterly drive them out. Neither did Ephraim drive out the Canaanites that dwelt in Gezer; but the Canaanites dwelt in Gezer among them. *See also* xviii, 28.

CHAP. xix, 47. And the coast of the children of Dan went out too little for them; therefore the children of Dan went up to fight against Leshem [called Laish in Judges, chap. xviii, v. 29], and took it and smote it with the edge of the sword, and possessed it and dwelt therein, and called Leshem, Dan, after the name of Dan their father.

This is the same affair, which is related more fully in the

18th chapter of Judges. According to the chronology given in the margin of our Bibles, and generally received by the learned, this happened about thirty years after the death of Joshua. The anachronism is explained in the following manner by the editors of the Bible, quoting from Bishop Patrick and Shuckford:

It is supposed that Ezra or some other, thought good in aftertimes to insert this verse here, in order to complete the account of the Danites' possession.

To receive this as sound criticism would bring down History to a level with the most worthless pastime that man can choose for his amusement: it would be, literally, no better than an almanach, which is altered year by year to adapt it to the existing state of things. If the Book of Joshua were indeed the work of the great man whose name it bears, no later historian would have ventured to impair its value by adding to or detracting from its contents.

CHAP. xxiv, 29, 30. And it came to pass after these things that Joshua the son of Nun, the servant of the Lord, died, being an hundred and ten years old. And they buried him in the border of his inheritance in Timnath-Serah, which is mount Ephraim, on the north side of the hill of Gaash.

As Joshua died at the age of 110 years, and his death is recorded in the book which passes by his name, we need no farther proof that this book could not have been written until after Joshua was dead. But this limitation of its origin to some period after the death of Joshua must be still further qualified: for in the next verse of the same chapter we read as follows:

CHAP. xxiv, v. 31. And Israel served the Lord all the days of Joshua, and all the days of the elders that over-lived Joshua, and which had known all the works of the Lord, that he had done for Israel.

How could Joshua write that Israel served the Lord a long time after he was dead, nay—after all those who outlived him were dead also ? If some later writer, as Samuel or Ezra, inserted all these additions to the original work of Joshua, he would certainly have not done so in a clandestine or covert manner, but with a note attached, that "so far is the work of Joshua, and the continuation is by a later hand."

In Mediæval times the monkish chroniclers have always displayed this species of common honesty: for we find a mark attached to those passages which begin the writing of a new author—"Hactenus dominus Radulfus scripsit Chronica, &c. So far is the Chronicle of Master Ralph, &c." Or " Explicit dominus Rogerus; incipit dominus Matthæus, &c. Here ends Master Roger of Wendover, and Master Matthew Paris begins."

Even the supposition of these additions made by later writers, goes far towards a concession of the fact which I would establish; namely, that we have not the Hebrew writings in their original state, but that they are a compilation, put together after the nation had returned, with fresh light and fresh intellectual force, from Babylon.

CHAPTER XVI.

THE BOOK OF JUDGES SIMILARLY EXAMINED.

An anonymous writer in one of our popular editions of the Bible gives an account of this Book, which contains many remarkable observations: I therefore copy it without abridgment:

The name of this book is taken from the title of the functionaries whose actions and administration it principally relates. This name is שופטים, shophetim, plural of שפט, shophet, a judge. This word designates the ordinary magistrates, properly called judges; and is here also applied to the chief rulers, perhaps because *ruling* and *judging* are so intimately connected in the east, that sitting in judgment is one of the principal employments of an oriental monarch (see Gesenius in שפט.)

It is remarkable that the Carthaginians, who were descended from the Tyrians and spoke Hebrew, called their chief magistrates by the same name: but the Latins, who had no such *sh*, as the Hebrews and Carthaginians had, and as we and the Germans have, wrote the word with a sharp *s*, and, adding a Latin termination, denominated them *Suffetes*.

These functionaries are compared to the Roman consuls, and appear in office as well as name, to have borne considerable resemblance to the Hebrew *Shophetim*, "judges." For some observations on the Hebrew "judges," and the nature of their administration, see the note on chap. ii, 16.

The book is easily divisible into two parts; one ending with chap. xvi, contains the history of the Judges, from Othniel to Samson; and the other, which occupies the rest of the book, forms a sort of appendix, relating particular transactions, which, not to interrupt the regular history, the author seems to have reserved for the end. If these transactions had been placed in order of time, we should probably have found them in a much earlier portion of the work, as the incidents related seem to have occurred not long after the death of Joshua.

The author of the book is unknown. Some ascribe it to Samuel, some to Hezekiah, and others to Ezra. The reason which has principally influenced the last determination of the authorship is found in chap. xviii, 30 :—" He and his son were priests to the tribe of Dan until the day of the captivity of the land." But this may have referred to the captivity of the ark among the Philistines, or to some particular captivity of the tribe settled in the north; or the reference may have been to both circumstances. It is also possible that the clause, "until the day of the captivity of the land," may actually have been added after the captivity. That the book itself was not then written is evident from the absence of Chaldee words, which so often occur in the books which we know to have been posterior to that event. Most of the Jewish and Christian commentators assign the authorship to Samuel; probably because internal evidence places it pretty clearly about his time, and in his time he is the most likely person to whom the authorship could be attributed. That it is written after the establishment of the monarchical government, appears from the habit which the author has of saying that the event he is relating happened in the time when "there was no king in Israel;" which renders it evident that there was a king when he wrote. But that it was written very soon after the establishment of kingly government is no less clear from other passages. Thus we see, from chap. i, 21, that the Jebusites were still in Jerusalem in the time of the author; but this ceased to be the case in the time of David, by whom they were expelled from that city. (2 Sam. v, 6.)* So also, in 2 Sam. vi, 21, there is a distinct and precise reference to a fact recorded in Judges ix, 53, which seems another proof that this book was written before the Second Book of Samuel: but this does not appear to be of a conclusive nature; as the fact may have been known to David, even had the Book of Judges not been then written. Upon the whole, there is little question that the book was composed, in its present form, either in the reign of Saul, or during the first seven years of the reign of David: and this renders it more probable that it was compiled, from the public registers and records, by Samuel, than by any of the other prophets, priests or kings, to whom it is assigned.

The chronology of this book is attended with much difficulty, and is stated by various chronologers with very serious difference. This chiefly arises from the period of servitudes, being by some counted as part of the years of the judges, while others count them separately; and also from judges being thought by some to have been successive, whom others consider to have been contemporary in different parts of Palestine. There are some also, who prolong the account by supposing several anarchies or interregnums, the duration of which the history does not mention. The result of Dr Hales's elaborate investigations gives 498 years (B.C. 1608 to B.C. 1110) from the passage of the Jordan to the election of Saul; and 400 years (B.C. 1582 to 1182) from the death of Joshua to the death of Samson, which is the period more peculiarly comprehended in the present book. The period is, however, frequently stated as little exceeding 300 years.

It may be gathered from this extract that those who assign an early date to this book, are obliged to admit that it could not at all events have been written earlier than the reign of Saul or David, that is, three or four hundred, and according to Dr. Hales, nearly five hundred years after the passage of the river Jordan. I shall proceed to enumerate the passages found in the book itself which give evidence of a late origin; among these are those texts which have led writers to limit its composition as not later, at all events, than the reign of David, but which may be shown by no means to warrant such an inference.

CHAP. i, 21. And the children of Benjamin did not drive out the Jebusites that inhabited Jerusalem: but the Jebusites dwell with the children of Benjamin in Jerusalem unto this day.

The Jebusites were certainly reduced to submission by David, but not *driven out:* they still dwelt in the land with the Israelites in the reign of Solomon; for we read in I KINGS, ix, 20:

And all the people that were left of the Amorites, Hittites, Perizzites, Hivites, and Jebusites, which were not of the children of Israel, their children that were left after them in the land, whom the children of Israel also were not able utterly to destroy, upon those did Solomon levy a tribute of bond service unto this day.

The writer of a book in which the name of Solomon is found must have lived during or after the time of Solomon. As the writer in this instance speaks of a later period, which evidently was after a long interval after the reign of Solomon, the words "unto this day" may reasonably be applied to the time after the Captivity. Some remarks concerning the Jebusites have already been made in the last chapter of this work.

CHAP. i, 26. And the man went into the land of the Hittites, and built a city, and called the name thereof Luz; which is the name thereof unto this day.

CHAP. xvii, 6. In those days there was no king in Israel but every man did that which was right in his own eyes.

CHAP. xviii, i. In those days there was no king in Israel: and in those days the tribe of the Danites sought them an inheritance to dwell in; for unto that day all their inheritance had not fallen unto them among the tribes of Israel.

CHAP. xviii, 30. And the children of Dan set up the graven image: and Jonathan, the son of Gershom, the son of Manasseh, he and his sons were priests to the tribe of Dan until the day of the captivity of the land.

CHAP. xix, i. And it came to pass in those days, when there was no king in Israel, that there was a certain Levite sojourning on the side of mount Ephraim, who took to him a concubine out of Bethlehem-judah.

Here we have five passages, in which the writer or compiler clearly points out that he is relating things which happened long before his own time. There was "no king in Israel," when three of these events took place: but the last of the three, according to the received chronology of our Bibles, is dated three hundred years before there was any king in Israel at all, and the writer, by the manner in which he speaks of that fact, seems to have lived at a still later period, when the people had become used to kingly government. But another of the extracts here given speaks of the "captivity of the land"; but by these words we must understand pre-eminently the Babylonish captivity. The plain meaning of the words cannot be evaded; and this book in which they occur must be taken, not as a contemporary record, but as written after the inhabitants of Judæa had been carried captives to Babylon.

CHAPTER XVII.

THE BOOK OF RUTH EXAMINED.

THE Book of Ruth, as has been already said, is properly part of the Book of Judges, from which it has been separated for no very obvious reasons. From its brevity it is not likely to contain many passages to aid us in our present enquiry. Those which I have discovered, are the following:

CHAP. i, 1. Now it came to pass in the days when the Judges ruled, that there was a famine in the land.

This was written after the Judges had ceased to rule; and consequently the work is not contemporary with Ruth, who lived "when the Judges ruled."

CHAP. iv, 21—22. And Salmon begat Boaz, and Boaz begat Obed, and Obed begat Jesse, and Jesse begat David.

Bishop Patrick's note to this is worthy of notice:

Salmon married Rahab, and therefore lived at the time of the Israelites' first entrance into Canaan. Now between this period and the birth of David, are computed 366 years. Thus, as only four generations are mentioned, we must either suppose that some names of persons, who come between, are omitted, (for which we have no warrant,) or that, as is more probable, Salmon, Boaz, Obed, and Jesse, all had their children born to them at a very advanced period of their lives.

Not only in this place may we conjecture that names of persons and things have been omitted, but the same may be said of almost every part of the Old Testament. The name of Salmon occurs under three forms in the Hebrew text; the passages where they occur in the original and in the various versions may be thus compared:

RUTH, iv, 20. *Hebrew* Salmah, *Gr. Septuagint* Salmon, *Lat. Vulg.* Salmon, *Syriac* Sela, *Arabic* Sela, *English* Salmon.

— iv, 21. *Hebrew* Salmon, *Gr. Septuagint* Salmon, *Lat. Vulg.* Salmon, *Syriac* Sela, *Arabic* Sela, *English* Salmon.

1 CHRONICLES, ii, 11. *Hebrew* Salma, *Gr. Septuagint* Salmon, *Lat. Vulg.* Salma, *Syriac* Salma, *Arabic* Salma, *English* Salma.

MATTHEW, i, 4. *Greek* Salmon, which appears in all the versions of St Matthew's Gospel.

The variations of this name are not very important, but may serve as a specimen of the uncertainty which prevails in other cases, especially in the Hebrew language, which is very defective in its alphabetic system. The genealogy of Ruth is probably very incomplete; and the book being compiled out of original papers, like all the rest of the Jewish History, after the captivity of Babylon, the compilers were likely to be puzzled by many discrepancies of this nature, and, choosing to preserve as much as possible the form of their original sources, they have retained even their errors also.

CHAPTER XVIII.

FIRST BOOK OF SAMUEL EXAMINED.

THE two Books of Samuel form but one in the Hebrew Canon. In the Septuagint and Vulgate translations they are called the First and Second Books of Kings, and those which we call the First and Second Books of Kings, are there termed the Third and Fourth Books. It is to be regretted that this diversity should exist; ancient histories should, as far as is possible, be kept in their original or earliest form. There seems to be no adequate reason for classifying these books, as they are classified in our Bibles: they contain quite as much of the history of David as of Samuel.*

* The impression may have prevailed that Samuel was their author; and as Protestants, in opposition to Roman Catholics, have magnified the importance of the Old Testament, exactly in proportion as they have decried the use of reason, the translators have so arranged the books as to produce the most striking effect; and thus a separate existence has been given to that which has none, but which really is only a part of the whole.

Yet notwithstanding the separation of Samuel from Kings, and its division into two parts, the work bears on the face of it the strongest evidence that it could not have been written by Samuel: for the twenty-fifth chapter of the first book begins with the words, "And Samuel died." Thus more than half of the book was obviously composed by a later writer. But we shall see, by an examination of the book in order, that the whole of it owes its origin to a date later than that of Samuel.

Chap. v, 5. Therefore neither the priests of Dagon, nor any that come into Dagon's house, tread on the threshold of Dagon in Ashdod unto this day.

Bishop Patrick has a note on the words "unto this day":

The day when Samuel wrote this book: when the events happened, he was a youth: but the book was written when he was advanced in years.

The space of time between this event and Samuel's death was about forty years,—not long enough to justify the expression 'unto this day.' It must not be taken for granted that Samuel wrote this book; and the verse before us tells as plainly as words can express, that Samuel must have been dead many years, perhaps centuries, when it was written: but the commentators have not seen the natural force of the words, on account of the erroneous opinion that Samuel was the writer, with which they would make the narrative harmonize.

Chap. vi, 18. And the golden mice, according to the number of all the cities of the Philistines belonging to the five lords, both of fenced cities, and of country villages, even unto the great stone of Abel, whereon they set down the ark of the Lord: which stone remaineth unto this day in the field of Joshua the Bethshemite.

Chap. vii, 15. And Samuel judged Israel all the days of his life.

Bishop Patrick's interpretation of this verse may be quoted, but to be as speedily rejected; because it perverts the plain meaning of words, seemingly for the purpose of making them support a pre-conceived theory:

As Samuel was the author of this book, he could not speak literally of "all the days of his life": the sense probably is, that he was so diligent in the discharge of his office, that he gave himself no rest, but sat to judge causes every day.

It is almost a waste of words to reply to such a manifest perversion of the meaning. "All the days of his life" means "the whole of his life," not "every day": and the use of these words shows that Samuel could not have been the author of the book. But the commentator, taking for granted that Samuel *was* the author of the book, has misinterpreted the words to suit this pre-conceived notion.

In I Samuel, ix, 9, 10, we read:

(Beforetime in Israel, when a man went to inquire of God, thus he spake, "Come and let us go to the seer:" for he that is now called a prophet was beforetime called a seer.) Then said Saul to his servant, "Well said; come, let us go." So they went unto the city where the man of God was. And as they went up the hill to the city, they found young maidens going out to draw water, and said to them, "Is the seer here?"

In explaining this passage, the Commentators try to make it appear that the words *now* and *before-time* imply no greater interval of time than that which passed in Samuel's own life-time. They quote as follows, from Bishop Patrick, Pyle, and Dr Gray:

The word *now* refers to the time when this book was written, probably the latter part of Samuel's life. The verse explains that, at the time when Saul was appointed king, the Hebrew word *Roeh*, "a seer of secret things," was usually applied to inspired persons; but that afterwards the word *Nabi* or "prophet," (which had been very anciently known, as appears from the books of Moses,) came into common use. *Bp. Patrick, Pyle.* The word *Nabi* "prophet," was in use in the time of Moses or Abraham; see Gen. xx, 7; but then it only implied a man favoured of God; whereas, in the time of Samuel, it was appropriated to one who foresaw future events.

These remarks contain both what is true and what is false. It is evident that the word *roeh* "seer" is the older term of the two, and we find that it is the word which Saul and his companions actually used—"Is the *seer* here?" The word *seer*, therefore, was used in Samuel's life-time, and there is no proof that the word *nabi*, "prophet," superseded it during the life of Samuel. Indeed there is a verse in the second Book of Samuel, which shows that the old word *seer* was still in use after the death of Samuel:

The king [i.e. David] said also unto Zadok the priest, "Art not thou a *seer?* return into the city in peace, and your two sons with you, Ahimaaz thy son, and Jonathan the son of Abiathar." II Sam. xv, 27.

The Book of Samuel was, consequently, not written by Samuel. The words *now* and *beforetime* denote too long an interval to allow room for such a supposition. But yet the word *nabi* "prophet"—not in use in the time of Samuel —actually occurs in the Pentateuch and other books of the Old Testament, as for example, in Genesis, xx, 7; Exodus, vii, 1; xv, 20; Numbers, xi, 29; xii, 6; Deuteronomy, xiii, 1, 5; xviii, 15; xxxiv, 10; Judges, iv, 4; vi, 8; I Samuel, iii, 20; ix, 9; II Samuel, vii, 2; I Kings, xiii, 11. In the later of these passages it is not to be wondered that the word rendered "prophet" should be found, because the writer of the First Book of Samuel tells us that it had come into use in his time, and therefore must have been a common word afterwards; but that it should occur in the Book of Genesis proves either that Genesis was written after the introduction of the word into the Hebrew language, or that the writer of the First Book of Samuel is wrong in describing the word as modern, or that the meaning of the word had changed. I believe that the word was actually a new word in the Hebrew language introduced after the Babylonish captivity, and consequently that the First Book of Samuel, as well as the Pentateuch, were written after that captivity.

The two next extracts cannot have been written by Samuel, on account of the terms of praise in which he is spoken of: and as they occur in the first part of the book, we may infer that no portion of the work was written by Samuel himself:

Chap. xii, 11. And the Lord sent Jerubbaal, and Bedan, and Jephthah, and Samuel, and delivered you out of the hand of your enemies on every side, and ye dwelled safe.

Chap. xii, 18. So Samuel called unto the Lord; and the Lord sent thunder and rain that day: and all the people greatly feared the Lord and Samuel.

The next extracts would prove, if proof were wanting, that at least Samuel could not have written the whole of this book, for his death is recorded in the extracts.

Chap. xxv, 1. And Samuel died; and all the Israelites were gathered together, and lamented him, and buried him in his house at Ramah.

Chap. xxviii, 3. Now Samuel was dead, and all Israel had lamented him, and buried him in Ramah, even in his own city.

Chap. xxx, 25. And it was so from that day forward, that he made it a statute and an ordinance for Israel unto this day.

There are also some passages, even in the First Book of Samuel, in which the distinction between Judah and Israel is clearly indicated. The book was therefore certainly written after the revolt of Jeroboam and the ten tribes. This took place about ninety years after the death of Samuel, the book, therefore, cannot be considered as a contemporary record. The passages which allude to the division of the kingdom, are these:

Chap. xviii, 16. But all Israel and Judah loved David, because he went out and came in before them.

Chap. xxvii, 6. Then Achish gave him Ziglag that day: wherefore Ziglag pertaineth unto the kings of Judah unto this day.

CHAPTER XIX.

SECOND BOOK OF SAMUEL EXAMINED.

The Second Book of Samuel labours under greater difficulties, as regards its authorship, than any of the preceding writings. Its narrative avowedly and manifestly begins long after the death of Samuel, who, consequently, had nothing whatever to do with writing it. The commentators have supposed Gad or Nathan to have been the author, but they might with more reason have referred it to the time of Ezra, Nehemiah, or some later writer. The internal evidence, furnished from an examination of its contents, will be found to confirm all that has been derived from an analysis of the preceding books of the Jewish Canon.

The allusions to the two separate kingdoms of Judah and Israel, which were noticed in the last chapter, occur again here:

Chap. ii, 4—10. And the men of Judah came, and there they anointed David king over the house of Judah......(v. 10.) Ishbosheth Saul's son was forty years old when he began to reign over Israel and reigned two years. But the house of Judah followed David.

CHAP. iv, 3. And the Beerothites fled to Gittaim, and were sojourners there until this day.

CHAP. v, 5. In Hebron he reigned over Judah seven years and six months, and in Jerusalem he reigned thirty and three years over all Israel and Judah.

This must have been written after the division of the kingdom.

In the seventh verse of the same chapter we are told that "David took the strong hold of Zion: the same is the city of David." The last words are introduced to explain, that the strong hold of Zion was the same which was called afterwards the city of David, and must have been written after that name was given to it.

In the ninth verse, again, of the same chapter, we read that "David dwelt in the fort, and called it the city of David. And David built round about from Millo and inward." Dr Pococke writes, that "from Millo" means from the place where Solomon afterwards built Millo; for it appears from I Kings, ix, 15, that it was not built till Solomon's reign.

If this be true, the Books of Samuel must have been written,—at least as late as the reign of king Solomon. So must the Book of Judges; for Millo is mentioned there also:

JUDGES, ix, 6. And all the men of Shechem gathered together, and all the house of Millo, and went and made Abimelech king, by the plain of the pillar that was in Shechem.

The house of Millo, or, as it is in the Hebrew, Bethmillo, occurs again in II Kings, xii, 20:

And his servants arose, and made a conspiracy, and slew Joash in the house of Millo, which goeth down to Silla.

II SAM. xvi, 23. And the counsel of Ahithophel, which he counselled in those days, was as if a man had enquired at the oracle of God: so was all the counsel of Ahithophel both with David and with Absalom.

CHAP. xviii, 18. Now Absalom in his life-time had taken and reared up for himself a pillar, which is in the king's dale: for he said, "I have no son to keep my name in remembrance": and he called the pillar after his own name: and it is called unto this day, Absalom's place.

The twenty-third chapter of II Samuel begins with these words:

Now these be the last words of David. David the son of Jesse said, and the man who was raised up on high, the anointed of the God of Jacob, and the sweet psalmist of Israel, said :

Then comes the song which David spake on this occasion; followed abruptly by the catalogue of David's mighty men of war: and in verse 1 of chapter xxiv begins a new subject, which shows that David was still engaged in the duties of active life :

And again the anger of the Lord was kindled against Israel, and he moved David against them to say, Go number Israel and Judah.

These abrupt methods of writing mark not an original author but a compiler, who collects original documents together, copies them one after another, and makes insertions, sometimes for the purpose of connecting them into one history, and at other times of explaining those passages which his readers might otherwise find it hard to understand. No other mode of interpretation will account for the inversions of order, the extraordinary repetitions, and unusual method of narration which the Books of the Old Testament present.

CHAPTER XX.

THE TWO BOOKS OF KINGS EXAMINED.

As it is generally admitted that the two Books of Kings and also the remaining Books of Chronicles, Ezra, Nehemiah, &c., were written after the return of the Israelites from Babylon, it is not absolutely necessary to examine them for the purpose of collecting the evidence which they furnish. But there are certain passages in all these books which, besides proving the assertion that has been made above, yield other evidence of a significant character respecting the true nature of Jewish History and Prophecy; and, besides, these passages are so remarkably similar to those gathered from the preceding books, that they warrant the inference of a common origin. Let us therefore take these books in order, and see what passages may be found in them upon our present subject.

Such are the following, in which the distinction between Judah and Israel is so plainly marked that it was evidently employed by the writer as a long established fact:

I Kings, i, 35. (*David speaks*) Then ye shall come up after him, that he may come and sit upon my throne; for he shall be king in my stead: and I have appointed him to be ruler over Israel and over Judah.

— iv, 1. So king Solomon was king over all Israel.

— iv, 20. Judah and Israel were many, as the sand which is by the sea in multitude.

— iv, 21. And Solomon reigned over all kingdoms from the river unto the land of the Philistines, and unto the border of Egypt; they brought presents, and served Solomon all the days of his life.

— iv, 25. And Judah and Israel dwelt safely, &c.

The *river* must here mean the Euphrates, not the Jordan; for Solomon reigned to a great distance beyond the Jordan eastward. This designation of the Euphrates as *the* river implies that the writer was well acquainted with it; that is to say, he wrote this account after the people for whom it was written had dwelt seventy years at Babylon upon its banks.

— ix, 11......(Now Hiram the king of Tyre had furnished Solomon with cedar trees and fir trees, and with gold according to all his desire,) that then king Solomon gave Hiram twenty cities in the land of Galilee......... 13. And he [Hiram] said, "What cities are these which thou hast given me, my brother?" And he called them the land of Cabul unto this day.

— xii,19. So Israel rebelled against the house of David unto this day.

— xiii, 2. And he cried against the altar in the word of the Lord, and said, "O altar, altar, thus saith the Lord; Behold a child shall be born unto the house of David, Josiah by name; and upon thee shall he offer the priests of the high places that burn incense upon thee, and men's bones shall be burnt upon thee."

As this prophecy concerning Josiah was recorded after the event had happened, the record of it may probably have received a species of colouring, and been written with more exactness, as is likely to occur in such cases. This consideration is of great importance in our estimate of such things: all original prophecies, known to have been written before their fulfilment, are found to be obscure, and even at present, after so many centuries have passed, it is uncertain whether many of them have been fulfilled or not.

I KINGS, xiv, 15. For the Lord shall smite Israel, as a reed is shaken in the water, and he shall root up Israel out of this good land, which he gave to their fathers, and shall scatter them beyond the river, because they have made their groves, provoking the Lord to anger.

II KINGS, viii, 22. Yet Edom revolted from under the hand of Judah *unto this day.*

To this passage, in the Commentary which has been so often quoted, is appended the following note:

unto this day] Unto the time when this book was written, which was not long after this revolt.

Yet the editors of that Commentary admit that the books were written probably by Ezra; and by the date B.C. 892, which they have attached in the margin to the revolt of Edom, it appears that nearly four hundred years, which certainly cannot be described as "not long," intervened between the revolt and this relation of it.

II KINGS, x, 27. And they brake down the image of Baal, and brake down the house of Baal, and made it a draught house *unto this day.*

—xiii, 23. And the Lord was gracious unto them, and had compassion on them, and had respect unto them, because of his covenant with Abraham, Isaac and Jacob, and would not destroy them, *neither cast he them from his presence as yet.*

—xiv, 7. He slew of Edom in the valley of salt ten thousand, and took Selah by war, and called the name of it Joktheel *unto this day.*

—xvii, 13. Yet the Lord testified against Israel and against Judah, by all the prophets and by all the seers, saying, "Turn ye from your evil ways, and keep my commandments and my statutes, according to all the law which I commanded your fathers, and which I sent to you by my servants the prophets.

—xvii, 29. Howbeit every nation made gods of their own, and put them in the houses of the high places, which the Samaritans had made, every nation in their cities wherein they dwelt. . . . 34 *Unto this day* they do after the former manners : they fear not the Lord, neither do they after their statutes, or after their ordinances, or after the law and commandment which the Lord commanded the children of Jacob, whom he named Israel.

—xxv, 27. And it came to pass in the seven and thirtieth year of the captivity of Jehoiachin king of Judah, in the twelfth month, on the seven and twentieth day of the month, that Evil-merodach king of Babylon in the year that he began to reign did lift up the head of Jehoiachin king of Judah out of prison.

The event recorded in the last of these extracts happened about the year B.C. 562, or twenty-six years before the date assigned for the return of the Jews from the Captivity of Babylon. The Books of Kings, in which this date occurs, could not have been written before, but after the events which are recorded in them.

CHAPTER XXI.

THE TWO BOOKS OF CHRONICLES EXAMINED.

THE fragmentary origin of the Old Testament is nowhere more evident than in the Books of Chronicles, in which whole chapters occur identical with others found elsewhere in various parts of the whole volume.

The first nine chapters of the First Book of Chronicles contain genealogies written it seems during the time of the Captivity of Babylon; for at I CHRON. v, 26, we read:

And the God of Israel stirred up the spirit of Pul king of Assyria, and the spirit of Tiglath-pilneser king of Assyria, and he carried them away, even the Reubenites, and the Gadites, and the half tribe of Manasseh, and brought them unto Halah, and Habor, and Hara, and to the river Gozan, *unto this day*.

The tenth chapter abruptly begins the historical part of the work, and is almost word for word the same as the thirty-first of the First Book of Samuel: and the first nine verses of the eleventh chapter correspond quite as closely with the first ten of the fifth chapter of the Second Book of Samuel.

Other coincidences may be briefly referred to as follows:

I Chron. xi, 10—47 corresponds to II Sam. xxiii, 8—39
„ xiii ... ... „ vi, 1—11
„ xiv ... ... „ v, 11—25
„ xv, 25—xvi, 3 ... ... „ vi, 12, 23
„ xvi, 7—36 ... ... Psalm, cv, 1—15, &c.

The seventeenth chapter, though not identical in its wording with II Samuel, chapter vii, is conceived so entirely in the same train of thought that it is impossible to regard them as distinct accounts, or as written by independent authors. The remaining chapters of the Chronicles are subject to the same remark. They seem to be a collection of historical fragments thrown together without order, from the inability of the compiler to put them in any other shape, and whilst they exhibit whole chapters taken out of the preceding writings, they in other places offer the most contradictory evidence on fact, which admits of no other explanation than that which long antiquity, if not oblivion, alone will furnish.

The genealogies, as well as other matters, found in these books, are in great part copied from the earlier books of the Bible, and partly also from other sources. The following table will enable the reader to compare the first nine chapters with those parts of the earlier scriptures from which they have been either taken or imitated, and in some cases either expanded or abridged.

I Chronicles i, 1—4 corresponds with Genesis, v.
„ i, 5—23 ... ... —— x, 2—29
„ i, 24—27 ... ... —— xi, 10, &c.
„ i, 29—31 ... ... —— xxv, 13—15
„ i, 32—33 ... ... —— xxv, 2—4
„ i, 35—54 ... ... —— xxxvi, 10—43
„ ii, 3, 4 ... ... —— xxxviii, 3—30
„ ii, 5 ... ... —— xlvi, 12
„ ii, 10—12 ... ... Ruth, iv, 19
„ ii, 13—17 ... ... I Sam. xvi, 6. &c.
„ iii, 1—9 ... ... II Sam. iii, 3—6, 11
„ iv, 24 ... ... Num. xxvi, 12

I Chron. iv, 28—31		corresponds with Josh. xix, 2—5	
,,	v, 1—10	... ...	Gen. xlvi, 9 : Num. xxvi, 5, Josh. xiii, 16, 17
,,	v, 27—29	...	—— xlvi, 11 : Ex. vi, 18—23 : xxviii, 1
,,	v, 30—41	... ...	Ezra, vii, 1—5
,,	vi, 1—4, 7	... ...	Exod. vi, 16—29, 23, 24
,,	vi, 39—66	... ...	Josh. xxi, 10—39
,,	vii, 6—12	... ...	Gen. xlvi, 21 : Num. xxvi, 38—40: I Chr. viii, 1, &c.
,,	vii, 13	... ...	—— xlvi, 24
,,	vii, 14—19	.. ...	Num. xxvi, 29 : xxvii, 1
,,	vii, 20—29	... ...	—— xxvi, 34—38
,,	vii, 30—40	... ...	Gen. xlvi, 17 : Num. xxvi, 44—47
,,	viii, 1—28	... ...	—— xlvi, 21 : Num. xxvi, 38—40: I Chr. vii, 6, &c.
,,	viii, 29—40 ix, 35—44	}	I Sam. ix, 1 : xiv, 49—51
,,	ix, 2—34	... ...	Neh. xi, 3—24

But there are reasonable grounds for surmising that those who put together the various documents which now pass under the name of Chronicles, have added to the facts which form the basis of the history, with reference to the state of things existing in their own time. This will be apparent from the following narrative.

When the plague was brought on King David as a punishment for unduly numbering the people, it is related that he was ordered by Gad the prophet to buy the threshing-floor of Araunah the Jebusite and to build there an altar unto the Lord.

So David bought the threshing-floor and the oxen for fifty shekels of silver. And David built there an altar unto the Lord, and offered burnt-offerings and peace-offerings. So the Lord was entreated for the land, and the plague was stayed from Israel.

This account is given in II Samuel, xxiv, 24, which forms part of the continuous history of the Jewish nation. But in Chronicles the narrative is much expanded. We are told at the end of the twenty-first chapter of the First Book that King David did not go to the high place at Gibeon where the Tabernacle was; "for he was afraid because of the angel of the Lord."

Then David said, "This is the house of the Lord God, and this is the altar of the burnt-offering for Israel."

The identification of Araunah's threshing-floor with the site of Solomon's Temple may be a fact that cannot be controverted; but there is nothing in the Books of Kings to show that David either pointed out the spot on which the Temple was to be built or provided cedar trees, as we read in I Chron. xxii, 4, for the building. It would seem that these later writers sought by additional details to elevate and adorn the memory of David as much as possible: and on the other hand, there are certain omissions, as of David's concubines at I Chron. xiv, 3 (though mentioned at II Sam. v, 13); of the chastisement threatened to his posterity, at I Chron. xvii, 13 (though recorded at II Sam. vii, 14); of his cruelty to Moab, at I Chron. xviii, 3 (though related at II Sam. viii, 2); and lastly, of his adultery with the wife of Uriah and his abominable treachery in procuring the murder of her husband.

Similar leniency is shown towards the whole royal house of Judah: as in the total silence of the chronicler about the harem of Solomon, and the troubles occasioned by the conduct of Amnon, and the rebellion followed by the death of Absalom. On the other hand the Chronicles omit everything which could tend to the honour of the kings of Israel, and they show such a disposition to exalt all the Levitical institutions that we cannot fail to discern in these particulars the strongest proof of their later origin.

CHAPTER XXII.

THE BOOKS OF EZRA, NEHEMIAH, AND THE APOCRYPHAL BOOKS OF ESDRAS EXAMINED.

It is necessary, in examining the contents of Ezra, Nehemiah, and the two Apocryphal Books of Esdras, to insist on a remark, which applies not only to these books, but to others also, namely, that for many years after the Christian era our canon both of the Old and New Testament has not been the same. We find that both the Vulgate and the Septuagint versions vary much from the Hebrew Text, and that almost all the writings which the English Bible regards as Apocryphal, are admitted as canonical by one or the other of these versions, although all are excluded from the Hebrew original. This remark applies to the four books, whose contents we are now briefly to pass in review.

The Book of Ezra takes up the history of the Jewish nation from the point at which the Book of Chronicles leaves off, and it actually repeats the last two verses of the concluding chapter. The Book of Nehemiah is somewhat confusedly connected with the preceding. The history comprised in the two extends over the space of about one hundred and thirty years, from B.C. 536 to 404. The fragmentary character of both the books is evident: they are made up of separate documents, joined together in an unartistic manner, and clearly have been derived from various sources and different authors.

The most striking of these documents, extending from Ezra, iv, 8, to vii, 27, is in what is called the Chaldee language; and like Daniel, ii, 4, consists chiefly of a letter and other original writings, which the compilers of these books thought best to retain in their primitive state. In chapter vii, 27, &c., Ezra speaks of himself in the first person, and as such is to be deemed the writer at all events of some parts of the work.

But a more important question arises from certain statements contained in these books. We read, at vii, 6:

> This Ezra went up from Babylon, and he was a ready scribe in the Law of Moses, which the Lord God of Israel had given: and the king granted him all his request, according to the hand of the Lord his God upon him.
>
> And there went up some of the children of Israel, and of the priests, and the Levites, and the singers and the porters, and the Nethinims, unto Jerusalem, in the seventh year of Artaxerxes the king.

Here, it appears, we meet with the Law of Moses named for the first time, by a writer, who although still anonymous and speaking of Ezra in the third person, may be considered as contemporary with most of the events which he describes.

The enlightened student of Ancient History cannot but see in the restoration of the Jewish State the designs of Providence wonderfully harmonizing with the policy of the world. For many hundred years the Jews, placed between the great Egyptian and Assyrian or other Asiatic monarchies as it were between the hammer and the anvil, had suffered from the various vicissitudes brought about by the rivalry between those states. For the last hundred years before the accession of Cyrus king of Persia, the Babylonians had got the better of their Egyptian rivals, and the Jewish people having become slaves to their conquerors, their land, reduced almost to a desert, was annexed to the empire of victorious Babylon. But the Egyptian kingdom retained some portion of its former vigour, and was still powerful enough to resist the ambitious designs of Cyrus, after he had destroyed the monarchy of their rivals the Babylonians. To restore the city of Jerusalem and the Jewish state was to erect a barrier against Egypt, and at the same time to fulfil the Divine decree, which the Jewish prophets had so often shadowed out in their predictions. Those who administered the Persian government knew the tenacious and obstinate nature of the Jewish people, and made use of their stern adherence to the religion and customs of their forefathers as the best bulwark against invasions from the Egyptians.

Nor was this foresight disappointed in the result. It is impossible to conceive a people more enthusiastic and even bigoted in carrying out the will of Providence and of Persia, than were the Jews, in restoring what had fallen and in establishing what was needed.

Hence we may observe that the most severe inspection was made into the conduct and manners of the people, and a series of ordinances now instituted, which having their origin in some remnants of the Mosaical Law still adhering to memory, or perhaps written in various documents still preserved among the people, found able exponents in Ezra, Nehemiah and others, to whom the government of the Jewish colony was intrusted by the Persian king.

Among other matters which occupied the attention of the government, a singular and harsh course seems to have been adopted as regards marriage. At chapter ix we read in the words of Ezra himself:

—1, 2. Now when these things were done, the princes came to me, saying, The people of Israel, and the priests and the Levites have not separated themselves from the people of the lands, *doing* according to their abominations, *even* of the Canaanites, the Hittites, the Perizzites, the Jebusites, the Ammonites, the Moabites, the Egyptians and the Amorites. For they have taken of their daughters for themselves, and for their sons : so that the holy seed have mingled themselves with the people of those lands.

On hearing these things Ezra prayed to God, confessing the sins which the people had committed, in terms which sound more in unison with the state of the Jews entering the land of Canaan for the first time under Joshua, than with a colony just dismissed from slavery and returning to their own land.

—ix, 10—12. And now, O our God, what shall we say after this? for we have forsaken thy commandments, which thou hast commanded by thy servants the prophets, saying, The land, unto which ye go to possess it, is an unclean land with the filthiness of the people of the lands, with their abominations, which have filled it from one end to another with their uncleanness. Now therefore give not your daughters unto their sons, neither take their daughters unto your sons, nor seek their peace or their wealth for ever; that ye may be strong, and eat the good of the land, and leave it for an inheritance for your children for ever.

In consequence of this, the princes and the people of their own accord made a covenant with Ezra, and all those who had taken strange wives put them away. The whole of chapter x, which concludes the Book of Ezra, is filled with the details of this subject, and suggests many reflections to the mind of the reader on the great similarity of proceeding to that which occurs more than once in the narrative of the first entrance of the Israelites into the promised land.

But our attention must now be turned to the Second Apocryphal Book of Esdras, or, as it is elsewhere otherwise called, the Fourth of Ezra. This work, existing now in Latin, Arabic, and Ethiopic MSS., and printed only in Latin, has evidently been translated from the Greek, possibly derived in its turn from the Hebrew. The only point with which we are concerned as regards its age and authorship, is that it is quoted by Clement of Alexandria and therefore cannot be later than the second century of our era. But there is in one passage of this book a tradition which has much to do with our present subject, and runs as follows :

II ESDRAS, xiv, 1—48. And it came to pass upon the third day, I sat under an oak, and behold, there came a voice out of a bush over against me, and said, " Esdras, Esdras !" And I said, " Here am I, Lord," and I stood up upon my feet. Then said he unto me, "In the bush I did manifestly reveal myself unto Moses, and talked with him, when my people served in Egypt. And I sent him...... 7, And now I say unto thee, That thou lay up in thy heart the signs that I have showed...... 13, Now therefore set thine house in order, and reprove thy people, comfort such of them as be in trouble, and now renounce corruption......" 19, Then answered I before thee, and said, " Behold, Lord, I will go, as thou hast commanded me, and reprove the people which are present : but they that shall be born afterward, who shall admonish them ! Thus the world is set in darkness, and they that dwell therein are without light. For THY LAW IS BURNT; therefore no man knoweth the things that are done of thee, or the works that shall begin. But if I have found grace before thee, send the Holy Ghost into me, and I shall write all that hath been done in the world since the beginning, which were written in thy Law, that men may find thy path, and that they which will live in the latter days may live." And he answered me, saying, " Go thy way, gather the people together, and say unto them, that they seek thee not for forty days. But look thou prepare thee many box-trees, [*or* box tablets to write on, *marg.*] and take with thee Sarea, Dabria, Selemia, Ecanus, and Asiel, these five which are ready to write swiftly ; and come hither, and I shall light a candle of understanding in thine heart, which shall not be put out till the things be performed which thou shalt begin to write. And when thou hast done, some things shalt thou publish and some things shalt thou show secretly to the wise : to morrow this hour shalt thou begin to write......" 37, So I took the five men, as he commanded me, and we went into the field, and remained there...... 42, The Highest gave understanding unto the five men, and they wrote the wonderful visions of the night that were told, which they knew not ; and they sat forty days, and they. wrote in the day, and at night they ate bread. As for me, I spake in the day, and I held not my tongue by night. In forty days they wrote two hundred and four books. And it came to pass, when the forty days were fulfilled, that the Highest spake, saying, " The first that thou hast written publish openly, that the worthy and unworthy may read it: But keep the seventy last, that thou mayest deliver them only to such as be wise among the people: For in them is the spring of understanding, the fountain of wisdom, and the stream of knowledge." And I did so.

It appears from this extract, which could not be given otherwise than complete, that Ezra was aided by five men endued with the spirit of God to re-write the Scriptures which had been lost, and that the work was finished in forty days. A large part of Christendom have indeed separated from the canon the book in which this narrative appears; but the greater number of Christians still retain it, and the objection which lies against it rests more on the language in which it is written and on the supposed want of inspired doctrine under which it labours, than on the want of antiquity as regards its origin or of historical accuracy as to its contents.

If then we assume that the history contained in the verses which have been quoted from the fourteenth chapter of the Second Book of Esdras is a legend, how are we to understand such a legend, appearing in a book as ancient as the second century of the Christian era, and ascribing to Ezra the compilation of a new edition of the Mosaical Law, seeing that the original had been burnt? It may be, as some writers have argued, that Jerome speaks of this book with contempt, but Irenæus, Clement of Alexandria, and Tertullian, who all lived and wrote many years before Jerome, speak of it with respect. Our English canon indeed rejects it, but more ancient canons than ours retain it.

The object of my work is to show that in our present volume of the Old Testament we have not the original writings of the Hebrew law-giver and Judges, but a compilation out of ancient Hebrew documents, begun by the very hand and continued by the successors of that Ezra, who is named in the legend just quoted, as having been inspired by God to perform this especial duty.

But there are testimonies which cannot be passed over, in support of what we read in the Second Book of Esdras, and those passages of their writings which furnish such testimony shall now be brought forward, and will form a fitting conclusion to the present chapter.

The first of these is Irenæus, but as his original work written in Greek is no longer extant, and the passage in which he bears clear testimony to the work of Ezra is found only as quoted in the Ecclesiastical History of Eusebius, it is not necessary to give the extract here, but to adduce it under the name of the historian in whose work it is found.

The second writer is Clement of Alexandria, in whose work entitled Stromateis, we read as follows:

Ἐν τῇ Ναβουχοδονόσορ αἰχμαλωσίᾳ διαφθαρεισῶν τῶν γραφῶν, κατὰ τοὺς Ἀρταξέρξου τοῦ Περσῶν βασιλέως χρόνους, ἐπίπνους Ἔσδρας ὁ Λευίτης ὁ ἱερεὺς γενόμενος, πάσας τὰς παλαιὰς αὖθις ἀνανεούμενος προεφήτευσε γραφάς. — CLEMENS ALEX., *Strom.* i, 22.

In the Captivity by Nebuchodonosor the writings having been destroyed, in the times of Artaxerxes king of the Persians, Esdras the Levite having become inspired, prophesied, restoring again all the old writings.

And in another place of the same work Clement briefly repeats the same statement.

Δι' Ἔσδραν γίνεται ὁ τῶν θεοπνεύστων ἀναγνωρισμὸς καὶ ἀνακαινισμὸς λογίων.— CLEM. ALEX., *Strom.* i, 21.

The recognition and renewal of the inspired oracles is made by Esdras.

The testimony of Tertullian, who wrote a few years after Clement, tends to establish the same conclusion.

Hierosolymis Babylonia expugnatione deletis, omne instrumentum Judaïcæ literaturæ per Esdram constat restauratum. *De cultu fœm.* c. 3.

Jerusalem having been destroyed by the Babylonian siege, it appears that every instrument of Jewish literature was restored by Esdras.

The historian Eusebius, whose date is A.D. 320, quotes from Irenæus the following passage, which bears a remarkable likeness to that previously cited from Clement of Alexandria:

Καὶ οὐδέν γε θαυμαστὸν, τοῦτο ἐνηργηκέναι τὸν Θεόν, ὅς γε καὶ ἐν τῇ ἐπὶ Ναβουχοδονόσορ αἰχμαλωσίᾳ τοῦ λαοῦ διαφθαρεισῶν τῶν γραφῶν, καὶ μετὰ ἑβδομήκοντα ἔτη τῶν Ἰουδαίων ἀνελθόντων εἰς τὴν χώραν αὐτῶν, ἔπειτα ἐν τοῖς χρόνοις Ἀρταξέρξου τοῦ Περσῶν βασιλέως, ἐνέπνευσεν Ἔσδρᾳ τῷ ἱερεῖ ἐκ τῆς φυλῆς Λευῒ, τοὺς τῶν προγεγονότων προφητῶν πάντας ἀνατάξασθαι λόγους, καὶ ἀποκαταστῆσαι τῷ λαῷ τὴν διὰ Μωσέως νομοθεσίαν.— EUSEB. *H. E.*, v. 8.

And it is not at all wonderful that God wrought this, who also in the captivity of the people in the time of Nabuchodonosor, when the writings had been destroyed, and the Jews came back after seventy years to their own land, then in the times of Artaxerxes the king of the Persians, inspired Esdras the priest of the tribe of Levi, to set forth all the words of the prophets who had gone before, and to restore to the people the legislation given through Moses.

Forty or fifty years later than Eusebius comes the celebrated Father of the Church Hieronymus, or Jerome, as in imitation of the French, he is more generally called by English writers. In his treatise against Helvidius is the following passage:

Certe hodiernus dies illius temporis æstimandus est quo historia ipsa contexta est, sive Moysen dicere volueris auctorem Pentateuchi, sive Ezram ejusdem instauratorem operis, non recuso. *Adv. Helvidium, tom.* iv, *p.* 134 *edit. Marcianæi.*	Certainly the "present day" is to be deemed of that time in which the history itself was put together: whether you choose to call Moses the author of the Pentateuch or Ezra the restorer of the same work, I make no objection.

Later than the foregoing indeed, but still valuable as keeping up the tradition, is the testimony of those well-known Fathers of the Church, Basilius, Chrysostom, Athanasius, and Leo Byzantinus, from whom I shall quote the following extracts; the inference to which their testimony leads,[*] must be plain to every reader.

"Ἐνταυθα πεδίον ἐν ᾧ ἀναχωρήσας Ἔσδρας πάσας τὰς θεοπνεύστους βίβλους προστάγματι Θεοῦ ἐξηρεύξατο.—BASIL., *Ep. ad Chilonem*.	There is there a plain in which Esdras retiring gave forth all the inspired books by the command of God.
Μετὰ δὲ ταῦτα προφήτας ἔπεμψε μυρία παθόντας δεινά. Ἐπῆλθε πόλεμος, ἀνεῖλον πάντας, κατέκοψαν, ἐνεπρήσθησαν αἱ βίβλοι. Ἑτέρῳ πάλιν ἀνδρὶ θαυμαστῷ ἐνέπνευσεν, ὥστε αὐτὰς ἐκθέσθαι, τῷ Ἔσδρᾳ λέγω, καὶ ἀπὸ λειψάνων συντεθῆναι ἐποίησε. Μετὰ δὲ τοῦτο ᾠκονόμησεν ἑρμηνευθῆναι αὐτὰς ὑπὸ τῶν ἑβδομήκοντα.—CHRYS. *Hom.* viii, *in Epist. ad Hebræos.*	But after these things he sent prophets who suffered numberless severities. War came on; they slew, they cut in pieces all men; the books were burnt. He again inspired another wonderful man to set them forth, I mean Esdras, and he caused them to be composed out of remains. And after this he managed that they should be translated by the seventy.

---

[*] Numerous other passages might be produced from the Fathers less forcible than those given in the text, but still pointing to Ezra and his successors as the compilers of the whole Hebrew Canon. Hilary, in his preface, says the Psalms were collected by Esdras, and Euthymius ascribes them to either Esdras or Ezekiel.

Πολλὰ τῶν προφητικῶν ἠφάνισται βιβλίων, καὶ ταῦτα ἐκ τῆς ἱστορίας τῶν Παραλειπομένων ἴδοι τις ἄν. 'Ράθυμοι γὰρ ὄντες οἱ 'Ιουδαῖοι, καὶ εἰς ἀσέβειαν συνεχῶς ἐμπίπτοντες, τὰ μὲν ἠφίεσαν ἀπόλλυσθαι, τὰ δὲ αὐτοὶ κατέκαιον καὶ κατέκοπτον. Καὶ τὸ μὲν 'Ιερεμίας διηγεῖται, τὸ δὲ ὁ τὴν τετάρτην συντιθεὶς τῶν Βασιλειῶν, λέγων μετὰ πολὺν χρόνον μόλις τὸ Δευτερονόμιον εὑρῆσθαι κατωρυγμένον που καὶ ἠφανισμένον. Εἰ δὲ οὐκ ὄντος βαρβάρου οὕτω τὰ βιβλία προὔδωκαν, πολλῷ μᾶλλον τῶν βαρβάρων ἐπελθόντων.—CHRYS. ad Matt. ii, ult. Hom. ix.

Many of the prophetical books disappeared, and this a man may see from the history of the Paraleipomena. For the Jews being slothful, and continually falling into wickedness, let some of them perish, and some themselves burnt and cut up. And Jeremiah describes the one fact, and he who composed the fourth book of Kings the other, saying that after a long time the book of Deuteronomy was found buried somewhere and put out of sight. But if they gave up their books when there was no barbarian, how much more would they do so when the barbarians invaded them.

The finding of Deuteronomy in this extract is probably another version of the finding of the Law in the reign of King Josiah.

'Ιστορεῖται δὲ καὶ τοῦτο περὶ τοῦ 'Εσδρα, ὅτι ἀπολομένων τῶν βιβλίων ἐξ ἀμελείας τῶν λαῶν καὶ διὰ τὴν πολυχρόνιον αἰχμαλωσίαν, αὐτός 'Εσδρας, φιλόκαλος ὢν καὶ εὐφυής, καὶ ἀναγνώστης, ἐφύλαξε πάντα καθ' ἑαυτόν, καὶ λοιπὸν προήνεγκε καὶ πᾶσιν ἐκδέδωκε, καὶ οὕτως διασώζεται τὰ βιβλία.— ATHAN. JUN. in Synop. S.S.

This also is related about Esdras, that whereas the books had perished from the carelessness of the people and through the long captivity, Esdras himself, being a lover of what is good, a clever man and a reader, treasured up all of them in himself, and at last brought them forth, and published them to all, and so the books are preserved.

'Ο μὲν "Εσδρας ἐλθὼν εἰς τὰ 'Ιεροσόλυμα, καὶ εὑρὼν ὅτι πάντα τὰ βιβλία ἦσαν καυθέντα ἡνίκα ἠχμαλωτίσθησαν, ἀπὸ μνήμης λέγεται συγγράψασθαι τὰ κβ' βιβλία ἅπερ ἐν τοῖς ἄνω ἀπηριθμησάμεθα. LEO BYZAN. de Sectis.

Esdras, having come to Jerusalem and found that all the books had been burnt when they were captured, is said from memory to have composed the twenty-two books which we have enumerated above.

A writer still later than these is one Josephus or Joseph, author of a book called *Hypomnesticon* or *Liber Memorialis*. He is thought by the learned Fabricius to have lived about

600 A.D., and his testimony on our present subject is only of use to show the continuity of opinion down to so late a date.

'Ομοῦ δὲ τῶν βασιλέων τὰς πράξεις καὶ τὰ τέλη. Ἐσδρας ὁ σοφὸς, ἐν τῇ ἐπανόδῳ γενόμενος τοῦ λαοῦ, τῇ ἀπὸ τῆς αἰχμαλωσίας, ἀποπνημονεύσας ἁπασαν τὴν βίβλον τῶν Βασιλέων τῶν τε εὐσεβῶς βιωσάντων τὰς πράξεις· μετὰ δὲ ταῦτα ἐπιγνοὺς τίνα ἐστι παραλειφθέντα αὐτῷ ἐν τῇ Βασιλειῶν βίβλῳ, ἰδίᾳ ταῦτα πάλιν ἀνενέγκας ἐξέθετο, ἐπείπερ ἡ προτέρα βίβλος ἡ ἐκδοθεῖσα παρὰ πολλῶν ἐξήλειπτο· ἦν τινα βίβλον ἐν δυσὶ τόμοις ἐγγραφεῖσαν Ἰουδαῖοι μὲν "Λόγοι ἡμερῶν," ἡ δὲ Ἐκκλησία "Παραλειπομένων βίβλον" ἐπέγραψεν.— JOSEPHI HYPOMNESTICON, ii, 131, in FABRICII Cod. Pseud. V. T., ii, 274.

At the same time the acts of the kings and their deaths, Esdras the wise living amid the return of the people from Babylon, writing from memory all the book of kings and the acts of those who lived religiously; and after this, noticing what things had been omitted by him in the book of the kings' acts, he again put forth and published these separately, since the former book put forth by him had been obliterated from many; which book, written in two volumes, the Jews entitled the "Words of Days," but the Church Book of Paraleipomena (things omitted).

CHAPTER XXIII.

THE PROPHETS.

AN important testimony to the recent formation of the Jewish canon is thought by some writers to be found in the discrepancies which they say exist between the teaching of the earlier prophets and the Mosaic law, as we now have it in the Pentateuch and elsewhere. These writers assert that the enactments of that law are more in harmony with the fierce spirit of the Jewish sacerdotalism after the re-establishment of their nation than with the character of their great lawgiver, who could not have maintained his influence over the multitude that escaped from Egypt, unless he had acquired a hold on their affections by his humanity as well as on their obedience by his power.

We are not able, it is true, to trace this class of evidence from the beginning; for the earliest prophets seem to have written nothing. In their time, no doubt, the living speech and action were more ready and useful whilst literature was not sufficiently advanced. The whole of the Old Testament, except the strictly historical portions of it, betrays a strong cast of poetry, and that is always found in the early state of all nations, especially in the East, where every product of the mind presents itself not only in a poetical, but in a dramatic form. Now the Jews were not less barbarous than the other nations by which they were surrounded, nor do they appear to have been less bigoted on that account in the worship of the true God, or more advanced in the observance of those humane laws and customs, which, not religion, but social culture can create. It is certain that there were prophets from the commencement of the Hebrew commonwealth, and fragments of their oracles appear throughout the early course of Jewish history, from Joshua to Joel; of which we probably have an instance in Judges, ii, 1, where an angel of Jehovah is said to have appeared and spoken to the people. The angel or messenger was probably a prophet, and in the same book (vi, 8) a similar messenger sent by God is denominated a prophet and not an angel.

Recurring then to our argument, we may observe some striking peculiarities in the form which all the prophetical books now bear. They are seventeen in number, and the authorship of the first five is ascribed to Isaiah, Jeremiah, Ezekiel, and Daniel, who are called the Major or Greater Prophets; whilst the twelve other books appear under the names of Hosea, Joel, Amos, Obadiah, Jonah, Micah, Nahum, Habakkuk, Zephaniah, Haggai, Zechariah, and Malachi, who are termed the Minor Prophets, not from any inferiority of style, but from the smaller quantity which has been handed down to us of their writings. The dates at which these prophets are supposed to have lived, have been already given in Chapter II of this volume, and at least five of them wrote either during the last years of the Captivity, or after the captives had returned to their own land.

An interesting subject of inquiry here arises. What was the essential difference between the priests and the prophets, and what were the duties of each class? It is the opinion of an able German critic, De Wette, that the teaching of the prophets was mostly spiritual, and that, holding no official position among the people like that of the priests, they were reverenced for such qualities as each of them exhibited in his own person, writings or prophecies, whilst the priests held a prominent official rank, which entitled them, as ministering according to the outward forms of the Temple service, to the reverence of the people, irrespective of any personal merit whatever. Thus, whilst the priests remained attached to the symbols of the faith, and retained or introduced all those ancient restrictions and narrow views which we still observe, the prophets broke through the symbolical forms, or rose to the spiritual conception of them, and served the cause of truth by proclaiming the Word of God, very much in the same way as Jesus of Nazareth did more than five hundred years afterwards. Indeed it has been suggested by Dr Donaldson and others, that, as the Jews have certainly tampered with their sacred books at various times, the "Law," which we now read, did not contain, in the times of the early prophets, many of the severe clauses and ceremonial requirements which appear in it since the Christian era.

It was the office of the prophets to purify and extend the influence of religion and morality: and they were moreover political teachers, natural philosophers, and workers of miracles. Their action on the public was kept up by religion, poetry, and music; all of which held an important place in their schools, and some of them, especially Samuel, seem to have united in their own persons, if not the names, yet all the functions, of prophet, priest, and king. Nor does this threefold character of Samuel, and perhaps of others, tend to weaken the theory which I am here endeavouring to point out, that the office of priest would tend towards exclusiveness and even bigotry, whilst the prophets would rather enlarge the bounds and spiritualize the duties of religious freedom. For whilst Samuel hewed Agag in pieces in vindication of the commands which emanated from religion, he accompanied the act with that noble maxim which accompanies the greatest freedom, "To obey is better than sacrifice and to hearken than the fat of rams!" It was difficult for Samuel to disconnect his various responsibilities. It was easier for the writer of the Fifteenth Psalm to proclaim the grand sentiments which it contains:

> Lord, who shall abide in thy tabernacle? Who shall dwell in thy holy hill? He that walketh uprightly and worketh righteousness, and speaketh the truth in his heart. He that backbiteth not with his tongue, nor doeth evil to his neighbour, nor taketh up a reproach against his neighbour.

Hosea also doubtless had good grounds for writing as we read in vi, 6:

I desired mercy and not sacrifice; and the knowledge of God more than burnt offerings.

In like manner Micah (vi, 8) asks a most important and pertinent question:

What doth the Lord require of thee, but to do justly, and to love mercy, and to walk humbly with thy God?

What says the greatest of the prophets, Isaiah, on this subject? In the very first chapter of his prophecies we read:

To what purpose is the multitude of your sacrifices unto me? saith the Lord. I am full of the burnt offerings of rams, and the fat of fed beasts; and I delight not in the blood of bullocks, or of lambs or of he-goats ... Bring no more vain oblations; incense is an abomination unto me; the new moons and sabbaths, the calling of assemblies, I cannot away with; it is iniquity, even the solemn meeting. ....Wash you, make you clean; put away the evil of your doings from before my eyes; cease to do evil; learn to do well; seek judgment, relieve the oppressed, judge the fatherless, plead for the widow. Come now, and let us reason together, saith the Lord.

These words might have proceeded out of the mouth of Jesus of Nazareth himself, nor can we doubt that the Laws of the Israelites, coming originally from Moses, have found true and faithful exponents in the prophets, who, at a time when sacerdotalism was beginning to exert its sway over the mind, uttered without fear the noble sentiments which we have here recited.

Now in what form do the writings of these prophets appear to us at present? Not apparently as separate and independent editions of each, like the works of authors, both ancient and modern, given to the world without any relation to one another, but as a collection made by some one who had got together all the remains of each which he could find, and who sends them forth to the public in one volume, with the names of the various authors attached wherever any of the writings could be ascribed with certainty or probability to each. Moreover, the explanations which are found at the beginning of almost all the prophets look very much as if they were prefixed by some compiler as introductions to the several portions of the work. Thus the prophecies of Isaiah begin as follows:

The vision of Isaiah the son of Amoz, which he saw concerning Judah and Jerusalem, in the days of Uzziah, Jotham, Ahaz, and Hezekiah, kings of Judah.

The introduction to the prophesies of Jeremiah is of the same kind:

The words of Jeremiah the son of Hilkiah, of the priests that were in Anathoth in the land of Benjamin: to whom the word of the Lord came in the days of Josiah, in the thirteenth year of his reign. It came also in the days of Jehoiakim the son of Josiah king of Judah, unto the end of the eleventh year of Zedekiah the son of Josiah king of Judah, unto the carrying away of Jerusalem captive in the fifth month.

The attempt to fix the exact date is here evident: but it can hardly be thought that prophets, who had to deal with such important political matters, or whose minds were inspired with such divine truths as were Isaiah and Jeremiah, would show much care to introduce their prophesies with such exact chronological minuteness.

The Books of Ezekiel and Daniel have no similar prefaces: but these again occur at the beginning of all the minor prophets. Thus we have:

The word of the Lord that came unto Hosea—The word of the Lord that came to Joel—The words of Amos—The vision of Obadiah—Now the word of the Lord came unto Jonah—The word of the Lord that came to Micah—The burden of Nineveh: the book of the vision of Nahum the Elkoshite—The burden which Habakkuk the prophet did see—The word of the Lord which came unto Zephaniah.—In the second year of Darius the king, in the sixth month, in the first day of the month, came the word of the Lord by Haggai—In the eighth month, in the second year of Darius, came the word of the Lord unto Zechariah—The burden of the word of the Lord to Israel by Malachi.

The only explanation which I can give of this remarkable identity of language by which these prophecies are prefaced, is that they were gathered from separate documents or traditions, and arranged by the zeal of those who, wishing to re-establish the existence of their nation, wished also to recover and re-establish at the same time its literature and its religion.

The Books of Ezekiel, Daniel, and some of the Minor Prophets are however distinguished from the rest by more striking marks than the want of a preface such as is prefixed to the writings of others. We will review in order certain peculiarities of their style.

The prophesies of Ezekiel are introduced by the mention of a date "in the thirteenth year," and the eighth chapter of the work, in like manner, is prefaced by the words, "And it came to pass in the sixth year." The same form recurs at the beginning of the twentieth chapter, "And it came to pass in the seventh year," as also at the beginning of chapter xxiv, "Again in the ninth year, in the tenth month, in the tenth day of the month." Chapters xxi and xxii mark the eleventh and the twelfth years apparently of the same series, but at chapter xl.we read, "In the five and twentieth year of our captivity," and "in the fourteenth year after the city was smitten." The enumeration of years goes no further, and the book ends with visions, in which the prophet sees a new commonwealth established, a new city, and a new temple. There are also great peculiarities in the style or rather in the mode of introducing and expressing the various prophesies. The language indeed is more debased than that of the earlier writings, but still is genuine Hebrew with such changes as happen to all people that have a prolonged national existence. But certain formulas recur to an enormous extent. "Thus saith the Lord God" occurs more than eighty, and the words "Son of Man," addressed to Ezekiel, more than ninety times in this book. The latter of these terms is found in no other part of the Old Testament except Daniel, and in the Christian Scriptures it occurs only in the Gospels according to St Matthew and St John, and in the Book of Revelation.

Of the minor prophets Haggai seems to have the least interest for the reader; his style is nerveless, and no high moral views are apparent in the two chapters which form his book.

Zechariah and Malachi partake of the sacerdotal spirit, which was already after the Exile beginning to show itself in the latest writings of the Jewish Canon. The former, like Ezekiel, repeats the formula, "Thus speaketh," or "Thus saith the Lord of Hosts," no less than forty-one times in eight chapters, and his Levitical tendency shows itself in repeated references to the Temple and the forms of worship. Moreover, as Ezekiel is the only one of the prophets who speaks of Angels, so is Zechariah the only one of them who speaks of Satan.

In like manner Malachi shows a disposition to limit religion to forms and ceremonies: he reproves the people for transgressing the rules of public worship, and neglecting other matters of the Mosaic law. We know absolutely nothing of the personal history of Malachi. Origen, by a remarkable fancy, supposed he might be an angel, and others have interpreted his name as an epithet or title of Ezra. He is placed by some writers, amongst whom are Bertholdt and Vitringa, as contemporary with Nehemiah, and these suggest a comparison of certain passages which occur in the books of Nehemiah and Malachi, as having reference to the same period of Jewish history. We read in Nehemiah (xiii, 10):

And I perceived that the portions of the Levites had not been given *them:* for the Levites and the singers that did the work, were fled every one to his field. Then contended I with the rulers and said, "Why is the house of God forsaken?" And I gathered them together, and set them in their place. Then brought all Judah the tithe of the corn and the new wine and the oil unto the treasuries.

Compare with this the words of Malachi (iii, 8).

Will a man rob God? Yet ye have robbed me. But ye say, Wherein have we robbed thee?" In tithes and offerings. Ye are cursed with a curse: for ye have robbed me, even this whole nation. Bring ye all the tithes unto the store-house, that there may be meat in mine house, and prove me now herewith, saith the Lord of Hosts.

The payment of tithe was no doubt always enforced as necessary for maintaining the public worship and the ceremonies that were customary in the Jewish Temple. But another particular, in which these later prophets harmonized with Nehemiah, was intermarriage between the Jews returning from exile and the people by whom they were surrounded.

In those days also [says Nehemiah, xiii, 23] saw I Jews that had married wives of Ashdod, of Ammon, and of Moab: and their children spake half in the speech of Ashdod, and could not speak in the Jews' language, but according to the language of each people. And I contended with them, and cursed them, and smote certain of them, and plucked off their hair, and made them swear by God, *saying,* "Ye shall not give your daughters unto their sons, nor take their daughters unto your sons, or for yourselves. Did not Solomon king of Israel sin by these things? Yet among many nations was there no king like him, who was beloved of his God, and God made him king over all Israel: nevertheless even him did outlandish women cause to sin. Shall we then hearken unto you to do all this great evil, to transgress against our God in marrying strange wives?

There can be no doubt—for History furnishes the most complete evidence of the fact—that the influence of women over the religious forms as well as feeling of the age, has always been most powerful; and to guard against such influence in the time of Ezra and Malachi, when Religion seems to have had much greater weight in the Jewish nation and government, was more needful than in the earlier times of Moses, Joshua, Solomon, and the kings his successors; for in their days war and rebellion were the alternate normal condition of the Israelites, far more than in any other nation in the history of the world. Taking then the passage above quoted from Nehemiah as a fair specimen of the legislation which then occupied the minds of the Jewish leaders, we may accede to the opinion of those writers who consider Malachi to have had the same thought, although his premises hardly bear out entirely his conclusion, when he writes as follows:

Have we not all one father? Hath not one God created us? Why do we deal treacherously every man against his brother by profaning the covenant of our fathers? Judah hath dealt treacherously, and an abomination is committed in Israel and in Jerusalem; for Judah had profaned the holiness of the Lord which he loved, and hath married the daughter of a strange god. The Lord will cut off the man that doeth this. MAL. ii, 10.

Thus much then may suffice on the subject of Malachi: it remains to make a few observations on the writings which are ascribed to the prophet Daniel; and here we meet with opinions the most opposite, and conclusions the most irreconcileable. Whilst one party regard the book which passes under his name, as a genuine work of the sixth century before Christ, written during the captivity of the Jews by the greatest man among those who shared in that state of exile, others have assigned its author to the times of the Syrian Antiochus, treating the work as a fiction, such as has often been published to the world at other times, in which Nebuchadnezzar and Belshazzar stand for the Syriac king, and the prophetic visions supposed to have been seen by the prophet Daniel, describe, not the return of his countrymen to their own country from Babylon and the consequent restoration of the Jewish state, but the victories and triumph which with divine aid they would obtain over Antiochus Epiphanes their oppressor. We will not here enumerate the objections which have been raised to the authenticity of this book, nor will it be needful to repeat the various conjectures by which these arguments have been met: for the fixed belief of the world in the received opinion of its authenticity needs no other support, and would probably reject any other support, than that faith which removes mountains, and which our Saviour wisely inculcated on his disciples as it is recorded in the Gospel history.

We learn from Jerome, in his Preface to his Commentary on Daniel, that Porphyry in his twelfth book assigns the work before us to the time of Antiochus Epiphanes, and says that it did not so much foretell things to come as relate things which had already happened. In modern times a large number of writers have assailed, whilst as many others have defended, this statement of Porphyry, but in a future chapter we shall have to review the whole question of age and authorship, and to consider whether the book of Daniel is to be regarded as a moral or a prophetic work. The book itself is disjointed, and consists of fragments with no such connection between them, as would probably be found in so short a work and written by so eminent a prophet.

We read in the first chapter: "In the third year of the reign of Jehoiakim king of Judah, came Nebuchadnezzar as king of Babylon unto Jerusalem and besieged it."

Chapter the second begins with these words: "And in the second year of the reign of Nebuchadnezzar, &c." The third and fourth chapters relate the story of the image of gold which Nebuchadnezzar set up, and the king's dream with the interpretation thereof given by Daniel, who was called among the Babylonians by the name of Belteshazzar. In the fifth chapter we read of Belshazzar the king who made a great feast, and of the hand-writing on the wall, which consigned his kingdom to the Medes and Persians. In the sixth chapter Darius the Median is introduced, and Daniel is cast into the lion's den, from which he comes out free, and his traducers are subjected to the fate which he had escaped. In the seventh chapter we recur to the first year of Belshazzar king of Babylon, when "Daniel had a dream and visions of his head upon his bed."

The eighth chapter begins thus:

In the third year of the reign of King Belshazzar a vision appeared unto me *even unto me* Daniel, after that which appeared unto me at the first. And I saw in a vision, and it came to pass, when I saw, that I *was* at Shushan *in* the palace, which is in the province of Elam; and I was by the river Ulai.

The beginning of the ninth chapter is as follows:

In the first year of Darius the son of Ahasuerus, of the seed of the Medes, which was made king over the realm of the Chaldeans: in the first year of his reign I Daniel understood by books the number of the years, whereof the word of the Lord came to Jeremiah the prophet, that he would accomplish seventy years in the desolation of Jerusalem.

The tenth chapter begins with the third year of Cyrus king of Persia, when "a thing was revealed unto Daniel whose name was Belteshazzar." The eleventh chapter begins, "Also I in the first year of Darius the Mede, *even* I, stood to confirm and to strengthen him:" and the twelfth chapter ends with reference to the daily sacrifice being suspended and the abomination of desolation set up, which are thought to have had their fulfilment by the act of King Antiochus, notwithstanding our Saviour's words in the Gospels, which seemed to imply that those events, and not other similar ones, were in his time still to come to pass.

But whatever may be the date assigned for the fulfilment of the prophesies, the book furnishes the strongest evidence that it is not one complete composition proceeding from the pen of the same inspired writer. We have nine chapters, out of the twelve which compose the work, all introduced by nine different dates, which it is impossible, except by unsupported conjecture, to harmonize with one another. The third year of Jehoiakim falls in the year before Nebuchadnezzar came to the throne of Babylon, and although this latter king is said to have reigned nearly fifty years, we come in the fifth chapter to Belshazzar, apparently the successor of Nebuchadnezzar, although no other writer knows any thing of a king bearing that name. Darius the Mede next occurs, and then the first and the third years of Belshazzar are spoken of, after which we have the first year of Darius the son of Ahasuerus, although it is not stated, nor can we ascertain from any other history, whether Darius the Mede before-named and Darius the son of Ahasuerus are one and the same person. We are then informed of the vision made to Daniel in the third year of Cyrus king of Persia, and lastly the history recurs to the first year of Darius the Mede.

That the incidents which fall under these several dates have very little connection with another, and are indeed wholly disjointed, did not escape the notice of the Seventy translators: they have in several places made the connection plain by insertions, needful, as they thought, to complete the sense. Thus between verses 23 and 24 in the third chapter they insert:

The angel of the Lord descended at the same time with these men who were with Azariah in the furnace, and drove out the flame of fire from the furnace, and made the midst of the furnace like the gently breathing spirit of dew, and the fire touched them not.

With a similar view of improving the book, the same translators have altered the king's threat, in verse 5, that a failure to explain his dream should be punished with a cruel death, into a simple threat that their property should be confiscated, and themselves made an example of.

The additions made to the Book of Daniel, which are found among the Apocryphal writings, Bel and the Dragon, the History of Susanna, and such like stories, are all valuable as original Greek works of a certain date, but the subject matter is too childish to arrest the attention of the reader.

CHAPTER XXIV.

THE KHETUBIM OR HAGIOGRAPHA.

THE Hebrew Scriptures, as is well known to almost every reader, were divided by the Jews into three parts. The most obvious mode of classifying them was the division into Historical, Poetical, and Prophetical Books. The same classification was often otherwise expressed by the names, the Law, the Psalms, and the Prophets, and this division seems to have been familiar to the Jews in the time of Christ, who says, as we read in the Gospel according to St Luke (xxiv, 14); "All things must be fulfilled which were written in the Law of Moses, and in the Prophets and the Psalms concerning me." How far these three names comprehended the books which we now should class under them is doubtful: for it would be difficult to say under which name the Books of Joshua, Judges, Kings, and Chronicles would be placed, and we learn from the Masora that under the same head as the Psalms were included eleven other works, which are mostly of a very different and wholly prosaic character, so that by no rule whatever could they be placed in the same class as our present Book of Psalms.

But all the three divisions of the Hebrew Bible have come down to us under names borrowed from the Greek. Every single book, indeed, has its proper Greek name. The Law and the Prophets are designated by the words which in Greek have the same respective meanings: but the third class, which originally bore in Hebrew the name of *Khetubim*, became in the Septuagint the *Hagiographa* 'Holy Writings,' and under this name were found twelve works—Psalms, Proverbs, Job, Solomon's Song, Ruth, Lamentations, Ecclesiastes, Esther, Daniel, Ezra, Nehemiah and Chronicles; and there is some force in the inference which Dr Donaldson has drawn from this fact, in his Christian Orthodoxy, where he says:

Genesis and Chronicles are the first and last books in the Jewish Canon. Accordingly there is presumptive evidence, that, at the Christian era, the Jewish collection was fixed and completed: and Josephus, who flourished in the first century A.D., mentions all the books in a division of twenty-two parts corresponding to the letters of the Hebrew alphabet.—Page 191.

It is with reason believed that the Hagiographa of the Greeks, the Khetubim of the Hebrews, and the Psalms of the New Testament, being one and the same collection, were compiled at a later period than either the Law or the Prophets. Not only does our Saviour name the Psalms last in referring to these books, but Jesus the Son of Sirach, who wrote the book which we call Ecclesiasticus about 150 years before our era, speaks thus in the second prologue to that book:

Whereas many and great things have been delivered unto us by the law and the prophets, and by others that have followed their steps, for the which things Israel ought to be commended for learning and wisdom; and whereof not only the readers must needs become skilful themselves, but also they that desire to learn be able to profit them which are without, both by speaking and writing; my grandfather Jesus, when he had much given himself to the reading of the law, and the prophets, and OTHER BOOKS OF OUR FATHERS, and had gotten therein good judgment, was drawn on also himself to write something pertaining to learning and wisdom; to the intent that those which are desirous to learn, and are addicted to these things, might profit much more in living according to the Law. Wherefore let me intreat you to read it with favour and attention, and to pardon us, wherein we may seem to come short of some words, which we have laboured to interpret. For the same things uttered in Hebrew, and translated into another tongue, have not the same force in them: and not only these things, but the law itself, and the prophets, and THE REST OF THE BOOKS, have no small difference, when they are spoken in their own language. For in the eight and thirtieth year coming into Egypt, when Evergetes was king, and continuing there some time, I found a book of no small learning: therefore I thought it most necessary for me to bestow some diligence and travail to interpret it; using great watchfulness and skill in that space to bring the book to an end, and set it forth for them also, which in a strange country are willing to learn, being prepared before in manners to live after the law.

There can be little doubt that the "other books of our fathers," which are named by Siracides in this prologue, as having been read by his grandfather, were those which are elsewhere and by other writers termed the Psalms in the New Testament, the Hagiographa in the Septuagint, and Khetubim according to the Hebrew text. It appears too from a passage in the Gospel according to St Matthew, that as the Book of Psalms stood first, so also the Books of Chronicles occupied the last place in the collection of the Hagiographa. Our Saviour, whilst castigating the Scribes and Pharisees, and referring to their cruelty and persecution of the Prophets whom God had at various times sent to them, uses the language which follows:

Ye serpents, ye generation of vipers, how can ye escape the damnation of hell? Wherefore, behold, I send unto you prophets and wise men and scribes: and some of them ye shall kill and crucify; and some of them shall ye scourge in your synagogues, and persecute them from city to city. That upon you may come all the righteous blood shed upon the earth, from the blood of righteous Abel unto the blood of Zacharias son of Barachias, whom ye slew between the temple and the altar.—MATT. xxiii, 33—35.

Our Lord, in this passage, refers to the narrative found in the Second Book of Chronicles:

And the spirit of God came upon Zachariah the son of Jehoiada the priest, which stood above the people, and said unto them, "Thus saith the Lord, Why transgress ye the commandments of the Lord, that ye cannot prosper? Because ye have forsaken the Lord, he hath also forsaken you." And they conspired against him, and stoned him with stones at the commandment of the king in the court of the house of the Lord. II CHRON. xiv, 20, 21.

Setting aside for a moment the difference of name by which the father of Zachariah is designated, our Saviour, dating his remark from the death of Abel, which he describes as the first act of slaying a prophet, evidently intends to comprehend the whole period of Jewish history, and the inference to be drawn from it seems not unreasonable, namely, that the Books of Chronicles stood last in the Jewish Canon.

If these and other facts treated of in these pages appear well grounded, the conclusion will be that the collection of books which form the Hebrew Canon began to be put together in the fifth century before the Christian era; that the Law was first published, with such additions and insertions in the original legislation of Moses, as were thought applicable to their own times, whether found in any ancient documents, or handed down by tradition, or dictated by their wish to produce a code suited to the emergencies of the age, the maintenance of their own authority, the due worship of God, and the good government of the people. All this, it seems, is due to the laborious zeal of Ezra and perhaps of Nehemiah, whilst we must look to a later date for the first appearance of the Prophets as they are now found, in an uniform collection, made probably soon after the year B.C. 400, when the prophet Malachi produced the short work which now stands last in the Hebrew Canon.

The third class of writings comprehending the twelve books before enumerated, is supposed by the most judicious critics to have been added to the canon about 150 years before the Christian era, when the Book of Daniel, which from internal evidence appears to be connected with the reign of Antiochus Epiphanes, is thought to have been compiled.

With these preliminary remarks we may proceed to examine the various books which passed under the general name of the Psalms, for no other reason than that the lyrical writings in that collection were the most important and interesting, and certainly many of them much more ancient than the other books which are classed with them under the same head.

CHAPTER XXV.

THE HISTORICAL BOOKS OF THE CHETUBIM OR HAGIOGRAPHA; NAMELY, RUTH, CHRONICLES, EZRA, AND NEHEMIAH.

To preserve the order in which the Books of the Bible are found in our authorised version, the attention of the reader has been already directed to Ruth, Chronicles, Ezra and Nehemiah in the XVIIth, XXIst, and XXIInd Chapters of this volume. Certain extracts have there been given, and references made to many peculiarities which serve to show that the origin of these books is in most respects similar to that of the others which precede them in the Canon of Scripture. But we must now regard these same books under a new aspect, not so much in the light of a continuation to the history and religious system comprised in those previous writings, as forming part of a third class of books, bearing the name of Chetubim or Hagiographa, collected perhaps two hundred years after the Law and the Prophets, and therefore possibly compiled at the same time that they were published, out of such documents and other sources as were then brought to light. That these books were then put forth in a separate form and not blended with the former was a natural process, such as has been often and almost universally adopted by those who have made large additions to works already existing. It must not, moreover, be forgotten that serious contradictions exist between some of these writings and the earlier histories. We may not be able fully to explain why such discrepancies should have been allowed to remain in two narratives, derived, it is true, from different sources, but ultimately put together in the same volume, and that volume forming a code of laws written for the political and religious government of God's chosen people. That these books were kept separate is a fact which seems, as we may reasonably infer, to limit the age within which they may be thought to have been written. No obvious reason can be assigned why the Book of Ruth was not at once added to the history of the Judges, to which it evidently belongs. The alternative is that those who formed the Canon into its ultimate state, thought it important to maintain the integrity of a book which had come into their hands as an integral and separate work. The same motives possibly influenced them in the case of the other books, Ezra, Nehemiah, and Chronicles. And another fact, which has already been mentioned, may have influenced them in the course which they adopted. The narrative in Ruth contains a beautiful episode of Hebrew domestic life, and is connected with the family of King David. The Chronicles too, as already stated, show a decided partiality towards the kings of Judah, and especially towards King

David. How long the Books of Chronicles may have circulated among the Jews before they were collected into the class of Chetubim, it is impossible for us to know, and useless to conjecture. They may have been circulated largely as separate works, and so acquired a notoriety which prevented them from being placed in the Canon under any conditions which altered the tenour of the narrative or destroyed their identity of form. If any earlier accounts form the basis of these works, we may still suppose that those who put together the documents may have added to the facts which form the basis of the history, with reference to the state of things existing in their own times. With these observations on the Historical portion of the Hagiographa, we may for the present conclude this part of our subject, and proceed to show that a similar view may be taken of the second portion, the Poetical Books, and lastly of those which are here proposed as forming what may be called works of Moral and Historical Fiction, forming the third part of the same collection.

The supposition that the writings known among the Jews by the name of Chetubim or Hagiographa, form the latest portion of the whole Hebrew Bible, will be found in remarkable harmony with the arrangement which prevails in almost all the editions of the perfect volume which we now possess.

The order in which those books are given by different authors, who have made mention of this third or additional collection of writings, is not universally the same, and need not be observed in the remarks which will here be made on the various books enumerated under this division of the Hebrew Scriptures. It will be more convenient and perhaps more fitting to divide the twelve books into three classes—Historical, Poetical, and works of Moral Fiction. The whole of them readily fall under this classification, and thus they coincide with the literature of other nations both of ancient and of modern times; but the same capability of being thus classified will account for the position which they now occupy in the Hebrew Canon, and in the various versions, both ancient and modern, which are still extant. If we suppose that Ezra, as has been seen in a previous chapter, rewrote from tradition and from remaining documents the Law of Moses, and that he or his successors accomplished a second task of gathering into one body the works which passed under the name of the Prophets, the third class of writings, of which we are now speaking, would find places in the Canon according to the nature of the several books of that class. The Books of Chronicles, Ruth, Ezra, and Nehemiah, are clearly historical, and it remains to justify the view which is here taken by some further remarks about the Poetical and also about the Moral Works, which are found in the collection of the Hagiographa.

CHAPTER XXVI.

THE POETICAL WRITINGS OF THE HAGIOGRAPHA; NAMELY, THE PSALMS, PROVERBS, ECCLESIASTES, SONG OF SOLOMON, LAMENTATIONS.

§ 1. *The Psalms.*

IN almost all countries the earliest writings have taken the form of poetry, which indeed seems to be peculiar to all primitive nations: for whilst they without doubt spoke in prose, and wrote, sung, or recited in verse, they seem for centuries to have been ignorant of prose, or of any kind of historical composition. It would be probable that the Hebrew nation, living and struggling through such a wonderful career as is related of them in their Scriptures, would not be an exception to the general rule. We might expect to meet with the highest flights of poetry among a people so enterprising, so energetic, so devoted to the religious sentiment, and, may I not add—so barbarous? Nor are we disappointed in this expectation. Whatever conclusion we may arrive at concerning the late origin of the volume which contains all that we now have of ancient Hebrew Literature, we certainly find therein specimens of a poetical spirit that surpass, or at all events vie with, everything that has come down to us from any other ancient source.

The Hebrew poetry which remains is indeed in form of

the lyric kind, but it combines much of the epic and of the didactic in its subject matter; and it exhibits the sentiment of devotion in every part of it more fully than does the poetry of other nations. The Book of Psalms found in the Hebrew Canon, contains one hundred and fifty separate hymns or songs, and besides these, there are ten or twelve others found in various parts of the Pentateuch and of the Historical Books. These last, or at least some of them, such as the Song of Moses and that of Deborah, are superior perhaps to any of the hundred and fifty that are included in the collection, and they rise to a height of grandeur and sublimity unequalled in all the rest of ancient or modern literature. It is indeed from such ancient remains, as well as other documents, that the Book of the Old Testament was compiled after the return from Babylon, and there can be little doubt that the collection of Psalms into one body was then made also.

It is somewhat perplexing to the mere English reader that the version of the Psalms of David found in the Book of Common Prayer is different from that given in the Authorized Version of the Bible. The two translations were made at different times and with different objects; the one to be inserted in the Prayer Book, which was to supersede the Roman breviary in the service of the Church, whilst the other was to be placed in the Authorized Version of the Bible, and to supersede the Latin Vulgate, which was not " understanded of the people," and therefore not according to the spirit of the Reformation. Those who were appointed to make these versions were no doubt also much perplexed by the difficulty of finding out the real meaning of the Hebrew original, which was obscured rather than cleared up by the translations that have come down to us from ancient times. A single instance of such a variance taken from the eighth verse of the sixtieth Psalm will suffice.

The Hebrew text is translated by Walton in the Polyglott Bible—" Over me, Peleseth [or Philistia], triumph."

The Septuagint has—" To me the foreigners have been subjected."

The Latin Vulgate follows the Septuagint.

The Targum or Chaldee paraphrase has—" Over the Philistines triumph, Oh congregation of Israel."

The Prayer-book has—" Philistia, be thou glad of me."
The Authorised Version has—" Philistia, triumph thou because of me."

In addition to this difficulty, the arrangement of the psalms which compose the separate collection is not the same in the different copies. The ninth and tenth, as they are numbered in the Hebrew, are united together and appear as Psalm ix in the Greek and Latin, and so the order is disturbed as far as Psalm cxiii, which stands cxii in the aforesaid versions. From this point other disturbances occur: Psalms cxiv, cxv become cxiii, &c.; and uniformity is only restored by the division of cxlvii into two parts, which consequently appear as cxlvi and cxlvii in the Septuagint and Vulgate translations. The Septuagint, moreover, has an additional or hundred and fifty-first Psalm, which occurs neither in the Hebrew nor in the Targums, but is found in the Syriac, Ethiopic, and Arabic versions. A literal translation of it may perhaps interest the reader.

A Psalm written by David's own hand, when he fought in single combat with Goliath.

I was a little one among my brethren, and younger in the house of my father: I used to feed my father's sheep. My hands made the organ, and my fingers put together the psaltery. And who shall tell it to my Lord? the Lord himself, himself hears. Himself hath sent his angel, and taken me away from my father's sheep and anointed me in the oil of his anointing. My brethren are beautiful and tall, and the Lord was not well pleased in them. I went out to the meeting with the foreigner, and he cursed me by his idols. [And I hurled at him three stones, against his forehead, in the strength of the Lord, and I laid him prostrate.]* And drawing his sword from him, I beheaded him, and took away the reproach from the children of Israel.

These peculiarities seem reasonably to point to a conclusion in harmony with the views here entertained concerning the whole of the Old Testament. We have a large number of poems formed into a collection or volume, and their arrangement in that collection is not uniform, but varies in the different copies that have been preserved. And there are still other facts concerning the Psalms which will require to be noticed. Although they now appear in

* The clause in brackets appears in the Arabic text only.

one volume, yet that they were not collected at one time, but at different times and by different persons, is evident from an examination of their contents. In the Masoretic copies and also in the Syriac they are divided into five books, having doxologies at the end of each.

The first of those books comprises from the first to the forty-first Psalm, and ends with the words, " Blessed be the Lord God of Israel, from everlasting to everlasting. Amen and Amen !"

The second book contains from the forty-second to the seventy-second Psalm, and concludes thus :—" Blessed be the Lord God of Israel, who only doeth wondrous things. And blessed be his glorious name for ever ; and let the whole earth be filled with his glory—Amen and Amen. The prayers of David the son of Jesse are ended."

The third book comprehends Psalms seventy-three to eighty-nine, and ends :—" Blessed be the Lord for evermore —Amen and Amen."

The fourth book contains from the ninetieth to the hundred and sixth Psalm, and ends with these words :—" Blessed be the Lord God of Israel from everlasting to everlasting ; and let all the people say Amen. Praise ye the Lord."

The fifth book consists of forty-four psalms, from the hundred and seventh to the end of the volume, and has these words at the conclusion :—" Let every thing that hath breath praise the Lord. Praise ye the Lord !"

It has been conjectured that these five books were collected at different times, according as fresh psalms became known to the collectors, and that they were put together into one volume by Ezra, when, as is said, the Jewish Canon was completed. But as we are informed by Mr Hartwell Horne in his " Introduction to the Critical Study and Knowledge of the Holy Scriptures," the fifth book " is supposed to have been collected in the time of Judas Maccabæus, but by whom it is impossible to conjecture." If this be true, it is impossible that Ezra could have collected into one volume all the Psalms which now appear there, seeing that forty-four of these are due to Judas Maccabæus nearly three hundred years after the time of Ezra.

Many attempts have been made to arrange the Psalms in the order of the times at which they were written. All these attempts however have ended in a failure which could not be avoided. The language of most of them is so vague, that it is in nearly every instance uncertain to what events the writer alludes: and unfortunately the Hebrew tongue is imperfectly known to even the best scholars; and lastly the five books, which have been thrown into one, contain each of them specimens, as is thought, of every age from the time of David almost to the time of Christ. There is also less certainty of arriving at a favourable conclusion if we go too deeply in examining the difference of style in the case of so many short poems like the Psalms. The thoughts which pervade the whole series are very much alike, and the way in which they are expressed is very similar in all. Writers have indeed observed that words of the Chaldee form abound in all of them, and this alone would make it safe to conclude that the collection of them into one body is due to the latest period of Jewish history, and that whilst they retain the thoughts and many expressions indicative of their remote origin, they were modernized, as nearly always is done in such cases, so as to make them intelligible in the later period to the generation for whose use they were collected.

§ 2. *The Proverbs.*

The Book of Proverbs, both from the love of proverbial philosophy which is so general among mankind, and from the variety of subjects which it takes within its range, is one of the most interesting parts of the Old Testament. It has from the earliest times been ascribed to King Solomon, but of late years, since the subject has been more fully investigated, this opinion has been abandoned. It is, indeed, highly probable, and might have been expected, that both David and Solomon should be named as the authors of many psalms, proverbs, and other books which they never wrote. And yet it is equally probable that of the books which are ascribed to them, some parts at least have really proceeded from their hands; and this is fully consistent with the fact, that all the works so ascribed to these two great kings have the appearance of being collections made from various sources rather than uniform works written each by a single author. This is pre-eminently the case with the Proverbs; under which name we have five divisions, each bearing its own appropriate title.

1. The first part is headed:—" The proverbs of Solomon the son of David king of Israel," and under this title are contained the first nine chapters.

2. After this we have another series, having a similar heading:—" The proverbs of Solomon," and this title contains fifteen chapters, from the beginning of the tenth to the end of the twenty-fourth.

3. The third division comprises chapters twenty-five to twenty-nine, and has for its inscription:—" These are also proverbs of Solomon, which the men of Hezekiah king of Judah copied out."

4. The fourth division contains the substance of only one chapter, the thirtieth, and is entitled:—"The words of Agur the son of Jakeh, even the prophecy; the man spake unto Ithiel, even unto Ithiel and Ucal."

5. The fifth and last division contains the thirty-first, which is the last chapter of the book, with the heading:—" The words of King Lemuel, the prophecy that his mother taught him."

Some of the proverbs contained under these five heads, are single unconnected sentences, whilst others are more argumentative, and form a series of admonitions, having for their object to inculcate the search after wisdom and the practice of the moral virtues.

This analysis of the book and its obvious division into parts lead us clearly to doubt its original character as a work of King Solomon, although it is highly probable that some of the proverbs which it contained may be as early as the reign of that great king. Such proverbs are found among all nations, current in the mouths of the people; but this is true of their substance only: the language in which they survive will generally be that which is spoken commonly by the people, and this never remains entirely the same for so long a space of time as a thousand years.

That the book still remaining is a miscellaneous collection of proverbs, augmented by additions made from time to time, seems also to explain the fact that many of the maxims and other sentences are repeated, and this would evidently not be so generally in the case of proverbs and short sentences, collected by a single author, but it would clearly be the duty of the editor or writer to take care that the same maxim should not occur more than once.

To those then who have gone through the earlier pages of this volume, it will be easy to see that we have no good reason for exempting the Book of the Proverbs from the judgment which applies to all the Hebrew Canon, and which ascribes them to the period between 450 and 150 years before the Christian era.

§ 3. *Ecclesiastes.*

The Book of Ecclesiastes, so called from the Greek word which means *preacher* or *orator*, one who speaks before a public assemby, has in Hebrew the title which we translate in our Authorized Version, "The words of the preacher, the son of David, king in Jerusalem." In the twelfth verse of the first chapter we read: "I the preacher was king over Israel in Jerusalem." These are all the references made by name to Solomon, who is generally supposed to have been the writer of the book. This opinion, however, has never been universally entertained. The Rabbi Kimchi ascribed it to Isaiah, and the Talmudical writers to Hezekiah. "Grotius, from some foreign expressions which he thinks are discoverable in it, conceives that it was composed by order of Zerubbabel for his son Abihud; Jahn, after some later German critics, for the same reason, thinks it was written after the Babylonish captivity; and Zirkel imagines that it was composed about the time of Antiochus Epiphanes, from some traces of the notions of the Pharisees and Sadducees which he conceives he has discovered in this book, and against which he supposes it to be directed."

Whilst these critics have thus, by conjecture only, assigned the book to various writers, others, omitting to define its authorship, have censured the sceptical and Epicurean tendency which seems to pervade the book. They accuse the author of teaching nothing that can be of value to mankind, but only, that all their hopes and actions are characterised by vanity and delusion.

It would be superfluous to quote, in support of this opinion, passages from the work itself, for they abound in every chapter, and it cannot add much to the lawful and proper enjoyment of human life, that the teacher should enumerate every source of pleasure open to mankind, and under the phrase "vanity of vanities, all is vanity," should condemn them all. But without inquiring how far this is a just estimate of the design of the book, and whether an alternative may not be found from passing so severe a sentence, it is fair to ascertain whether the sentiments expressed in the book are such as would seem likely to come from the Israelitish king to whom it is ascribed.

The history of Solomon is contained in the First Book of Kings, from chapter ii, verse 12 to the end of the eleventh chapter, and is given after much the same manner in the first nine chapters of the Second Book of Chronicles. In both of these narratives the life of the king is represented as an uniform series of unbroken prosperity. No complaint of vanity ever came from his lips; on the contrary, he seems to have thoroughly enjoyed the good things which Providence had thrown in his way. His daily allowance of fine flour (I Kings iv, 22), fat oxen (23), his chariots and horses (26), his wisdom (29), and other gifts, supplied everything which could render life happy. He had dominion over "all kingdoms from the river unto the land of the Philistines" (21).

Judah and Israel were many, as the sand which is by the sea in multitude, eating and drinking and making merry.

In the midst of all this prosperity there was little room for the sentiment that all is vanity—unless the king had discovered the vanity of fearing God, and keeping his commandments; for the author of Ecclesiastes tells us at the end of his work, that this is the only thing which is not vanity, and that "this is the whole duty of man." Let us then see how far Solomon practised this duty: we read that, as time went on, he loved many strange women, and then the usual results followed.

I Kings, xi, 4—10. For it came to pass, when Solomon was old, that his wives turned away his heart after other gods; and his heart was not perfect with the Lord his God, as was the heart of David his father. For Solomon went after Ashtoreth the goddess of the Zidonians, and after Milcom the abomination of the Ammonites. And Solomon did evil in the sight of the Lord, and went not fully after the Lord, as did David his father. Then did Solomon build an high place for Chemosh the abomination of Moab, in the hill that is before Jerusalem, and for Molech the abomination of the children of Ammon. And likewise did he for all his strange wives, which burnt incense and sacrificed unto their gods. And the Lord was angry with Solomon because his heart was turned from the Lord God of Israel, which had appeared unto him twice, and had commanded him concerning this thing, that he should not go after other gods: but he kept not that which the Lord commanded.

The reign of King Solomon lasted forty years, and the whole of that time was prosperous beyond the experience of any other king. The kingdom of Israel, from having been a small weak state, exposed to enemies on every side, and hardly able to defend itself from their attacks, became, under the two able kings David and Solomon, an absolute monarchy, one of the most powerful states of Asia, and not very likely to inspire its monarch with the sentiments of despondency which run through the Book of Ecclesiastes. To suppose that Solomon repented of his wickedness, and committed such sentiments to writing that others might avoid following his examples, is a vain conjecture. The Scriptures say nothing that warrant such an inference: we only read that "Solomon slept with his fathers, and was buried in the city of David his father: and Rehoboam his son reigned in his stead."

§ 4. *The Canticles or Song of Solomon.*

The Song of Solomon, or as it is otherwise called the Song of Songs, is the only specimen of amatory Hebrew poetry that has come down to us; and it has been explained by various writers both ancient and modern in so many different ways and on such different principles of interpretation that any one who has examined all of these will probably find himself less competent than at first to form a reasonable judgment of its drift and meaning.

The first ancient writer who gives us any information about it is Jerome, who says, in his Preface to Ezekiel, that the reading of this book as well as others was forbidden to young men until the age of thirty years. The reason of this prohibition may have been of a moral or of a mystical character. If the latter, we can understand the allegorical meaning which was ascribed to it by Origen, Theodoret, Epiphanius, and many German critics, among whom Herder is most conspicuous. Bishop Lowth says it is a pastoral poem, and that the two principal personages appear as shepherds; and he describes it as an allegory in which the universal church is depicted. Bishop Horne, taking it in the same sense, applies it spiritually to all believers. Bishop Horne's namesake, the author of the "Introduction to the Critical Study of the Scriptures," forgetting that the indelicacy of one author can receive no support from the example of another, quotes Ezekiel and makes the following comparison between the two:

His [Ezekiel's] great freedom in the use of this image is particularly displayed in two parables (xvi and xvii), in which he describes the ingratitude of the Jews and Israelites to their great protector, and their defection from the true worship, under imagery assumed from the character of an adulterous wife and the meretricious loves of two unchaste women. If these parables (which are put into the mouth of God himself with a direct allegorical application, and in which it must be confessed that delicacy does not appear to be particularly studied, according to our refined notions of delicacy) be well considered, we are persuaded that the Song of Solomon (which is in every part chaste and elegant) will not appear unworthy of the divine sense in which it is usually taken, either in matter or style, or in any degree inferior either in gravity or purity to the other remains of the sacred poets.

The opinion of Bishop Horsley, in the first volume of his Sermons (p. 73), is equally grotesque with that which has been cited.

In the prophetical Book of the Song of Solomon the union of Christ and his church is described in images taken entirely from the mutual passion and early love of Solomon and his bride. Read the Song of Solomon, you will find the Hebrew king, if you know anything of his history, produced indeed as the emblem of a greater personage; but you will find *Him* in every page.

Volumes have been written to explain this short incoherent Song of Solomon, and to show the meaning of what is called its imagery and typical allegories. What allegory can be discovered in the following verses?

vii, 1—3. How beautiful are thy feet with shoes, O prince's daughter! the joints of thy thighs are like jewels, the work of the hands of a cunning workman. Thy navel is like a round goblet, which wanteth not liquor; thy belly is like an heap of wheat set about with lilies.

Is not the imagery vivid enough to fill the mind of the reader with its meaning? or is it necessary to search for any divine sense in which such an apostrophe can be taken? Is the Union between Christ and the Church hallowed by the use of such language as this, or can we suppose that even Solomon, in the midst of his crowded harem and surrounded by Oriental state, has left for the edification of posterity a poem containing such passages as this? But the apostrophe in those lines is from a man to a woman. We have, however, in the first chapter of the song, a specimen of the language in which one of the other sex, apparently a beautiful negro, addresses her beloved, at one time in the second, at another in the third person.

i, 1—5. The song of songs, which is Solomon's. Let him kiss me with the kisses of his mouth: for thy love is better than wine. Because of the savour of thy good ointments, thy name is as ointment poured forth, therefore do the virgins love thee. Draw me, we will run after thee: the king hath brought me into his chambers: we will be glad and rejoice in thee, we will remember thy love more than wine: the upright love thee. I am black but comely, O ye daughters of Jerusalem, as the tents of Kedar, as the curtains of Solomon.

But our inquiry now is not into the moral character and tendency of this or any other portion of the Hebrew Canon, except incidentally, but to show when and by whom the various books which form that Canon were compiled. With this view one more extract may be given comprising the last verses of chapter viii, with which the book concludes.

viii, 8—14. We have a little sister and she hath no breasts: what shall we do for our sister in the day when she shall be spoken for? If she be a wall, we shall build upon her a palace of silver: and if she be a door, we will enclose her with boards of cedar. I am a wall and my breasts like towers: then was I in his eyes as one that found favour. Solomon had a vineyard at Baal-hamon; he let out the vineyard unto keepers; every one for the fruit thereof was to bring a thousand pieces of silver. My vineyard, which is mine, is before me: thou, O Solomon, must have a thousand, and those that keep the fruit thereof two hundred. Thou that dwellest in the gardens, the companions hearken to thy voice: cause me to hear it. Make haste, my beloved, and be thou like to a roe or to a young hart upon the mountains of spices.

It remains to point out the reasons why this Song of Songs cannot be accepted as the work of Solomon, but must be ascribed to the same age to which all the other Jewish Scriptures are more justly assigned.

1. The title the "Song of Songs, which is Solomon's," shows the hand of a later writer, as in the case of the prophets mentioned in page 184 of this volume.

2. The way in which Solomon is named not only in the title and in the two passages already quoted, but in a fourth (iii, 11) where the writer says, "Go forth, O ye daughters of Zion, and behold King Solomon with the crown wherewith his mother crowned him in the day of the gladness of his heart."

3. The incoherence and the obscurity which attach to every chapter of the book, especially to iii, 6—11; to vi, 10, &c.; and to viii, 8—10; which seem to be out of place, and have led Herder, Paulus, and other critics to think that we have in it a collection of fragments put together with little of either order or design.

4. The person named in the Song, whether the writer or otherwise, seems to be at one time in Jerusalem (i, 5; ii, 7; iii, 1; v, 7), and immediately afterwards among the flocks (i, 7, 8); on the mountains (ii, 8); and among the vineyards (vii, 12; viii, 12—13).

5. A fifth argument is drawn from the appearance of Chaldaisms in the book, and as these are found in almost every book of the Old Testament, it is unnecessary to particularise those which occur in this Song, with one exception, the word פרדס PRDS from the Persian, signifying a paradise or park, and occurring so often in those Greek writers who were thrown into connection with the Persians during the four hundred years which immediately precede the Christian era.

The conclusion then at which I have arrived, respecting the Song of Solomon, is that it is a collection of fragments and snatches of songs that had been handed down from earlier times, and being current among the people, were put together by some one or other of those who, in the latest age of the Hebrew Commonwealth, collected together these and similar compositions, and out of them compiled the third great division of Hebrew Literature, which passed generally under the name of the Psalms, and as such is quoted by our Lord in the New Testament.

§ 5. *The Lamentations.*

The authorship of this short book is generally ascribed to Jeremiah; and Jerome, who wrote about 400 years after Christ, says that the Prophecy of Jeremiah and the Lamentations count for only one book in the Canon. But this remark was made after the new or present arrangement of the Hebrew Scriptures was established: its first appearance in the Hagiographa denotes an origin later than the time of Jeremiah, although portions of it may have been written by him, and afterwards published at the time when the collection of the Chetubim was made. An argument in support of this view is derived from the fact that this work is not quoted in the historical books which entered into the Law or first portion of the Hebrew Canon; whereas it is quoted as follows in the Book of Chronicles:

And Jeremiah lamented for Josiah: and all the singing men and the singing women spake of Josiah in their lamentations to this day, and made them an ordinance in Israel: and, behold, they are written in the Lamentations. II Chron. xxxv, 25.

It is hardly possible to conjecture the style or character of the lamentations which these singing men and singing women chanted over the death of King Josiah, but there seems little doubt that the present book represents all that could be recovered of what Jeremiah wrote or sung about the death of that king. Whether other words of mourning have been mingled with those of the prophet, although suspected by some, has been doubted by others, but many such surmises have been made, and conjectures hazarded, for which not the slightest grounds can be assigned. It is hardly worth while to pay attention to such conjectures, but only to notice the salient points which connect the book with our present subject.

Those who have endeavoured to analyse more minutely

the five chapters of which this book consists, have fancied that they detect five separate poems or elegies, joined together in one series, and that in some of these the prophet, in others the Jewish people, and in one or two passages the city of Jerusalem personified, is made to utter a complaint to God. That there is but slight connection between these several portions did not escape the notice of Bishop Lowth, whose contributions to our knowledge of Hebrew literature must always be remembered with respect and gratitude. According to Gregory's translation of his Latin Lectures on Hebrew poetry, he says that the Book of the Lamentations "bears rather the appearance of an accumulation of corresponding sentiments than an accurate and connected series of different ideas arranged in the form of a regular treatise."

The Septuagint translation of this book prefixes a verse which is also found in the Latin Vulgate and in the Arabic version, but has no counterpart in the original Hebrew text.

The only other remark which I shall here make is that there are certain acrostic and alphabetic fancies in various parts of the book, which will be dwelt on more fully in a future chapter, as indicating its later origin.

CHAPTER XXVII.

WORKS OF MORAL AND HISTORICAL FICTION IN THE HAGIOGRAPHA; NAMELY JOB, ESTHER, AND DANIEL.

§ 1. *The Book of Job.*

THE Book of Job has been the subject of more discussion and the cause of more divergent opinions among scholars and theologians than any other part except Daniel of either the Old or New Testament. The author of the book is entirely unknown, and the age in which it was written is equally uncertain. If indeed, according to Mr Hartwell Horne,[*] "we allow Job himself to have been the writer of the book,

---

[*] "Introduction to the Critical Study and Knowledge of the Holy Scriptures," Fifth Edition, 1825, vol. iv, p. 77.

two important advantages will be evidently obtained:—
First, all objections to historical truth will vanish at once; no one could tell us his own story so well as Job: nor have we any reason to question its veracity. The dialogue too will then appear to have been the substance of a real conversation, &c. ... The *second* advantage alluded to is this, —that if Job himself were the writer of the book, then every point of history and every doctrine of religion here treated of, which coincide with those delivered in the Books of Moses, are an additional proof and confirmation of the latter, as being evidently derived from some other source, not borrowed from the Pentateuch."

But we are unfortunately not justified in ascribing an anonymous book to any particular author, merely because we should thereby obtain the first advantage here pointed out, and it is somewhat doubtful how far the certainty of procuring the second advantage is secured by adopting the supposition that Job himself was the author of the book which relates his history. We have no means of knowing who was the author of the work, otherwise than by the internal evidence which it may furnish, and the fact that it forms part of the class of writings that were added last of all to the Hebrew Canon.

It is unnecessary to summarize the contents of the book itself. We have it in the original Hebrew, in the Syriac, Arabic, Greek Septuagint, and Latin Vulgate translations. Little need be said about the various readings which are found in these various copies; they are as numerous or as few as those which occur in other parts of the Bible, and in many classical works which time has spared.

But the Septuagint version has an additional paragraph at the end of the book, which is adduced by some critics as a proof that Job was really an historical person. The additional paragraph is here subjoined that the reader may answer this question for himself.

But it is written that he shall rise again with those whom the Lord raises [from the dead]. He is translated out of the Syriac book, dwelling in the land of Ausitis, on the frontiers of Idumæa and Arabia; but his first name was Jobab. Then having taken an Arabian wife, he begets a son whose name was Ennon. But he himself was son of Zare his father, [one] of the sons of Esau, and of Bosorrha his mother, so that he was the fifth from Abraham: and these the kings who reigned in Edom, of which he also was ruler: first Balak the son of Beor, and the name of his city was Dennaba; and after Balak, Jobab who was called Job; and after him Asom who was governor from the country of Thæmanitis; and after him Adad son of Barad, who cut off Madiam in the plain of Moab, and the name of his city was Gethaim. But the friends who came to him were, Eliphaz of the sons of Esau, king of the Thæmanians, Baldad the tyrant of the Sauchæans, Sophar the king of the Minæans.

As the Septuagint translation of the Bible is thought to have been made in the third century before Christ, it is not probable that the passage which it adds to the original text of the Book of Job can date from an earlier period. The same subscription, it is true, appears in the Arabic version, but not in the Targums, and it is safe to conclude that the genealogy which it contains is based on no better authority than many others, which have been framed by credulous men with no evil intent, and have afterwards been set aside as of no historical value or importance. But the whole work which passes under the name of Job is open to remarks militating strongly against the antiquity which some writers have wished to ascribe to it, and also against its acceptance as a real history.

The poem opens with a few lines descriptive of the daily life and prosperity of the patriarch. We are then introduced into the court of Heaven, where among the sons of God who appeared on a certain day to do obeisance, Satan, as we are told, "came also among them." Now this appearance of the Evil One in the court of heaven itself, though highly imaginative and admissible in a religious poem, may fairly be looked upon as not coming within the range of fact, and the conversation which ensues between Satan and the Almighty may justly be compared with the plan of other religious poems, and especially of our own Milton, who deals not only with Satan, but with all Pandemonium in his immortal epic. That God suffers us, his creatures, to be tempted by the principle of Evil, embodied and personified in Satan, the fallen angel, cannot be denied, but that he should give up one man's family to be tested not only by moral temptation but by severe and apparently undeserved calamity can only be accepted as an imaginative thought, framed to bear the superstructure of a moral and religious tale, although it may be admitted that from such tales great moral and religious good often undoubtedly is derived. But the introduction of Satan at all into a Hebrew book implies that the work is later than the date of the Captivity: for the idea of Evil and Good personified, the one in the Creator of the world and the other in the Devil, can be traced satisfactorily to those eastern nations with which the Jews never came closely into contact, until their country was laid waste, their city destroyed, and the people carried captive into a land where their habits, language, and religion derived many new features from those of the Medes, the Persians, and the Babylonians. If these remarks should be thought well founded, we might still receive the Book of Job as one of the most valuable documents which have come down to us, and worthy of being admitted, as it was into the Hebrew, so now also into the Christian Canon.

This conclusion, however, has other supports than that which has just been named. The great age, to which the patriarch is said to have lived, presents another difficulty which seems to admit of solution only in harmony with its later and poetical origin. The history, in our Authorized Version, concludes with these words:

After this lived Job an hundred and forty years, and saw his sons, and his sons' sons, *even* four generations. So Job died, *being* old and full of days.

But the Septuagint translation varies the narrative as follows:

Job lived after his affliction an hundred and seventy years, and all the years that he lived were two hundred and forty; and Job saw his sons and his sons' sons, the fourth generation. And Job died an old man and full of days.

According to the later account the patriarch was seventy years old when evil befel him, and so far the narrative is consistent with the average duration of man's life. But the addition which the Authorized Version following the Hebrew text, as well as the Septuagint translation, make to this number of years, an hundred and forty in the one case, and an hundred and seventy in the other, deserves a more minute examination than implicit faith in the narrative or in the integrity of an ancient text would warrant. It is indeed true that the patriarchs who lived before, and even for some generations after the flood, are said to have lived three times as long as either of the two periods assigned to Job; but it may justly be inquired, and has indeed been doubted, whether the ages of those patriarchs are to be taken as defined by the same denomination of years as that which at present holds good among mankind. I have never seen it remarked, but have often made the observation to myself, that the great age assigned to the patriarchs was a device adopted by the writer to give dignity to the character and to exalt the person of ancient men in the estimation of those for whom those writings were compiled. Nor is this supposition without a parallel: for in those great pictorial works which have been discovered lately in Assyria, and which now ornament the walls of the British Museum and other places, the kings and chieftains are always represented as three or four times as tall and large as the soldiers and dependants who accompany them. The oriental style indeed is fond of such pictures and of such descriptions. If dignity is increased by the device of increasing personal size, why may it not be further elevated by attaching other qualities, such as longer life and similar powers, to the description of those whom the poet, the painter, and the historian equally delight to honour?

Thus the patriarchs of the Bible history would receive additional honour from the Jews, who certainly were not the most enlightened people of antiquity, by the length of age which the writer assigned to them, just in the same way as the gigantic portraits of the Assyrian kings not only now give us a clear idea of their higher rank, but no doubt struck a sort of awe and respect formerly into the eyes of the beholders for whom they were first painted. If this device was adopted by Ezra in the case of the early patriarchs, we may perhaps refer to the same origin the great age of Job, as related in the extract which has here been quoted.

The subject of the work, though based upon the slight framework which the history of Job furnishes, is essentially metaphysical, and as such is different from that of most other books in the Hebrew canon. It abounds indeed with moral maxims, which doubtless were of much practical benefit to the Jewish nation, but the poem turns chiefly on questions concerning the ways of Providence and the moral government of the world. In several parts of it the line of thought runs parallel with that of the Psalms, especially the thirty-seventh and the seventy-third Psalms, and some modern German critics have thought that they could detect a difference of style and breaks here and there, which might have arisen from its having been compiled out of separate compositions blended into one didactic poem. It is the opinion of DeWette, that chapters xxxii—xxxviii have been interpolated, for several reasons, the most striking of which is that a new speaker, Elihu, is introduced instead of Eliphaz: it is also asserted that there is a discrepancy and inconsistency in the doctrine concerning the punishment of the wicked; that in one part of the work, as in chapters xxi and xxiv, they seem to prosper in life and to suffer little by death, whereas elsewhere, as in chapter xxvii, they are described as generally meeting with the reward of their disobedience. These remarks point to the inference that a later date must be taken than that which is commonly assigned—an inference which the introduction of Satan as an actor, and the chief incidents of the drama, as well as the long didactic nature of the book, seem clearly to confirm. Nor is this view refuted or even weakened by the mention which Ezekiel makes of the name Job in that well-known passage,

Though these three men, Noah, Daniel, and Job, were in it, they should deliver but their own souls by their righteousness, saith the Lord. EZEKIEL, xiv, 14.

For it has been well remarked by Mr. Parker, the American editor, that there may have been an ancient tradition of such a character as Job, which was known to Ezekiel, although the book which records the wonderful episode of his life had not then been written. A similar explanation may be given of those passages in Tobit (iv, 12), and in the Epistle of St James (v, ii), where the former simply names him in conjunction with other prophets, and the latter reminds the readers that they have heard of Job's great fame for patience.

But in investigating subjects of ancient history, particularly Jewish history, for which so few records have come down to us, no opinions or suggestions may be slighted, however opposed to the opinions which now exist, and have been always taken for granted among mankind. There are some who, led away by too bold an imagination, believe that not only Job, but Noah also and Daniel, with whom Job is so often connected, and notably by Ezekiel in the passage which has just been quoted, are not to be looked upon as historical, but as legendary characters, round which mythical incidents have been thrown, to teach moral lessons to a people intensely alive to the charms of mythology and wonderful tales of fiction.

§ 2. *The Book of Esther.*

The short book which bears this name contains the history of a Jewish lady, who by her beauty, and perhaps also by her wit, attracted the notice of the King of Persia, and was by him chosen to be his queen. The story may be briefly told as follows:—

Ahasuerus, king of Persia, in the third year of his reign, made a great feast, and with that unseemly vulgarity of conduct, to which we have a parallel in the life of another Asiatic sovereign, sent for his wife, Vashti, that the assembled nobles might see and admire her beauty. The queen, however, more sensible than her husband of the propriety which became her rank, refused to come, and the king appealed to the nobles who were his guests, to know how he should act in such a case. By their advice a foolish decree was passed, and letters sent into all the empire of Persia, "That every man should bear rule in his own house, that Vashti come no more before King Ahasuerus," and that the king should "give her royal estate unto another that is better than she (i, 19—22)." After this the king appointed officers to "gather together all the fair young virgins unto Shushan the palace," that the king might choose one of them to be his queen in the place of Vashti. Among those who came was Hadassah, or Esther, niece to Mordecai, a Jew, whose great grandfather, Kish, had been carried captive to Babylon by Nebuchadnezzar with Jeconiah king of Judah. The king's choice fell upon Esther, and "in the tenth month, which is the month Tebeth, of the seventh year of his reign" (ii, 16), she was taken into the palace.

About this time Haman was the king's favourite, and a great man at his court, and every one did him homage except Mordecai the Jew. In revenge for this slight, Haman laid plans for putting to death all the Jews throughout the kingdom of Ahasuerus, and with this object in view, he had recourse to the prevailing science of those times and of that country.

In the first month, that is the month Nisan, in the twelfth year of King Ahasuerus, they cast Pur, that is, the lot, before Haman from day to day, and from month to month, to the twelfth month, that is, the month Adar (iii, 7).

The lots, we may suppose, were until then unfavourable, but in that month Haman offered the king ten thousand talents of silver, and obtained permission to do what he pleased with all the Jews throughout Persia.

Letters were sent by posts into all the king's provinces, to destroy, to kill, and to cause to perish, all Jews, both young and old, little children and women, in one day, even upon the thirteenth day of the twelfth month, which is the month Adar, and to take the spoil of them for a prey (iii, 13).

Mordecai now goes to the queen, and at his urgent request, Esther, risking her life, as it is related, by appearing unsummoned in the presence of the king, presents herself before him, has the golden sceptre held out towards her, and invites the king to meet Haman at a banquet which she has prepared. Haman, anticipating the success of his schemes against Mordecai, erects a gallows, seventy feet high, on which to hang his rival, but is checked in his ambition by having to do public honour to Mordecai for the discovery which the latter made of a conspiracy against the king's life. This check reverses the course of things. Esther obtains from the king permission that the Jews should defend themselves against those who were to assail them by virtue of the king's previous decree.

Thus the Jews smote all their enemies with the stroke of the sword, and slaughter, and destruction, and did what they would unto those that hated them. And in Shushan the palace the Jews slew and destroyed five hundred men. . . . . The ten sons of Haman, the son of Hammedatha, the enemy of the Jews, slew they; but on the spoil laid they not their hand (ix, 5—10).

It seems this was not enough to gratify the vindictive spirit of the queen. Another day was given up to the slaughter; three hundred more were killed in the palace, and the bodies of Haman's ten sons were hanged upon the gallows.

But the other Jews that were in the king's provinces gathered themselves together, and stood for their lives, and had rest from their enemies, and slew of their foes seventy and five thousand, but they laid not their hands on the spoil.

After these events we are not surprised to read that Haman was himself hanged on his own gallows, that Queen Esther was confirmed in the influence she had obtained over the king, and that Mordecai the Jew was "next unto King Ahasuerus and great among the Jews, and accepted of the multitude of his brethren, seeking the wealth of his people, and speaking peace to all his seed."

Such is a short outline of the narrative contained in the Book of Esther, but it labours under such patent difficulties that it is impossible to regard it as a history of events which really happened, and its legendary character, if sufficiently established, may be accepted as an additional proof, if any further proof be wanted beyond the fact of its being found among the Hagiographa, that it was written in the later days of the Jewish Commonwealth. That the work is a moral tale and not a real history, will appear from the following remarks :

No such king as Ahasuerus ever reigned in Persia. Darius the Mede, who conquered the Babylonians, lived only two years afterwards. Cambyses reigned too short a time ; for we read in chapter iii, verse 6, of the twelfth year of the reign of King Ahasuerus. Of those who succeeded to the throne of Persia, Darius might be supposed to be meant, if we took the name of his queen, Atossa, to be represented by Hadassah, the other name of Esther; but Atossa had four sons born after she became queen, and nothing is said of her husband, Darius, having divorced a previous queen. Xerxes also has been thought likely to be described under the name of Ahasuerus, and those who think so suppose that the expedition into Greece occupied the three years of his reign between the third when Vashti was divorced and the seventh when Esther was raised to the throne in her stead. But this delay seems improbable, and the narrative seems to exclude the possibility of such a solution. The king apparently remained at Shushan, and the young women from whom he was to select his queen, became in the meanwhile his concubines: for we read at ii, 12—13:

Now when every maid's turn was come to go in to King Ahasuerus, after that she had been twelve months, according to the manner of the women (for so were the days of their purifications accomplished, to wit, six months with oil of myrrh, and six months with sweet odours, and with other things for the purifying of the women;) then thus came every maiden unto the king; whatsoever she desired was given her to go with her out of the house of the women unto the king's house. In the evening she went, and on the morrow she returned into the second house of the women, to the custody of Shaashgaz, the king's chamberlain, which kept the concubines; she came in unto the king no more, except the king delighted in her, and that she were called by name.

But if Xerxes was Ahasuerus, and if he was absent in Greece during these three or four years, the whole story of Vashti and Esther is not true; for Herodotus (ix, 108—110) tells us that he had his queen, Amestris, with him whilst he was at Sardis, organizing and directing the expedition against Greece: nor does the apparent similarity of sound between Esther and Amestris help us out of the difficulty which the appearance of the latter in the narrative creates. But to return to the course of events.

The turn of Esther came, and, as has been already said, she was raised to be queen in the tenth month of the seventh year of the king's reign, and no exception can be taken to the mode of selection which the king adopted, or to its result, however repugnant it may be to our modern European notions.

But the proclamation that every man should bear rule in his own house is too absurd to have ever issued from the court of a Persian king. And it cannot be believed that any monarch, either of an eastern or western empire, would allow a whole nation of his subjects to be cut off in one day by their fellow-subjects for no pretext or crime at all, and it is thought that the Jewish people at that time may have amounted to two or three millions. Nor would the king have given back to Haman the ten thousand talents, which is three millions of our money, even if Haman had been so rich or so foolish as to offer them. Nor again is it likely that a king, having issued an unwise order that one part of his people should be put to death without a cause, would endeavour to remedy it by giving counter orders that they should defend themselves by slaying the others. It is only in a legend that we read of seventy-five thousand having been slain in one day, whilst not one Jew appears to have fallen. Nor is there the slightest proof in history or probability, from the nature of the case, that the laws of the Medes and Persians were unalterable. The nobility who surrounded the king may have wished occasionally to hold him to a decree which gratified them: but no civilized nation or absolute monarch would ever bind themselves to a law which forbade them to retract or remedy any previous error they might have committed.

These and many other minor inconsistencies compel us to relegate the Book of Esther to the realm of fiction, and the more so that no other work in the Hebrew Canon has less reference to the power of the Creator: it has indeed been remarked that the name of God does not once occur in the whole of this book. But, whilst we maintain that it is a moral fiction, written probably to show that virtue will finally emerge from trial and from distress, there are certain passages in the book which point to real facts, and may lead us to interpret truly the meaning and drift of this fictitious narrative.

In the Second Book of Maccabees (xv, 36) we read of the "thirteenth day of the twelfth month, which in the Syrian tongue is called Adar, the day before Mardocheus's day." Mardocheus is the Greek name for Mordecai, and it appears from the words above quoted that the fourteenth day of the month Adar was called Mardocheus's day at the time when the second book was written, that is, later than 160 B.C., the date of the last event which is related in that book. Still later than this date is the notice by Josephus that two days, the 14th and the 15th of Adar, were kept sacred by the Jews. The feast of Purim, so called from Pur, a lot, was then celebrated, and we need not doubt that its object was to perpetuate the memory of some deliverance of the Jews from evil which had been brought about by means of a Jew named Mordecai, and we may accept the narrative contained in the Book of Esther as correctly fixing the scene of the deliverance and the residence of Mordecai in Susa, the capital city of the Persian empire.

The feast of Purim was then introduced among the Jews. We read in Esther, ix, 30—32 :

He (Mordecai) sent the letters unto all the Jews, to the hundred and twenty and seven provinces of the kingdom of Ahasuerus, with words of peace and truth, To confirm these days of Purim in their times appointed, according as Mordecai the Jew and Esther the queen had enjoined them, and as they had decreed for themselves and for their seed, the matters of the fastings and their cry. And the decree of Esther confirmed these matters of Purim; and it was written in the book.

So far it appears that the feast of Purim was established at some time before Alexander conquered the Persian empire, and probably between the years 400 and 500 B.C. But at this point, however, we must cease to follow the narrative of Esther. The Jewish nation, oscillating during its whole existence beyond rebellion and superstition, were never lower in the scale of intellectual humanity than during the three centuries which immediately preceded the Christian era, and it is probable that the origin of the feast of Purim was soon lost among the Jews who lived at Jerusalem and in Judea, especially as the events which led to its institution had happened at the court of Persia. The feast itself was still kept, whilst its origin was forgotten. The mass of the people in all countries think little of the signification of those solemnities, holidays, and rejoicings which give them pleasure. But where history fails, legend steps in and occupies the vacant ground. The forefathers of the Jews had found many such stories to explain why certain names Gilgal, Bethel, and others had been given to certain sacred places, and in like manner the legend of Esther was evolved out of certain well-known facts amplified by the desire to do honour to their forefathers, and so to relieve their ancestry from the dark shadows which hovered over them since the cessation of their ancient scriptures, and the more humble dependent situation which they occupied among the surrounding nations.

§ 3. *The Book of Daniel.*

In a previous chapter of this work the Book of Daniel has been placed among those which form the Second or Prophetical Portion of the Hebrew Scriptures. But, as was then remarked, it is proposed also to present the work under different points of view, with the sanction, it is believed, of those who deem it not only lawful, but desirable to examine every part of the Canon with that freedom of inquiry which alone can elicit truth.

The literary history of the Ancients, as well as that of the Moderns, shows that Fact and Fiction are equally the vehicles of Morality and Religion, and there is no want of examples in which the two elements are blended in the same work. The celebrated Greek historian Xenophon is thought to have indulged his imagination in many particulars of the Life of Cyrus, which do not seem to agree well with what is considered the more authentic narrative of Herodotus. The history of Alexander the Great also is less certainly ascertained from the want of agreement between the historians Arrian and Quintus Curtius, the only authors who have written expressly about his life. There seems to be room for supposing that Historical and Moral Fiction is not alien from the genius of the Hebrews, and that works of that character may have been admitted into the volume which contains all their remaining literature, as well as all the records and documents of their religion. The Books of Job and Esther, as already stated in the first and second sections of this chapter, have been proposed as examples, the first of a pure Moral Fiction, and the second of a Fiction, based upon a solemnity existing among the Jews, connected with historical names and well-known countries, but derived from an origin of which the nature and all its circumstances had been effaced by time. If then the Book of Daniel should be found to bear marks of a similar origin and of similar authorship, we should be relieved from that mass of conjectures by which the subject has been for ages surrounded, and the whole Canon would be brought under a reasonable view consistent with the nature of things, and in harmony with what we know both of Jewish history and that of other nations.

Some writers have indeed asserted that the fictitious character of this book cannot be maintained even in its circumstantial details, and that the collectors of the canonical books would not have been so credulous as to receive among the sacred writings, held by the people to be divine, a supposititious book ascribed to the old prophet Daniel, which appeared in the Maccabæan period. But Dr Davidson, in his "Introduction to the Old Testament" (iii, p. 162) justly replies that the Jewish Synagogue would have admitted any book belonging to the national collection, however inferior to Daniel, and that the testimony of the Jewish Synagogue is often insecure and worthless.

I have treated, cursorily it is true, of the Book of Daniel in the chapter assigned to the Greater Prophets generally, amongst whom Daniel stands the fourth, because, whatever may be our opinion of the writing which bears his name, we need not deny that he was a real prophet, who had been carried captive when a boy to Babylon, and was afterwards esteemed by his countrymen for his piety and talents. But, as in the case of the other three Greater Prophets, so also in that of Daniel, it has been disputed whether the book has come down to us in its original state, and whether parts of it have not been lost, which would have given to it more the appearance of a connected narrative. This question however seems to be of greater weight in the case of Daniel from the fact that certain additions to the narrative, which did not exist in the Hebrew text, are found in the Greek version of the Septuagint. To the other works which pass under the names of the Prophets, whether Greater or Lesser, no such appendices are to be found, unless we regard in that light certain portions of Isaiah, Jeremiah, and perhaps Ezekiel, which are thought by some critics to present marks of later and more feeble authorship.

Before we proceed to consider the reasons which may be alleged in favour of the views which have been expressed above concerning this book, it is desirable that we should meet the argument which lies against it from the mention made of Daniel by our Saviour in the New Testament. The only two passages occur in the Gospels according to St

Matthew and St Mark in almost similar words as they here follow:

MATTHEW, xxiv, 15. When ye therefore shall see the abomination of desolation, spoken of by Daniel the prophet, stand in the holy place, (whoso readeth, let him understand :) then let them which be in Judæa flee unto the mountains.	MARK, xiii, 14. But when ye shall see the abomination of desolation, spoken of by Daniel the prophet, standing where it ought not, (let him that readeth understand,) then let them that be in Judæa flee to the mountains.

The words of our Lord have been supposed to sanction the belief that Daniel, as author of the book which bears his name, had prophesied a certain abomination of desolation which was to happen to Jerusalem, and that Jesus himself adopting the words of Daniel made them his own, and prophesied that the same was on the point of immediate fulfilment. But this is by no means the only interpretation of our Lord's words which they admit, nor does our Saviour's quotation of words from the Book of Daniel imply that Daniel must on his authority be deemed to be the writer of the book. It was the practice of our Lord at all times to fall in with the belief, whether erroneous or not, of his countrymen, on all matters of science and of literature. The writers of the Gospel, as well as St Paul, and indeed all the Apostles, adopted this mode of speaking and of acting. Demoniacal possession, the water following the camp of the Israelites, alluded to in a previous page, the sun standing still, besides other matters, are all facts which were universally accepted in their strict literal form; and the numberless passages quoted from the prophets and other writers of the Old Testament to confirm things related in the New, all furnish illustrations of my present meaning. An instance of this may be given in the quotation applied to our Lord in St Matthew's Gospel:

ii, 15. That it might be fulfilled which was spoken of the Lord by the prophet, Out of Egypt have I called my son.

The only passage in the Old Testament which is at all similar to this occurs in the prophecy of Hosea (xi, 1), where we read:

When Israel was a child, then I loved him, and called my son out of Egypt.

No one can affirm and it is impossible to believe, that Hosea, when he wrote those words, intended to foretell that Jesus the Messiah was represented by Israel, and would in process of time be called out of Egypt. The writer in the Gospel merely institutes a comparison between Israel personified and Jesus Christ. He quotes the words of the prophet in the same way as we quote lines of poetry which seem well to represent our immediate subject, without the remotest idea that the lines had reference to it in the mind of the original writer. Thus our Saviour, foretelling the destruction which in a few years was about to happen to Jerusalem, describes it as an "abominable devastation, to use the words of the prophet Daniel," and not as the very devastation to which allusion is made in the book of that prophet.

But there are two other passages, one in Ezekiel (xiv, 14—20) and the other in the First Book of Maccabees, in which the name of Daniel is mentioned with respect, as that of an eminent prophet: and whilst the former of these, in which Daniel is joined with Noah and Job as characters highly esteemed for piety by the people, has no relation whatever to any book passing under his name, the latter, although apparently quoting from the book itself, will be found by no means to refer to an earlier date than the latter half of the second century before the birth of Christ. The words of the writer are these:

I MACCABEES, ii, 59, 60. Ananias, Azarias, and Misael, by believing were saved out of the flame. Daniel for his innocency was delivered from the mouth of lions.

If the narrative of events which led to Daniel's being cast into the den of lions, as well as that which is told of Ananias, Azarias and Misael, who were cast into the fiery furnace, shall appear to be Moral Fictions composed for the purpose of showing God's protection of his faithful servants amid the evils and temptations of the world, the words of the writer just cited might still be as applicable as if they referred to the most indisputable history.

The youthful Daniel and his three companions were taken

into the palace of Nebuchadnezzar, and, having been made eunuchs, as Josephus tells us, *Ant.* x, 10, and as we gather from the Book of Daniel (i, 3, &c.), they rose at once into great favour with the king. That they had aspirations of ambition from the first is evident from one particular of their conduct which Josephus tells us in his History. They adopted a vegetarian diet, and gave the other more costly kinds of food allowed them to Ashpenaz, the keeper of the eunuchs, thereby securing the favour of this official, which might greatly aid them afterwards in their ambitious views.

Soon after this, King Nebuchadnezzar dreamed a dream, and forgot what it was about. The Chaldæans and wise men were summoned, and naturally disclaimed all power to explain a dream which the dreamer himself had forgotten. The alternative was that all the wise men of Babylon should be put to death, and we read that "they sought Daniel and his fellows to be slain also." From this fate they were however saved by the prayers of the four Hebrew youths. God revealed to Daniel in a vision the secret of the dream, and the Chaldæans were saved.

But the chronology of this period is not in perfect harmony with the narrative. Nebuchadnezzar, it seems, carried Daniel a youth to Babylon in the third year of Jehoiakim king of Judah. But this was not the first year of Nebuchadnezzar's reign, and if the dream was explained in the second year of Nebuchadnezzar, Daniel was still a youth, and his position in the palace was such that he could hardly have discharged the duty of interpreter of dreams recorded of him. Neither would the king have allowed those who were admitted to such intimacy in the palace to be destroyed without a cause, even if Oriental tyranny could have gone so far as to consign to death the other Chaldæans who were unable to do what no human intellect could ever have succeeded in doing. We are therefore driven to the alternative already named, that the narrative of the king's dream proceeded from the invention of the writer to do honour to a man who had risen to eminence during the evil days of the Jewish commonwealth, and whose name had come down to posterity as that of one of their greatest prophets.

Difficulties of the same nature attend, not only the three fabulous and childish stories which are given in Greek in the Apocrypha, but also the remaining chapters of the Hebrew book. The king, who had witnessed the superior power of Jehovah, the god of the Hebrews, in interpreting his dream, could hardly, save in an Oriental fable, have set up an image for men to worship, and have condemned to the burning fiery furnace those very men who worshipped Jehovah, and would not approach the image "which Nebuchadnezzar the king had set up."

I shall not proceed further in examining the details of this book. The subject has been so fully entered into by some of the first writers of the day that there is no difficulty in ascertaining whatever can be said in favour of the late origin of the work, or in favour of its having been written by the hand of Daniel himself.

That it was written about the middle of the second century before Christ, may fairly be deduced from the following arguments:

1. That it consists of separate short narratives very inartistically put together, and inconsistent with themselves in many particulars.

2. That the prophetical passages are in every respect different from those which are found in the earlier prophetic writings, being confused in meaning, and arithmetical in form.

3. That they look like prophecies of the evils which befel the Jews from Antiochus, the Greek king of Assyria, and which the writer, then alive and cautious what he wrote, ascribed to the pen of an old well-known prophet, who was safe from suffering any punishment for the boldness of his predictions.

4. That parts of the book are of an apocalyptic character, turning much on the agency of dreams, and visions, such as rarely occur in the previous books, but which belong to the whole period of the later Jewish state for 200 years down to the Christian era.

5. That its first appearance in conjunction with other writings in the Hagiographa or latest portion of the Jewish Canon seems due to no other cause than that it was only first compiled or collected when it was first published.*

* I have here in this chapter on Daniel not thought it needful to enter more largely into the subject; as it forms only a portion of this work,

CHAPTER XXVIII.

FURTHER DISCREPANCIES, ANACHRONISMS, ERRORS, LAWS AND CUSTOMS NEGLECTED OR FORGOTTEN IN THE BOOKS OF THE OLD TESTAMENT GENERALLY, SHOWING THAT THEY ARE NOT CONTEMPORARY RECORDS, BUT COMPILED LATER THAN THE BABYLONISH CAPTIVITY.

IN the preceding chapters I have attempted to prove from internal evidence, discoverable in the several Books of the Old Testament, that they are not the productions of Moses, Joshua, Samuel, and others, to whom they are commonly attributed, but are rather to be taken collectively as a compilation from original records, made at a time when the Israelitish people began to show a disposition, common to all nations, to inquire into the history of their remote ancestors. That this view of the matter is well founded seems fairly to result from the examination to which the Books of the Old Testament have been severally submitted. The same inference will follow from other instances of internal evidence gathered from the same books taken collectively, differing partly somewhat in character from those already brought forward, but equally valuable for the purpose of establishing my present argument.

Under this head will fall all those historical narratives, involving errors, discrepancies, anachronisms, laws and customs, neglected or not observed, and other inconsistencies, which Moses, Joshua, and Samuel, *may* undoubtedly have written, but which it is extremely improbable that teachers and prophets such as they were *would* have written. The collective weight of these passages will be as great as is

---

which embraces many other points, all combining, it is thought, to establish the same conclusion; but the reader who wishes to enter more fully into the subject may consult the "Sibyline Oracles," the Books of Esdras in the Apocrypha, besides the modern treatises which have been written about the Book of Daniel.

furnished by those which have been produced in the foregoing chapters, and which certainly could not have been written by the authors to whom they are ascribed.

§ 1.

Close connexion of the narrative from Genesis to the Second Book of Kings—The Prophets and the Psalms similarly classified.

One of the arguments which have been adduced in this work for the assertion that the Old Testament is up to a certain point a continuous narrative—i.e. continuous as far as a compilation can be, which gives many of the several legends entire, and puts them together without much art to conceal the joining—is the close historical connection observable between the various divisions of the volume. Now, as it is evident that the Second Book of Kings must have been written after the Babylonish Captivity, because it relates things which happened many years after that event, and the narrative up to that point is continuous from Genesis, it follows that the whole Bible to the end of the Second Book of Kings must have been compiled at a later period than the captivity of Babylon. It has the decided appearance of being one complete work, written nearly at the same time. Such would be the generally received opinion of those who are conversant with books and the various questions which relate to them.

So much then having been said for these books, we may notice in the second place, that a similar classification was made of the Prophets, although these, being not historical but didactic, could not be put into a similarly connected narrative as the books which precede them. They were however placed one after another in a series according to their greater or lesser importance, and were from their first publication known by the name of the Prophets, to indicate the nature of the contents.

The remaining works were at a still later period collected, forming the third portion of the present Canon, and these, taking the name from the chief book comprised in the class and the chief writer of that book, were denominated the Psalms of David.

This view of the structure of the Old Testament has been already adverted to in a previous chapter. But we are now able to explain the position of some of these books which otherwise might seem anomalous. Twelve books, it appears, were put forth to form the last portion of the Canon: but it was not possible that all these should be embodied with the preceding books, some of which were not only dissimilar, but even in some instances contradictory. Wherever indeed this was possible, when the last classification of the Scriptural volume was arranged, the narrative was made continuous, as in the case of Ruth, which, although discovered and published later, was placed at the end of Judges, of which it forms a portion and an episode. The Book of Daniel also was placed after Ezekiel, as being next to that prophet in quantity of matter and importance, but before the twelve shorter books which pass under the name of the Minor Prophets. This, however, was the limit, beyond which the arrangement could not farther be carried out. The Books of Chronicles were of a different character and tendency in every respect from the Kings. It was necessary to place them distinct from the others, and they are followed by Ezra and Nehemiah, the former of which singularly begins with the same two verses which conclude the history of the Chronicles. Thus then six of the miscellaneous productions of a later date being accounted for, the remaining six, Esther, Job, Psalms, Proverbs, Ecclesiastes and the Song of Solomon, were placed together in the Canon in the order in which they are here enumerated. It may be difficult to say why they were placed before the prophets, nor indeed is it necessary to go into all the minutiæ connected with such a subject. The literary or antiquarian student will be satisfied that such a Book as the Bible has come down to our times, although he may be unable to answer questions which might be asked respecting its contents; and the theologian will think it unimportant to entertain even wider questions than the present, satisfied that he has in this Book a higher and more complete system of morality and religion than any other that has yet been promulgated among mankind. I shall, however, venture hereafter, when entering on the subject of the Christian books of the New Testament in the second volume of this work, to propose a theory, which would explain why the three divisions of the Old Testament are placed in their present order, so similar as it is to that which is found in the later Christian canon. In the meanwhile we will revert to those further points in the Hebrew writings which it is proposed to investigate in the present chapter.

§ 2. *Inconsistencies concerning Abraham and Sarah.*

Two extraordinary inconsistencies are found in the history of Abraham and Sarah, which, as far as I can discover, have not been noticed by any of the commentators. Abraham is said to have been 100 years old, and Sarah 90, at the birth of Isaac, as appears by Genesis, xvii, 17:

Then Abraham fell upon his face, and laughed, and said in his heart, Shall a child be born unto him that is an hundred years old, and shall Sarah, that is ninety years old, bear?

Soon after this, as we read in the next chapter three men of a mysterious character, supposed to be angels, were entertained by Abraham under a tree.

9. And they said unto him, Where is Sarah thy wife? And he said, Behold, in the tent. 10. And he said, I will certainly return unto thee according to the time of life; and lo, Sarah thy wife shall have a son." And Sarah heard it in the tent door which was behind him. 11. Now Abraham and Sarah were old and well stricken in age, and it ceased to be with Sarah after the manner of women. 12. Therefore Sarah laughed within herself saying, After I am waxed old shall I have pleasure, my lord being old also?

It seems then that Abraham and Sarah both laughed at the promise of a son, seeing that her husband was in his hundredth year, and she ninety years old, when Isaac was born. In fact she was already an old woman; and this is repeated in Genesis, xxi, 2:

For Sarah conceived, and bare Abraham a son in his old age, at the set time of which God had spoken to him.

But it would appear that the birth of Isaac did not follow close upon the promise which had been made to his father and mother. Between the events which occurred under the tree in the plains of Mamre, related in chapter xviii, and the birth of Isaac, as told in Chapter xxi, 1, we find that Sarah is made to pass for Abraham's sister and carried away to the court of King Abimelech, no doubt on account of her beauty, which would render her fit to be admitted into the harem of an eastern king. Through fear of God's wrath however she is restored, and Abraham explaining the deception which he had practised, receives large presents from the king for interceding with God in his behalf.

This surely did not happen after she was ninety years old. The events have probably been misplaced by a compiler; as has also been the case with the second discrepancy which occurs in the same part of the history.

Sarah lived thirty-seven years longer, as we learn from what follows:

GEN. xxiii, 1—2. And Sarah was an hundred and seven and twenty years old: these were the years of the life of Sarah. And Sarah died in Kirjath-arba: the same is Hebron in the land of Canaan: and Abraham came to mourn for Sarah, and to weep for her.

Abraham was therefore 137 years old when Sarah died: yet he is said to have married again, and to have begotten six children.

GEN. xxv, 1—2. Then again Abraham took a wife, and her name was Keturah. And she bare him Zimran, and Jokshan, and Medan, and Midian, and Ishbak, and Shuah.

This account is repugnant to what went before. If Abraham, at the age of 100 years, laughed at the idea of his having a son, how does it happen that, when he is thirty-seven years older, he marries again and begets six children? We may easily believe that he was unlikely to have a son at the age of one hundred years, and this improbability would increase with every succeeding year. There is no reason for believing that the children, which were born to Abraham from Keturah, were children of promise, like Isaac; and the only supposition by which the inconsistency can be explained, is that Abraham had taken Keturah to wife at an earlier period of his life; for polygamy was common in those days, and no less likely to have been practised by Abraham than it confessedly was by Abraham's grandson, Jacob, in the case of Leah, Rachel, and their two handmaids his concubines.

This explanation, however, compels us to believe, not that Moses wrote the narrative, but a compiler in a later age, who ranges in successive dates events which really were contemporaneous.

§ 3. *Inaccuracies concerning Jacob's children.*

In Genesis, xxxv, 26—after the names of Jacob's children, we read, "These are the sons of Jacob, which were born to him in Padan-Aram." But it is well known that Benjamin was born, some years after Jacob came back into Canaan. The text therefore is inaccurate, and creates a serious difficulty, if we suppose that Moses, writing in the presence of God, could have been liable to such an error. If, again, "some careless or injudicious transcriber," as Dr Shuckford supposes, "finding the words *in Padan-Aram* in Genesis xlvi, 15, might add them here also," our want of confidence is merely transferred from Moses to the book itself; it is impossible to fix limits to this work of interpolation, and the only safe ground for the inquirer is furnished by the supposition that the compiler put together his account long after the events had happened, and when no more certain information could be procured.

An error is found also in the other catalogue of Jacob's children, who accompanied him into Egypt. At Genesis, xlvi, 8—25, we have their names, and in verse 26 it is said:

All the souls that came with Jacob into Egypt which came out of his loins, besides Jacob's sons' wives, all the souls were three score and six.

This total is erroneous, for the names really amount to sixty-seven; and a still greater difference is found between the Hebrew text and the Septuagint in the 27th verse; the former makes "all the souls of the house of Jacob" to be "three score and ten;" whereas the latter states them to have been seventy five.

We might set aside the authority of the Septuagint as inferior to that of the Hebrew in such a matter, were it not that in St Stephen's speech, in the seventh chapter and fourteenth verse of the Acts of the Apostles, the number 75 is repeated, and an awkward dilemma is created, from which it is impossible to extricate ourselves, if these conflicting accounts are to be considered as having come down to us in their original state. This may with justice be called in question; for Dean Shuckford, who supposes that the transcribers have added something in the thirty-fifth chapter, accuses them of having omitted something in the forty-sixth, of having added verse 27 to the forty-sixth chapter in the Septuagint, which is more full than the Hebrew, and lastly of having altered 70 into 75 in the seventh chapter of the Acts. It is difficult to imagine how a book, with which such liberties have been taken, can properly be regarded as an immaculate record. Nor can these different copies be both regarded as undoubtedly free from the charge of dishonesty; for it is easy to suppose that copyists may by accident or want of care omit sentences of limited length from the work which they are copying or translating. But it is difficult to believe that a translator can with singleness of purpose insert additional sentences not found in the original text. When therefore we find, in more than one instance, in the Septuagint a verse which is omitted in the Hebrew Bible, it is a fair inference that some copyist of the latter has inadvertently passed over that verse, whereas the Septuagint writer found it in that copy of the Hebrew Bible which he was using when he made the Greek translation where it now appears.

But the interpretation, which turns upon the addition or the omission of a verse in different copies or translations of the same book, is wholly inapplicable to explain such remarkable facts as the enumeration of ten sons of Benjamin and two grandsons of Judah, among those who went down with Jacob into Egypt. The famine throughout the land of Canaan was what drove the patriarch and his family out of that country; and Benjamin, if we may trust the chronologers, was under twenty years of age. Yet in the forty-sixth chapter of Genesis, verse 19, where the family of Jacob are reckoned by name, to make up the whole number of those who accompanied their father into Egypt, we read as follows:

The sons of Rachel Jacob's wife; Joseph and Benjamin. And unto Joseph in the land of Egypt were born Manasseh and Ephraim, which Asenath the daughter of Potipherah, priest of On, bare unto him.

And the sons of Benjamin were Belah, and Becher, and Ashbel, Gera, and Naaman, Ehi, and Rosh, Muppim, and Huppim, and Ard.

These are the sons of Rachel, which were born to Jacob : all the souls were fourteen.

Compare with this the account given in I Chronicles, vii, 6:

"The sons of Benjamin: Bela, and Becheor, and Jediael, three."

And again compare with it chapter viii, 1, of the same book of Chronicles.

Now Benjamin begat Bela his first-born, Ashbel the second, and Aharah the third, Noah the fourth, and Rapha the fifth.

From a comparison of these texts, it is doubtful whether Benjamin had three, five, or ten sons, but, if our tables of chronology have any claim to accuracy, it is certain that none of them were born before the family went down to Egypt, and that the Jewish mythical number of seventy persons must have consisted of others than the ten children of a young man who had not yet reached his twentieth year. A similar case of inaccuracy is found in the twelfth verse of the same forty-sixth chapter of Genesis. The grandsons of Judah, Hezron and Hamul, are also reckoned among the "seventy," but these two could not have been born until many years later; for Pharez their father was only two or three years old, when the whole family first entered the land of their servitude.

§ 4.

Different accounts of the length of time which the Israelites sojourned in Egypt.

Among the many chronological difficulties which meet the reader of the Old Testament, may be noticed the uncertainty about the length of time which the Israelites spent in Egypt. The first impression which the Bible narrative tends to convey is that 400 years passed between the settling of Jacob's family in Egypt and the Exodus under

Moses. This was the period of time foretold to Abraham in Genesis.

But there is a variation from this number in other passages where the subject is referred to: for in Exodus, xii, 40-41, the number is stated to be, not four hundred, but four hundred and thirty years. The same variation is observable in two places of the New Testament, Acts, vii, 6, where we read four hundred, and in Galatians, iii, 17, four hundred and thirty years. The difference between these numbers is not important, if the book in which it occurs is to be judged by the same standard as other works of history; but if, on the other hand, not only its spirit but also its letter and style are to be considered as possessing an original authority which commands our belief without inquiry, and forbids us to test its accuracy, the variation of thirty years becomes a serious discrepancy, militating greatly against the pretension of infallibility.

It remains to adduce the passages where the subject is mentioned, and to endeavour to solve the difficulty which they present.

EXODUS, xii, 40-41. Now the sojourning of the children of Israel, who dwelt in Egypt, was four hundred and thirty years. And it came to pass at the end of the four hundred and thirty years, even the self-same day it came to pass, that all the hosts of the Lord went out from the land of Egypt.

The obvious inference is that 430 years passed between the arrival of Jacob with his children and the Exodus under Moses, and that the two events, the coming and the going, took place on the same day of the year.

But in the popular Commentary on the Bible the following note occurs:

The sojourning of the children of Egypt.] This includes their fathers Abraham, Isaac, and Jacob; and their sojourning in the land of Canaan as well as in Egypt. From the time of Abraham's coming from Charran into the land of Canaan, when this sojourning began, till the going of his descendants out of Egypt, was just 430 years. From this arrival in Canaan to the birth of Isaac was 25 years; Isaac was 60 years old when he begat Jacob: and Jacob was 130 years old when he went down into Egypt, making together 215 years: and from his family's coming into Egypt till their departure was just 215 more.

This note alters the language of the text, but does not explain it. How can the "sojourning of the children of Israel who dwelt in Egypt" be supposed to begin 215 years before any of the children of Israel ever were in Egypt? Abraham certainly visited Egypt two hundred and fifteen years before, but he did not sojourn there, and in his time there were no children of Israel; for this name was first given to his grandson, Jacob. Besides which it is plainly written that the "hosts of the Lord," i.e., the children of Israel, came *out* of Egypt, "on the self-same day," i.e., as they had gone *in*, four hundred and thirty years before. This cannot apply to Abraham, whose visit to Egypt had nothing to do with the slavery of his posterity in that country so many years afterwards.

Neither is it certain that two hundred and fifteen is the correct number of years between the visit of Abraham and the journey of Jacob, when he went to settle with his family in Egypt. We find in Genesis, xii, 4, that "Abram was seventy-five years old when he departed out of Haran:" but we are not told that he went directly into Egypt: he may have resided some years in Canaan before he went down into Egypt, and so the interval would have been less than two hundred and fifteen years by the exact number of years that he first remained in Canaan.

It is also without good grounds that the commentators calculate two hundred and fifteen years to have passed between the settling of Jacob's family in Egypt and the time of the Exodus. The Bible furnishes but very slender data for ascertaining the exact length of this interval. In Exodus, vi, 16—20, we learn that Levi lived 137 years, his son Kohath 133, whose son Amram lived 137 years, whose son Moses was 80 years old, when he led the Israelites out of Egypt. But these dates do not supply a total of 215 years; though they seem, by exhibiting four generations, to bear some reference to Genesis, xv, 13, where the promise, made originally to Abraham, is found:

GEN. xv, 13. And He said unto Abram, Know of a surety 'hat thy seed shall be a stranger in a land that is not theirs, and shall serve them; and they shall afflict them four hundred years: And also that nation, whom they shall serve, will I judge: and afterward shall they come out with great substance. And thou shalt go to thy fathers in peace; thou shalt be buried in a good old age. But in the fourth generation they shall come hitherto again: for the iniquity of the Amorites is not yet full."

Here we have a notice of 400 years, extending, it would seem, through four generations; which must clearly be counted from Jacob and not from Abraham, for if we reckon from Abraham, we make six generations, Isaac, Jacob, Levi, Kohath, Amram, Moses. Thus we are involved in a double difficulty: if the sojourning lasted 430 years, it runs through six generations; but if it runs through only four generations, it may have lasted no more than 215 years. Bishops Patrick and Kidder have annotated on the last passage, as if it were clear and intelligible like any other part of history ancient or modern, and presented no difficulty whatever to the critical inquirer.

And he said unto Abram, &c.] Three things were to befall Abram's seed: 1st, That they "should be a stranger in a land not theirs;" and they sojourned partly in Canaan, partly in Egypt: 2dly, That they should "serve;" and they did serve the Egyptians: 3dly, They should be "afflicted;" and so the Israelites were in a great degree, a long time before they came out of Egypt. The time from the birth of Isaac to the deliverance of the Israelites from Egypt was 400 years.

But this is an evasion, not an explanation of the text—for the "affliction," the "servitude," did not begin in Canaan, but in Egypt, and it was to last, either 400 years, in round numbers, or 430 years, if the calculation is exact. This point, however, cannot now be cleared up, and the same variation is found in the New Testament also, where a reference is made to the sojourning in Egypt.

ACTS, vii, 6. And God spake on this wise, That his [Abraham's] seed should sojourn in a strange land; and that they should bring them into bondage, and entreat them evil 400 years.

But this evil-entreating according to the commentators lasted much less than even 215 years, for Jacob was treated well by the Egyptians whilst he was in Egypt, and so were his family for many years, until the new king arose "who knew not Joseph." From this difficulty, it might be thought, we are relieved by a passage in Saint Paul's Epistle to the Galatians.

GALATIANS, iii, 17. And this I say, that the covenant that was confirmed before of God in Christ, the law, which was four hundred and thirty years after, cannot disannul, that it should make the promise of none effect.

But St Paul's authority, great as it might be on a matter touching morals or religion, is not to be taken as conclusive on a subject of history or chronology. The text before us only shows his view of the case. His words only imply the current opinion, or possibly that he also had remarked the impossibility of compressing 430 years into the interval between Jacob's descent into Egypt and the Exodus of his descendants; and that he solved it by reckoning that number of years from the call of Abraham: *if*, at least, St Paul *did* so reckon them. For his words are doubtful. He may, after all, have supposed that the children of Israel were actually 430 years in Egypt; for he only says that the Law given by Moses, i.e., at the Exodus, was 430 years later than the Promise which had been before given by God. But the Promise was given to Isaac and Jacob, as well as to Abraham, and it is at all events doubtful whether St Paul refers to the first time or to the last time that it was given. We conclude, then, from these conflicting data, that '430 years' describes the interval between the Call of Abraham and the Exodus, and that the language of Genesis which speaks of the *children of Israel*, and of their going out the *self-same day* as they went in, is not to be too minutely criticized. The items which make up the 430 years are as follows:

	Call of Abraham when 75 years old .	B.C. 1921
25	Birth* of Isaac, 25 years afterwards when Abraham was 100 years old . . .	1896
37	Death of Sarah, who was 90 years old when Isaac was born, and lived to the age of 127—Isaac being 37 years old at her death. GEN. xxiii, 1, 2. . . .	1859
—		
62		

* In this date, also, we have to deal with round numbers, for Abraham says in Gen. xvii, 17, " Shall a child be born unto him that is an hundred years old ?" to which God answers, in verse 21, " Isaac, which Sarah shall bear unto thee at this set time in the next year." The 100 years, therefore, would seem to be, more accurately, 101.

62 *brought over.*

3	Marriage of Isaac at the age of 40, i. e., 3 years after his mother's death. GEN. xxv, 20	1856
20	Birth of Esau and Jacob, when their father Isaac was 60 years old, i. e., 20 years after his marriage. GEN. xxv, 26 . . .	1836
30	Jacob,* at the age of 130, goes into Egypt, GEN. xlvii, 9	1806
215†	years—the assumed interval between Jacob's descent into Egypt, and the exode of his descendants	1591

430 total.

From all these texts taken together we might draw the inference that 400 or 430 years is the space of time that passed, whilst the Israelites were in Egypt and not whilst they were *partly* in Egypt. The difficulty which these inconsistencies present can only be solved by the supposition that the book was written long after the events which it records, and at a time when it was impossible to arrive with certainty at the exact chronology of an age so remote.

§ 5.

The expressions ON THIS SIDE JORDAN, BEYOND JORDAN, *examined.*

It has been noticed in page 74 that the expression "on

---

* The intermediate events of the life of Jacob may be thus arranged:

91 years—Jacob's age when Joseph was born, for Joseph was 30 when he first came before Pharaoh; and 9 years afterwards [i.e. 7 years of plenty and 2 of famine] was 39 years old, when his father Jacob stood before Pharaoh. Gen. xlvii, 9.

30 years afterwards, Joseph was brought before Pharaoh. When he had been 2 years in Egypt.

7 years of plenty.

2 years of famine, at the end of which Jacob and his family went down into Egypt.

130

† There is no positive basis for the length of this interval. All we know is that Levi (son of Jacob) was probably about 40 years old when he accompanied his father into Egypt; his son Kohath, a child at the time of the descent, died at the age of 133, leaving Amram his son, who died at the age of 137, leaving Moses, who was 80 years old, and Aaron, who was 83 years old, at the time of the Exodus.

this side Jordan" in Deuteronomy, i, 1, has been considered as an indirect testimony that the book, in which it occurs, was written by Moses, because the words denote that the writer was on the eastern side of the river Jordan, and Moses died before the Israelites crossed to the western side of that river. But the words "on this side" have been wrongly translated, and Dr Shuckford has made the following observations on them, showing that the inaccuracy of our translation in this passage has already occurred to the notice of others:

DEUTERONOMY, i, 1. These be the words which Moses spake unto all Israel on this side Jordan in the wilderness, in the plain over against the Red Sea, between Paran and Tophel, and Laban, and Hazeroth and Dizahab.

I might here answer a trifling cavil offered concerning the Book of Deuteronomy, raised from the words here cited. It is pretended that *be neber ha Jarden*, which we translate *on this side* Jordan, do rather signify *beyond* or *on the other side* Jordan, and consequently, that these words imply Moses not to have wrote the book of Deuteronomy, for that the book so called was wrote by a person who had passed over Jordan, and could, according to the intimation of these words, remark that the words of Moses were spoke on a different side the river from the place where the book was written. But were there no other, the 10th and 13th verses of the 50th chapter of Genesis are sufficient to show the word *beneber* to have the signification we take it in. When Joseph went up out of Egypt to bury his father, they journeyed from Goshen into Canaan, and came to the cave of Macpelah before Mamre, in their way to which they stopped at the threshing-floor of Atad *beneber ha Jarden*, not *beyond*, but *on this side* Jordan; for they did not travel into Canaan, so far as to the river Jordan. SHUCKF. CONNECTION, vol. iii, preface, page ix.

Dr. Shuckford does not much improve his case by citing a second passage in which the same Hebrew words occur: for his explanation implies that they are wrongly translated in the second passage, if not in the first. The question how we should interpret the Hebrew word in these cases depends on the place where the writer was when he wrote, and on the meaning which he intended to convey. The exact grammatical signification of the word must first be ascertained; and then we may inquire, if any particular circumstances, habits of life, or figure of speech, has in later times modified this meaning.

It appears that our translators have rendered the same Hebrew words *be neber ha Jarden* by two contradictory English expressions. This is an important question, and requires to be fully investigated, for, as our knowledge of the Old Testament is derived, for the great body of our people, from a translation only, it is of vital importance that the translation of it should be scrupulously accurate and faithful.

The words *be neber ha Jarden* are written in the Hebrew character without points, thus: בעבר הירדן. The first of these words, as we read from right to left, according to the Hebrew manner, is compounded of *be* and *neber*. The prefix *be* is a kind of preposition, meaning *in*. The second part of the compound *neber* is thus explained in Dr Winer's Hebrew Lexicon, 8vo, Leipzig, 1828, page 690:

עבר m. 1) regio *ulterior (das Jenseitige)* : עבר הירדן *regio trans-jordanensis*, Gen. 1, 10. 11. Deut. i, 1.

Here we have the very two passages which Dr. Shuckford refers to, adduced as illustrations that *neber* means *trans*, "beyond," and not *on this side*. Our translators, then, have mistranslated one of the verses in question, namely Deut. i, 1; for in the other passage, Gen. l, 10, the word is rightly rendered "beyond." It may be inquired, to what source so serious an error is to be ascribed; for that they have intentionally given a false interpretation to any passage in the Old Testament, is not for a moment to be imagined. We shall see, from a collation of other passages where the same word *neber* occurs, that the cause of its mistranslation in one of the passages before us may be traced beyond the reach of doubt.

(1) GENESIS, l, 10, And they came to the threshing floor of Atad, which is beyond Jordan, and there they mourned with a great and very sore lamentation : and he made a mourning for his father seven days.

(2) NUMBERS, xxi, 13. From thence they removed, and pitched on the other side of Arnon, which is in the wilderness that cometh out of the coast of the Amorites : for Arnon is the border of Moab, between Moab and the Amorites.

(3) DEUTERONOMY, i, 1, already given in page 241.

(4) DEUTERONOMY, xxx, 13. Neither is it beyond the sea, that thou shouldest say, Who shall go over the sea for us, and bring it unto us, that we may hear it and do it?

(5) JOSHUA, xiv, 3. For Moses had given the inheritance of two tribes and an half tribe on the other side Jordan: but unto the Levites he gave none inheritance among them.

(6) JOSHUA, xxiv, 2. 3. And Joshua said unto all the people, Thus saith the Lord God of Israel, Your fathers dwelt on the other side of the flood in old time, even Terah, the father of Abraham, and the father of Nachor: and they served other gods. And I took your father Abraham from the other side of the flood, and led him throughout all the land of Canaan, and multiplied his seed, and gave him Isaac.

(7) II SAMUEL, x, 16. And Hadarezer sent, and brought out the Syrians that were beyond the river: and they came to Helam; and Shobach the captain of the host of Hadarezer *went* before them.

(8) I KINGS, iv, 24. For he had dominion over all the region on this side the river, from Tiphsah *(Thapsacus)* even unto Azzah, over all the kings on this side the river: and he had peace on all sides round about him.

(9) I CHRONICLES, xxvi, 30. And of the Hebronites, Hashabiah and his brethren, men of valour, a thousand and seven hundred, were officers among them of Israel on this side Jordan westward, in all business of the Lord, and in the service of the king.

(10) EZRA, viii, 36. And they delivered the king's commission unto the king's lieutenants, and to the governors on this side the river: and they furthered the people, and the house of God.

(11) NEHEMIAH, ii. 7. Moreover, I said unto the king, If it please the king, let letters be given me to the governors beyond the river, that they may convey me over till I come into Judah.

(12) ———— iii, 7. And next unto them repaired Melatiah the Gibeonite, and Jadon the Meronothite, the men of Gibeon, and of Mizpah, unto the throne of the governor on this side the river.

(13) ISAI. vii, 20. In the same day shall the Lord shave with a razor that is hired, *namely*, by them beyond the river, by the king of Assyria, the head, and the hair of the feet: and it shall also consume the beard.

In these thirteen passages the Hebrew word *neber* is the same: and in *eight* of them it is correctly rendered by the words 'beyond' 'on the other side of,' whilst in the other *five*, Nos. 3, 8, 9, 10, 12, the same word is wrongly translated *on this side of*.

There can be no doubt that the Hebrew word *neber* communicates to all its compounds the signification of *beyond, further, ulterior,* or *on the other side of*: and I find a remark in Dr Winer's Hebrew Lexicon which explains the difficulty. He observes that the word means usually 'trans Jordanem' *beyond Jordan*, i. e. 'ab oriente Palæstinæ' *on the eastern side from Palestine;* but that in I Chron., xxvi, 36, 'ex seriorum Judæorum usu,' *according to the later practice of the Jews,* it means 'ab occidente Jordanis' *on the western side of Jordan.*

In other words the expression *beyond Jordan* or *beyond the flood* (i. e. the river Euphrates), must obviously convey a different meaning, according to the position of the person speaking or writing: and as a large number of the Israelites were carried to Babylon, where they appear to have emerged from their bondage, and to have gained favour at court, they would then naturally describe their own land Judæa as lying beyond Jordan, whereas in former times Babylon would have been spoken of as lying *beyond,* and Palestine as lying *on this side* Jordan. Let us see how this explanation applies.

In I Kings, iv, 24, Solomon is said to have held dominion over all the country on this side the river [the Euphrates]. But Dr Winter says that it ought to be rendered *beyond* the river:

Libros enim Regum post exilium Babylonicum scriptos esse, vix dubitatur. Cf. DE WETTE, EINLEITUNG, p. 280.	For it is scarcely doubted that the Books of Kings were written after the Babylonish Captivity.
Sed videtur scriptor ex eo in quo ipse constitutus erat loco rem metiri, vel appellatione tum usu recepta uti.	But the writer seems to write with reference to the place where he had formerly been, or to use the description to which he had been there accustomed.

We may illustrate this very just remark of Dr Winer by an instance which will be at once familiar to every school-boy. The northern part of Italy was anciently inhabited by Gauls and called by the Romans Gallia Cisalpina, *Gaul on this side of the Alps.* The name was proper in the mouth of every one living on the same side of the Alps as the country which he was describing. But in process of time foreigners began to call it "Cisalpine Gaul," even though they themselves resided on the other side of the Alps. Many other examples of this practice may be cited from modern history. Part of the kingdom of Portugal is called *Tras-os-Montes* Beyond the Mountains; we have *Abruzzo Ulteriore* The Farther Abruzzo; the *Cis-Padane* and the *Cis-Alpine* Republics were separate Italian States in the time of Napoleon; *Gallia Citerior* and *Gallia Ulterior* were provinces of the Roman empire; and these names underwent no change from those who spoke or wrote of them, on whichever side of the frontiers the speaker or writer lived. This, then, is precisely the case with the Israelites: their expressions Trans-Jordan, and Trans-Euphratean, in early times denoted the eastern, but after the Babylonish captivity, either the eastern or western side of the rivers, according as they retained or abandoned, when they returned to their own country, the new use of the term which they had acquired at Babylon.

The same explanation of these conflicting meanings of a Hebrew word has been given by Dr Hengstenberg (p. 246) and other leading anti-rationalists. But they seem to confound the origin of this diversity of meaning with the use of it when an uniform history of the past was consigned to writing. If Moses wrote the very text which we now read, he would have used the Hebrew word, which means *on this side*, and not the word which means *on the other side*; because he had never been there. Yet we may notice what can be said in opposition to this view.

" Who does not see," says Dr Hengstenberg, " that the situation of the places named in I Kings, iv, 24, is determined by their relation to the central point of the Chaldee-Persian empire, without regard to the writer's personal point of view ? . . . . . The *other side* is to be explained by the circumstance that the Israelites had not yet gained a firm footing "*on this side*" Jordan; and therefore, the designation, which strictly speaking was only suitable for them as long as they had not crossed over Jordan, still continued in frequent use. They had still their fixed position on *the other side* Jordan, so that what was outwardly taken *on this side*, was inwardly taken still on the other side for them. That almost all the instances, in which *beneber* occasions any difficulty, are found in the Pentateuch and Joshua, appears, according to our view, quite natural. For, when the occupation of the land was completed, the personal point of view coincided with the general.

Thus Dr Hengstenberg refers the confused use of these terms, not, as I have done, to the Babylonish captivity, but to the very brief time which the Israelites passed on the eastern bank of the Jordan, before they crossed into the land of Canaan. As this space of time was less than two years— for the other thirty-eight were spent, not on the eastern bank of the Jordan, but in the wilderness to the south of Judæa—and the Israelites had, then, never passed into the country to the west of the Jordan, it cannot be allowed that so remarkable a confusion of terms could have arisen in so short a time.

But the writer adds that, he would unhesitatingly decide in favour of this interpretation rather than admit that the Pentateuch is not the work of Moses, an admission which, if it has any significance at all, implies that he would not yield even to the truth, if he could only find the smallest ground to stand upon in defence of his favourite theory.

We must then restore the word 'beyond' in the five passages before quoted, and everything becomes consistent: it must be inquired in every particular case whether the eastern or western side of the river was intended by the writer. I leave the reader to institute this inquiry for himself, only cautioning him to observe that the compilers who united all the original chronicles and fragments, from which the Old Testament is composed, may have retained or altered the word rendered *beyond* according to their particular notions of propriety or perhaps by pure accident. The use which can be derived to our present inquiry from the foregoing remarks, is the inference that as this confusion of terms originated in the Babylonish Captivity, the Old Testament must have been compiled after or during that period.

§ 6. *Ordinance of the Scape-goat.*

I have already endeavoured to show that the original laws of Moses were really of a less harsh and severe character than they now appear in the five books which pass under his name, and which formed the civil as well as religious code of the Jewish nation. In contrast with the law of burnt offerings and sacrifices which entered into their ritual, appear certain declarations of the prophets which can be reconciled with those things only if we remember that the Israelites twice started into a national existence, and that their institutions were necessarily varied to suit the altered circumstances of their condition. Further testimony to this view is furnished by Jeremiah, who says in chapter vii, verse 22—23:

I spake not unto your fathers, nor commanded them in the day that I brought them out of the land of Egypt, concerning burnt-offerings or sacrifices. But this thing commanded I them, saying, Obey my voice, and I will be your God, and ye shall be my people: and walk ye in all the ways that I have commanded you, that it may be well unto you.

It must be inferred from these words that the law of the burnt-offerings and sacrifices on the Sabbaths, new moons, and other occasions, was less prominent in the Law of Moses than those weightier matters, of which our Saviour speaks in the Gospel, and of which Samuel gives a general hint when he says that "to obey is better than sacrifice, and to hearken than the fat of rams!"

The only explanation which will reconcile the Law and the Prophets on this head, is to believe that the Mosaic Law, as we now find it, was intended to apply to the modern commonwealth of the Jews as well as to their former state, and that it regulates and sanctions observances not contemplated by Moses, and not originally forming part of his code.

There are, however, some particulars in this code which may here be worthy of notice, because they form a connection between Israel and Egypt, the latter of which countries has in all ages of the world been closely connected with the former, and exercised much influence over its political relations. The three subjects to which I refer are, the ordinance of the Scape-goat; the observance of the Seventh day; and the rite of Circumcision.

The ordinance of the Scape-goat is briefly spoken of in one only passage of the Bible:

LEVIT. xvi, 8. And Aaron shall cast lots upon the two goats; one lot for the Lord, and the other lot for the scape-goat, and Aaron shall bring the goat upon which the Lord's lot fell, and offer him for a sin offering. But the goat, on which the lot fell to be the scape-goat, shall be presented alive before the Lord, to make an atonement with him, and to let him go for a scape-goat into the wilderness. . . . 26. And he that let go the goat for the scape-goat shall wash his clothes, and bathe his flesh in water, and afterwards come into the camp.

Whether Moses wrote these words or not, it is certain that the ordinance of the Scape-Goat was borrowed from the customs and institutions of Egypt, out of which the Jewish nation had just escaped. We have the proof of this in the history of Herodotus, who writes as follows:

The mode of sacrifice established among them is this: having led the cattle which they have marked to the altar, where they sacrifice, they light a pile of wood. And then having poured wine down over the victim upon it, and having invoked the god, they slay it, and having slain it, they cut off its head. They then skin the body of the animal, and having uttered many imprecations upon that head, those who have a market and Grecian traders dwelling among them, carry it to the market and sell it to them; but those who have no Greeks living among them, cast it into the sea. Now they utter the imprecations, saying these words over the heads, that if any evil is about to befal either themselves who offer the sacrifice or the whole of Egypt, it may be turned away upon this head. As regards then the heads of the beasts that are offered in sacrifice and the libation of wine, all the Egyptians use the same customs in all sacrifices alike; and from this custom no Egyptian will taste the head even of any other animal. HEROD. ii, 39.

It would appear from this extract that the ordinance of the goat applied to every sacrifice of this kind offered up by the Egyptians, whereas among the Israelites it was only on the great day of atonement that the lot was drawn between the two goats, to determine which should be sacrificed to Jehovah, and which should be set free, carrying the sins of the people into the wilderness. But the silence which is observed on the subject of this ordinance throughout the whole existence of the Jewish commonwealth, from the time of Moses to the early years of the Christian era, together with the variations from the Biblical narrative, which are found in the Talmud, are too remarkable to be passed over unnoticed. From the promulgation of the Mosaic law fifteen hundred years before Christ, nothing is said of the scape-goat until we reach the first century of our era, at which time it is believed that the Mishna and the Gemara, collectively called the Talmud, began to be written.

The account given by the writer of the Gemara states that, when the lot had determined which of the two should be the scape-goat, the people treated it with cruelty until it was taken away by the man appointed for the purpose; and he further adds that this man led the goat to the top of a high precipice and threw him down backwards so as to dash him to pieces. It was intended no doubt, when the law was promulgated, that the animal should be set free, but it may well be doubted whether a law, from which so remarkable a deviation is described by writers so strictly national as those who compiled the Talmud, could have been current previously among the people for the space of fifteen hundred years or more.

We will proceed to notice the second of the three ordinances, to which the attention of the reader is invited.

§ 7. *Circumcision.*

The rite of circumcision, from the influence which it has exercised on Christians and Mahometans, equal if not superior to that which it exercised among the Jews themselves, must not be passed over in any work that concerns the religion and literature of that people. The origin of it, as practised among other nations, has never been clearly ascertained, nor would it be important to the Western nations to ascertain it, were it not still kept in memory by the Church, which assigns the first of January in every year to celebrate the Feast of the Circumcision of our Lord. The idea that this rite drew its origin from considerations of health and cleanliness seems now to have been abandoned, for the custom is by no means universal in hot countries, and does not seem ever to have prevailed among the Hindoos who inhabit India, which is the hottest country in the world.

Herodotus, in the second book of his History (104) gives us the following account:

The Colchians, the Egyptians, and the Ethiopians, are the only nations of the world, who from the first have practised circumcision. For the Phœnicians, and the Syrians in Palestine, acknowledge that they learnt the custom from the Egyptians; and the Syrians about the Thermodon and the Parthenius, with their neighbours the Macrones, confess that they very lately learnt the same custom from the Colchians. But of the Egyptians and the Ethiopians, I am unable to say which learnt it from the other, for it is evidently a very ancient custom. And this appears to me a strong proof that the Phœnicians learnt this practice through their intercourse with the Egyptians, for all the Phœnicians, who have any commerce with Greece, no longer imitate the Egyptians in this usage, but abstain from circumcising their children.

The first mention of Circumcision in the Bible occurs in the seventeenth chapter of Genesis, verse 10; where God says to Abraham:

This is my covenant, which ye shall keep, between me and you and thy seed after thee; Every male child among you shall be circumcised.

Now it appears that this covenant was entered into with Abraham immediately after he had come back out of Egypt into the land of Canaan.

Agreeably with the command, Abraham and his family underwent the process of circumcision, and to the fact that Ishmael took part in the ceremony his descendants in Arabia, now professing the Mahometan religion, refer their perpetual observance of the rite down to the present day.

Passing over the barbarous vengeance which the sons of Jacob took of Shechem the Hivite for the affront done to their sister, as recorded in Genesis (xxiv) we find the law of circumcision mentioned again in Exodus (xii, 48), where it is commanded that no uncircumcised person shall eat of the passover; and again in Jeremiah (ix, 25):

Behold the days come, saith the Lord, that I will punish all them that are circumcised with the uncircumcised.

Between the time of Moses and Jeremiah only one notice occurs on this subject, in the book of Joshua (v, 2) where the origin of the name Gilgal is explained. Here the great captain of the Lord's chosen people, following a second command from God, is said to have "rolled away the reproach of Egypt" from among the people, by performing on them the rite of circumcision, which had been neglected forty years during the whole time of their sojourn in the wilderness.

Besides the foregoing, there are three other passages, two in the Book of Deuteronomy (x, 16; xxx, 6), and one in the Prophet Jeremiah (iv, 4), in which reference is made to the rite of circumcision. But the reference here is made in a figurative sense, which, as regards Deuteronomy, we should hardly expect to find in the earliest age of a nation who had just escaped from slavery in Egypt, and much more in harmony with the ideas and train of thought which occur in more recent writings.

"Circumcise therefore the foreskin of your hearts," says Moses in the course of those long warnings and admonitions which he is dramatically represented as speaking to all Israel, when he had called them together (v, 1) to hear his parting words. "And the Lord thy God will circumcise thine heart," is the form in which the warning is conveyed in the second passage of that book. The same metaphor is used by Jeremiah in the exhortation which he addresses to them about the time when destruction was already hanging over their city and nation.

Circumcise yourselves to the Lord, and take away the foreskins of your heart, ye men of Judah and inhabitants of Jerusalem: lest my fury come forth like fire, and burn that none can quench it, because of the evil of your doings.

We need not doubt that a Divine command was given to Abraham that all his posterity should practise the rite of circumcision: nor is it to be gainsaid that Moses was commissioned to include this rite amongst the laws which he gave for the children of Israel to observe. But their recent sojourn in Egypt makes it probable that Moses, knowing well the prevalence of such a practice among the Egyptians, would lay less stress on it as a mark to distinguish his own people, than would be laid by Ezra, who came from Babylon after the power of Egypt had been broken, and the rivalry of the Egyptians had been extinguished. The neglect of it indeed by Moses and by the Israelites, whom he led within sight of the promised land, is a strong presumption against its continued existence among them whilst sojourning in Egypt. Like many other laws and customs of the Israelites, it assumes importance in the few passages where it occurs, but again slumbers through the many centuries which passed until the beginning of the Christian era.

In contrast with these improbabilities we turn to the age of Ezra and his successors. We have seen the spiritual view which the prophet Jeremiah has taken of this subject. Granting that the rite existed from the first among the descendants of Abraham, no other use is made of it by one of the prophets than that which we find in the words of Jeremiah already quoted. But if, as suggested, we may refer the first authorship of the Canonical Jewish Scriptures to Ezra, we may understand how he would combine the stern enactments of the Jewish law, its pains and penalties, with such spiritual applications as were already beginning to show themselves in the religion of the Jews, when they returned to their own land instructed in the learning which in those days seems to have had Babylon for its centre. The religion of the Jews, although emanating in a peculiar manner from the Almighty, was not necessarily free from those blemishes and defects which are common to that of all the nations of the world; and it is quite consistent with the Divine government that the most favoured nation should attain to whatever perfection mankind is capable of by following the same course of toil and difficulty which belong to all human things.

Such then were the ordinance of the scape-goat and the rite of circumcision, both clearly imitated from the Egyptians, and by God's command enjoined on the practice of his chosen people. The former continued probably to be kept up as long as the Israelites, wandering in the wilderness, were able literally to send into that wilderness the victim charged with the burden of their sins; but we nowhere read that the institution was maintained after they were finally established in the land of their inheritance. The rite of circumcision however has had a longer duration. Mentioned only once historically for the long space of fifteen hundred years between the times of Abraham and Ezra, it recurs to the notice of the historian in the later part of the Jewish commonwealth, and is even now retained in full force by the descendants of that extraordinary nation in the various countries where they are dispersed.

§ 8. *The Sabbath.*

But the third ordinance to which our attention must now be directed, that of the Sabbath, though involved as to its origin in mystery equally with the other two, and equally uncertain as to its observance for many centuries, has firmly held its place among the people where it seems chiefly to have prevailed, and is still observed not only by their descendants, but in some form or other by all the civilized nations of the earth. An analysis of the various notices of the Sabbath, which occur in the Books of the Old Testament, will furnish the most abundant proof of the fragmentary origin of those books, and that consequently they owe their existence not to contemporary writers but to a compiler who lived when the Jewish people were struggling to maintain their position as a nation among the larger states which were growing up around them. The relation which Abraham held towards Chedorlaomer king of Elam and Tidal king of nations, and even that which the kings of Judah and Israel held toward the Syrians and Sidonians, have no counterpart in the position of the later Jews toward the great empires of Persia, Egypt and Greece. The smaller states of Asia, like those of Europe in modern times, had been swallowed up one by one, and the Jews alone, although in defence of their national independence they had fought successfully at intervals against the successors of Alexander, were doomed in the end to be annexed to the universal dominion of the Romans.

The formal institution of the Sabbath is recorded in the twentieth chapter of Exodus, and copied thence into the code of the Ten Commandments, is well known to the members of every Christian community. "The seventh day is the Sabbath of the Lord thy God" are the words of the enactment, and the same form of words is observed in the fifth chapter of Deuteronomy where those Commandments are repeated. We shall presently have to consider the case of the Ten Commandments as a whole; but have now only to notice the Sabbath, with reference to its observance during the many centuries which mark the duration of the Israelitish state.

The promulgation of the whole law of the Decalogue took place after the people had removed to Sinai, but we read in a previous chapter of Exodus (xvi, 25) that Moses had already instituted the Sabbath in connection with the gift of manna:

To-day is a sabbath unto the Lord: to-day ye shall not find it in the field. Six days ye shall gather it; but on the seventh day, *which is* the Sabbath, in it there shall be none . . . . See, for that the Lord hath given you the Sabbath, therefore he giveth you on the sixth day the bread of two days; abide ye every man in his place, let no man go out of his place on the seventh day. So the people rested on the seventh day.

After this distinct utterance, followed by the general code of laws delivered by God himself after a short interval from Mount Sinai, as recorded in the twentieth chapter of Exodus, there would seemingly be no further need that such a law should be repeated. Yet in the same book (xxiii, 12) after the mention of the law which provided that the land also should lie fallow and rest every seventh year, we again read:

Six days thou shalt do thy work, and on the seventh day thou shalt rest: that thine ox and thine ass may rest, and the son of thy handmaid, and the stranger, may be refreshed.

Thus we have three distinct statements of the law of the Sabbath within a few chapters of one another, and yet we find a fourth and a fifth within a short distance further on, couched in almost the same words:

xxxi, 14, 15. Ye shall keep the sabbath therefore; for it *is* holy unto you: every one that defileth it shall surely be put to death: for whosoever doeth *any* work therein, that soul shall be cut off from amongst his people. Six days may work be done; but in the seventh *is* the sabbath of rest, holy to the Lord: whosoever doeth *any* work in the sabbath day, he shall surely be put to death.

xxxv, 1. And Moses gathered all the congregation of the children of Israel together, and said unto them, These *are* the words which the Lord hath commanded, that *ye* should do them. Six days shall work be done, but on the seventh day there shall be to you an holy day, a sabbath of rest to the Lord: whosoever doeth work therein shall be put to death."

These passages are conceived in general terms, and are practically illustrated by the mode in which offences against the law were treated in the wilderness. In contravention of what Moses had proclaimed, some of the people kept until the morning a portion of the manna which they had gathered and it stunk, "and Moses was wroth with them." (Exod. xvi, 20.) But others went out on the sabbath day as on other days, to gather manna, having neglected to provide themselves with a double portion the day before. We do not however find that these were put to death. They were left to abide the natural consequence, which was that "they found none ... So the people rested on the seventh day."

Far different was the fate of one who in the course of the next year was found gathering sticks upon the sabbath day.

They put him in ward, because it was not declared what should be done to him. And the Lord said unto Moses, The man shall be surely put to death: all the congregation shall stone him with stones without the camp. And all the congregation brought him without the camp, and stoned him with stones, and he died; as the Lord commanded Moses. NUMB. xv, 34.

Thus the offended law was vindicated, and the lawgiver, by divine command, turns his attention to other matters of a somewhat singular nature; he bids the people "to make them fringes in the borders of their garments throughout their generations, and that they put upon the fringes of the borders a ribband of blue."

In the Book of Leviticus (xxiii and xxv) we read that as every seventh day was to be a sabbath or a day of rest, so every seventh week, month, or year was to be a sabbatical week, month, or year of rest, but in no part of the Jewish history before the Babylonish Captivity do we meet with any record that these sabbaths were observed at all.

In Leviticus (xxvi, 30) we have indeed a minute picture of the punishment which would be inflicted on the people if they would not obey the law of God—so minute indeed as to be a true picture of what did actually befal them when they were carried into captivity by Nebuchadnezzar, and here we find an account of the result, worded however in the form of a prophecy, which looks very much as if it had been written after the event.

Your land shall be desolate, and your cities waste. Then shall the land enjoy her sabbaths, as long as it lieth desolate, and *ye* be in your enemies' land; *even* then shall the land rest, and enjoy her sabbaths. As long as it lieth desolate, it shall rest; because it did not rest in your sabbaths, when ye dwelt upon it.

The prophet Amos, however, in his prophecy (viii, 5) written about seven hundred years after Moses, asks a question which seems to show that the law of the sabbath in his time was observed somewhat strictly: "When will the new moon be gone, that we may sell corn? and the sabbath, that we may set forth wheat?" But Jeremiah (xvii, 21), two hundred years later than Amos, complains that whereas the Lord said, "Take heed to yourselves and bear no burden on the sabbath day, &c," the people "obeyed not, neither inclined their ear:" nor do we find any words in the law of Moses, as we now have it, to authorize such an appeal as that which Jeremiah then made. When however we come to a later period, after the return of the people from Babylon, the observance of the Sabbath already begins to show itself with all that harshness which received the well-merited censure of our Lord so beautifully recorded in the gospel history.

If the people of the land bring ware, or any victuals on the sabbath day to sell, *that* we would not buy it of them on the sabbath or on the holy day: and *that* we would leave the seventh year, and the exaction of every debt. NEHEM. x, 31.

And in the same Book of Nehemiah (xiii, 15) we have an instance of the attention which was then paid to the observance of this article of the law:

In those days saw I in Judah *some* treading wine-presses on the sabbath, and bringing in sheaves and lading asses; as also wine, grapes, and figs, and all *manner of* burdens, which they brought into Jerusalem on the sabbath day: and I testified *against them* in the day wherein they sold victuals .... 19. And it came to pass, that when the gates of Jerusalem began to be dark before the sabbath, I commanded that the gates should be shut, and charged that they should not be opened till after the sabbath: and *some* of my servants set I at the gates, *that* there should no burden be brought in on the sabbath day. So the merchants and sellers of all kind of ware lodged without Jerusalem once or twice.

Here, however, owing perhaps to the greater intelligence of the age, there is no thought of inflicting the punishment of death by stoning, and from this time till the beginning of the Christian era the institution of the Sabbath becomes the important feature of the Jewish law. The calamities which befel both the nation and individuals under the Maccabee princes, from the tyranny of Antiochus, and in consequence of their persevering adherence to the law of the Sabbath, are too well known to require that we should notice them in this place.

But a passage found in the history of Dion Cassius may be here quoted in confirmation of the theory that the observance of the Sabbath, like that of the two preceding ordinances, was copied by the Israelites from the Egyptians, with whom the inhabitants of Palestine have in all ages been closely connected.

Κεχωρίδαται δὲ ἀπὸ τῶν λοιπῶν ἀνθρώπων ἔς τε τὰ ἄλλα τὰ περὶ τὴν δίαιταν πάνθ' ὡς εἰπεῖν, καὶ μάλισθ' ὅτι τῶν μὲν ἄλλων θεῶν οὐδένα τιμῶσιν, ἕνα δέ τινα ἰσχυρῶς σέβουσι· οὐδ' ἄγαλμα οὐδὲν ἐν αὐτοῖς ποτε τοῖς Ἱεροσολύμοις ἔσχον· ἄρρητον δὲ δὴ καὶ ἀειδῆ αὐτὸν νομίζοντες εἶναι, περισσότατα ἀνθρώπων θρησκεύουσι καὶ αὐτῷ νεών τε μέγιστον καὶ περικαλλέστατον, πλὴν καθ' ὅσον ἀχανής τε καὶ ἀνώροφος ἦν, ἐξεποίησαν.

But they [the Jews] are separated from the rest of mankind both in all other things that concern their mode of life, so to speak, and most of all because they honour none of the other gods, but mightily worship one certain god: nor did they ever have any statue in Jerusalem itself, but deeming him to be unutterable and invisible, they worship him most of all men and made for him a temple both very great and surpassingly beautiful except so far that it was both open and without a roof.

Καὶ τὴν ἡμέραν τὴν τοῦ Κρόνου καλουμένην ἀνέθεσαν, καὶ ἄλλα τε ἐν αὐτῇ ἰδιαίτατα οὐ ποιοῦσι καὶ ἔργου οὐδενὸς σπουδαίου προσάπτονται. Καὶ τὰ μὲν κατ' ἐκεῖνον, τίς τ' ἐστὶ καὶ ὅθεν οὕτως ἐτιμήθη, ὅπως τε περὶ αὐτὸν ἐπτόηνται, πολλοῖς τε εἴρηται καὶ οὐδὲν τῇδε τῇ ἱστορίᾳ προσήκει. Τὸ δὲ δὴ ἐς τοὺς ἑπτὰ τοὺς πλανήτας ὠνομασμένους τὰς ἡμέρας ἀνακεῖσθαι, κατέστη μὲν ὑπ' Αἰγυπτίων, πάρεστι δὲ καὶ ἐπὶ πάντας ἀνθρώπους οὐ πάλαι ποτέ, ὡς λόγῳ εἰπεῖν, ἀρξάμενον.—DION CAS. xxxvii, 17, 18.

And they have dedicated to him that which is called the day of Saturn; and they do not do in it their other most private affairs, nor engage in any serious work. And as regards himself, both who he is and whence he has been so honoured and how they are in awe about him, has both been told by many and does not belong to this history. But the fact that the days are set apart to the seven planets so called, was established by the Egyptians, and is found also over all mankind, having begun, to speak in a word, not long ago.

The conclusion to which the foregoing argument leads is of the same character as that which is insisted on generally in this work, that the records of the Jews are of later origin, and that the national customs of that remarkable people, drawing their origin from the Mosaical law, received from the zeal of their leaders Ezra and his successor a tone which has come down to the present time, and continue to maintain the isolation of the Jews in the countries where they now dwell in a manner that has no parallel in the history of any other nation.

§ 9. *The two versions of the Ten Commandments.*

The observance of the Sabbath day among the Jews from a very early date, and kept up among ourselves even to the present day, has been thought worthy of a separate consideration in this work. But the Ten Commandments, among which the Sabbath occupies a prominent place, next indeed to the worship of one only God, furnish certain varieties of reading which, though not of a nature to invalidate their historical truth, yet show plainly that the writer of one of the original documents, out of which the Bible was compiled, had not seen other parts in which the same subjects had been differently described.

Such a discrepancy is found between the Ten Commandments, as they are noticed in the 20th chapter of Exodus, and again in the 5th chapter of Deuteronomy.

The two copies of the commandments are here subjoined in parallel columns:

Exodus, xx, 1—17.	Deuteronomy, v, 7—21.
1. Thou shalt have no other gods before me.	1. Thou shalt have none other gods before me.
2. Thou shalt not make unto thee any graven image, or any likeness of any thing that is in heaven above, or that is in the earth beneath, or that is in the water under the earth. Thou shalt not bow down thyself to them, nor serve them: for I the Lord thy God am a jealous God, visiting the iniquity of the fathers upon the children unto the third and fourth generation of them that hate me: And showing mercy unto thousands of them that love me, and keep my commandments.	2. Thou shalt not make thee any graven image, or any likeness of anything that is in heaven above, or that is in the earth beneath, or that is in the waters beneath the earth. Thou shalt not bow down thyself unto them nor serve them: for I the Lord thy God am a jealous God, visiting the iniquity of the fathers upon the children unto the third and fourth generation of them that hate me: And showing mercy unto thousands of them that love me, and keep my commandments.

3. Thou shalt not take the name of the Lord thy God in vain; for the Lord will not hold him guiltless that taketh his name in vain.	3. Thou shalt not take the name of the Lord thy God in vain: for the Lord will not hold him guiltless that taketh his name in vain.
4. Remember the Sabbath day, to keep it holy.	4. Keep the Sabbath day, to sanctify it, as the Lord thy God hath commanded thee.
Six days shalt thou labour and do all thy work: But the seventh day is the Sabbath of the Lord thy God: in it thou shalt not do any work, thou, nor thy son, nor thy daughter, thy man servant, nor thy maid servant, nor thy cattle, nor thy stranger that is within thy gates.	Six days thou shalt labour and do all thy work: But the seventh day is the Sabbath of the Lord thy God: in it thou shalt not do any work, thou, nor thy son, nor thy daughter, nor thy man-servant, nor thy maid-servant, nor thine ox, nor thine ass, nor any of thy cattle, nor thy stranger that is within thy gates: that thy man-servant and thy maid-servant may rest as well as thou.
	And remember that thou wast a servant in the land of Egypt, and that the Lord thy God brought thee out thence, through a mighty hand, and by a stretched out arm:
For in six days the Lord made heaven and earth, the sea and all that in them is, and rested the seventh day:	
Wherefore the Lord blessed the Sabbath day and hallowed it.	Therefore the Lord thy God commanded thee to keep the Sabbath day.
5. Honour thy father and thy mother:	5. Honour thy father and thy mother: as the Lord thy God hath commanded thee
that thy days may be long	that thy days may be prolonged, and that it may go well with thee
upon the land which the Lord thy God giveth thee.	in the land which the Lord thy God giveth thee.
6. Thou shalt not kill.	6. Thou shalt not kill.

7. Thou shalt not commit adultery.	7. Neither shalt thou commit adultery.
8. Thou shalt not steal.	8. Neither shalt thou steal.
9. Thou shalt not bear false witness against thy neighbour.	9. Neither shalt thou bear false witness against thy neighbour.
10. Thou shalt not covet thy neighbour's house, thou shalt not covet thy neighbour's wife, nor his manservant, nor his maidservant, nor his ox, nor his ass, nor anything that is thy neighbour's.	10. Neither shalt thou desire thy neighbour's wife, neither shalt thou covet thy neighbour's house, his field or his man-servant, or his maidservant, his ox, or his ass, or anything that is thy neighbour's.

These two copies of the same document must have been handed down in two separate works; and the compiler, whoever he was, that drew up the existing collection which forms the canon of the Old Testament, inserted both of them because they seemed to be of equal authority, without being deterred by the somewhat inconsistent reasons which they give for the observance of the Fourth Commandment.

§ 10.

Inconsistency between Samuel's picture of a king and that ascribed to Moses in Deuteronomy.

The description of a king, in the seventh chapter of Deuteronomy,* has nothing offensive to the feelings or injurious to the happiness of the people; nor does it seem to imply that the Almighty would disapprove of the Israelites choosing for themselves a king when they should be settled in the land of promise. On the contrary it conveys an idea that the request would be a natural one, and it explains the mode in which the petition should be complied with. Is it then likely that Samuel had read this description when he cautioned the people against choosing a king, by giving the following picture of his tyranny and his rapacity?

I SAMUEL, viii, 11—18. This will be the manner of the king that shall reign over you: he will take your sons, and appoint them for himself for his chariots, and to be his horsemen; and some shall run before his chariots.

And he will appoint him captains over thousands, and captains

---

* See the extract in pages 267, 268, where it is more conveniently placed.

over fifties, and will set them to ear his ground, and to reap his harvest, and to make his instruments of war, and instruments of his chariots. And he will take your daughters to be confectionaries, and to be cooks, and to be bakers. And he will take your fields, and your vineyards, and your olive-yards, even the best of them, and give them to his servants. And he will take the tenth of your seed, and of your vineyards, and give to his officers and to his servants. And he will take your men-servants and your maid-servants, and your goodliest young men, and your asses, and put them to his work.

He will take the tenth of your sheep; and ye shall be his servants.

And ye shall cry out in that day because of your king which ye shall have chosen you; and the Lord will not hear you in that day.

These words of Samuel will seem reasonable to those who know the nature of oriental despotism, if we only suppose that Samuel had never read the seventeenth chapter of Deuteronomy, which deals so much more leniently with the same contingency.

It is something also to our present point that neither does Samuel cause Saul to copy out the Book of the Law, as ordered by Moses; and this seems to prove that there was no Book of the Law, besides the two tables of stone, then in existence.

But the people were tired of the Sacerdotal Government, and insisted on the election of a king. The *seer* complied with their wishes, and declared to the people that Saul was the king whom the Lord their God had chosen:

And Samuel said to all the people, See ye him whom the Lord hath chosen, that there is none like him among all the people? And all the people shouted and said, God save the king! Then Samuel told the people the manner of the kingdom, and wrote it in a book, and laid it up before the Lord. And Samuel sent all the people away, every man to his house. I SAMUEL, x, 24, 25.

§ 11. *Discrepancies in the history of David and Saul.*

Another discrepancy is observable between the two accounts of David's introduction to Saul, as related, the one in the sixteenth, the other in the seventeenth chapter of the First Book of Samuel.

I SAMUEL xvi, 14—21. But the spirit of the Lord departed from

Saul, and an evil spirit from the Lord troubled him. And Saul's servants said unto him, Behold now, an evil spirit from God troubleth thee. Let our lord now command thy servants, which are before thee, to seek out a man who is a cunning player on an harp: and it shall come to pass, when the evil spirit from God is upon thee, that he shall play with his hand, and thou shalt be well. And Saul said unto his servants, Provide me now a man that can play well, and bring him to me. Then answered one of the servants, and said, Behold, I have seen a son of Jesse the Bethlehemite, that is cunning in playing, and a mighty valiant man, and a man of war, and prudent in matters, and a comely person, and the Lord is with him. Wherefore Saul sent messengers unto Jesse, and said, Send me David thy son, which is with the sheep.

And Jesse took an ass laden with bread, and a bottle of wine, and a kid, and sent them by David his son unto Saul. And David came to Saul, and stood before him: and he loved him greatly, and he became his armour-bearer.

It is difficult to reconcile this with the account given in the seventeenth chapter of the same book, where are related the circumstances which preceded and followed the battle between David and Goliath. The reader will remember that the two armies were drawn up in array, when Goliath of Gath challenges the Israelites to single combat. At this moment, the stripling David comes to see his brothers, and asks what shall be given to the man who should kill the Philistine. Then follows this narrative:

I SAMUEL, xvii, 28. And Eliab his eldest brother heard when he spake unto the men; and Eliab's anger was kindled against David, and he said, Why camest thou down hither? and with whom hast thou left those few sheep in the wilderness? I know thy pride, and the naughtiness of thine heart; for thou art come down that thou mightest see the battle. And David said, What have I now done? Is there not a cause? And he turned from him towards another, and spake after the same manner: and the people answered him again after the former manner. And when the words were heard which David spake, they rehearsed them before Saul: and he sent for him. And David said to Saul, Let no man's heart fail because of him; thy servant will go and fight with this Philistine, &c.

Passing over the battle in which David slays the Philistine, at verse 55 we read:

And when Saul saw David go forth against the Philistine, he said unto Abner, the captain of the host, Abner, whose son is this youth? And Abner said, As thy soul liveth, O king, I cannot tell. And the king said, Enquire thou whose son this stripling is. And as David returned from the slaughter of the Philistine, Abner took him, and brought him before Saul with the head of the Philistine in his hand, and Saul said to him, Whose son art thou, thou young man? And David answered, I am the son of thy servant Jesse the Bethlehemite.

These two accounts do not agree together. If David, according to the first of them, was already "a mighty valiant man, and a man of war, and prudent in matters," before he played on the harp to Saul, how could he be afterwards described as a "stripling" and as unused to armour, when he fought with the Philistine? Again: If David had been the armour-bearer of Saul, who "loved him greatly," how should Saul afterwards have been ignorant of his very name? The explanation of the discrepancy may be this. The two narratives were originally independent of one another, and were afterwards united by some compiler who did not perceive that they were irreconcilable in the points above mentioned, although, in their main features, equally founded upon fact.

It is not, however, impossible that the compiler has added details by way of ornament to his narrative: for he gives us a dialogue as having passed between the champions: but does not tell us in what language they spoke. The Philistines and Israelites certainly did not at this time speak the same, or we should not find them speaking differently five or six centuries afterwards, as we read in Nehemiah, xiii, 23:

In those days also saw I Jews that had married wives of Ashdod, of Ammon, and of Moab. And their children spake half in the speech of Ashdod, and could not speak in the Jews' language, but according to the language of each people.

Ashdod was one of the five cities of the Philistines, and its inhabitants, having always maintained their independence, retained also their native language, still distinct from that of the Israelites as late as the time of Nehemiah.

The dialogue between David and Goliath is similar to those which we find in Homer as passing between the various champions of Greece and Troy: but neither can these be received as other than the embellishments of the poet:

for Hector and Achilles, Ajax and Æneas, spoke different languages, and could not have understood a word of the taunts and threats which, according to the poem, they so liberally discharged the one against the other.

§ 12. *Error in the number of Solomon's officers.*

In the First Book of Kings, ix, 23, we read:

These were the chief of the officers that were over Solomon's work, five hundred and fifty, which bare rule over the people that wrought in the work.

The number of officers is very different in II Chronicles, viii, 10;

And these were the chief of king Solomon's officers, even two hundred and fifty, that bare rule over the people.

The explanation which Bishop Patrick gives of this discrepancy, in a note on I Kings, ix, 23, is simply a conjecture, founded on no fact or reason whatever:

At II Chronicles, viii, 10, the number is stated at 250. The most probable solution is that there were 250 set over those who wrought in the temple; and the rest had the superintendence of public works in other places.

Numbers, expressed by short ideagraphic signs, such as Arabic or Roman numerals, which denote whole words, and are not compounded of separate letters, are always liable to corruption; but the care taken by the Jews to preserve their scriptures from error, renders it unlikely that these scriptures should have been corrupted like other books. Yet we find so many disagreements in numbers between Kings and Chronicles, that it is necessary to assign some reason for the fact. One general explanation may be given of all these discrepancies. The separate documents differed originally because they proceeded from different authors who wrote independently, and, like all historians, differed from each other in the minor details of their histories. The compilers who collected those records, retained the narratives in their original form, and with all these inaccuracies uncorrected.

§ 13.

Error in the number of talents brought from Ophir.

In I Kings, ix, 28, it is said that the ships built by King Solomon " came to Ophir, and fetched from thence gold, four hundred and twenty talents, and brought it to King Solomon."

Bishop Patrick writes the following note on this verse:

> It is said at II Chronicles, viii, 18, that they brought 450 talents; a difference which is of little importance, whether we attribute it to a variation in the value of the talent, or in the quantity of the metal, the one referring to the quantity of pure gold, the other of gold with alloy: or whether we suppose 450 talents to be the gross produce of the voyage, 420 the produce with the deduction of expenses.

Such annotations as these are unworthy the importance of the subject, and the positive nature of the statements. The difference of thirty talents is decided; it arose, no doubt, from an inaccuracy in the ancient records, and this inaccuracy has been perpetuated by the compiler, who valued and preserved the genuineness of his materials, even though they were slightly discrepant the one with the other.

§ 14. *Concerning the situation of Tharshish.*

The passages of the old Testament, in which Tharshish is named, involve a doubt whether that city was situated on the Red Sea or the Mediterranean:

> I KINGS, x, 22. For the king [Solomon] had at sea a navy at Tharshish with the navy of Hiram: once in three years came the navy of Tharshish, bringing gold and silver, ivory, apes, and peacocks.

The Tyrians, whose king was Hiram, certainly had their navy in the Mediterranean, and not in the Red Sea, from which they were separated by the Israelites, the Philistines, and other tribes.

> I KINGS, xxii, 48. Jehoshaphat made ships of Tharshish to go to Ophir for gold: but they went not; for the ships were broken at Ezion-geber.

Now Ezion-geber was a port on the Red Sea, and, if we might judge from this verse alone, the city of Tharshish was situated there also. This is confirmed by the parallel passage in II Chronicles, xx, 36, 37:

And he [*Jehoshaphat*] joined himself with him [*Ahaziah*] to make ships to go to Tarshish; and they made the ships in Ezion-geber. Then Eliezer the son of Dodavah of Mareshah prophesied against Jehoshaphat, saying, Because thou hast joined thyself with Ahaziah, the Lord hath broken thy works. And the ships were broken, that they were not able to go to Tarshish.

It is not unimportant to notice the various kinds of merchandize which were imported into Palestine. Gold, silver, and, perhaps, ivory, apes, and peacocks might be got from the northern coast of Africa, but certainly all of them, and especially peacocks, point to India and the east as the countries where they principally are produced.

§ 15.

Excessive accounts of the population of the Holy Land.

In the Second Book of Samuel, xxiv, 9, we meet with the assertion that the number of soldiers in David's army was one million three hundred thousand men:

And Joab gave up the sum of the number of the people unto the king: and there were in Israel eight hundred thousand valiant men that drew the sword; and the men of Judah were five hundred thousand men.

If these numbers are correct we must suppose that all the men in Israel and Judah capable of bearing arms, whether soldiers by profession or not, were included in the calculation. Now, computing those capable of bearing arms as one out of three—a very large proportion—it results that the whole number of males in Israel and Judah was nearly four millions. There would be, in the next place, the same number of females of all ages, or rather the number of females would be greater, as is found to be the case in nearly all countries. We may then conclude that the population of David's dominions amounted to at least eight millions, a very large number indeed for so small a country as Judæa, which is in size hardly greater than Holland or

Belgium, and yet these two kingdoms, though thickly peopled, contain together little more than half of the above mentioned estimate taken from the census of King David's dominions. Let us now compare with this the account given in I Chronicles, xxi, 5.

And Joab gave the sum of the number of the people unto David. And all they of Israel were a thousand thousand and an hundred thousand men that drew sword: and Judah was four hundred three score and ten thousand men that drew sword.

These numbers make a total of one million five hundred and seventy thousand men, capable of bearing arms, and after the same rate, the population of the Holy Land, in the reign of David, amounted to nine millions four hundred and twenty thousand persons, which is even greater than the total, afforded by the account given in the book of Samuel.

§ 16.

The Law of Moses not observed by the Israelites, and especially by King Solomon.

It is difficult to imagine that the Law of Moses, as we now have it, could have been in public and active operation during the times of the Hebrew commonwealth and monarchy; for in the history of the kings we find the most flagrant breaches of that law without any marks of censure from the writer; who, as far as we learn by his narrative, appears to have known little more than the name of Moses or of his Laws.

We have already noticed in sections 6, 7, 8, the neglect of the sabbatical institution, the silence respecting the scape-goat, and the apparent neglect of circumcision, and now we may notice the way in which the kings, even Solomon himself, seem to have been wholly ignorant of what Moses had commanded, or if they knew it, to have treated it wholly with contempt.

Thus, in Deuteronomy, xvii, 14—20—a passage which, according to the theory now proposed, was written after the events there suggested had been realized,—we find the following:

When thou art come unto the land which the Lord thy God giveth thee, and shalt possess it, and shalt dwell therein, and shalt say, I will set a king over me, like as all the nations that are about me; thou shalt in any wise set him king over thee whom the Lord thy God shall choose: one from among thy brethren shalt thou set king over thee: thou mayest not set a stranger over thee, which is not thy brother.

But he shall not multiply horses to himself; nor cause the people to return to Egypt, to the end that he should multiply horses; forasmuch as the Lord hath said unto you, Ye shall henceforth return no more that way.

Neither shall he multiply wives to himself that his heart turn not away: neither shall he greatly multiply to himself silver and gold.

And it shall be when he sitteth upon the throne of his kingdom, that he shall write him a copy of this law in a book, out of that which is before the priests the Levites: and it shall be with him, and he shall read therein all the days of his life: that he may learn to fear the Lord his God, to keep all the words of this law and these statutes, to do them: that his heart be not lifted up above his brethren, and that he turn not aside from the commandment, to the right hand or to the left: to the end that he may prolong his days in his kingdom; he, and his children, in the midst of Israel.

Such were the commands of Moses on three specific points: 1. Horses; 2. Wives; and 3. Copying out the Law. The following texts show how Solomon obeyed these commands:

I Kings, iv, 26. And Solomon had forty thousand stalls of horses for his chariots, and twelve thousand horsemen.

—xi, 3. And he had seven hundred wives, princesses, and three hundred concubines: and his wives turned away his heart.

The writer of this history censures, it is true, the multiplication of wives, but he does not point out the flagrant breach of the Law which Solomon committed; and as regards the copying of the Law, he observes a deep and total silence upon the subject.

§ 17.

The Captivity and Assyria are actually mentioned in the early books of the Old Testament.

In Numbers, xxiv, 21—24, we read:

And he [Balaam] looked on the Kenites; and took up his parable, and said, Strong is thy dwelling-place, and thou puttest thy nest in a rock. Nevertheless the Kenite shall be wasted, until Asshur shall carry thee away captive. . . . And ships shall come from the coast of Chittim, and shall afflict Asshur, and shall afflict Eber, and he also shall perish for ever.

To this passage are appended the following notes in the popular Commentary on the Bible, to which the attention of the reader has been so often invited.

21.— *the Kenites*,] Not one of the Canaanitish nations, mentioned in Gen. xv, 19, but probably a tribe of the Midianites: Jethro, the father-in-law of Moses, being called in one place "the priest of Midian," Exod. iii, 1, and in another, "the Kenite," Judges i, 16. *Bp Newton*.

22. *Nevertheless the Kenite, &c.*] The Amalekites were to be utterly destroyed, but the Kenites were to be carried captive. And accordingly, when Saul was sent to destroy the Amalekites, he ordered the Kenites to depart from among them, 1 Sam. xv, 6. This shows that they were "wasted" and reduced to a low and weak condition. And, as the kings of Assyria carried captive, not only the Jews, but also the Syrians, II Kings, xvi, 9, and several other nations, II Kings, xxi, 12, 13, it is highly probable that the Kenites shared the same fate as their neighbours; especially as some Kenites are mentioned among them after their return from captivity. *Bp Newton*.

In Deuteronomy, xxix, 25—28, are described the evils that should happen to the Israelites in case of their not observing the law which had been given by Moses:

Then men shall say, Because they have forsaken the covenant of the Lord God of their fathers, which he made with them when he brought them forth out of the land of Egypt. For they went and served other gods, and worshipped them, gods whom they knew not, and whom he had not given unto them. And the anger of the Lord was kindled against this land to bring upon it all the curses that are written in this book. And the Lord rooted them out of their land in anger, and in wrath, and in great indignation, and cast them into another land, as it is this day.

Here is an allusion to the great downfall of the first Israelitish monarchy, too plain to be interpreted merely as a supposed case of a misfortune which might befall them, if they should be disobedient to God's commandments. The impression, which the words irresistibly leave on the mind, is that the calamity of defeat and transportation into a strange country had actually befallen them when those words were written.

§ 18.

Allusion in Genesis to the Babylonish mode of building.

A remarkable passage, which furnishes internal evidence that the Old Testament was written after the Babylonish captivity, occurs in Genesis, xi, 3, where the building of the tower of Babel is described:

And they said one to another, Go to, let us make brick, and burn them thoroughly: and they had brick for stone, and slime had they for mortar.

The last words of this verse are not correctly translated; the Hebrew is,

והחמר היה להם לחמר

and it is observable that the letters חמר enter into the composition of the first and last of the four words. The meaning of this triliteral root is threefold, as a verb *to bubble up*, as a noun *bitumen* and *slime* or *clay*. According to the vowel-points the proper translation of the passage is "and bitumen had they for mortar (cement or clay)." What gives particular importance to this passage is the fact that bitumen is found in Mesopotamia or Chaldæa, where it oozes out from the ground and is found floating upon the water. We have this fact on the testimony of Herodotus, who says of a well near Susa:

They draw bitumen and salt and oil out of it, in such manner as this: it is drawn with a pole, to which half a skin is bound instead of a bucket; with this they dip and draw up, and then pour the contents into a receiver: from this it is poured off into another vessel, and turned into three different channels. HERODOTUS, vi, 119.

Elsewhere also (i, 179), speaking of a river named Is, he says: "This river, the Is, casts up with its water many lumps of bitumen, from whence the bitumen was fetched to build the wall at Babylon."

Thus it appears that the Babylonians used bitumen for

cement in building, and it is well known that they used bricks also, because their country does not produce stone. The writer of the passage in Genesis must have himself seen or heard from others that the Babylonian buildings were constructed of brick and bitumen. The fact described in the text before us is named as something remarkable because different from the customs of the people for whose use it was written. But surely, if this was written just after the Israelites had escaped out of Egypt, it would be more novel for them to hear of stone being used than brick, for the hardship of their own slavery in Egypt had consisted in the compulsory and severely exacted manufacture of this article; and it is most probable that they had never seen or heard of bitumen, and would therefore know nothing about it. But if the text before us was written after the Babylonish captivity, the account would come with propriety from a writer who knew of the remarkable nature of Babylonian architecture, and would be highly intelligible to the readers, as well known to be applicable to Babylon, but not to their own country Judæa.

§ 19.
Silence concerning the mode in which the Book of the Law was preserved during the captivity.

We have an indirect testimony to the non-existence of the Pentateuch before the Captivity in the remarkable silence which all the Hebrew Scriptures observe concerning the mode in which this valuable national relic may have been preserved during the convulsions which tore the Jewish state and ended in the temporary destruction of its nationality. Either the book was conveyed to Babylon or it was left in Judæa. But Judæa was deprived of its chief inhabitants: those who remained were too ignorant to appreciate such a volume as the Pentateuch and unlikely to have preserved it. Those of the nation who were carried to Babylon may have conveyed it with them in secret, though it is not likely that such an ancient and important document should have escaped the hands of Shishak, Nebuchadnezzar, and others, who so often pillaged the Jewish Temple. We read of the silver and the gold, with other valuables, which were carried away by those invaders, either into Egypt or to Babylon, but it is not related that they got possession of any book held in reverence by the Jewish people, or that the priests used any device to prevent their sacred books from falling into the hands of the enemy. In all these cases of plunder the historian is very explicit in describing the nature and extent of the booty which they carried off. When Shishak returned to Egypt after the invasion of Palestine, of which we read in the 12th chapter and 9th verse of the Second Book of Chronicles, he "took away the treasures of the house of the Lord, and the treasures of the king's house; he took all: he carried away also the shields of gold which Solomon had made." And again, when Nebuchadnezzar returned to Babylon, the treasures which accompanied him are also described in the thirty-sixth chapter, and verses 7—10, of the same book:

Nebuchadnezzar also carried off the vessels of the house of the Lord to Babylon, and put them in his temple at Babylon. . . . . . And, when the year was expired, king Nebuchadnezzar sent, and brought him to Babylon, with the goodly vessels of the house of the Lord.

In neither of these passages, though so many valuable articles of plunder are enumerated, is there the least notice taken of the Book of the Law, or, indeed, of any book at all. This surely gives rise to a strong suspicion that the sacred books of the Jews, such as we now have them, did not then exist; for books were in ancient times not only not disregarded, but actually held in the highest esteem. A copy of the Hebrew bible, written by the hand, on vellum or any other valuable substance, would even in the present day cost a considerable sum of money, certainly as much as several pairs of silver, or even gold candlesticks; and we know from history, that manuscripts have been considered, even by kings, as the most costly and valuable of their treasures. If the original manuscript of Moses, or even an authentic copy of it had been preserved down to the time of Nebuchadnezzar, we should certainly have learnt from later writers that it was seized and carried to Babylon by the invaders, or they would have triumphantly described the interposition of

Providence, by which their national relic was preserved from profane hands.

But no information has been preserved to us on this very important question; and in the absence of such authentic data, modern writers, who treat of this period of Jewish history, are compelled to interweave such facts as are recorded with conjectures of their own, in order to account for the appearance of the book of the Old Testament in its present totality. The most liberal and intelligent account of this matter that I have seen is given by Dr Milman:

Ezra, who had been superseded in the civil administration by Nehemiah, had applied himself to his more momentous task—the compilation of the Sacred Books of the Jews. Much of the Hebrew literature was lost at the time of the Captivity; the ancient Book of Jasher, that of the wars of the Lord, the writings of Gad and Iddo the Prophet, and those of Solomon on Natural History. The rest, particularly the Law, of which, after the discovery of the original by Hilkiah, many copies were taken; the historical books, the poetry, including all the prophetic writings, except those of Malachi, were collected, revised, and either at that time, or subsequently, arranged in three great divisions: the Law, containing the five Books of Moses; the Prophets, the historical and prophetical books; the Hagiographa, called also the Psalms, containing Psalms, Proverbs, Ecclesiastes, and the song of Solomon. At a later period, probably in the time of Simon the Just, the books of Malachi, Ezra, Nehemiah, and Esther, were added, and what is called the Canon of Jewish Scripture finally closed. It is most likely that from this time the Jews began to establish synagogues or places of public worship and instruction, for the use of which copies of the sacred writings were multiplied. The law, then revised and corrected, was publicly read by Ezra, the people listening with the most devout attention; the feast of Tabernacles was celebrated with considerable splendour. After this festival a solemn fast was proclaimed; the whole people, having confessed and bewailed their offences, deliberately renewed the covenant with the God of their fathers. An oath was administered, that they would keep the law; avoid intermarriages with strangers; neither buy nor sell on the Sabbath; observe the sabbatical year, and remit all debts according to the law; pay a tax of a third of a shekel for the service of the temple; and offer all first-fruits, and all tithes to the Levites. Thus the Jewish constitution was finally re-established.

In the twelfth year of his administration Nehemiah returned to the Persian court. But the weak and unsettled polity required a prudent and popular government. In his absence affairs soon fell into disorder. Notwithstanding the remonstrances of Malachi, the last of the prophets, the solemn covenant was forgotten; and on his return, after a residence of some time in Persia, Nehemiah found the High Priest, Eliashib himself, in close alliance with the deadly enemy of the Jews, Tobiah the Ammonite, and a chamber in the temple assigned for the use of this stranger. A grandson of the High Priest had taken as his wife a daughter of their other adversary Sanballat. Others of the people had married in the adjacent tribes, had forgotten their native tongue, and spoke a mixed and barbarous jargon; the Sabbath was violated both by the native Jews and by the Tyrian traders, who sold their fish and merchandize at the gates of Jerusalem. Armed with the authority of a Persian satrap, and that of his own munificent and conciliatory character—for as governor he had lived on a magnificent scale, and continually entertained 150 of the chief leaders at his own table—Nehemiah reformed all these disorders. Among the rest he expelled from Jerusalem Manasseh, the son of Joiada (who succeeded Eliashib in the high priesthood), on account of his unlawful marriage with the daughter of Sanballat the Horonite. Sanballat meditated signal revenge. He built a rival temple on the mountain of Gerizim, and appointed Manasseh High Priest; and thus the schism between the two nations was perpetuated for ever. The Jews ascribe all the knowledge of the law among the Samaritans, even their possession of the sacred books, to the apostacy of Manasseh.* The rival temple, they assert, became the place of refuge to all the refractory and licentious Jews, who could not endure the strict administration of the law in Judæa. MILMAN's *History of the Jews*, vol. ii, p. 25.

There are many other inaccuracies and contradictions in the Old Testament, which prove that the books are not contemporary with the events which they describe. Those, however, which have been enumerated may suffice; the reader who wishes to examine the others for himself will have no difficulty in finding them out, particularly the following:

In I Chronicles, iii, 16, Zedekiah, who was Mattaniah, is called the son of Jehoiakim, but in II Kings, xxiv, 17, he is stated to have been his uncle.

* One would think that no other proof could be wanting, to show the absurdity of the supposition that the Samaritan Pentateuch is older than the Hebrew. See page 108, chapter xiii, of this volume.

In II Kings, xxiv, 8, Jehoiachin is said to have been 18 years old when he began to reign, but in II Chronicles, xxxvi, 9, his age is stated to have been 8 only, as will be further noticed in p. 288.

In Ezra, ii, 64, is a wrong total, being considerably more than the several items before enumerated amount to.

The chronology of sovereigns given in the books of Kings will also be found in so many instances contradictory to that given in Chronicles, that it is impossible to harmonize them, and a forcible impression is left upon the mind that both may be wrong, because neither is contemporary.

CHAPTER XXIX.

PREHISTORIC RECORDS—ALLEGORICAL READINGS OF EARLY ISRAELITISH HISTORY—PHILO THE JEW—SHISHAK OR SESOSTRIS—PHARAOH NECHO—DETAILS OF THE BABYLONISH CAPTIVITY—ASSYRIAN KINGS, PUL, TIGLATH-PILESER, SHALMANESER, AND ESARHADDON—NEBUCHADNEZZAR KING OF BABYLON.

The Israelitish people were subject to the same passions and liable to the same vicissitudes as other nations; nor need we doubt that their history also may be similarly divided into periods corresponding to those of Greece, Rome, and all the other nations of the world. To trace back the deeds of our forefathers to remote antiquity has been a favourite pursuit both in ancient and modern times, and many of those writers who treat of the early ages of their countrymen, have ventured to carry back their investigations even to the origin of things and the creation of the world itself. The annals of the Hebrews are more minute than others on this interesting subject, and they profess to form a chain of events connecting the race with the first man and woman that ever existed upon the earth. But if the observation just made is well-founded, and the Hebrew annals are to be illustrated by those of our own and other nations, we must divide the accounts which have been handed down to us into two parts. There is a point in the duration of every people at which the light seems to break upon their history, whilst all the preceding portion of their existence is more or less obscure. The name of Mythical or Prehistoric is given to those early years, to denote the uncertainty which generally exists respecting times of which the records are necessarily short and few. Nor is this an exception to the general law of nature: the origin of the various species in the physical world, whether animal, vegetable, or mineral, has always been enveloped in obscurity hitherto impenetrable to science. It is, therefore, hardly to be expected that the early years of the human race, spread into numerous families over the face of the whole earth, and influenced not only by physical but by moral laws, are exempt from the lot which excludes the remote past as well as the distant future from the circle of human knowledge. The portion of time which man can clearly scan with the eye of the intellect may be clearly visible and susceptible of being described for the benefit of future ages; but the intellectual as well as the visual eye is limited in its operations: the lamp of history is constantly moving onward, and as fresh regions are opened for it out of the dark future which lies in front, so those through which it has passed become gradually obscure, and in process of time are again numbered with the unknown. As regards that remarkable people with whose history and literature we are now concerned, it has always been doubted at what point of time the strictly historical period may be supposed to begin. The narrative of the creation found in the Book of Genesis takes cognizance of things that happened before there was a man living to know or to relate them, and it is not unreasonable to believe that such a subject as the creation and origin of the universe would be found to be in any case beyond the power of man to describe. It was perhaps partly from the conviction of this truth that writers have introduced the theory of allegory into narratives which they found it difficult to realize as describing actual and objective occurrences. Nor can it be said that this mode of dealing with the subject is due to the incredulity of foreign and perhaps hostile critics. For one of the most eminent of the Jews, Philo, and one so decidedly national that he bears the surname of "the Jew," has left us long treatises on the subject, in which it is his object to explain the laws and early history of his countrymen as an outward dramatic representation of inward spiritual religion.

It is best, [*says he*,] to trust in God, and not in uncertain reasonings or uncertain conjectures. Abraham trusted in the Lord, and it was counted to him for righteousness. . . . . . If we distrust our own reason, we shall prepare and build for ourselves a city of the mind which will destroy the truth. For Sihon, being interpreted, means destroying. . . . . . Moses says, "there is a fire gone out of Heshbon, and a flame from the city of Sihon. . . . . And it devours even as far as Moab;" that is to say as far as the mind. . . . . The pillars are Arnon, which, being interpreted, means the light of Arnon, since every one of these facts is made clear by reasoning. . . . . "Woe to thee, Moab." . . . . The "people of Chemosh," that is to say, thy people and thy power, have been found to be mutilated and blinded. For Chemosh, being interpreted, means feeling with the hand. And this action is the especial characteristic of one who does not see. Now, their sons are particular reasonings—exiles,—and their opinions are in the place of daughters, being captives to the kings of the Amorites, that is to say, of those who converse with the sophist. For the name Amorites, being interpreted, means talkers, being a symbol of the people who talk much. . . . . Sihon, then, who destroys the sound rule of truth, and his seed also, shall both perish; and so shall Heshbon, namely the sophistical riddles, as far as Debon; which, being interpreted, means adjudication. PHILO, *Alleg.* iii, 81.

This is but an illustration, one out of many, of Philo's arguments, which he still more clearly develops in his remarks on the history of Joseph and the wife of Potiphar.

To those who do not treat the words of the law with reference to allegory, there will result the appearance of a difficulty. . . . . Joseph, that is the disposition of continence, when Pleasure says to him, "Lie with me, and as you are a man, yield to man's passions, and enjoy the pleasures of life," opposes her, saying, "I shall sin against God, who loves virtue, if I become a lover of pleasure." PHILO, *Alleg.* iii, 84.

Thus then, it is not without reasonable grounds, if Jewish writers of reputation explained their early records allegorically, that many modern writers have adopted the same interpretation. Philo indeed, standing face to face with the intellect of Greece and Rome, was probably like Josephus unwilling that the learned men of those nations should look too minutely into the miraculous events which filled every page of his country's story; and whilst Josephus, in his works, has smothered as much as possible the less credible features of that miraculous narrative, Philo boldly adopts and represents it as a drama, in which the virtues and vices, the wisdom and the follies of his forefathers, are represented under the assumed characters which appear in the early Hebrew Records.

Neither then is it without reason that we also should hesitate to be dogmatic, where there was thought to be room for doubt so many hundred years ago. Nor is it unreasonable to pay respect to the opinions of those who consider a portion of the Jewish history to lie beyond the limits of what is called the Historic Period. At what point, however, in this case the Historic Period may be thought to begin, we have no certain data that will enable us to discover. During the many centuries which elapsed before the great empires of Assyria, Babylon, and Persia appear in the eastern world, the little state of Judæa seems to have kept its ground with tolerable security among the other smaller states which divided with them the possession of Palestine and the adjoining countries. We have, it is true, remarkable accounts of the wealth and power of the Israelites at that time, but these accounts come from Israelites alone, and are not confirmed by the statements of any foreign writers. It is, therefore, reasonable to suppose that these accounts have been amplified as much as possible in order to give greater dignity to the ancestral history of the nation. Is it unreasonable to believe that the records of God's chosen people become, like those of all nations, more obscure and shadowy, the farther back we go in the age of the world, and that the most remote pages of those records, let us say nineteen hundred years before Christ, are to be viewed, as Philo viewed them, and not equally descriptive of stern fact with other narratives which record the actions of mankind nineteen hundred years since the great Christian epoch?

But the empires of Assyria, Babylon, and Persia exercised much influence over the fortunes of the Jews. Whatever may have been the real dimensions of their state, whether under the Judges or under the Kings, they are found to have played a very inferior part during the long rivalry between the Egyptian and the Asiatic empires. It is, however, from this very point that the annals of the Jewish nation date their origin: all that preceded has been preserved by the zeal of men, derived and learnt in a great measure during the time of their subjection to foreign conquerors, and to that time is to be ascribed the compilation of those histories from which alone all our knowledge of previous events is derived. Of the monarchs who contended for the empire of the eastern world, the Egyptian appear first in connection with the Jews. The short notices of Chedorlaomer, Tidal king of nations, and other petty chieftains bearing sonorous titles, connected with Abraham and the early Israelites, are too unimportant to arrest our attention. Nor does any foreign power appear to disturb the peace of the Hebrews until the kingdoms of Egypt and Assyria begin to overstep their natural boundaries and to choose the fertile lands of Palestine and Syria as a battle-field on which to contend for empire. In the time of Solomon we read of Pharaoh's daughter becoming his wife (I KINGS, iii, 1), and later in Solomon's reign, we are told that Pharaoh received Hadad Solomon's enemy, "gave him an house, and appointed him victuals, and gave him land" (xi, 18), in resentment perhaps for the affront put upon Pharaoh's daughter on account of the numerous rival wives and concubines that Solomon had introduced. In the reign of Rehoboam, Solomon's son, the alliance between the two nations was rudely broken.

It came to pass in the fifth year of king Rehoboam, that Shishak king of Egypt came up against Jerusalem: and he took away the treasures of the house of the Lord, and the treasures of the king's house; he even took away all: and he took away all the shields of gold which Solomon had made. I KINGS, xiv, 25, 26.

Shishak is no doubt the Sesostris of profane history, who according to Herodotus carried his arms through all the tract of territory which lay on his line of march from Egypt through Palestine to Colchis on the eastern coast of the Euxine sea.

A more full account of this event is given in the Second Book of Chronicles (xii, 2—10), but with particulars which indicate that the writer of that book tempered his narrative to the necessities, even so as to gratify the national vanity and encourage the religious faith of his readers. The Egyptian king limited his proceedings to plunder, and left the inhabitants of Jerusalem to themselves, and the prophet Shemaiah proclaimed that the "people had humbled themselves," that the "Lord would grant them some deliverance," and that his wrath should not be "poured out upon them by the hand of Shishak:" so King Rehoboam "strengthened himself in Jerusalem" and the nation rose again from its fall. The invasion was indeed no more than a violent and sudden storm, which damaged the material welfare of the city for a moment, and compelled the people to replace the treasures which Solomon had accumulated in the Temple and which now had become the spoil of the Egyptians.

After Shishak, we read of no Egyptian expedition against Israel for three or four hundred years, until the time of Necho who again invades Palestine; as Herodotus briefly relates it:

Neco, having come to an engagement with the Syrians on land at Magdolus, conquered them, and after the battle took Cadytis, which is a large city in Syria. HEROD. ii, 159.

The city of Cadytis is elsewhere named by Herodotus in his third book, where he is speaking of the invasion of Egypt by Cambyses, and of the different routes by which an army might be led into that country from Asia: his words are these:

From Phœnicia to the confines of the city of Cadytis, which belongs to those who are called the Syrians of Palestine, and from Cadytis, which is a city in my opinion not much less than Sardis, the sea-ports as far as the city of Jenysus belong to the king of Arabia. HEROD. iii, 5.

The city of Cadytis was the city of Jerusalem, if at least the modern names of places furnish a clue to the designation under which they went in ancient times. The city of Jerusalem probably often owed its safety to its sacred character as much as to its arms and powers of defence. The Arabs still call it El-kuds "The Holy," and in this word we detect the base on which the Greeks formed their more euphonious epithet of "Cadytis." But the short account here quoted from Herodotus gives a very imperfect knowledge of Necho's expedition. It is more fully related in the Books of Kings and Chronicles, which here differ in no other respect than that the latter is more abundant in its details than the former. This will be evident from a comparison of the two narratives which are here subjoined in parallel columns.

In his [Josiah's] days Pharaoh Necho king of Egypt went up against the king of Assyria to the river Euphrates.	After all this when Josiah had prepared the temple, Necho king of Egypt came up to fight against Carchemish by Euphrates.
And king Josiah went against him; and he slew him at Megiddo when he had seen him. II KINGS, xxiii. 29.	And Josiah went over against him, but he sent ambassadors to him, saying, What have I to do with thee, thou king of Judah? I come not against thee this day, but against the house wherewith I have war: for God commanded me to make haste: forbear thee from meddling with God, who is with me, that he destroy thee not. Nevertheless Josiah would not turn his face from him, but disguised himself, that he might fight with him, and hearkened not unto the words of Necho from the mouth of God, and came to fight in the valley of Megiddo. And the archers shot at King Josiah; and the king said to his servants, Have me away, for I am sore wounded. His servants therefore took him out of that chariot, and put him in the second chariot that he had; and they brought him to Jerusalem, and he died, and was buried in one of the sepulchres of his fathers. II CHRONICLES, xxxv, 20—24.

The battle of Magdolus described by Herodotus, may be taken as identical with the Scriptural battle of Megiddo: but if so, the unwisdom of the Jewish king is doubly apparent from the position of the places and the march of the Egyptian army. King Josiah needlessly provoked the encounter in which he met his death. Megiddo was a town in the direction of Mount Carmel, beyond the borders of the king of Judah, and lying in the territory of Israel, which had already been thrice conquered by the Assyrian king. The moderation, therefore, of the Egyptian Necho was remarkable for that age of the world: he seems to have spared Jerusalem in his advance, to have at first defeated his Assyrian enemies, and to have taken Carchemish on the Euphrates. His success however was shortlived: in the third year he was obliged to abandon his conquest, and on his return to Egypt, took Jerusalem, the Cadytis of Herodotus, dethroned Jehoahaz, leaving in his stead as a tributary king his brother Eliakim, whose name he changed to Jehoiakim, and retreated into his own land. Thus this Egyptian invasion, keenly as it was felt by the Jews, and beautifully as it is lamented with still a ray of hope by Jeremiah in the forty-sixth chapter of his prophecies, produced no other effect on the fortunes of Judah than to weaken that sole remaining state in resisting the Babylonians, who now without a rival rapidly prosecuted the entire conquest of the land.

But whilst the state of things was such as we have seen on the side of Egypt, the kingdom of Israel was in a far different case. Its position to the north of the Holy Land exposed it most to be attacked by the Assyrians, and not only by the Assyrians finally, but by the Syrians in still earlier times. "Shall we go to Ramoth-Gilead to battle or shall we forbear?" was the question put to Micaiah the prophet by Ahab king of Israel. The history of that and of other unfortunate campaigns against the smaller states which surrounded Israel, is well known: but soon a more formidable foe appears against them. About the year B.C. 770 and in the reign of Menahem:

> Pul the king of Assyria came against the land: and Menahem gave Pul a thousand talents of silver, that his hand might be with him to confirm the kingdom in his hand. II KINGS, xv, 19.

The thousand talents of silver procured peace for Menahem during the remainder of his short reign of ten years; but his son Pekahiah who succeeded, was slain after a reign of two years only, and Pekah who slew him occupied the throne for twenty years.

In the days of Pekah king of Israel came Tiglath-pileser king of

Assyria, and took Ijon, and Abel-beth-maachah, and Janoah, and Kedesh, and Hazor, and Gilead, and Galilee, all the land of Naphtali, and carried them captive to Assyria. II KINGS, xv, 29.

In this narrative we have the details of what is termed the FIRST CAPTIVITY OF ISRAEL; soon after which event Pekah underwent the same fate which he had inflicted on his predecessor. "Hosea the son of Elah ... smote him and slew him and reigned in his stead;" but apparently it was Pekah himself who dealt this blow to the declining fortunes of the Hebrews by an alliance which he made with Rezin king of the Syrians, against Ahaz, the contemporary king of Judah. The course which Ahaz took to defend himself was sanctioned by the example of his enemies, and could not perhaps be avoided, but it served still more to shake the stability of both monarchies and to prepare the way for their ultimate extinction.

Ahaz sent messengers to Tiglath-pileser king of Assyria, saying, I am thy servant and thy son: come up and save me out of the hand of the king of Syria, and out of the hand of the king of Israel, which rise up against me. And Ahaz took the silver and gold that was found in the house of the Lord, and in the treasures of the king's house, and sent it for a present to the king of Assyria. And the king of Assyria hearkened unto him; for the king of Assyria went up against Damascus, and took it, and carried the people of it captive to Kir, and slew Rezin. II KINGS, xvi, 7—9.

With this must be compared the corresponding narrative from the Second Book of Chronicles (xxviii, 16); from which it appears that the whole country was at this time in a state of what might be almost termed a civil war. Every little commonwealth and tribe was in arms against its neighbours, and it may well be imagined that the Assyrian Conquest did on the whole as much good as harm to the unhappy country which became its victim. The two monarchies into which the Hebrews were divided had passed through all the various stages of change to which nations are subject. The patriarchs of the earliest times gave way, when the people were become too numerous for tribal independence, to Judges chosen to rule the whole free commonwealth of the twelve tribes, and these were afterwards replaced by kings, some of whom ruled their countrymen with justice and regard to law: but the example set by Solomon and so easily followed by some of his successors on Asiatic soil, led to an absolute monarchy, wherein the possession of the throne and the right of inheriting it were decided by the sword alone. Thus the whole land of Palestine, which at no time has ever been able long to maintain its independence, was ready at almost all times to fall a victim to any great power like that of the Assyrians, by which it was now assailed. But the writer of Chronicles tells us Tiglathpileser came to Ahaz, "and distressed him, but strengthened him not." This might have been expected: the Æsopian fable, in which one animal invokes the aid of man against another which attacked him, has been often illustrated by such alliances as that which was cemented so unhappily between the Assyrian giant and the Israelitish dwarf.

Omitting, however, further remarks upon this subject, let us proceed to speak of what is called the SECOND CAPTIVITY of the house of Israel.

Whilst the events above named were progressing against the Syrians, Hoshea the successor of Pekah was reigning wickedly, and "did that which was evil in the sight of the Lord." Shalmaneser was now king of Assyria, and Hoshea "became his servant, and gave him presents." But this state of things did not last long. Hoshea at length "brought no present to the King of Assyria," and the necessary result ensued.

In the ninth year of Hoshea, the king of Assyria took Samaria, and carried Israel away into Assyria, and placed them in Halah and in Habor by the river of Gozan, and in the cities of the Medes. .... So was Israel carried away out of their own land to Assyria unto this day. And the king of Assyria brought men from Babylon, and from Cuthah, and from Ava, and from Hamath, and from Sepharvaim, and placed them in the cities of Samaria instead of the children of Israel: and they possessed Samaria, and dwelt in the cities thereof. II KINGS, xvii, 6—24.

The invasion of Shalmaneser is not mentioned in the Books of Chronicles, but it is again named in the Second Book of Kings, more fully than before, and indeed in a way which would seem to indicate that the writer was forgetful of what he had previously written. His words are these:

And it came to pass in the fourth year of King Hezekiah, which was the seventh year of Hoshea son of Elah king of Israel, that Shalmaneser king of Assyria came up against Samaria and besieged it. And at the end of three years they took it, even in the sixth year of Hezekiah, that is the ninth year of Hoshea king of Israel, Samaria was taken.

From this time the monarchy of Israel disappears from the page of history: and its territory was perhaps annexed to the Assyrian kingdom. A THIRD CAPTIVITY of Israel is assigned by some writers to the reign of Esarhaddon who succeeded to the throne of Shalmaneser: but the biblical records made no mention of any events worthy to be so described: they only allude to the settlement in Samaria and Galilee of colonists, brought by Esarhaddon about the year B.C. 678 to occupy the territory in the place of the exiled Israelites, and to maintain with greater security the domination of the Assyrian king. These colonists, amalgamating with the native inhabitants, formed that race of Samaritans who seventy years afterwards interfered with the builders of the temple, and who appear in the New Testament as antagonistic to the Jews in the time of Christ.

We must now turn our attention to the more important, although the smallest in size, of the two Jewish kingdoms. The events which befel the city of Samaria and its territory, beginning with the tribute paid to Pul in 770 B.C. and ending in the total ruin of the state, extended through little more than fifty or sixty years: but Jerusalem, although pillaged by Shishak in 971, remained in safety for 360 years, until the time of Necho, who captured Jerusalem, but carried his vengeance, for the trouble which Josiah had needlessly caused him, no further than to set on the throne of that city a king of his own choice. It is true that the Assyrian Sennacherib, 100 years before Necho, had attacked the monarchy of Judah and approached the city of Jerusalem, but the word of the Lord was spoken by Isaiah the son of Amoz to king Hezekiah concerning the king of Assyria, and the storm which threatened the city passed away.

He Sennacherib shall not come into this city, nor shoot an arrow there, nor come before it with shield, nor cast a bank against it. By the way that he came, by the same shall he return, and shall not come into this city, saith the Lord. For I will defend this city to save it, for mine own sake, and for my servant David's sake. And it came to pass that night, that the angel of the Lord went out and smote in the camp of the Assyrians an hundred fourscore and five thousand: and when they arose early in the morning, behold, they were all dead corpses. So Sennacherib king of Assyria departed and went and returned, and dwelt at Nineveh. And it came to pass, as he was worshipping in the house of Nisroch his god, that Adrammelech and Sharezer his sons smote him with the sword: and they escaped into the land of Armenia. And Esarhaddon his son reigned in his stead. II KINGS, xix, 32—37.

With this may be compared the narrative which Herodotus gives of the same events in the Second Book of his history, where he speaks of the Egyptian kings.

After this, Senacherib, king of the Arabians and Assyrians, marched a large army against Egypt; whereupon the Egyptian warriors refused to assist him [Sethon], and the priest, being reduced to a strait, entered the temple, and bewailed before the image the calamities he was in danger of suffering. While he was lamenting, sleep fell upon him, and it appeared to him in a vision, that the god stood by and encouraged him, assuring him that he should suffer nothing disagreeable in meeting the Arabian army, for he would himself send him assistants. Confiding in this vision, he took with him such of the Egyptians as were willing to follow him, and encamped in Pelusium: for here is the entrance [into Egypt]. None of the military caste followed him, but tradesmen, mechanics, and suttlers. When they arrived there, a number of field mice, pouring in upon their enemies, devoured their quivers and their bows, and moreover the handles of their shields; so that the next day, when they fled bereft of their arms, many of them fell. HEROD. ii, 141.

The Grecian historian, who wrote these words, has cautioned his readers that his narratives are based, not upon his own testimony or belief, but upon the authority of his informants, and are to be taken, as each reader may determine, upon their intrinsic credibility alone. The Jewish narrative would commend itself to Jewish belief as based upon the authority of their sacred books, and the well-known fact that Jehovah wrought miracles for the preservation of his chosen people. The modern reader of this history can hardly fail to observe that the apparently natural explanation, furnished by the Grecian historian, of the destruction which overwhelmed the Assyrian army, is not less miraculous than that which the Hebrew writers record, and that we have in the account of these events only one more instance of the difficulties under which we labour to explain things of which insufficient data have been preserved. We may therefore pass on to those further events which hung like clouds over Jerusalem, and threatened soon to overwhelm it in the destruction that had befallen Samaria.

The military failure of Sennacherib, followed by his parricidal murder, and by convulsions in the state, as often is the case when great crimes are committed in the royal house of a despotic monarch, may explain the inactivity of an hundred years which now ensued. At the end of that time the city of Nineveh had disappeared from the face of the earth, and Nebuchadnezzar was reigning in Babylon.

Hardly three years had passed away since Eliakim was placed on the throne of Judah, and his named changed to Jehoiakim by Pharaoh-Necho. But the power of Egypt was now waning, and Jehoiakim had to contend against the great king of Babylon.

In his [i.e. Jehoiakim's] days Nebuchadnezzar king of Babylon came up, and Jehoiakim became his servant three years: then he turned and rebelled against him. And the Lord sent against him bands of the Chaldees, and bands of the Syrians, and bands of the Moabites, and bands of the children of Ammon, and sent them against Judah to destroy it, according to the word of the Lord, which he spake by his servants the prophets. Surely at the commandment of the Lord came this upon Judah, to remove them out of his sight, for the sins of Manasseh, according to all that he did; and also for the innocent blood that he shed: for he filled Jerusalem with innocent blood; which the Lord would not pardon. II KINGS, xxiv, 1—4.

Where was the king of Egypt at this crisis to protect the tributary king whom he had placed upon the throne? We are told in the seventh verse of the same chapter what had occurred:

The king of Egypt came not again any more out of his land: for the king of Babylon had taken from the river of Egypt unto the river Euphrates all that pertained to the king of Egypt.

Judah was thus left to face the enemy alone; the country was overrun by hostile bands, and what is termed the FIRST

Captivity of Judah was the result. King Jehoiakim, however, "slept with his fathers, and Jehoiachin his son reigned in his stead." The year 606 B.C. is fixed on as the date of the first Babylonian invasion, more for the sake of making the 70 years of slavery complete than because the date is strictly accurate. For it does not appear that any of the Jews were carried to Babylon by Nebuchadnezzar at the time when Jehoiakim "became his servant three years." In the reign of Jehoiachin, the son of Jehoiakim—if, indeed, there has not been some confusion of name between the two—calamity fell with much greater force upon the Jewish people, in what is called the SECOND CAPTIVITY of Judah.

We are told in the Second Book of Kings, (xxiv, 8,) that Jehoiachin was eighteen years old when he began to reign and that he did that which was evil in the sight of the Lord. This was no more than his father and many previous kings had done, and he was, according to the same account, carried to Babylon in the eighth year of his reign. But in the corresponding chapter of the Second Book of Chronicles (xxxvi, 9,) it is stated that

Jehoiachin was eight years old when he began to reign, and he reigned three months and ten days in Jerusalem, and he did that which was evil in the sight of the Lord.

It is easy to imagine that a child of eight years might do much mischief in almost any situation where he was unwisely placed; and that the formula "in the sight of the Lord" might be applied to denote what was done amiss: but it is more important to point out the variation in the two accounts, which is best explained by the fact that they were both written at a later date than the events which they record, and one of them at a date still more recent than the other. But we will return to the narrative of events.

Nebuchadnezzar, king of Babylon, came against the city, and his servants did besiege it. And Jehoiachin, the king of Judah, went out to the king of Babylon, he and his mother, and his servants, and his princes, and his officers, and the king of Babylon took him in the eighth year of his reign. And he carried out thence all the treasures of the house of the Lord. . . . . And he carried away all Jerusalem and all the princes, and all the mighty men of valour, even ten thousand captives, and all the craftsmen and smiths: none remained save the poorest sort of the people of the land. And he carried away Jehoiachin to Babylon, and the king's mother, and the king's wives, and his officers, and the mighty of the land, those carried he into captivity from Jerusalem to Babylon. And all the men of might, even seven thousand, and craftsmen and smiths a thousand, all that were strong and apt for war, even them the king of Babylon brought captive to Babylon (II Kings, xxiv, 11—16).

But even now the monarchy of Judah was not destroyed, nor the existence of the state extinguished. Mattaniah, uncle to Jehoiachin, was placed upon the throne, and his name changed to Zedekiah. It might be thought that the danger of rebellion would by this time have been fully impressed upon all the inhabitants of Jerusalem, if not upon their king himself. But the example of the preceding monarchs was lost upon Zedekiah:

He *also* did that which was evil in the sight of the Lord his God, and humbled not himself before Jeremiah the prophet, speaking from the mouth of the Lord. And he also rebelled against King Nebuchadnezzar, who had made him swear by God; for he stiffened his neck and hardened his heart from turning unto the Lord God of Israel (II Chron. xxxvi, 12).

The measure of Judah's calamities was now full. The treasures, which remained in the house of the Lord and of all his princes, were carried to Babylon.

And they burnt the house of God, and brake down the wall of Jerusalem, and burnt all the palaces thereof with fire, and destroyed all the goodly vessels thereof. And them that had escaped from the sword carried he away to Babylon; where they were servants to him and his sons until the reign of the kingdom of Persia. To fulfil the word of the Lord by the mouth of Jeremiah, until the land had enjoyed her sabbaths: for as long as she lay desolate she kept sabbath, to fulfil threescore and ten years (xxxvi, 19).

CHAPTER XXX.

SLAVERY AMONG THE TRIBES OF SYRIA AND PALESTINE—THE BABYLONIAN CAPTIVITY GROWING OUT OF POLITICAL MOTIVES—ITS LIMITED NATURE AS TO SLAVERY.

In the last chapter has been given a concise account of the various invasions of Judæa, which ended in the destruction of the Israelitish monarchy and the subjection of their territory to the Babylonians for the conventional period of seventy years. It is the common belief that the whole population of Palestine was carried away into captivity, and this, in the opinion of the Israelites themselves, was sufficiently accounted for by the wrath of God, that the land might recover her sabbaths, or in other words might lie fallow and have rest from cultivation, to make amends for the neglect of the sabbatical year, throughout the whole period during which the people had been in possession of the promised land. The fact that the sabbatical year had not been observed cannot be disputed; nor can it be denied that such an observance might be extremely beneficial, in an agricultural point of view, to a rude and untaught people, too apt to follow the impulse of their wild nature, and probably ignorant of those principles of farming which turn upon a succession of crops, such as in modern times keeps up the fertility of land even without the occasional intervention of a fallow. The Israelites referred all their laws to divine command. Even the commonest operations of nature are said to indicate the personal action of God himself, and the impulses, which so often influenced the minds of the Judges, the Prophets, and the Kings, are declared to have been communicated by the living voice and in the personal presence of the Almighty. If this devout peculiarity of the Jewish race be clearly understood, the interpretation of their books becomes comparatively easy. Those books are sacred because they develope a religion which in its progress has ended in the Christian duties and obligations that bind us now: but they are also to be read with the same care and regard for the truth and accuracy of fact as other books in which we read the history of the past. If we examine carefully the accounts which have come down to us, we shall find that an erroneous notion prevails on the subject we are now discussing, and that the captivity of Babylon has been magnified beyond its real extent. The kings of Assyria and Egypt, as we have seen, contented themselves with carrying away plunder and slaves, but did not destroy the city of Jerusalem. Those rival monarchs knew well enough that the Jewish city would be a powerful outwork of their kingdoms, and so its allegiance was transferred from the one to the other by the chances and as the result of war: its king too was deposed and another set up according as the one empire or the other prevailed at the moment over its rival.

The whole tenour of the narrative towards the latter part of the Kings and Chronicles shows the barbarous condition of all the petty states into which Palestine and Syria were divided. Our attention must be directed to the slavery which was at this time a recognised institution in those countries. The inhabitants of Syria and of Israel could hardly complain of the measure that was dealt out to themselves, seeing that they had served the people of Judah, as we read in the following extract:

Ahaz king of Judah sacrificed also and burnt incense in the high places, and on the hills, and under every green tree. Wherefore the Lord his God delivered him into the hand of the king of Syria; and they smote him, and carried away a great multitude of them captives, and brought them to Damascus. And he was also delivered into the hand of the king of Israel, who smote him with a great slaughter. For Pekah, the son of Remaliah, slew in Judah an hundred and twenty thousand in one day, which were all valiant men; because they had forsaken the Lord God of their fathers. .... And the children of Israel carried away captive of their brethren two hundred thousand, women, sons, and daughters, and took also away much spoil from them, and brought the spoil to Samaria. II CHRON. xxviii, 4—8.

So wholesale a deportation of slaves might have been tolerated between two nations of different race, but there were still some in Samaria who protested against the slavery of their brethren, and their protest was listened to. The "hundred and twenty thousand, all valiant men," who were slain in one day—an exceedingly large number unless Judæa still was thickly peopled—could not be recalled to life, but the two hundred thousand captives were released and sent back by the agency of certain persons "who were expressed by name."

They rose up and took the captives, and with the spoil clothed all that were naked among them, and arrayed them, and shod them, and gave them to eat and to drink, and anointed them, and carried all the feeble of them upon asses, and brought them to Jericho, the city of palm-trees, to their brethren: then they returned to Samaria (xxviii, 15).

Whilst such was the conduct of their own brethren in the northern kingdom, worse might be expected from those of a different race, and the same narrative, in which we read of the treatment, tempered with a certain merciful change of mind, which the Jews in Jerusalem experienced from the Samaritans, informs us that "the Edomites had come and smitten Judah and carried away captives;" and an invasion of the Philistines followed with still more serious results.

The Philistines also had invaded the cities of the low country, and of the south of Judah, and had taken Beth-shemesh, and Ajalon, and Gederoth, and Shocho with the villages thereof, Gimzo also and the villages thereof, and they dwelt there (xxviii, 18).

The system of carrying away captives from a conquered people to become the slaves of their captors was as well known among the inhabitants of Palestine as we find it was from time immemorial among the Greeks, the Romans, and almost every other people. Nor had it in its origin any thing more than a tendency to humanity and mercy: the slaughter of defeated enemies does not commend itself to the feelings even of the most hard-hearted and cruel nations. To relieve themselves from toil by the forced work of others was naturally suggested to the mind of those who had a number of defeated enemies absolutely at their disposal, and the slavery, to which these were consigned, became an institution which had the effect of gradually softening the manners both of the master and the slave.

The comedies of Plautus and Terence show that the slaves, though wholly at the disposal of those whom they served, enjoyed much freedom of intercourse both with the public and with their own masters. Nor has the case been different in any other age of the world or in more modern times. Tyranny indeed is not exercised over any class of men without a reflex of loss or inconvenience to the tyrant: it carries with it its own punishment and insures its own ultimate destruction. The advantages of free labour have become manifest, at one time or other, to all slaveowners, and the intimacy and even friendship which have grown up between the master and his slave have been productive of results worthy not only of the approbation of the humane, but to be recorded in the pages of the historian.

The destruction of Jerusalem by Nebuchadnezzar put an end to the Jewish monarchy for many years, but the people of Judah were not all slain or carried away as slaves. There were probably two millions of people at that time, on the very lowest calculation, in the two kingdoms of Judah and Israel. The army of Uzziah king of Judah about the year B.C. 760, was enormous for so small a state, no less than "three hundred thousand and seven thousand and five thousand that made war with mighty power" (II Chron. xxvii, 13), and this number indicates a proportionately large population for the whole kingdom. The army of Sennacherib lost one hundred and eighty-five thousand men in one night. But the country which required so large a force to overrun it must have counted a proportionately large army of soldiers to act in its defence. Notwithstanding these numbers, the captives carried away to Babylon by Nebuchadnezzar were by no means numerous, nor does it appear that they were carried away solely as slaves: they seem rather to have been the chiefs and higher orders only who were then carried away.

He [Nebuchadnezzar] carried away all Jerusalem, and all the princes, and all the mighty men of valour, even ten thousand captives, and all the craftsmen and smiths: none remained save the poorest sort of the people of the land. And he carried away Jehoiachin to Babylon, and the king's mother, and the king's wives, and his officers, and the mighty of the land, those carried he into captivity from Jerusalem to Babylon. And all the men of might, even seven thousand, and craftsmen and smiths a thousand, all that were strong and apt for war, even them the king of Babylon brought captive to Babylon. II KINGS, xxiv, 14—16.

The object of the king of Babylon was not so much to make slaves as to disable the Jews from again rebelling against him. The menial, or at all events, laborious duties of slaves would have been better discharged by the poorest people of the land: but these were not made captives. The wealthy, the mighty men of valour, and the princes were taken away, that no leaders of rebellion might be left: the craftsmen and men were captured that no weapons of war might be manufactured, and the poorest people of the land were left that so fair a portion of Nebuchadnezzar's empire might still be inhabited, and produce the ample crops of which it was capable. That these were the merciful motives of the great king is evident from his further measures. He gave the Jews another king, Mattaniah, thenceforth called Zedekiah, and belonging to the former royal family. But he, too, either by his own ambition or instigated by his turbulent people, rebelled against the Babylonian monarch; and that king now was determined to crush a city, whose loyalty it was impossible to trust. After two years' siege, Jerusalem was destroyed; the king and the men of war who defended it, fled: the king was taken prisoner, and together with those who were unable to flee out of the city, carried captive to Babylon. But the number of these second prisoners of war must not be set at too high a figure. The capture of prisoners defeated in war is much modified by circumstances such as always arise to modify great evils. A small proportion of the whole number will be found to suffer from the harsh law. Flight will save many: the capacity of the victors to secure their prisoners will certainly be limited, even if the desire to enslave continue without limits, and the very worthlessness of some will cause the captors to forego their prize. A victorious army cannot be encumbered, and will indeed be endangered by an unlimited train of captives. To these causes may be ascribed the small numbers "ten thousand" and "seven thousand" of Hebrew captives compared with the whole population. The highly wrought picture of this great overthrow must be qualified by the bitter feelings which actuated that wonderful people when they were carried away, and by the vigour with which they resumed their national existence when the period of their bitterness was past. If, indeed the whole Israelitish people had been removed to Babylon and again suffered to return, the event would have been even greater in magnitude than the greatest migrations which history has recorded. The exode from Egypt would have been repeated on a still more gigantic scale: the great movements of the Cimmerian and northern nations would no longer pass for the most remarkable instances of the migratory powers of man; and the mighty army of Xerxes, which shook the world, and filled Asia and Europe with wonder, would have been paralleled by a still more numerous host issuing from the same plains of Babylonia, not a hundred years before, and moving with all the excitement of renewed life and buoyant hopes, to reoccupy the territories of their forefathers, and to rebuild what had been a mighty city. But the real fact of these events was on a much less extended scale, the people still inhabited the land, and still cultivated the soil; and in the first year of Cyrus, King of Persia, an edict went forth that those who had been brought to Babylon seventy years before should now return to their native country. In the Books of Ezra and Nehemiah we have a detailed account of their return and of the number of those who went back:

The whole congregation together was forty and two thousand three hundred and threescore, besides their servants and their maids, of whom there were seven thousand three hundred thirty and seven: and there were among them two hundred singing men and singing women. EZRA, ii, 64—65.

It is unnecessary to dispute the accuracy of these numbers: the purpose which they were meant to serve would require such a number of emigrants, and the people of the land who were left would help speedily to make up a fit population for the city which was to be built.

But the people of the land were of two kinds: there were the people of Judah and the people of Israel. Of the latter class some had been placed in the land by Esarhaddon, and though they had, it seems, become assimilated to the native Israelites, were offensive as aliens and schismatics to those who now came from Babylon with all the authority of the sovereign and all the sanction of Babylonian religion and literature. The political state of the country was soon reconstituted, but the royal name and government were gone. The seventy years had truly regained for the nation the sabbaths which they had previously neglected. The laws of Moses were re-enacted with such additions as the times suggested, and that government by priests was established which lasted, more or less controlled by temporal leaders, and, more or less checked by foreign invaders, still exercised such sway over the mind of the Jews till the time of Christ.

CHAPTER XXXI.

REFERENCES TO FACTS OF WHICH NO RECORDS HAVE BEEN PRESERVED.

THE course of events which, beginning with the year B.C. 721, when Samaria was taken, ended with the restoration of the Jews and the rebuilding of Jerusalem about the year 500, together with the political motives which influenced those events, have been briefly described in the last two chapters. The zeal and even impetuosity, with which the Jews hurried on and completed the re-establishment of their nation, was likely to show itself in investigating the history of their ancestors. There was indeed now little scope for the arts of war. The opposition of the Samaritans, who had been refused permission to join in the work of restoration, caused temporary obstruction and inconvenience to the builders, some of whom were obliged, as appears by a passage of Nehemiah, (iv. 16—17), to work in relays, whilst others with one of their hands "wrought in the work, and with the other hand held a weapon." This opposition, however, was rather of the nature of a civil disturbance; no foreign army was able to march against the rising nation. The great king of Persia, combining in one the Assyrian, the Median, the Babylonian, and other smaller communities, overshadowed all Asia, and deterred the various states from interfering with the decree which had gone forth that the Jewish nation should be reconstituted, and Jerusalem, valuable as an outwork against Egypt, be rebuilt. Thus, there being no possibility of an attack from without, the attention of the people was turned to the arts of peace, and all the records of their past history would naturally be sought out and brought together. The books which still remain of their literature, comprised within the limits of our present Old Testament, are yet remarkably abundant in the information which they furnish on the subjects of which they treat; and they refer to other books in terms which seem to imply that those others were still in existence when the Pentateuch and the rest of the Jewish Canon were published. In relating the acts of the kings, both of Israel and Judah, the writer breaks off as if from a superfluous task, and tells us that the rest of the acts of that king and all that he did, "Are they not written in the book of the Chronicles of the kings of Judah?"

It is probably owing to this that in several parts of the Old and New Testaments, and especially the latter parts of the former, we find a reference made to events said to have happened in earlier times, of which no trace can be found in the books where we should expect them to be mentioned. Every one of these Chronicles, Acts, and other writings, referred to in our Bibles, has perished, unless a book, which bears the title of Enoch, and has been discovered in very recent times, may be regarded as the same which is quoted once in the New Testament, in the Epistle which bears the name of Jude.

The disappearance of so many works of the ancient Hebrew literature has no doubt left us without sufficient information towards thoroughly understanding many parts of the history of the nation; nor have we any right to question such obscure statements which occur in our books, seeing that the needful explanation might have been found in some of those writings which have been lost. Reference has been already made in page 38 of this volume to several of those lost treatises, and it may now be desirable to notice a few passages of the Bible where allusion is made to facts of which no record is found, but which possibly were related in some of those works which have been lost.

§ 1. *The Call of Abraham.*

The first instance of an incomplete narrative, which shall be adduced, relates to the Call of Abraham. It is the general belief that the Call to leave the native land of Chaldæa and to go into Canaan was addressed to Abraham, and we read in the Epistle to the Hebrews (xi, 8) what here follows:

By faith Abraham, when he was called to go out into a place which he should after receive for an inheritance, obeyed; and he went out, not knowing whither he went.

The writer of this Epistle, who is thought to have been no other than the Apostle Paul, derived this statement no doubt from the first verse of the twelfth chapter of Genesis:

Now the Lord had said unto Abram, Get thee out of thy country, and from thy kindred, and from thy father's house, unto a land that I will show thee, &c. . . . So Abram departed, as the Lord had spoken unto him; and Lot went with him: and Abram was seventy and five years old when he departed out of Haran.

Bishop Patrick remarks that this happened before Abraham came to Haran, and while he lived in Ur of the Chaldees. But this could not have been so; for in chapter xi, 31, we read:

And Terah took Abram his son, and Lot the son of Haran, his son's son, and Sarai his daughter in law, his son Abram's wife, and they went forth with them from Ur of the Chaldees, to go into the land of Canaan; and they came to Haran, and dwelt there.

Thus it appears that it was Abraham's father Terah, and not Abraham, who led the family out from Ur of the Chaldees; and that, too, with the intention of entering the land of Canaan. Abraham only continued the migration which his father had begun. The account of this transaction is noticed in the book of Judith, in terms that seem to show that there were once more full accounts which are now lost.

This people are descended of the Chaldæans: and they sojourned heretofore in Mesopotamia, because they would not follow the gods of their fathers, which were in the land of Chaldæa. For they left the way of their ancestors, and worshipped the God of heaven, the

God whom they knew: so they cast them out from the face of their gods, and they fled into Mesopotamia, and sojourned there many days. JUDITH, v, 6—8.

The author of the Book of Judith, as well as the writer of the Epistle to the Hebrews, seem to have had a more complete account than now remains of what is termed the Call of Abraham, and the translators of our Authorized Version, trusting perhaps too much to one part of the Scriptures to explain difficulties in another, have inserted the little word 'had' in the first verse of the twelfth chapter of Genesis. By this insertion they make it appear, as remarked by Bishop Patrick, that the Call of Abraham had been made whilst still in Ur of the Chaldees. This, however, is contrary to the other passage cited from Genesis, unless, which is hardly probable, two calls were made, one to the Father Terah and the other to the son, whilst still a youth in his father's house.

Our translators had no authority for rendering the Call of Abraham in the pluperfect tense: every other version but ours has it simply in the past tense, 'And God said unto Abraham;' the Vulgate translates it *dixit*, and the Septuagint ειπε; and the meaning becomes clear. The family of Terah, Abraham's father, quitted Ur of the Chaldees, for the reason given in the Book of Judith, and the only call made at that time was the obligation to worship the 'God of Heaven,' and not to join in the ceremonies of the idolatrous Chaldæans. How long they sojourned at Haran in Mesopotamia, half-way between Chaldæa and Canaan, whither Terah himself had intended to go, we are not informed: but it was at Haran that the Call was made to Abraham, and he, in obedience to God, departed into the land of Canaan, which was promised to be the dwelling-place of his descendants.

§ 2. *Bedan.*

In many parts of the Old Testament are found names which occur nowhere else in that volume; these are generally found in genealogies, which would naturally contain names of sons and relatives who play no part in the history of their times, and in such cases these names would attract no notice from the reader. But in the First Book of Samuel (xii, 11), we meet with Bedan, named together with other famous heroes, as having himself also delivered his countrymen from some of the neighbouring tribes which oppressed them.

And the Lord sent Jerubbaal, and Bedan, and Jephthah, and Samuel, and delivered you out of the hand of your enemies on every side, and ye dwelled safe.

Bishop Patrick has the following note on this passage:

It is remarkable that there is no such name as Bedan mentioned in the book of Judges.

Dr Hales, with singular boldness of criticism, observes on the same: "Perhaps Barak may be meant."

This supposition might pass, if it were certain that the book of Judges contained a full history of all that period of the Jewish national existence; but, as it certainly is a very brief history, and occasionally changes with great abruptness from one subject to another, it is probable that there once were other writings, which perished before the present book of Judges was compiled, and that in those writings the achievements of Bedan would be found.

§ 3. *The appointment of a captain to lead the Israelites back to Egypt.*

A similar mode of interpretation may be applied to a passage of Nehemiah, ix, 16, as compared with Numbers, xiv, 4.

NEHEMIAH, ix, 16. But they and our fathers dealt proudly, and hardened their necks, and hearkened not to thy commandments, and refused to obey, neither were mindful of thy wonders that thou didst among them; but hardened their necks, and in their rebellion appointed a captain to return to their bondage, &c.

In Numbers, xiv, 4, we are told:

And they said one to another, Let us make a captain, and let us return into Egypt.

But it is not stated that the people actually chose a captain to lead them back into Egypt. The alternative is evidently this: Nehemiah either quotes erroneously from the book of Numbers, or he had a more full account of the matter to which he referred than has been handed down to us, and he found in that history, whatever it was, that the rebellious Israelites actually appointed a captain who should lead them back to Egypt.

§ 4. *Sprinkling the Book.*

Again; in the Epistle to the Hebrews, ix, 19, we read thus:

> For when Moses had spoken every precept to all the people according to the law, he took the blood of calves and of goats, with water, and scarlet wool, and hyssop, and sprinkled both the book and all the people.

The writer of this epistle must also have had more sources of information than we now possess: for the account which he gives in the verse before us does not exactly tally with any of the various verses in the Levitical Law, where the subject is related. In the fourteenth chapter of Leviticus is found a description of the ceremony by which lepers should be cleansed; both hyssop and scarlet are used in the rites which accompanied the cleansing, but no mention is made of a book as used in that ceremony, nor is there any other passage in the Law of Moses, to which the writer, whether St Paul or some other, might have referred as an authority for what he has stated about sprinkling the book in the Epistle to the Hebrews.

§ 5. *The Contest between Michael and the Devil.*

Another remarkable instance, bearing upon the present argument, is the account which St Jude gives of a contest between Michael and the Devil:

> Yet Michael the archangel, when contending with the Devil he disputed about the body of Moses, durst not bring against him a railing accusation, but said, The Lord rebuke thee! JUDE, 9.

It is not known to what St Jude alludes in this verse: nothing is said, in the Old Testament, of any contest between the Devil and the archangel Michael; and the remark, which is quoted from Dr Hales in a commentary on Deuteronomy, xxxiv, 10, rather embarrasses than clears up the subject:

From an obscure passage in the New Testament, in which Michael the archangel is said to have contended with the devil, about the body of Moses, Jude 9, we may collect, that he was buried by the ministry of angels, near the scene of the idolatry of the Israelites; but that the spot was purposely concealed, lest his tomb might also be converted into an object of idolatrous worship among the Israelites, like the brazen serpent.

It is dangerous to hazard such a conjecture, because it leads to the inference that a man admitted to such intimate converse with God, should, after death, run the risk of being carried away by the Devil, and only be rescued by the interposition of an archangel. The passage of St Jude may be left in its original obscurity, rather than that we should attempt to solve it by compromising the power and goodness of the Almighty. St Jude probably had other writings to refer to, which recorded the contest between the powers of good and evil, but are now lost.

§ 6. *The Magicians Jannes and Jambres.*

In St Paul's Second Epistle to Timothy, (iii, 8,) are found the names of two of the magicians who competed with Moses in magical arts, in the presence of Pharaoh king of Egypt.

Now, as Jannes and Jambres withstood Moses, so do these also resist the truth; men of corrupt minds, reprobate concerning the faith.

These names, Jannes and Jambres, occur nowhere in the existing Hebrew Scriptures, and were probably taken out of other Jewish writings. They are meant no doubt to designate the wise men, sorcerers, and magicians, who imitated Moses and Aaron when they changed their rods into serpents, and "did in like manner with their enchantments." (Exod. vii, 11.) From what source St Paul got these names is uncertain. Theodoret, in his note on the text, says it was from the unwritten teaching, or learning, of the Jews. This is equivalent to saying that he got them from tradition. At all events, they appear to have been known among the Greeks and Romans. Eusebius tells us in his Præparatio Evangelica (ix), that Jannes and Jambres, or Mambres, were Egyptian writers who practised magic and opposed Moses in the presence of Pharaoh. Pliny also, in his Thirtieth Book, chapter 3, writes thus :

There is also another school of magic derived from the Jews, Moses, Jannes, and Lotapea, but many thousand years later than Zoroaster.

If Pliny supposed Moses to have lived many thousand years later than Zoroaster, he must have referred the Persian philosopher to very remote prehistoric times, but it is probable that the classical writers, who have so briefly alluded to Jewish history, considered the origin of that people to belong to an age not very remote from their own times.

The name of Lotapea, whom Pliny connects with Moses, is otherwise entirely unknown, and it is fair to presume that the names " Jannes " and " Jambres," not found in the books of Moses, may have become known to St Paul through the medium of other writings in which many particulars of Jewish history were recorded, but which are now no longer in existence.

§ 7. *Moses not the son of Pharaoh's daughter.*

Several circumstances of the life and acts of Moses are known to us only because they are noticed in the New Testament, no mention being made of them in the old Jewish Scriptures. For instance, there is no authority in the Pentateuch for the remark which occurs in Hebrews, xi, 24 : " By faith Moses, when he was come to years, refused to be called the son of Pharaoh's daughter." And in the Acts of the Apostles (vii, 22) we are told that :

Moses was learned in all the wisdom of the Egyptians, and was mighty in words and in deeds. And, when he was full forty years old, it came into his heart to visit his brethren of Israel, &c.

But in the Book of Exodus the account of these things is much shorter, and nothing is said of the age of Moses, at the time referred to.

These circumstances make it probable that there were other original records in the time of St Paul, which have since perished.

This conclusion is supported by the admitted fact that many books, which have perished, are quoted in the Old Testament itself. Such are the books of Jasher, Enoch, the Wars of the Lord, and many others, of which mention has been already made in this work.

A perplexing train of argument opens to us from a consideration of these facts. If the books, which have perished, were of value, why have they perished? if they were of no value, why have valuable writers like St Paul quoted them? It is supposed that they were of inferior authority, but this point has not been proved. If the existing books are genuine relics of a high antiquity, yet some of the lost books were more ancient still. The same Providence which has preserved the ones, has suffered the others to sink, even though those which have floated down the stream of time are imperfect on many points which the others would have supplied. I think these observations coincide with the opinion which has been advanced, that those which remain are not original contemporary records but have been copied from more ancient sources.

CHAPTER XXXII.

GRAMMATICAL SUBTLETIES ARE A PROOF OF A LATER AGE.

It is a favourite theory with philosophers of every school, and, indeed, is admitted by almost all mankind, that nothing which has had a beginning can fail at some time or other to have an end. The comparatively short space of time over which History extends, shows us that the greatest empires, as well as the smallest tribes, are alike due to decay—gradually or otherwise, as it may be—and, ultimately, to extinction. Nor is it an argument against this view that some races of men, as some departments of the material world, have an existence prolonged far beyond that of others, whose nature is more frail, or is exposed to greater wear and tear. In this particular, at all events, we may recognise the struggle between species, although we are not bound to infer that the first origin of those which survive is to be ascribed to the similar theory of development. Every ancient nation of which we have records has passed away almost totally from the face of the earth; the traces of them, and the ruins of their works which still remain, are daily becoming fewer and more faintly marked, and it is still nearer to our present purpose to remark that these remains in every branch of art, architecture, numismatics, painting, and sculpture, become worse and worse as time goes on, when they have once begun to degenerate from the excellence to which they had previously attained. In this particular mind seems to be subject to the same law as the physical universe, for it blooms or withers according to the favourable or adverse circumstances in which it is placed. Those who have studied the ancient history and literature of Greece and Rome, have observed that, when those countries began to give signs of decay, the style of their writers also began to decline, and to exhibit symptoms of decrepitude and bad taste. Certain plays on words, with grammatical and verbal subtleties, were then introduced into Greek and Roman versification, adapted, perhaps, to amuse for a moment even those whose minds were capable of deriving pleasure from more noble writings; but certainly not to be encouraged as models on which a national literature should be formed. No one would venture to compare those subtleties of words and grammatical fancies which have prevailed in later ages with the noble simplicity of Homer, Æschylus, or Pindar, and, as we know that the later period of Greek and Roman literature produced these plays on words and other poetical fancies, we may reasonably infer that the same peculiarities occurring in the Bible owe their existence to the fact that they were produced in the latest period of Jewish literature. A few instances of the bad taste, which always marks a degenerate age, may here be of use to those who have not time to read the Classics for themselves.

About the year 200 before Christ, lived one Simmias, a native of Rhodes, who is generally considered the inventor of the style of versification to which I refer, for it does not appear to have existed before his time, and, indeed, could hardly have been conceived except in an age when the public taste had become exceedingly corrupt: it consists in arranging verses in such a way as to form figures of various objects. Six such poems have been preserved, forming an axe, a pair of wings, two altars, an egg, and a pan-pipe. The last of these is sometimes ascribed to Theocritus, but, no doubt, erroneously. It consisted of twenty verses, arranged in ten pairs, each pair of the same length, but shorter than the preceding pair, the whole representing ten pipes, each shorter than the other.

The Latin poets indulged abundantly in conceits of this kind. The poet Ausonius was not free from the infection. Among his Idyllia is a poem so constructed that the last word of every line is the first word of the following line. In our own country Venerable Bede improved upon this thought, and wrote an elegy in such a manner that the last half of each verse was the first half of the next verse. Ausonius also wrote poems in which every line ended with monosyllables, denoting the members of the body, the names of Gods, of the virtues, the letters of the alphabet, &c. But

Ausonius belonged to a declining age, and Bede, although he was the author of the Ecclesiastical History of our nation, from which we derive the knowledge we possess of our earliest forefathers, is never placed on a level in the list of poets with Virgil, Horace, or Juvenal.*

These facts have their parallel in the Hebrew writings. Thus, in the third chapter of Zephaniah, verse viii,† are found all the letters of the Hebrew alphabet, together with the vowel points, and almost all the grammatical marks invented to facilitate the reading of the Hebrew language. Some may suppose that this curious circumstance could not be the result of accident; and that the fact of *not quite all* the grammatical marks being found there seems to imply that those which do not occur have been invented since.

There are several other instances of this play on letters in the Old Testament. Its grand division into twenty-two books, corresponding to the number of letters in the alphabet, is the most striking, and it is notorious that the 119th Psalm is divided into twenty-two parts, designated by the names of the letters, *aleph, beth, gimel, daleth,* &c. It is also otherwise peculiar. Each of the twenty-two divisions contains eight verses, and in these eight verses occur the same eight Hebrew words in every one of the twenty-two divisions of which the psalm consists.

The twenty-fifth Psalm contains twenty-two verses, each of which begins with a different letter of the alphabet, from *aleph* to *tau*.

The thirty-fourth contains twenty-two verses, besides the title *A Psalm of David*, &c. Each verse begins with a fresh letter; but *vau* is omitted, and to fill up the number the last verse begins with *pe*.

Several other psalms are constructed on similar principles. For instance, Ps. xxxvii, cxi, cxii, and cxlv; but in Ps. cxlv

---

* These fancies did not end with Ausonius or Venerable Bede—they have lasted down to the present day; and even the stagnation of a Papal Court has been enlivened by their quaint wit. The Synod of Dort produced nothing of an ecclesiastical stamp to create much interest in the present day, but the epigram which probably most often brings it to our remembrance, touches upon the subject of this chapter—

Dordrechti sy*nodus nodus*—chorus inte*ger æger*.
Conv*entus ventus*—sessio stra*men amen !*

† See Lee's "Hebrew Grammar," page 31.

one letter ס is omitted; in Ps. xxxvii צ is repeated, and ע is omitted. This kind of composition is found also in Proverbs, where the last twenty-two verses of the thirty-first chapter are also alphabetic; but, as the latter part of this chapter treats of a totally different subject from the former half, they probably were at first different chapters altogether. The same form of composition is found still more remarkably in the lamentations of Jeremiah, where each chapter or elegy is divided into twenty-two periods, to correspond, as in the Psalms, with the letters of the Hebrew alphabet. The first four chapters, moreover, are in the form of acrostics. In the first three chapters each verse contains three lines, and the initial letters are, with a slight variation, in the order of the alphabet. In the fourth chapter each verse consists of four lines; in the third the alphabet is repeated three times, but in the fifth none of these peculiarities are found.

This species of writing occurs, therefore, in four books of the Old Testament, Psalms, Proverbs, the Prophecy of Zephaniah, and the Lamentations of Jeremiah. In such late poets as the last two, who are supposed to have flourished about the year 600 before Christ (see p. 23), this metrical conceit is less remarkable; but in the Psalms and Proverbs, the works of David and Solomon, who are represented as first-rate poets—the former called the "sweet psalmist of Israel"—we cannot believe that such puerile absurdities could be found. It will, possibly, be replied, that some of the Psalms were not written by David, and that some of the Proverbs were not written by Solomon; but it is worthy of notice that the twenty-fifth and thirty-fourth Psalms, in which these alphabetic fancies occur, are superscribed "A Psalm of David." We must, then, infer, either that the Psalms in question were not written by David, or that the reputation of David as a poet was not so great as has been represented. But the consent of the whole Israelitish nation has awarded to David the same honours in Israel which Homer enjoyed among the Greeks, Tasso in Italy, Aldhelm among the Anglo-Saxons, Taliessin in Wales, Ossian in Scotland, and many other bards, in different countries, whose songs have inspired their countrymen to deeds of valour in the field, and of conviviality at the banquet. These Psalms, therefore, were not composed by David, but rather by some imitator in a later age, when the glories of past times had faded, and the increased facilities, which about the fifth and sixth centuries before Christ were opened by the more general use of writing, led to the composition of many pieces both in prose and verse, which were afterwards—ignorantly or otherwise—ascribed to the great masters of the heroic ages.

But our notice of this subject would not be complete without a further remark on the examples of degenerate taste which have here been pointed out. With the exception of the single chapter of Zephaniah, in which all the Hebrew letters and vowel points occur, possibly, after all, the result of accident, all the other examples are found in the books which form the Hagiographa, and we have every reason for ascribing these writings to the latest period of the Jewish Commonwealth. Thus a variety of reasons concur to support our argument concerning the time when these writings were first produced. Such pedantic forms imply a degenerate age, and all the external evidence which can be brought to bear upon the subject tends to show that the books in which these forms of writing occur were first published in that very age in which such pedantries in every country have abounded.*

CHAPTER XXXIII.

THAT THE ISRAELITES SPOKE EGYPTIAN IN EGYPT, AND AFTERWARDS ACQUIRED THE CANAANITISH OR HEBREW LANGUAGE BY A LONG RESIDENCE IN CANAAN.

THE inexperienced zeal of theologians has sometimes sought to magnify the importance of the Israelitish nation by

---

* I have somewhere met with the following calculation of the number of books, chapters, verses, words, and letters found, both in the Old and in the New Testaments:—

	In the Old.	In the New.
Books	39	29
Chapters	929	260
Verses	23,214	7,959
Words	592,439	181,253
Letters	2,728,100	838,380

This table, including the New as well as the Old Testament, is probably due identifying Hebrew as the original language of mankind. Such an opinion needs no refutation in these days, and, if there were the slightest ground for such a theory, yet, as is justly remarked by the author of the *Celtic Researches*,* "That any living language whatsoever should have remained in the same state, from the Creation to the time of Moses, is a thing in itself of the utmost improbability." Those who have advanced the contrary opinion have argued that the Hebrew is a sacred language, and, consequently, free from those causes which have changed and corrupted all the other languages of the earth. The sacredness of character is supposed to be derived from the circumstance of its having been selected as the vehicle of communication from God to man. But the Bible contains much more than the laws and institutions commanded by God, and delivered by Moses and the Prophets to mankind; and the language in which the Bible is written was common to others beside the Jews. The inscriptions discovered in modern times at Carthage, are in the language of Canaan, which is known to have been the same as that which was spoken by the Jews. There could, therefore, be no inherent sacredness in that tongue, even though our oldest sacred books are written in it. Like all other languages, it was merely a medium for the expression of human ideas, and for communicating information on all subjects to the human intellect. No reason can be assigned why one language should be more sacred or more incorruptible than another, or why the most ancient language should be more sacred or more incorruptible than the

---

to some modern calculator; but I believe the doctors of the later period of the Jewish Commonwealth kept a similar account of the Old Testament, in order to preserve the purity of its text.

* Davies's *Celtic Researches*, p. 91. It has been suggested from time to time during the last hundred years or more, that the Celtic languages were closely connected with the Hebrew, if not wholly derived as dialects from that tongue. No thorough confirmation of this theory has been furnished, and the likeness between them may be no other than is found or imagined to exist between languages spoken in different countries but in the same age of the world. Whatever similar words or expressions may be discovered between the old British languages and Hebrew were probably due to the trade carried on, perhaps for centuries, between the Celtic nations in the north-west of Europe and the Phœnicians, who certainly spoke the language of the Jews, as their remaining inscriptions found in Carthage and in Palestine fully testify.

most modern. On the contrary, there is every reason why the ancient languages should be more liable to decay than those which have grown up in modern times. It is a patent fact that all the ancient languages that were spoken before the Christian era have died out, and been replaced by new dialects that have risen upon their ruins. The language in which the books of the Old Testament were written has had its day, and for more than fifteen hundred years has been dead. If we may believe those writers who possess the greatest knowledge of the subject, that language underwent a change even during the existence of the nation who spoke it.

"Originally," says Mar Sutra, "the law was given to Israel in Ibri writing, and the holy (Hebrew) language. It was again given to them in the days of Ezra, in the Ashurith writing and the Aramaic language." DEUTSCH's *Remains*, p. 321.

If so, the present Hebrew being the law which was given to Ezra—for it is the only law that remains—is comparatively modern, and there was one earlier still, in what is called the Ibri writing, and the holy (Hebrew) language. We may, therefore, examine it in the same manner as we should examine any other ancient or modern language, and test it by all the various modes which criticism can supply. When, therefore, we find that the Hebrew nation (which comes into contact with Europeans for the first time in the age of Alexander the Great, about three hundred years before Christ), claim for their sacred books an antiquity of twelve hundred years precedent to that date, it becomes necessary to inquire how far the mutability of all human languages is consistent with such claims.

On the authority of the Old Testament itself, it is said that the Hebrews derive their name from their ancestor Heber,* one of whose descendants, Abraham, left his native country Chaldæa, and settled in the land of Canaan. Now

---

* *Heber* or *Eber* was the great-great-great-great-great-grandfather of Abraham, and, as far as we know, never had any intercourse with the land of Canaan. Surely the *five greats* which mark the interval of kinsmanship between him and Abraham, may be thought sufficient to exempt him from having given name to the Hebrew nation. There can be no doubt that they were so called because they were foreigners, from the Hebrew word which means *over* or *beyond* the river.

we have a complete demonstration in Genesis, xxxi, 47, that the great stock of the family of Heber, which remained in Mesopotamia, spoke the Chaldaic and not the Hebrew dialect.

Laban, who had been brought up in the house of his fathers, denominates the heap of witness, certainly in his native tongue, Jegur Sahadutha. This name is composed of three Chaldaic words, *jegur*, a heap, *sahad*, a witness, and *dutha*, an appointment. Had Moses literally transcribed all the words of Laban, he could not have furnished us with a more satisfactory proof of the language he used.

Jacob, on the other hand, who had been born in a foreign country, and had lived there from his infancy, till he was upwards of seventy years of age, describes the same heap in a language different from that of his relations. He calls it Galeed, using two Hebrew terms, one of which implies a *heap* and the other a *witness* or testimony. The name is synonymously recorded in both languages,* and therefore in the languages which Laban and Jacob respectively used. The Hebrew was not then the general dialect of the children of Heber. And it is equally clear that it was not peculiar to his family. The prophet Isaiah, in the nineteenth chapter, emphatically calls it the *language of Canaan*: "In that day shall five cities in the land of Egypt speak the language of Canaan, and swear to the Lord of hosts; one shall be called The city of destruction." Isaiah, xix, 18.

In addition to this testimony, we have the names of men and places amongst the old Canaanites, in the time of Abraham, in pure Hebrew. We have Phœnician inscriptions, the fragment of the Punic language in the Pænulus of Plautus and the remains of that language in the island of Malta, as undeniable proofs, that the Hebrew was the genuine language of Canaan, which preserved it with little variation to a late age.

This language could by no means have been communicated by Abraham to the natives of the country. It is certain that he found it, and very probable that he learnt it there. In his conversation with the inhabitants, he must have used

---

* Bishop Patrick says, "The one is a Syriac, the other a Hebrew name, both having the same signification." Syriac and Chaldaic may be considered as the same language.

their language. It is easy and natural for a stranger to acquire the language of the people amongst whom he settles, especially if it differs from his own only as a dialect. But it is an absolute impossibility for several independent kingdoms suddenly to accommodate themselves to the dialect of a single sojourner: and the language of the old Canaanites, and of the posterity of Abraham, at least, the house of Jacob, was the same.*

Thus Laban, who had always lived in the land of Chaldæa, naturally spoke the language of his kindred and nation, whilst Jacob, who had been educated in the land of Canaan, as naturally spoke the language of that country. It is a popular error to suppose that Jacob was a young man when he fled to his cousin Laban, that he might escape from his brother Esau. He was, in fact, nearly eighty years old, as may be seen by comparing the dates given in the margins of our Bibles; and consequently the language of Canaan, i.e. the Hebrew language, would be familiar to his ear. His father Isaac, and his grandfather Abraham, had been settled nearly two hundred years in the land which their posterity afterwards occupied.

Jacob, after parting from Laban, would naturally resume the use of his paternal language, and all his family and tribe would learn it also. Otherwise he could not have associated with the people of Canaan, in the manner described in the

* The native tongue of Abraham must have been that which was spoken by his family, in Chaldæa and Mesopotamia. The former name of this very patriarch seems to be referable to the Chaldaic *Ramah, to be dejected* or *cast down*, rather than to the Hebrew *Ram, Exalted, Lofty*. He had been born in the declining years of his father. His lot was only that of a younger son. His own wife was barren, and he had long been *cast down*, as to the hope of a progeny. He consequently seems to have been regarded in his native country as a *dry branch*. No separate patrimony had been assigned to him. His residence was in a city which had received the name of his brother Haran. This must have been an afflicting circumstance, in an age when the sons regularly shared the paternal estate, and became the heads of families, and the chiefs of the little cities : and it seems to have weighed heavy upon Abraham's heart. "Lord God," says he, "what wilt thou give me, seeing I go childless !—Behold, *to me thou hast given no seed*, and lo, one born in mine house is mine heir." He had hoped to become the father of a family ; but from that hope he was *cast down*. To the mortifying epithet which reminded him of his affliction, his new *Hebrew* name, *A father of Multitudes*, which was conferred upon him several years after he had been in the land of Canaan, must have presented a very pleasing contrast. To the title of *Exalted father*, it would have no contrast at all.—*C. B.*

Bible, where no mention is made of an interpreter to communicate between them. But we need not suppose that his family lost the use of the Chaldaic, for Jacob had lived about 20 years in Chaldæa,

Where he married Chaldean or Aramæan wives and here his children were born and partly educated. These children could have heard the Hebrew only from their father's mouth, even if we suppose that he used it in conversing with them. Their *mother* tongue was the Chaldaic, the same which was spoken in the family of their grandfather Laban. Jacob, with his household, again returned into the land of Canaan. Here the young men married wives who spoke the Canaanitish language. So that, when the whole family went down into Egypt, about thirty-three years after their return from Mesopotamia, they must have carried with them both the Chaldaic language and that of Canaan.

But, as the latter was the dialect most familiar to Jacob himself, and perhaps the only dialect of the younger and more numerous branches, it prevailed over the other.—*Celtic Researches.*

If this argument should be thought to rest too much on probability, having nothing to support it but the diversity of name, which Laban and Jacob give to the same pillar,—confessedly two names taken from different languages or dialects,—yet we now come to an ascertained fact, which leads to an inference of much importance to our argument. When the sons of Jacob first went down to Egypt to buy corn, the services of an interpreter were required to enable them to transact their business. It is clear, therefore, that the languages of the Egyptians and the Hebrews were different, the one from the other. But, when Jacob went to dwell in Egypt, his tribe consisted of sixty-six persons only; and as from this time to the Exodus, a period of more than 200, if not more than 400 years, they continued to reside in Egypt, it becomes almost a physical certainty that they lost the use of their native tongue, Hebrew, and adopted that of the people among whom they dwelt.

There is an important passage in the book of Nehemiah, which shows how soon a language is lost when a small number of persons fix themselves for permanent residence in a strange country.

In those days also saw I Jews that had married wives of Ashdod, of Ammon, and of Moab. And their children spake half in the speech of Ashdod, and could not speak in the Jews' language, but according to the language of each people. NEHEMIAH, xiii, 23, 24.

Let us see what facts may be brought forward from the books of Genesis and Exodus, in support of the assertion, above made, that the Israelites in Egypt exchanged their native language for that of the Egyptians.

We read that, when the Hebrews arrived in Egypt, they came into the land of Goshen, the province of Egypt, which travellers, coming from Canaan by the usual route, ordinarily arrive at. The narrative continues,

And Joseph said unto his brethren, and unto his father's house, I will go up, and show Pharaoh, and say unto him, My brethren, and my father's house, which *were* in the land of Canaan, are come unto me; and the men are shepherds, for their trade hath been to feed cattle; and they have brought their flocks, and their herds, and all that they have. And it shall come to pass, when Pharaoh shall call you, and shall say What is your occupation? that ye shall say, Thy servants' trade hath been about cattle from our youth up even until now, both we *and* also our fathers: that ye may dwell in the land of Goshen: for every shepherd is an abomination to the Egyptians. GENESIS, xlvi, 31—34.

In pursuance of this plan, Joseph prepares Pharaoh for the reception of Jacob, who afterwards has an interview with the king.

And Joseph placed his father and his brethren, and gave them a possession in the land of Egypt, in the best of the land, in the land of Rameses, as Pharaoh had commanded. GENESIS, xlvii, 11.

Again we read, at verse 27 of the same chapter, that "Israel dwelt in the land of Egypt, in the country of Goshen; and they had possessions therein, and grew and multiplied exceedingly."

It has been argued, on the strength of this separate residence of the Hebrews in Egypt, that they still retained the use of their native language. This theory is found in the *Celtic Researches*, page 100; the writer of which rejected many popular errors, and would, if he had lived in the present day, have rejected the view which, as learnt from others, he has retained in the following passage:

During the former part of the two centuries that the Israelites remained in Egypt, they were appointed a residence and establishment, separate from the inhabitants of the country. In this time their tribes became numerous. They expanded from a family into a nation. Their language obtained the stability of a national language, and from henceforth they preserved it with considerable purity.

But the author who writes thus, almost retracts in the next sentence what he has so written.

But the condition to which they were at last reduced, must have rendered it almost impossible for them to preserve it absolutely immaculate. New habits of life and new occupations must have introduced new ideas, and demanded new terms, and those which were already current amongst the Egyptians would, in general, be employed on such occasions.

If it can be proved that so small a number of persons as sixty-six, all of one family, ever yet in the history of the world, remained more than 400 or even 200 years in the midst of a large, dense and highly civilized people, as the Egyptians then were, without adopting the language of that country instead of their own; then may we admit that the Hebrews spoke, at the Exode, precisely the same language which they carried with them into Egypt. But there are several facts which militate against this inference.

We have seen that, of the family of Jacob, some were Canaanitish Hebrews by birth, others Chaldaic Hebrews, and that they spoke different dialects. There was, then, a struggle between these rival dialects, which would very much smooth the way for the extinction of both by the obvious mode of adopting a third, which would be of greater use, and in fact essential to them, in the country where they were come to reside.

But even before Jacob came into Egypt, this change of language was already beginning. For in Genesis, xlviii, 5, we read that Jacob says to Joseph his son:

And now thy two sons, Ephraim and Manasseh, which were born unto thee in the land of Egypt before I came unto thee into Egypt, are mine; as Reuben and Simeon they shall be mine.

What language, it may be asked, were these children

taught to speak? Their mother was an Egyptian lady, and we read of their birth in Genesis, xli, 50.

And unto Joseph were born two sons BEFORE THE YEARS OF FAMINE CAME, which Asenath the daughter of Poti-pherah priest of On bare unto him.

It was in the third year of the famine, Genesis, xlv, 6, that Jacob and his family entered Egypt: so that the two children were at least three or four years old, when their grandfather settled there. It is natural to suppose that they spoke the Egyptian language, and had no sufficient reason for learning the Hebrew tongue at all. Their father was well acquainted with Egyptian, and in fact used it continually in discharging his duties as prime minister of Pharaoh. These offices he continued to discharge until his death, and therefore, he was continually in the habit of speaking the Egyptian language, and this, by a natural law of which there are exemplifications in the world at present, became the language of his children after him.*

But it is said that the Israelites resided in the land of Goshen, separate from the native inhabitants. It must first, however, be observed that we know nothing about the land of Goshen, save this fact, that the Israelites were placed to dwell in it. What, therefore, may have been the peculiar circumstances which caused it to be selected, we can only conjecture. But it is of no importance to our present inquiry. For it is quite certain that they were not alone in the land of Goshen, and did not live there during the whole of their residence in Egypt. Moses, who led them out of Egypt, was eighty years old at the time of the Exodus, and before his birth, his countrymen, having been made slaves, certainly did not occupy the land of Goshen all to themselves. The circumstances related of the birth of Moses show plainly

---

* It is well-known that there are many consuls, ambassadors and others, in England and elsewhere, whose families have completely adopted the language of the people among whom they dwell. The English chaplain at Brussels some time ago had a large family of children, some of whom could not speak English, although there were several thousand English residents in that city. There was also in France a Roman Catholic clergyman, with whom I used to converse, and who occupied a high post in the office of censorship of ecclesiastical books printed in the diocese of Paris, who, though an Irishman by birth, had almost lost the use of his native tongue in consequence of his long residence in Paris.

that the Hebrews in Egypt were in a state of bondage under the task-masters of Pharaoh. It is probable that they had been in this state many years, ever since the death of Joseph; for we read in Exodus, i, 8: "That there arose up a new king over Egypt, which knew not Joseph."

Joseph is supposed to have died about 1635 before Christ, at least this is the date marked in the margin of our bibles. As the same system of chronology places the Exode in 1491 before Christ, it appears that the Hebrews remained in Egypt 144 years after the death of Joseph, and sixty years before the birth of Moses. During by far the greater portion of this time, perhaps all of it, they were in a state of grinding slavery, reduced to the occupation of brick-making, and other hard service, as we read in Exodus, i, 13:

And the Egyptians made the children of Israel to serve with rigour: and they made their lives bitter with hard bondage, in mortar, and in brick, and in all manner of service in the field: all their service, wherein they made them serve, was with rigour.

Neither can it be said that the Hebrews abstained from intermarrying with the natives during their residence in Egypt; for we read in Leviticus, xxiv, 10:

And the son of an Israelitish woman, WHOSE FATHER WAS AN EGYPTIAN, went out among the children of Israel: and this son of the Israelitish woman and a man of Israel strove together in the camp.

Is it possible that in this condition the Israelites should have retained the use of the same language, which their ancestor Jacob spoke 200 years before when he first came into Egypt, but which even Jacob's own children did not speak as their mother tongue, because his wives were Chaldean women, and nearly all his children were by birth Chaldeans also?

The effects which slavery will produce may still be seen in the West Indies and America, where millions of negroes now exist, all speaking the language which they have learnt since their captivity began. In the English settlements some of these speak a broken English, others have formed a base dialect, which an Englishman could not understand, and so different from the language of the blacks in other parts of the settlement that it has been thought necessary, or advisable to translate the Bible expressly for their use. In none of the American settlements have the blacks retained the language which they carried with them from Africa, except a few words and names which here and there, in consequence of peculiar circumstances, have been preserved.

And yet, be it remembered, the colonies of black slaves in America have been yearly augmented by fresh importations from Africa, consisting, in some years, of almost as many individuals as went out of Egypt at the time of the Exode. It may then be fairly inferred that the Israelites lost the use of their original language during the space of more than 200—if not 400—years that they resided in Egypt.

Let us, however, inquire into the early history of Moses himself. It is unnecessary to repeat the story of his being placed in the ark of bulrushes and found by Pharaoh's daughter. But the mode in which he was brought up is deserving of notice. The mother of Moses was, by a device of his sister, introduced to be his nurse.

And the child grew, and she brought him unto Pharaoh's daughter, and he became her son. And she called his name Moses : and she said, Because I drew him out of the water. Ex. ii, 10.

We learn from a Biblical note that the word Moses in the Egyptian language signifies one saved or drawn out of the water. *Mo* or *Mou* was the Egyptian for water. *Calmet, Bryant.*

Thus, then, the young child Moses, was bred up in the house of Pharaoh's daughter, who assumed the charge of his education, gave him an Egyptian* name, and adopted him for her son. Is it not, then, a moral, nay, a physical certainty, that he learnt Egyptian as his mother tongue ? Is it likely that a princess would have bred up a foundling to speak any other language than her own ? Is it not a more obvious explanation of these difficulties to assert that the Egyptians and the Hebrews spoke at this time the same language—the language which prevailed at that time in the

---

* Dr. Lee says it is doubtful whether the word is Egyptian or Hebrew. "Moses is so called on account of his having been taken out of the water, as the text shows, whether the word itself be Egyptian or Hebrew, for on this subject learned men differ." *Heb. Gram.* art. 178, 2, 3, page 153.

land of Egypt, where the one people acted as imperious masters, the other were treated as vile and ignominious slaves?

When, therefore, the Israelites, escaping from this tyranny, found themselves once more in the open wilderness of Arabia, where their forefathers, Abraham, Isaac, and Jacob, roamed as independent chiefs, among other kindred Arab tribes, they carried with them the dialect, not of Canaan, but of Egypt. And it must not be forgotten that from the nature of their service in Egypt, there were, probably, few men of literary acquirements among them. The circumstances of the case do not admit of any other inference: they were a nation of slaves, and their slavery had been peculiarly severe. We have no record of any one, in the whole number of the Jewish people, better than a slave, with the exception of Moses himself, who had been educated in all the learning of the Egyptians. But the new mode of life, into which they were thrown, would soon produce a corresponding change in the habits and character of the people. They dwelt no longer in houses of brick or stone, but in canvas tents, which could easily be struck and transferred to another place. Their wealth consisted in their flocks and herds, and especially camels, those natives of the desert, which thrive the most where every other animal would starve. With the altered habits of the nation, their language, which was probably limited to a very narrow vocabulary—certainly much narrower than that of the Egyptians, from which it was in the most part taken—must have immediately begun to adapt itself to the situation in which they were placed; and at the end of the forty years, which elapsed before they crossed the Jordan, would, in all probability, be much changed from what it was when they went forth from Egypt—changed, I mean, not in general principles, but by the introduction of new terms to express the new objects which surrounded them and the new wants which they daily felt.

We must not suppose that the Israelites, during their passage through Arabia, were entirely secluded from the world, or held no intercourse with the other tribes, who roamed the desert like themselves. So far was this from being the case that Moses, their leader, had frequent cause to censure them for their proneness to associate, and even to form matrimonial alliances with other tribes. The following are the passages from the Pentateuch which allude to the intercourse between the Israelites and other tribes in the desert.

Exodus xvii, 8. Then came Amalek, and fought with Israel in Rephidim. And Moses said unto Joshua, Choose us out men, and go out, fight with Amalek: to-morrow I will stand on the top of the hill with the rod of God in mine hand. So Joshua did as Moses had said to him, and fought with Amalek, &c.

Exodus xviii, 1–5. When Jethro the priest of Midian, Moses' father-in-law, heard of all that God had done for Moses, and for Israel his people, and that the Lord had brought Israel out of Egypt; . . . Jethro, Moses' father-in-law, came with his sons and his wife unto Moses into the wilderness, where he encamped at the mount of God.

Numbers xii, 1. And Miriam and Aaron spake against Moses because of the Ethiopian woman whom he had married: for he had married an Ethiopian woman.

Thus the Israelites were by no means lonely sojourners in the wilderness. Within two months after they had escaped as fugitive slaves out of Egypt, they make war against the Amalekites, a powerful tribe, who appear constantly in connection with the Israelites, as late as the time of Saul and David. Moses also was able, notwithstanding the weight of his public duties, to attend to many domestic matters. He entertains his father-in-law Jethro, who was led to visit him in the wilderness by the fame of his wonderful achievement of leading his countrymen out of Egypt. But we are somewhat surprised that about the same time that he entertained Jethro,* the father of his wife Zipporah, he should have added to his domestic cares the charge of another wife, the Ethiopian woman, and may admit as reasonable the unpleasantness which this act may have caused to his brother Aaron, and Miriam his sister. But the narrative cannot be thus summarily dismissed. Who was this Ethiopian woman, whose marriage with Moses produced a schism in the family, and caused Miriam to become a leper?

* See Numbers x, 29, where the father-in-law of Moses is called Raguel; and the remarks made on it in page 140 of this work.

The country, to which this wife of Moses belonged, here called Ethiopia, in the original Hebrew is Cush, which may be interpreted in a very wide sense. Ethiopia also, in Grecian history, designated not only the modern Ethiopia, but parts of Egypt, Arabia, and perhaps other neighbouring countries. It might then be said that the Ethiopian woman here mentioned was the same person elsewhere described as Jethro's daughter, but the manner in which her name is here introduced, is perfectly incompatible with her having been already described, and that so fully, in Exodus ii, as the daughter to the priest of Midian, and married to Moses, possibly several years before the strife which Miriam and Aaron now stirred up on this account. This leads to the following conclusion: either that the two accounts of the wife of Moses were written by two distinct authors, or that the Ethiopian woman whom Moses married, was not the same as the daughter of Jethro, priest of Midian. In the former case, the whole Pentateuch, as it now is, cannot be considered as the work of Moses; in the latter case, the mixture of the Israelites with other tribes would appear to have begun very early after the Exodus, and to have been carried to a very great extreme.

In pursuing the summary of events which seem to bear upon our present subject, we notice the following facts. Moses sends messengers from Kadesh to the king of Edom, for leave to pass through his territories, but that king refused the permission, and they were not strong enough to force a passage. Numbers xx, 14; xxi, 35.

In the next chapter, we read that the Israelites are defeated by Arad, king of the Canaanites. But in the next war which they waged they were more successful. The king of Sihon, having refused to allow them a free passage through his territories, was defeated; and the result of this battle is remarkable, for it shows that they already began to occupy the land, and to abandon the wandering habits which they had practised forty years previously in the wilderness.

Israel smote him with the edge of the sword, and possessed his land from Arnon unto Jabbok, even unto the children of Ammon; for the border of the children of Ammon was strong. And Israel took all these cities: and Israel dwelt in all the cities of the Amorites, in Heshbon, and in all the villages thereof. . . . Thus Israel dwelt in the land of the Amorites.

And Moses sent to spy out Jaazer, and they took the villages thereof and drove out the Amorites that were there. And they turned and went up by the way of Bashan; and Og the king of Bashan went out against them, he and all his people, to the battle at Edrei. . . . So they smote him and his sons, and all his people until there was none left him alive: and they possessed his land.

We have next in Numbers, from chapter xxii to xxv, the narrative of Balak and Balaam: but though the Moabites, whose king was Balak, seem disposed to make common cause with the Midianites against the Hebrews, yet nothing of a hostile nature immediately ensues; for we read in chapter xxv, 1—3:

And Israel abode in Shittim, and the people began to commit whoredom with the daughters of Moab. And they called the people unto the sacrifices of their gods: and the people did eat, and bowed down to their gods. And Israel joined himself unto Baal-peor: and the anger of the Lord was kindled against Israel.

Then we read of Zimri, the Simeonite, who was slain with Cozbi, the Midianitish woman. When these excesses were checked, a detachment of a thousand men from each tribe defeated the Midianites; and all the adult male captives were put to death; but they spared the females and children, for which Moses afterwards censured them, and gave this severe command:

Now, therefore, kill every male among the little ones, and kill every woman that hath known man by lying with him. But all the women children, that have not known a man by lying with him, keep alive for yourselves. NUMB. xxxi, 17—18.

The reason for sparing alive all the women who were virgins is, that slavery and concubinage were the lot of those young females, whose lives, with that very object, the fury of the war had spared.

By this summary, then, we see that the conquest of their destined country was gradually effected by the Israelites. Before the death of Moses they had taken possession of the kingdoms of Bashan, Sihon, and portions of the Moabitish territories. These were assigned to the tribes of Reuben, Gad, and half of the tribe of Manasseh, and were at once occupied by them before the death of Moses. It is not necessary to detail all the events which followed. The death of

Moses is generally placed in the year before Christ 1451, and in that year, or the following, Joshua led the Israelites over the river Jordan. The conquest of the land occupied, it is said, twenty-nine years; but this is one of those conventional dates which are adopted for the sake of forming a system of chronology. It is difficult to say when the conquest of the Holy Land was complete; for the various nations which possessed it were alternately defeated and victorious, whilst the Israelites were, in consequence of these vicissitudes, sometimes tributary to their enemies, sometimes in the receipt of tribute from them. These alternations of fortune arose from their neglect of the command of Moses, to destroy all the inhabitants of Canaan, and to leave none alive. But this command was too hard for human nature to obey. The most ruthless band of savages that ever perpetrated the most terrible deeds of blood, would have been unequal to the execution of such a sentence. For it was the avowed intention of the Israelitish people to occupy, not to ravage, the land of Canaan; and, if all the inhabitants of the land had been destroyed without mercy, the whole of it would have returned to a state of nature, and become a dense wilderness. Hence we read in the first chapter of Judges the following narrative:

Verse 21. And the children of Benjamin did not drive out the Jebusites that inhabited Jerusalem; but the Jebusites dwell with the children of Benjamin in Jerusalem unto this day.

Verse 27. Neither did Manasseh drive out the inhabitants of Beth-shean and her towns, nor Taanach and her towns, nor the inhabitants of Dor and her towns, nor the inhabitants of Ibleam and her towns, nor the inhabitants of Megiddo and her towns: but the Canaanites would dwell in that land.

Verse 29. Neither did Ephraim drive out the Canaanites that dwelt in Gezer; but the Canaanites dwelt in Gezer among them.

Verse 30. Neither did Zebulun drive out the inhabitants of Kitron.

Verse 31. Neither did Asher drive out the inhabitants of Accho.

Verse 33. Neither did Naphtali drive out the inhabitants of Beth-shemesh.

We repeatedly meet with the descendants of the Canaanitish tribes throughout all the history of the Jews. Some of the chief officers of the kings both of Judah and Israel, as

Uriah the Hittite, belonged to these native races; and in I Kings ix, 20—21, they are described as being very numerous:

And all the people that were left of the Amorites, Hittites, Perizzites, Hivites, and Jebusites, which were not of the children of Israel, their children that were left after them in the land, whom the children of Israel also were not able utterly to destroy, upon those did Solomon levy a tribute of bond-service unto this day.

It may reasonably be supposed that the Israelitish host, however numerous when they crossed the Jordan, were yet not as numerous as all the inhabitants of Canaan put together. Even after they had destroyed so many thousands of the natives, the remainder probably still surpassed them in number. The Norman Conquest of England is in many respects analogous to the occupation of the Holy Land by the Israelites. The enmity between the English and Normans was intense, and years passed away before their animosities were allayed. Yet the Normans were remarkably few when compared with all the inhabitants of England; and their occupation of the country was as complete as that of Palestine by the Israelites. We do not find that the Normans exterminated, or even tried to exterminate, the English. On the contrary, the English have so completely overgrown and amalgamated the foreign race, that no difference is now observable between the two nations. Their language, also, is the same, and, what bears more closely upon our argument, the present language of England is different from the Norman-French on the one hand, and the Anglo-Saxon on the other, which were spoken by the contending parties at the time of the Norman Conquest.

In the same way, it may be argued, the language which the Israelites brought with them out of Egypt, must have come into collision, when they entered Canaan, with that which was spoken by the inhabitants of that country. The natural result is evident. A gradual union of the two would be effected, which in process of time would produce a third, different, but yet not totally different, from both. This has always happened in every country where two hostile races of people have sunk down into a quiet and peaceful population.

From the date, then, at which we have now arrived, B.C. 1451, when the Israelites entered Canaan, to the time when they were carried captive to Babylon, about 600 before Christ, nearly nine hundred years elapsed. This is a hundred years more than have passed since the Norman Conquest to the present time. Was, then, the language of Joshua and his invading host the same as that afterwards spoken by Hezekiah and the other kings who reigned in Israel just before the Babylonian Captivity? The question may be solved by reference to our own country. During the 800 years that have passed since the Norman Conquest, the English language has changed so much that a book, written in English at the time of the Conquest, would be now unintelligible to a common reader. Indeed, many such books have been preserved, and they are unintelligible to all but scholars. Yet England has received no importation of foreigners since the Conquest—not even an invading army has ever remained a day amongst us—and the nations, Norman and Saxon, began from the first to amalgamate. But in the case of the Holy Land all is different. The country was continually exposed to the ravages of foreign armies, and a hundred years before the last exportation of the Israelites to Babylon, colonies of Assyrians, and a rabble of every description, began to occupy the lands from which the Israelitish masters had been displaced. Again, in the year B.C. 560, when the Israelitish captives who had been carried to Babylon were all dead, leaving behind them the children which, by a law of Nature, are born even to captives and to slaves—when these children having reached the age of manhood were allowed after years of slavery to return to Palestine, is it to be supposed that their language was still the same, after the vicissitudes through which it had passed?

I shall pursue the argument no further, but briefly recapitulate the facts to which it has led us.

1. The patriarchs Abraham, Isaac, and Jacob spoke the language of the Canaanites, among whom they dwelt, whatever that language may have been.

2. Jacob, by his residence in Mesopotamia, acquired a knowledge of the Chaldaic dialect, which was the principal language of all his family, who were born and educated in Mesopotamia.

3. Jacob's descendants in Egypt lost their native tongue, and acquired that of the Egyptians.

4. The Israelites again underwent a change or modification of their language by admixture with the inhabitants of Canaan.

5. The lapse of 900 years, from the entrance into Canaan to the return from captivity in 536 B.C., effected another change of dialect so decided, that two persons, living, one at the beginning, the other at the end of this period, could not have understood one another.

6. In conclusion, and as the consequence of the former five propositions, it follows that Moses must have written whatever he wrote, in the Egyptian language, or that what he wrote would have been unintelligible to those for whose use he wrote. So that either the Pentateuch, which we now have, is not the original work of Moses, or it is written in the Egyptian language—a theory which no writer has yet ventured to affirm.

CHAPTER XXXIV.

THAT THE CHALDEE LANGUAGE WAS THE RESULT OF A LATE GRADUAL CHANGE, AND FINALLY OF THE ROMAN CONQUEST OF JUDEA, AND NOT OF THE BABYLONISH CAPTIVITY.

THE Hebrew Scriptures, as has already been remarked in the second chapter of this work, are written mostly in the Hebrew, but partly in a different language, called *Chaldee;* and I propose now to examine this point a little more minutely. To determine the nature of this second language, called *Chaldee*, is of the utmost importance to our argument, because it is affirmed, but without any evidence of fact to support the affirmation, that the Chaldee was, from the time of Ezra to that of Christ, the common language of the Jews, who had forgotten the old Hebrew language during the Babylonish Captivity.*

* "The language," says Dr Farrar in his *Life of Christ*, vol. i, p. 90, "which our Lord commonly spoke, was Aramæan, and at that period Hebrew was completely a dead language, known only to the more educated, and only to be acquired by labour; yet it is clear that Jesus was acquainted

In the first place it must be observed that the portions of the Old Testament written in this Chaldee dialect consist of only 283 verses altogether.

These are: Jeremiah, x, 11; Daniel, ii, 4, to vii, 28; Ezra, iv, 8, to vii, 27.

A serious difficulty here immediately presents itself. Ezra and others after the Captivity still wrote in Hebrew, and not in Chaldee; and save the verses above named, all the rest is in pure Hebrew. But, if the Israelites during the Babylonish Captivity had forgotten the old Hebrew language, why did not Ezra, who wrote nearly 100 years after the Jews had returned from Babylon, write *all* his books in the old Chaldee language, which the people, according to this theory, could have understood, rather than in the old Hebrew, which they had forgotten? Again, if Ezra wrote the books of Chronicles; or, if they were written after his time, why were they also not written in Chaldee? As regards Daniel and Jeremiah, it may be said that, being among those who were carried captives to Babylon, they had not forgotten the Hebrew, in which language they accordingly wrote their books, if indeed they did write them. But this solution proves too much, for the Babylonish Captivity was not effected at once: it took place at different times, as may be seen by the chronological table given in page 50, and those who were carried captive the last time, B.C. 588, may—at least some of them—have been alive when the decree of Cyrus permitted them to return. But this point would almost require a separate treatise. Let us recur at present to the consideration of the extraordinary fact that Ezra, who pro-

---

with it, for some of his Scriptural quotations directly refer to the Hebrew Original."

It is impossible to speak too highly of Dr. Farrar as a writer and biographer; but as regards critical difficulties he must not be taken as an authority. It has long been the fashion to talk of the Aramæan and Syro-Chaldæan languages as having replaced the Hebrew in Palestine: but we have no remains of those languages and cannot correctly judge of them. The Hebrew itself is an Aramæan language, and there were probably as many separate dialects as there were tribes in Syria and Palestine, as there were no doubt in the British Isles in the earliest times. Even in the present day there are two principal branches of the Welsh language, the Northern and the Southern, and these again both diverge into numerous subordinate dialects. In the same way almost every county in England has its peculiar words and sounds, and those persons who live at the farther extremities of the island, can hardly understand one another.

fessedly wrote books for popular use, is said to have employed a language which the people, for whom he wrote them, had entirely forgotten. And not only Ezra, but Haggai, Zechariah, and Malachi, all of whom wrote after the Captivity, are supposed to have used a language which their countrymen no longer understood. This circumstance did not fail to arrest the attention of Dean Prideaux, and he has, in his learned "Connection of the History of the Old and New Testament," taken notice of the fact, but not of its inconsistency. Following the received opinion, and not appearing to think that it was a difficulty, he has given the following account of the matter:

The common people, by having so long conversed with the Babylonians, learned their language, and forgot their own. It happened indeed otherwise to the children of Israel in Egypt. For, although they lived there above three times as long as the Babylonish Captivity lasted, yet they still preserved the Hebrew language among them, and brought it back entire with them into Canaan. The reason of this was, in Egypt they all lived together in the land of Goshen: but on their being carried captive by the Babylonians, they were dispersed all over Chaldea and Assyria, and being there intermixed with the people of the land, had their converse with them, and therefore were forced to learn their language; and this soon induced a disuse of their own among them; by which means it came to pass, that after their return, the common people, especially those of them who had been bred up in that captivity, understood not the Holy Scriptures in the Hebrew language, nor their posterity after them. And, therefore, when Ezra read the law to the people, he had several persons standing by him, well skilled in both the Chaldee and Hebrew languages, who interpreted to the people in Chaldee what he first read to them in Hebrew.

The whole of this author's dissertation on the subject now before us is well worthy of the reader's attention, but sufficient has been quoted for the present to show the nature of the explanation which the author means to give of the remarkable fact before us. This explanation would, no doubt, be admissible, if Ezra had confined himself to *reading* the Scriptures for the benefit of the people, but, as he *wrote* a large quantity of new Scriptures and revised the old ones, adding, as is said, many explanatory interpretations of his own, it seems preposterous that he should adopt the language which had been forgotten, and reject that in which alone the people could understand him, a plan no less troublesome to himself—for he also had never spoken the Hebrew—than pernicious to the best interests of the people.

But we are told that, notwithstanding this inconsistency, it is a fact that Ezra did, out of reverence, perhaps, to the old Law, adopt the Hebrew language for his own compositions, and that the interpretations of the whole book of the Law, which he caused to be read along with the Hebrew text, in order that the people might understand him, are those very Targums, or Chaldee paraphrases, which are still in existence, and have often been published in the Polyglott and other editions of the Hebrew Bible.

This then is the case of those who argue that the Jews spoke the Chaldee language after the Babylonish captivity. It remains to see what may be said on the opposite side of the question; and I shall endeavour to show, on evidence which cannot be gainsaid, that the Jews as a nation did not forget the Hebrew tongue in consequence of the Babylonish Captivity, but continued to speak it down to the time of the Christian era—or, more correctly speaking, that the Hebrew, such as we now have it, was the language spoken by the Jews, not *before* but *after* the return of that people from Babylon. It is not however denied that it was also very similar to the language spoken before the Captivity, but less and less similar the nearer we approach to the time of Moses and the Exodus. In short, the language of the Israelites, like that of every people upon earth, was a flowing and changing stream of words and thoughts, gathering from all sides as it went, until the Egyptian which they spoke in Egypt became, a thousand years after, the Hebrew; the last form of the language spoken by the Jews before the Romans subverted their commonwealth never to be restored.

1. In the first place then the use of the Hebrew tongue by Jeremiah, Daniel, Ezra, Haggai, Zechariah and Malachi, who lived between 606 and 456, during or after the Captivity, in a continuous and contemporary series, shows, if these books were written by the supposed authors, and at the periods of time here assigned to them, that the Hebrew was then a living tongue, and the purity of style in their writings is not surpassed by that of the books of Moses, Joshua, or Samuel.

2. The introduction of 283 verses in the Chaldee dialect may be otherwise explained. The single verse in Jeremiah, x, 11, is as follows:

Thus shall ye say unto them, The gods that have not made the heavens and the earth, even they shall perish from the earth, and from under these heavens.

This verse is in what is called the Chaldee language. I imagine it is a quotation from some book in that language, and that Jeremiah quoted the original words as more forcible than a Hebrew translation of them would be. Dr W. Lowth's commentary on this verse is as follows:

This verse is written in Chaldee, as if the prophet designed to put these words in the mouths of the Jews, wherewith they might make a public profession of their own faith in the true God, and be able to answer the heathens that would entice them to idolatry.

The Chaldee verses in Daniel and Ezra may be also satisfactorily explained. Let us turn to the first of these in the second chapter of Daniel, which begins thus:

And in the second year of the reign of Nebuchadnezzar, Nebuchadnezzar dreamed dreams, wherewith his spirit was troubled, and his sleep brake from him. Then the king commanded to call the magicians, and the astrologers, and the sorcerers, and the Chaldeans, for to show the king his dreams. So they came and stood before the king, and the king said unto them, I have dreamed a dream, and my spirit was troubled to know the dream.

Verse 4 begins:

Then spake the Chaldeans to the king in *Syriac*, O king, live for ever! tell thy servants the dream, and we will show the interpretation.

These words are in Chaldee or Syriac, as is declared in the words themselves; for what is usually called Chaldee is the same, possibly with slight dialectic variations, as the Syriac which was spoken at Damascus, in Mesopotamia, and among many of the nations to the north and east of Palestine. The reason why these parts of Daniel, from chapter ii to the end of chapter vii, are written in this Syriac or Chaldee language, is partly explained by Bishop Newton, as quoted in the "Notes to the Bible."

Hitherto the prophecies of Daniel, that is, from the fourth verse of the second chapter to this [the sixth] chapter, are written in Chaldee. As they greatly concerned the Chaldeans, so they were published in that language. But the remaining prophecies are written in Hebrew, because they treat altogether of affairs subsequent to the times of the Chaldeans, and relate not at all to them, but principally to the Church and people of God.

I do not dispute this reasoning, but am content with a different explanation, namely, that the Old Testament is a compilation from various sources, and that the passage before us, forming a body of separate facts, and existing in the Syrian language, was transferred, in its totality, into the book of the Old Testament.

The passages in Ezra, which are in the Syriac or Chaldee tongue, admit of a still more ready explanation.

And in the days of Artaxerxes wrote Bishlam, Mithridath, Tabeel, and the rest of their companions, unto Artaxerxes king of Persia; and the writing of the letter was written in the Syrian tongue, and interpreted in the Syrian tongue. Rehum the chancellor and Shimshai the scribe wrote a letter against Jerusalem to Artaxerxes the king in this sort: Then wrote Rehum the chancellor, and Shimshai the scribe, and the rest of their companions; the Dinaites, the Apharsathchites, the Tarpelites, the Apharsites, the Archevites, the Babylonians, the Susanchites, the Dehavites, and the Elamites, and the rest of the nations whom the great and noble Asnapper brought over, and set in the cities of Samaria, and the rest that are on this side the river, and at such a time. This is the copy of the letter that they sent unto him, even unto Artaxerxes the king; Thy servants the men on this side the river, and at such a time. Be it known unto the king, that the Jews which came up from thee to us are come unto Jerusalem, &c. EZRA iv, 7.

This is the beginning of what is termed the Chaldee portion of the book of Ezra, and it extends to the 27th verse of the seventh chapter.

But here also, as in Daniel, the extract of itself says that it is in the Syrian tongue, and neither in Daniel nor Ezra is any mention made of any distinct Chaldee language at all. But it is easy to be perceived why this portion of Ezra is not in Hebrew. The whole of it consists of authentic documents, the first of which is the letter of Rehum and the others above-mentioned. Is it remarkable that their letter to the Persian king should be written in the Syriac language, which, (whether the same as the Chaldee or not) they all certainly were familiar with? On the contrary, it would be most remarkable if their letter had been written in any other language, seeing that they were the colonists placed in Samaria when that city was taken; as has been mentioned already in page 285 of this work. That the king of Persia might understand it, we find that it was not only written in the Syrian but also accompanied by a translation in the Syrian language, i. e., as all agree, from the Syrian tongue into the Persian. It is evident that the Persian translation could be of no use to Jews, but the Syrian original has been preserved, and it surely would be unreasonable to expect that it should be written in Hebrew, or, indeed, in any other language than the Syrian.

The question then is reduced into a very narrow compass. Did Daniel, Ezra, Jeremiah, Haggai, Zechariah, and Malachi write 283 verses only in the language which the Jews could understand, and deliver all the mass of their writings in a dead language, whilst on the other hand their Syrian neighbours and enemies wrote in the language of the Jews, or did these Jewish writers compose their writings in their own language, leaving the letters which their Syrian enemies wrote against them, to tell their own story in the Syrian tongue? The question may, it would seem, be answered with little or no hesitation.

But what was the nature of the Syrian or Chaldee dialect? To answer this question we must consider who were the Syrians, by whom it was spoken. Now it is well known that the kingdom of Syria has always been the territory bounding Israel on the north and north-east, and itself bounded on the west by the Mediterranean Sea, and on the east by the desert, into which however it stretches much farther than the corresponding eastern frontier of the Israelites. The kings of Syria were often in arms against the kingdom of Israel, after its separation from Judah. Even before that time we read of their kings fighting against king David, but with small hopes of success whilst the twelve tribes were united under one king: for

> David slew of the Syrians two and twenty thousand men. Then David put garrisons in Syria of Damascus, and the Syrians became servants to David and brought gifts. II SAMUEL, viii, 5, 6.

The names of Benhadad and Hazael, kings of Syria, are well known to the readers of Jewish history: for the nation was powerful among the small states of that age and country, until it was destroyed by the kings of Assyria, who, as it is recorded in II Kings, xvi, 9, "went up against Damascus, and took it, and carried the people of it captive to Kir, and slew Rezin."

The king of Assyria, who destroyed the kingdom of Syria, was Tiglath-pileser, to whom Ahaz king of Judah, as before related, about the year 742 before Christ, sent messengers,—saying, "I am thy servant and thy son: come up and save me out of the hand of the king of Syria, and out of the hand of the king of Israel, which rise up against me."

It was an unlucky request of Ahaz: it would have been wiser to make peace with the petty kings who molested him, than to call in the aid of the gigantic power which was at this very time extending its limits over all Asia. But sovereigns, in their wars, have no care but to extricate themselves from their immediate distress or to gain the object of their immediate pursuit. Tiglath-pileser came with speed, and destroyed Rezin king of Syria; two years afterwards he began to cut Israel short, and to carry away its people for slaves: but like his precursor Polyphemus, he granted his friend the king of Judah a respite, and devoured him the last of the three.

From this time Syria continued to be part of the Assyrian empire, and afterwards passed with the other provinces into the hands of the Median and Persian monarchs.

It might then seem remarkable, that there should be a confusion between the Chaldee and the Syrian languages; for Chaldæa and Syria were certainly not exactly the same country, though the later kingdom of Syria contained part of Chaldæa if not all of it, within its frontiers. The first instance of confusion between these two countries occurs in Judges, iii, 8:

Therefore the anger of the Lord was hot against Israel, and he sold them into the hand of Chushan-Risathaim king of Mesopotamia; and the children of Israel served Chushan-Risathaim eight years.

The word Mesopotamia seems inappropriate here, as a

translation of the Hebrew word *Aramnaharaim*; in the Septuagint version it is rendered Συρίας ποτάμων *Syria of the rivers*. Our translators have apparently followed the Latin Vulgate "regis Mesopotamiæ," but the name Mesopotamia is a Greek word, and Alexander was the first Greek who explored those countries, several hundred years after the time of Chushan-Risathaim.

The language spoken by the Syrians and the Assyrians was almost if not wholly the same, for when " Sennacherib king of Assyria came up against all the fenced cities of Judah and took them," II Kings, xviii, 13, he sent a detachment of his army to besiege Jerusalem, and when Rabshakeh spoke to the soldiers who were manning the walls in Hebrew, so that all might understand him, Eliakim the son of Hilkiah, and Shebna, and Joah, fearful lest their soldiers might be tempted by fear or promises to submit, said unto Rabshakeh, "Speak, I pray thee to thy servants in the Syrian language, for we understand it: and talk not with us in the Jews' language in the ears of the people that are on the wall."

Dean Prideaux also, "Connection of the History of the Old and New Testament" (ii, 497), speaking of the Chaldee in which the Jewish paraphrases of the Old Testament were written, says that this " language was anciently used through all Assyria, Babylonia, Mesopotamia, Syria, and Palestine; and is still the language of the churches of the Nestorian and Maronite Christians in those eastern parts, in the same manner as the Latin is the language of the Popish churches here in the west."

Thus then we obtain the following fact: that the Syrian language spoken by the tribes and various people on the north-east of Palestine as far as Babylon, was in existence long before the captivity of the Jews; that it continued to exist after the return of the Jews, and throughout the whole of its duration it was different from the language of the Jews: that it was the language afterwards called Chaldee, and still spoken by the aliens placed in the Holy Land after the Captivity; that the Jewish writers have written 283 verses in this language, consisting almost entirely of matters concerning foreigners alone, and especially of documents, letters and papers, which could not have been originally written in Hebrew, and that these same writers have nevertheless written the greater part of their books in the Hebrew language. Do not these facts amount to a demonstration that the Jews still spoke Hebrew after the Babylonish Captivity, notwithstanding all the suppositions and hypotheses which writers, having a theory to maintain, have advanced to the contrary?

CHAPTER XXXV.

THAT THE CHALDEE PARAPHRASES CALLED TARGUMS, TOGETHER WITH THE VOWEL-POINTS AND ACCENTS ARE LATER THAN THE TIME OF CHRIST.

BUT it has been said that there are still in existence the Targums or Chaldee paraphrases which were read at the same time with the Hebrew text, that the people who had forgotten the Hebrew, might understand the meaning of their sacred books. This assertion may be met with evidence still more conclusive than the former.

Although a greater antiquity is assigned by some, yet the oldest Targum that has come down to us is thought by Professor Eichhorn to have been written in the second century of the Christian era. It is clear, then, that none of these Targums could have been read, concurrently with the Hebrew Text, 500 years before they were written. No mention is made of them by Jerome, who lived in the fourth century after Christ, or by any other of the Christian Fathers of the Church. Most of them are loose paraphrases, which convey an imperfect idea of the original, and contain tales taken out of the Talmud, a well known collection of legends and marvels, written hundreds of years after the date of the Hebrew Canon.

The Targums were certainly written many years after the destruction of Jerusalem, when the Israelites, expelled from their country, had forgotten the Hebrew language, but still managed to maintain the appearance of a school of learning among the inhabitants of Syria and Babylonia, where they were principally scattered, and where they naturally forgot the Hebrew and learnt the Chaldee or Syriac language spoken in those countries. We shall see that the same inference may be obtained with equal clearness from the case of the vowel-points which are next to be considered.

The following is a list of the Targums which now remain, together with the names of their supposed writers:

1. That of Onkelos, on the five books of Moses. 2. That of Jonathan Ben Uzziel on the prophets, that is, on Joshua, Judges, the two books of Samuel, the two books of Kings, Isaiah, Jeremiah, Ezekiel, and the twelve minor prophets. 3. That on the Law which is ascribed to Jonathan Ben Uzziel. 4. The Jerusalem Targum on the Law. 5. The Targum on the five lesser books called the Megilloth, *i.e.*, Ruth, Esther, Ecclesiastes, The Song of Solomon, and the Lamentations of Jeremiah. 6. The second Targum on Esther. 7. The Targum of Joseph the one-eyed on the book of Job, the Psalms, and the Proverbs; and 8. The Targum on the first and second books of Chronicles.

All these Targums are now almost universally admitted to have been written long after the time of Christ, even the first, to which, from its similarity of style to the Chaldee verses found in the Bible, an earlier date had been assigned.

In the mature state of an alphabetic language, such as now exists in every civilized part of the world, except China and the countries immediately adjoining it, we find two classes of written characters, grammatically designated as vowels and consonants. Vowels are generally defined to be such letters as can be sounded by themselves, whereas consonants can only be sounded with the help of vowels. Notwithstanding this apparent superiority of vowels over consonants, yet there can be no doubt that consonants have preceded vowels, in the first formation of every language, and for good reasons. The vowels, generally considered to be five in number, express sounds which hardly can be called articulate, but are rather similar to the utterances of irrational animals: they are, in fact, a mere expiration of the breath, modified by the various shape of the lips and tongue. The consonants, however, b, k, l, m, &c., though requiring the aid of a vowel sound, give that wonderful distinctness and variety to human language, which forms the predominant advantage of our species over the brute creation.

In illustrating the gradual progress of the literary art from the first rudiments to the present perfection of alphabetic writing, which will form the subject of a future chapter I have placed the Hebrew as the first approach to a phonetic system, in distinction to the older ideagraphic modes. That it is properly placed in this intermediate position arises from that peculiarity of formation which gave to it consonants but not vowels. It is true that the Hebrew now no longer retains this singularity, for the vowel-points, as they are termed, render it capable of expressing every vowel sound as perfectly as any modern language. This however, according to the best authorities, was not at first the case.

Originally [says Professor Stuart, *Heb. Gr.* p. 17] the Hebrew alphabet consisted only of consonants. Some learned men have maintained the contrary, and averred that *aleph, vau,* and *yod* were originally designed to be *vowels*. But the fact, that these letters constitute essential parts of the *triliteral* roots in Hebrew, and that they are susceptible of forming syllables by union with every sort of vowel sound, proves, beyond all reasonable doubt, that they are essentially *consonants*.

That a language should possess no characters to designate vowel-sounds would certainly, at first sight, seem to present a great impediment to its free use; but this difficulty was little felt by the Hebrews themselves, who learnt to speak their language whilst they were children, for probably very few persons, from the scarcity of books in those days, learnt to read and write at all. Even foreigners, learning the language mostly by the ear, would care very little in what manner the words were expressed on paper; and native Hebrews, who began to learn the art of reading, would easily supply the vowel-sounds from their former perfect knowledge of the language. An illustration of this may be drawn from the English tongue, in which the vowel sounds are, indeed, expressed by certain characters, but so loosely, that in some cases the latter serve rather to mislead than to guide, and to a foreigner are often the source of error. Thus the words *side, give,* and *river* furnish different modes of pronouncing the letter i, and a foreigner would probably find it not more difficult to pronounce those words, if they were written without any vowels at all, thus *sd, gv, rvr*.

The account which Professor Lee gives of the introduction of the vowel-points into the Hebrew, is supported by the opinion of most philologists who have written on this subject. In his Hebrew grammar, Art. 39, page 15, he writes thus:

When the Hebrew and Syriac tongues were vernacular, the vowels would only be wanted in words which would otherwise be ambiguous; and we find in the old Syriac Estrangelo manuscripts, that these vowel marks are mostly added, when this would be the case. Thus a participle present has almost invariably a point placed over the first radical letter, directing the first consonant to be pronounced with an *o*; the preterite, in like manner, has a single point under one of its radicals, mostly the second, directing that consonant to be pronounced with an *a*. The same is observed in other words, which have the same consonants with each other, but which ought to be pronounced with different vowels. This is sufficient, even now, to guard against any ambiguity which might arise in reading the Syriac text. In most of the Arabic manuscripts, if we except the Koran, a few vowels only are added for a similar purpose: which has also been done by some of the best editors of Arabic books in modern times. In these cases, no one will object, that every danger of ambiguity is sufficiently removed; and it may hence be inferred, that a similar practice would be quite sufficient, so long as the Hebrew language continued to be generally spoken. When, however, it became a dead language, and the Jews, dispersed as they were, into different nations of the earth, would naturally forget the true pronunciation of the sacred text, no less than its meaning in many important passages, it became almost necessary that every word should be fully pointed, so as to leave no doubt on the mind of the reader, as far, at least, as such a system of punctuation would go. For this purpose, additional vowel-marks were added, and some new ones invented. To which also a system of accents seems to have been added, which, taken in the aggregate, composes the system of Hebrew orthography as we now have it. At what exact period this began to take place, it is impossible to say; there is, however, good reason for believing, that it must have been after the time of Jerome, as he makes no mention whatever of it. That it was completed later than the twelfth century is scarcely possible, as the names of most of the vowels and accents are found in the Rabbins of that period. The school of Tiberius, and about the period A.D. 500, has generally been fixed upon as the place and time of their invention; and it is not improbable that they were there and then first partially introduced, and afterwards augmented to the number which we now have.

As these remarks of Professor Lee bear with great force on an inference which will presently be drawn from them, it will be desirable first to confirm them by adducing the testimony of Professor Stuart, in whose Hebrew grammar, page 17, we find the following:

When the diacritical signs, which distinguish the later alphabet and increase the number of letters, together with all the vowel-points and accents, were first introduced, no historical documents satisfactorily show. But it is now generally agreed, that the introduction was a *gradual* one; and that, however early some few particular things in the general system may have been commenced, yet the whole system of diacritical signs, vowel points, and accents, was not completed, so as to exist in its present form, *until several centuries after the birth of Christ; pretty certainly not until after the fifth century.* In regard to reading MSS. destitute of all this system of helps, there is no serious difficulty, at least none to any one who well understands the language. The same thing is habitually done at the present day, by the Arabians, the Persians, and the Syrians, in their respective tongues: and in Hebrew by the Jewish Rabbis and all the learned in the Shemitish languages.

Thus, then, it appears, from the concurrent evidence of these two learned Hebrew scholars, that the language of the Israelitish people neither had nor required characters to denote the vowel sounds, whilst it continued to be a vernacular or living language; but that, when the Hebrew was no longer a spoken or living language, the vowel-points were introduced for the sake of guiding the pronunciation. But the introduction of these points did not take place until after the Christian era. It certainly follows, as a necessary deduction from these premises, that the Hebrew language was a living language at the beginning of the Christian era, and if we turn to the New Testament, we shall find, not by supposition or mere inference, but by the strong evidence of facts, that such undoubtedly was the case. This point is of sufficient importance to form the subject of a new chapter.

CHAPTER XXXVI.

THAT THE JEWISH NATION SPOKE HEBREW AS LATE AS THE TIME OF CHRIST—PROVED FROM THE NEW TESTAMENT.

It is much to be regretted for many reasons, and those not merely literary, that our knowledge of the Jewish history in the time of Christ is extremely scanty and imperfect. The reduction of almost all the known world into one immense empire under the Romans checked that free growth of the intellect which is sure to arise in smaller states, where institutions of freedom have been formed. A large empire is liable to stagnate, as an unwieldy animal, whatever may be its species, is unable to move with that agility which more limited dimensions would allow. The most brilliant actions of our race have sprung from the clash of contending principles, and the exertions which competing interests create. But those who govern large empires love repose rather than competition—they restrain enterprise, and sometimes dignify languor with the name of order—*solitudinem faciunt, pacem appellant.* From the moment that the Roman emperors had firmly fixed themselves in their despotic seats, manly sentiment began to disappear from the earth, and for five hundred years hardly a writer arose whose works can be put in competition with those which the golden age of Greece and Rome produced. The Jews at this time were certainly not behind the rest of the world in a desire to maintain their nationality and freedom. They were the same turbulent people as ever, and by no means submitted readily to the Roman domination.

The Jewish nation were bigoted beyond our experience of any other people; and they showed this bigotry most from the time they came into contact with Europe under Alexander the Great down to the very day when their city was taken and their nationality destroyed by the arms of the Roman Titus. "Neither the violence of Antiochus," says

Gibbon (ii, 113), quoting from Cicero (*pro Flacco*, c. 28), "nor the arts of Herod, nor the example of the circumjacent nations, could ever persuade the Jews to associate with the institutions of Moses the elegant mythology of the Greeks." If their subjection had been deferred a few years later, so that Josephus, the only Jewish writer who came into close contact with the literature of the West, might have signalised his talents in the service of his own country and in his own language, we should not have had to lament the want of Hebrew books, which now drives us to the New Testament for all our information concerning the language of the Jews at this period of their commonwealth.

It has been already observed that some writers have referred the oldest of the Targums to the earliest period of the Christian era. But this opinion is rejected by others, and it is not safe to build upon a basis of doubtful stability. We are therefore obliged to recur to the New Testament for whatever indications it may furnish that the Jews still spoke the language in which the books of the Old Testament were composed, and which was as much entitled to be called the Hebrew then, as it was in the days of David, Daniel, or Malachi.

In making these observations I claim due allowance for the changes which lapse of time, even without external causes, will invariably produce in the most stable language that ever has been spoken. But this allowance may be conceded without prejudice to either side of the question: for those who entertain a different view of the matter argue that the change of language from Hebrew to Chaldee was effected, comparatively speaking, instantaneously, in consequence of that great national calamity, the Babylonish Captivity. Let us then see what evidence the New Testament will yield to clear up this disputed part of history.

1. Hebrew is expressly mentioned in the New Testament as being still the language of the people, as is evident from the following texts:

JOHN v, 2. Now there is at Jerusalem by the sheep-market, a pool, which is called *in the Hebrew tongue* Bethesda, having five porches.

JOHN xix, 17. And he, bearing his cross, went forth into a

place called the place of a skull, which is called *in the Hebrew* Golgotha.

If the Hebrew tongue had become obsolete, why did the writer of this gospel explain the names of these places in that language? It is not customary with those who write books for popular use in England to explain foreign or other names by adding their meaning in the Anglo-Saxon language, which was spoken 800 years ago, but in the English language, which is still spoken in England.

The inference which these texts furnish is confirmed by the inscription placed over the cross. This is mentioned by all the four evangelists; but only Luke and John tell us the languages in which it was written:

LUKE xxiii, 38. And a superscription also was written over him in letters of Greek, and Latin, and *Hebrew*, THIS IS THE KING OF THE JEWS.

JOHN xix, 19. And Pilate wrote a title, and put it on the cross. And the writing was JESUS OF NAZARETH THE KING OF THE JEWS. This title then read many of the Jews; for the place where Jesus was crucified was nigh to the city: and it was written in *Hebrew*, and Greek, and Latin.

It may be asked, with reason, why the title should be written in three languages? The answer is ready: it was inscribed in Latin, because Pilate, who was a Roman, his court, and his guards spoke Latin, the language of the government; in Greek, which was the language of literature, of the better classes, and perhaps of a large part of the Roman army; and in Hebrew, because that was the language of the natives. No other explanation is admissible: for it is absurd to suppose that an inscription, which it was of course intended that all should read and understand, would be written in an obsolete dialect, which would be intelligible to no one but the priests. In fact we find that it was not written in an obsolete language, for it is said that "this title read many of the Jews," and there can be no doubt that they understood it with as much ease as the citizens understand the proclamations which are sometimes fixed by the agents of the government upon the walls of the Mansion-house in London.

Nor is there wanting proof that Hebrew was still spoken at Jerusalem thirty years after the crucifixion of our Lord. In the twenty-first chapter of the Acts it is related that St Paul was saved from death at the hands of a mob at Jerusalem, by the intervention of the chief captain. He was rescued, it appears, by main force, and was ordered to be taken into the castle for safety. We then read what follows:

And as Paul was to be led into the Castle, he said unto the Chief Captain, " May I speak unto thee ?" Who said, " Canst thou speak Greek ? Art not thou that Egyptian, which before these days madest an uproar, and leddest out unto the wilderness four thousand men that were murderers ?" But Paul said, " I am a man which am a Jew of Tarsus, a city in Cilicia, a citizen of no mean city : and I beseech thee, suffer me to speak unto the people." And when he had given him license, Paul stood on the stairs, and beckoned with the hand unto the people. And when there was made a great silence, he spake unto them in the Hebrew tongue, saying, " Men, brethren, and fathers, &c. . . ."

We have here the statement that St Paul made a speech to an assembled multitude at Jerusalem in the Hebrew language. This could hardly have been the case if the people to whom he spoke could not understand the language which he used; and it would seem, also, that St Paul was expected to speak in Hebrew, or at all events in some language not familiar to the chief captain: for, when he naturally asked permission to speak to this Roman military officer, who had rescued him, he is asked whether he can speak Greek. The chief captain was probably himself a Greek (for there were many both officers and private men of that nation in the Roman army), and would naturally wish to know whether he could converse with St Paul in a language which both of them understood; and if Paul used the Greek language when he asked permission to address the chief captain himself in his own defence, that officer would naturally be surprised to hear what he had so little expected. Whatever explanation may be given of these details, it is evident that St Paul could speak in Greek to the chief captain, in Hebrew to the multitude, and that they could readily understand him.

In the next place Hebrew words are found in the New

Testament. The following are examples of words and sentences used by Christ and others in the course of their daily and familiar conversation:

MARK iii, 17. And James the son of Zebedee, and John the brother of James; and he surnamed them *Boanerges*, which is, The sons of thunder.

"This word," says Dr Whitby, "is compounded of two Hebrew words explained in the text." If so, the Hebrew language must still have been the language of the inhabitants of Judæa.

MATTHEW xxi, 9. And the multitudes that went before, and that followed, cried saying, "*Hosanna* to the son of David: blessed is he that cometh in the name of the Lord: Hosanna in the highest!"

"The word Hosanna," says Bishop Pearce, "is an abbreviation of two Hebrew words which signify 'save now:' they are found at Psalm cxviii, 25, and were a customary acclamation of the common people on solemn occasions."

MARK xiv, 36. And he said, "*Abba*, Father, all things are possible unto thee; take away this cup from me: nevertheless not what I will, but what thou wilt."

"Abba is the Chaldee for father," says Dr Lightfoot in the note on this verse, in the commentary on the Bible. But is it not the Hebrew, also, for the same word? Abba is plainly the Greek form of the Hebrew *ab*, which denotes father.

MARK v, 41. And he took the damsel by the hand, and said unto her, *Talitha cumi*, which is, being interpreted, "Damsel, I say unto thee, arise."

ACTS i, 19. Insomuch as that field is called in their proper tongue *Aceldama*.

These words, *Talitha cumi*, and *Aceldama*, are also Hebrew, with little dialectic variation the same as they would have been if they occurred in the Pentateuch or the books of Joshua and Judges.

JOHN i, 41. He first findeth his own brother Simon, and saith unto him, "We have found the *Messias*," which is, being interpreted, the Christ.

JOHN i, 42. And he brought him to Jesus. And when Jesus beheld him, he said "Thou art Simon the son of Jona; thou shalt be called *Cephas*," which is by interpretation, a stone.

MARK iii, 22. And the scribes, which came down from Jerusalem, said, "He hath Beelzebub, and by the prince of the devils casteth he out devils."

Compare with this the following verse, from the gospel of St Matthew:

MATTHEW xii, 24. But when the Pharisees heard it, they said, "This fellow doth not cast out devils, but by *Beelzebub* the prince of the devils."

For an explanation of the name of Beelzebub, we are referred to the notes in the Commentary on II Kings i. 1—2, where the name Baal-zebub occurs. The text of that passage runs thus:

Then Moab rebelled against Israel after the death of Ahab. And Ahaziah fell down through a lattice in his upper chamber that was in Samaria, and was sick: and he sent messengers, and said unto them, "Go, enquire of Baal-zebub the god of Ekron, whether I shall recover of this disease."

The note to this passage tells us that

The word Baal-zebub signifies the "god of flies," but how this idol came to obtain that name, it is not so easy a matter to discover. Several are of opinion that this god was called Baal-semin, the Lord of Heaven, but that the Jews, by way of contempt, gave it the name of Baal-zebub, or the lord of a fly, a god that was nothing worth, &c."

The opinion is puerile, and the commentator who quotes it, Dr Stackhouse, afterwards more reasonably suggests that the name may have been given to the deity who protected the people from the flies, which molest the Asiatics as much as the mosquitoes in the West Indies.

But whatever may have been the origin of the word, it appears to have been a Hebrew name, in use before the Babylonish captivity, and still in use in the time of Christ.

JOHN i, 38. Then Jesus turned, and saw them following, and saith unto them, "What seek ye?" They said unto him, "*Rabbi* (which is to say, being interpreted, Master) where dwellest thou?"

JOHN xx, 16. Jesus saith unto her "Mary." She turned herself, and saith unto him, "*Rabboni*," which is to say Master.

I copy the following note on this verse from Dr Carpenter's Apostolical Harmony of the Gospels, p. 194, second edition, 8vo, Lond. 1838.

Rabboni My teacher (*or* Master). The received text has 'Ραββονι, which is the Syro-Chaldaic form of the pure Hebrew 'Ραββι, My Teacher, (*or* Master). The most approved reading is 'Ραββουνι, which represents the Galilæan pronunciation of 'Ραββονι. The Rabbinical writings say that *Rabboni* is more dignified than *Rabbi*, and this than *Rab*, which simply signifies Master or Teacher. See Schleusner.

MATTHEW xxvii, 46. And about the ninth hour Jesus cried with a loud voice, saying, "*Eli, Eli, lama sabacthani?*" that is to say, My God, my God, why hast thou forsaken me? Some of them that stood there, when they heard that, said, "This man calleth for Elias."

The account is very similar in the gospel according to St. Mark;

MARK xv, 34. And at the ninth hour Jesus cried with a loud voice, saying "*Eloi, Eloi, lama sabachthani?*" which is, being interpreted, My God, my God, why hast thou forsaken me? And some of them that stood by, when they heard it, said, "Behold, he calleth Elias."

Let us hear Dr Lightfoot's interpretation of these texts:

St Matthew gives the words Eli, Eli, in the Hebrew, exactly the same as they occur at Ps. xxii, 1. St Mark gives them according to the Syro-Chaldaic dialect; which was in common use at the time of our Saviour.

From which it appears that the Syro-Chaldaic dialect, as Dr Lightfoot terms it, was remarkably similar to the Hebrew if it differed from it no more than by the addition of the letter *o* to the sentence "Eli, Eli, lama sabachthani." But the truth is, we know nothing of the Syro-Chaldaic dialect, or of any other dialect than the Hebrew, as spoken at Jerusalem about the period of time when our Saviour was crucified. It is more reasonable to suppose that Eloi and Eli are merely the forms by which two different translators have rendered the same word from Hebrew into Greek; and this supposition is strengthened by the usage of many modern Greeks, who pronounce *Eli* and *Eloi* in the same manner, *Ailee*. It is also to be remembered that the quotations from the Old Testament are invariable copied in the New Testament from the Greek Septuagint, and in no instance translated afresh from the Hebrew. This alone renders nugatory all attempts to distinguish the Hebrew from the so-called Syro-Chaldaic in tracing the origin of these quotations. As regards the words Eli and Eloi, a dilemma is unavoidable: the word, as it occurs in the Psalm of David, is Eli: does Dr Lightfoot imply that Christ altered the word into another and a more corrupt dialect? He could not have used both forms: which then did he use? If Eloi, why has St Matthew put Eli into his mouth? if however Eli is the word which he ejaculated, why has he been made to use the other form Eloi in the gospel according to St Mark? No other solution seems so reasonable as to ascribe the discrepancy to the peculiarities of different translators.

It is necessary however to notice another observation which has been made on these texts, resting on no better foundation than the former. Some of those who stood by thought that Christ called for Elias. This, according to the views of some commentators, is supposed to prove that the Hebrew was no longer spoken in Jerusalem at this time; for otherwise, say they, everybody who stood by would have understood the meaning of his words. This however would not necessarily be the case; for a man in the last agonies of death would not be likely to speak with sufficient distinctness to make his words intelligible, particularly to the lower classes, who alone are in the habit of attending on such occasions. Nor is it likely that a quotation from the Psalms would be very intelligible to an ignorant multitude who knew little about the Bible in general, and perhaps nothing at all about the Psalms of David. The immense labour of writing out books with the pen in those days leaves us little ground for believing that the copies of the

Hebrew Bible were then either numerous or extensively circulated.

3. The proper names of persons and places also which occur in the New Testament are of the same character as those which occur in the Old. Thus we have Zechariah the father of John, Joseph the reputed father of Christ, Simeon and Anna, who received Christ, when he was presented in the temple, Jonah, Barabbas, Bar-Jona, Bar-timæus (with a Latin termination), Zebedee, Eli, occurring in one genealogy as the grandfather of Christ, and Jacob who occurs in the other genealogy: whilst the name of Jesus himself is only a Greek form of Joshua, and is therefore identical with that of the great captain who lived fifteen hundred years before.

Again, we have names of places in the purest Hebrew, although we should always remember that they come to us through the medium of a Greek translation. Such are Golgotha, Bethesda, Bethsaida, Bethlehem, and many others compounded of that remarkable word Beth, describing the idea of *house*, locality or *residence*, which is as characteristic of the Hebrew nation, as the *dune* marks the Celts all over the west of Europe, as the *ville* denotes a Norman origin, and as *ham, bourne, stead* and *wich* denote Anglo-Saxon etymology throughout the whole of England.

The names of places would not, it is true, furnish so strong an argument in every case, because the same name may remain in use for many centuries, provided that the same race of people inhabit the spot which bears it. It is, indeed, said that the whole of Palestine underwent a more violent change of masters than countries in general are fated to undergo. If so, the names would have been changed, as has happened in other similar cases. But the names in the Old Testament and in the New belong to the same language, which must therefore have been the same from the period of the Babylonish captivity down to the beginning of the Christian era.

4. Lastly, Christ himself reads from the book of the Old Testament, as appears from the gospel according to St Luke, iv, 16—17:

And he came to Nazareth, where he had been brought up: and as his custom was, he went into their synagogue on the sabbath day, and stood up for to read. And there was delivered unto him the book of the prophet Esaias. And when he had opened the book, he found the place where it was written, The Spirit of the Lord is upon me, because he hath anointed me to preach the gospel to the poor, &c.

Some of the commentators say that it was customary in Judea to read the original text of the Hebrew Bible verse by verse, alternately with the Targum or Chaldee paraphrase. If this was the case, why is no mention made of it in the passage before us? No notice whatever is taken of such a remarkable custom, and who was there that would assist a reformer like Jesus in interpreting what he read? There was evidently no such custom, or the writers of the four gospels would have related it. It is unlikely that the scribes and Pharisees would have let slip such favourable opportunities to "entangle him in his talk."

But we have not the slightest indication of any discussion having arisen with regard to the interpretation of Hebrew words and sentences. It is more probable, therefore, that both Christ himself and the people, as well as the Scribes and Pharisees, still spoke Hebrew, and consequently understood the language in which their scriptures were originally written.

CHAPTER XXXVII.

SUCCESSIVE CHANGES IN THE RELIGION OF THE HEBREWS RESULTING FROM THEIR CONTACT WITH FOREIGN NATIONS.

PECULIARITIES of speech have a sensible influence on the manners and customs of nations. Religion is, perhaps, of less weight than language in its effects on national character; but it must not be neglected, in an inquiry into either the social or intellectual state of the Hebrew people, and may contribute something to illustrate the subject now before us.

A trite but somewhat indistinct observation has been often repeated by all the commentators on the Old Testament, that the Israelites were prone to fall aside from their allegiance to the Lord God. It is certainly remarkable that this wayward people could, in defiance of the Almighty, and almost in his very presence, fall into religious extravagances which in no degree fall short of the lowest idolatries of the most heathen nations. But these excesses were not without the connection of cause and effect, which might be discovered, if we could only trace it, in all the actions, however apparently strange, both of individuals and of nations. We see, throughout the Old Testament, in the religious observances of the Hebrews, evident marks of the external circumstances to which they were exposed. I use the name *Hebrews*, as more extensive than Israelites: Abraham, Isaac, Esau, and Jacob were Hebrews, but Israelite is a term applied to the posterity of Jacob alone.

The Old Testament, in various passages, plainly indicates that the religion of Abraham, and that of the nation which descended from him were not in every particular the same. Setting aside those points in which they agreed, let us notice those in which they differed, and we shall find these are far from trivial, though not greater than might be anticipated in a nation exposed to many extraordinary vicissitudes running through so long a space of time.

The religious belief of Abraham was extremely simple. He worshipped an Almighty Being, the Lord God, Jehovah Elohim,* to whom he looked for the fulfilment of hopes long held out to himself and his posterity. To the worship of God was attached the practice of expiatory sacrifice, common, as it appears, to all the Canaanitish nations, and the offering of Isaac bears a fearful relation to the devotional enthusiasm which prompted the people of that country to give up their dearest pledges in submission to the Divine will. Another feature which may be detected in the religious belief of the patriarchs, Abraham, Isaac, and Jacob, is that to which the name of Anthropomorphism, *likeness to man*, has been given. The opinion which represents God in the form of a man, is exceedingly liable to rise in the minds of beings like ourselves endued with narrow powers of comprehension,

---

* The identity of Jehovah with the Jove of the ancient Etrurians was known as early as the time of Diodorus. And the Ali and Allah of the Mahometans shows the same affinity to Elohim of the Jews. Some think Jehovah to have been first used by Moses, as copied from the Egyptian mysteries.

and yet always aspiring to that which is above us. The belief is not universal; some nations are notorious for having worshipped deities under the form of the most degrading species of the brute creation; of which one of the most revolting examples that I know of is found among the inhabitants of Bubastes in Egypt, who worshipped God under the image of a cat. If we could investigate the origin of these peculiar creeds, some extenuating circumstances might possibly be discovered, which would render even these cases no longer exceptions, but fresh instances, or at least illustrations, of the general rule. The whole of the Grecian and Roman mythology describes a host of deities, whose human forms flattered the vanity of their votaries, even whilst the intellect was humbled by the rites which accompanied their worship.

The mind of man, as it surveys the material universe around, seeks in vain for an agency superior to its own organization: it is conscious of powers to which everything within its range is inferior, and by an easy and natural extension of these powers, man, in his thoughts, soon arrives at the idea of a God. Even the negative of man's positive qualities suggests new faculties by which a species of omnipotence might be gained. The power of sight suggests the idea of invisibleness: space leads the mind to reflect on infinity; and whilst the principle of gravity presses us down to the earth with the greatest force, we aspire in our imaginations to that freedom from the trammels of matter which would carry us, without weight and buoyant in spirit, above the starry spheres. As a corollary to this theorem, man not only aspires to God's heavenly seat, but dares to bring down God to the level of himself. The Lord God walked in the garden in the cool of the day, when he would enquire into the particulars of Adam's transgression. He was repeatedly seen by Abraham, Isaac, and Jacob—so was the report current among their posterity—and the last of these patriarchs is represented as having personally wrestled with the Lord. Many tribes of ignorant savages have been known to beat the images of their gods, to make them listen more readily to their prayers. Jacob's wrestling with God, and prevailing, either falls under the same category, or in a spiritual sense denotes the influence and success of his prayers.

From the nature of their Deity, and what may be called the essentials of the patriarchal religion, we naturally turn to the subordinate but still important particulars which characterised their worship. These are, 1. the persons whose duty it was to perform their rites and ceremonies: and 2. the places in which those ceremonies were performed. As regards the ministers of religion, we do not find that any existed among the Hebrews before the sojourn in Egypt, and this fact cannot but be looked upon as of the utmost importance to a clear understanding of the history and polity of the Israelites. There is no mention of priests or ministers of religion even from the creation of the world down to the time of Moses and Aaron—that is to say, among the Hebrews; for in Canaan Melchisedec, according to a Biblical expression, which has not hitherto been satisfactorily explained by the commentators, was the "priest of the most high God;" and in Egypt we know that the priestly office existed in the time of Joseph, who is related to have married the daughter of Potipherah, priest of On. The duties which in later days devolved upon the priests were, in the time of Abraham, performed by the patriarch himself. Each separate society consisted, in those days, of a single clan or family, who knew no other superior than the head of the clan, whose word was their law, no doubt modified by custom, into which the ideas of justice and equity more or less entered, according to the peculiar circumstances of the clan. The head of this family was also their priest, and discharged for them the few religious offices which their simple theology demanded; and this he did from the light of nature, rather than from any code of laws and canons like those which, from the age of Moses, have been continually growing and branching out in various directions, until they have caused the utmost perplexity and embarrassment to mankind.

The places in which the religious rites of the Hebrew patriarchs were performed were generally places which the majesty of Nature rather than the graces of architecture pointed out: and these were afterwards indicated by rude but lasting monuments, some of which still survive, not to tell us any history of the past, but only that they had a history, which we now shall never be able to unfold.

The earliest monuments of all nations seem to be those

which belong to the rites and ceremonies of religion. Pillars, sometimes standing singly, sometimes formed into enclosures, as at Stonehenge, Avebury, the temples of Karnac, and others in Egypt, and almost everywhere in the ancient world, attest a similarity of construction, for many of which no other use has been imagined than the worship of a Supreme Being, which is so natural to the human breast. Of these massive remains, the oldest model is probably the *monolith*, as it is termed, because it consisted of a single stone; though the term is not applicable, when the object was a lofty tree, of which the stone pillar was perhaps an imitation. Though the Hebrew patriarchs "worshipped not in temples made with hands," yet they generally selected some spot shaded by the foliage and marked by the aspiring trunk of some stately tree.

When Jacob hides the teraphim, the idols of his wife, he selects, as a sacred place, "under the oak by Shechem." Deborah, Rebecca's foster-mother, was buried with pious carefulness beneath the stones of Bethel, under an oak, and the name of it was called the oak of weeping. So also Saul and his sons were interred under the oak in Jabesh: Gideon's angel came and sat under an oak which was in Ophrah; the erring man of God rests under an oak; as if these were in the nature of consecrated trees and religious stations. In Joshua, xxiv, 26, we read that the successor of Moses took a great stone and set it up there under an oak, which was by the sanctuary of the Lord; and this selection of oaks and setting up of monolithic pillars might be illustrated by numerous other examples.

But the inhabitants of Canaan had already, in the time of Abraham, begun to improve on the original idea of worshipping under the single tree,—standing perhaps in the centre of a surrounding plain. They already were used to plant whole groves of trees in honour of the Deity, and Abraham apparently imitates them in this particular; for we read in Genesis, xxi, 23, that he "planted a grove in Beersheba, and called there on the name of the Lord, the everlasting God."

This grove, according to a note by Bishop Patrick, was planted as a solemn and retired place wherein to worship God; and he adds:

Hence, some think, the custom of planting groves was derived into all the Gentile world; who so profaned them, by images and filthiness, and sacrifices to demons, that God commanded them, by the law of Moses, to be cut down.

This is probable, for it does not appear that the Lord God objected to the groves themselves, but only to their being consecrated to other gods than himself. But it may be doubted that this was the first instance of a grove being planted, or that the nations of Canaan learnt this usage from a single stranger, sojourning among them. It is far more likely that Abraham planted the grove, in honour of Jehovah, on the same principle of solemnity and mysterious awe which dense foliage conveys, as influenced the other people of Canaan, each to honour his own god in the same manner.

High places, also, we find, were chosen by the nations of Canaan, as peculiarly fitting for the worship of their gods. To ascribe idolatry universally to those who frequented the summits of lofty hills as sites of religious worship, would be to draw a premature and unjust conclusion from such premises. It cannot be denied that the ancient Persians were wholly averse to every appearance of idolatry, and their descendants, the modern Parsees, imitate their forefathers in this particular, and yet they pay peculiar respect to hills and high places; as if these localities especially raised them nearer to the heavens, to which all the good in every age have aspired to go. Nature, majestic in all her works, is more majestic still, viewed from the top of the heaven-pointing hill; the spirits expand with the degree of elevation which is attained; earth's toils and the cares which oppress us in the valley, are for the moment left behind, and the soul feels or fancies that it is nearer than before to the Great Being from whom it is derived. But when the soul has become sunk in superstition, and reason, which is our first guide to truth, is overlaid with the inhuman tenets of a barbarous ritual, when the mountain air has been polluted by the unhallowed offering of the child to demons by its misguided parents, and when other profane or indecent ceremonies have desecrated the mountain-top, it then would be the duty of the Israelite to abandon the "High Places," which the patriarchs selected whereon to devote themselves to the worship and service of their Maker.

The sojourn in Egypt gave a new character to the faith of the tribes of Israel. They went down into that land holding a species of Deism, purer perhaps than any other form which has existed among men. But they came out of Egypt so many years later, greatly altered in this particular: as they speedily evinced by their conduct, hardly one month after they had escaped across the Red Sea. The golden calf furnishes a striking instance of the effect which their residence in Egypt had produced; the worship of the bull-god Apis, an Egyptian superstition, is too well known to be here repeated; it is sufficient to remark that the golden calf was the natural resource of a degraded nation of slaves, who finding themselves, as they supposed, without a god to protect them, speedily constructed such an one as they had seen worshipped by their former masters the Egyptians. Whether, as some think, the Cherubim of the Jews was a more open manifestation of the symbolism which represented the spiritual deity under the likeness of Apis the bull, may not now be easy to determine. But when the people were suffering from the bite of the fiery serpents, it is related that Moses erected a brazen serpent, and "put it upon a pole, and it came to pass, that if a serpent had bitten any man, when he beheld the serpent of brass, he lived," Numbers, xxi, 9.

The reason why God commanded Moses to adopt this course has not been recorded: but the fact would probably be susceptible of a satisfactory explanation, if we were acquainted more fully with the serpent-worship which existed among the ancient people of Egypt. Many modern writers have indeed written treatises on this subject, but their arguments are mostly conjectural, and their conclusions rather addressed to the imagination than commended to the solid judgment of the reader. In the absence of certain information, it may be supposed that the Israelites had been taught to hold serpents in great respect whilst they were in Egypt, and that Moses availed himself of their superstition to bend them the better to his will. But a serious statement concerning this brazen serpent is recorded in II Kings, xviii, 4:

He [Hezekiah] removed the high-places, and brake the images, and cut down the groves, and brake in pieces the brazen serpent that Moses had made; for unto those days the children of Israel did burn incense to it: and he called it Nehushtan.

The Israelites were still idolaters as late as the year 726 before Christ. It is possible that the Judges and Kings may have found this superstition too firmly fixed in the minds of their people, and may have silently acquiesced in its continuance, if not actually allowed it to continue as a mode of keeping up some kind of religious observance, in retired places perhaps removed from the more immediate inspection of the central government. At all events, the Popes, in more modern times, have not scrupled to adopt many particulars of the ancient heathen ritual, as a mode of converting the nations of Europe to the Christian faith.

A third feature, common to both the Egyptian and the Israelitish religion, was the ceremony relating to the scape-goat: the customs of the two nations, as already stated in page 246 of this work, though not perfectly the same, are so nearly similar that the one appears to have been derived from the other. The import of both is certainly the same: for in both, the goat is made use of as a substitute,* to draw away calamity from the party sacrificing, in the one case being sent into the wilderness, and in the other consumed by fire.

The next particular in which the Egyptians and Israelites bore a resemblance to one another, has also been already noticed, in page 249, namely, the remarkable rite of circumcision. In modern times it is known as the distinguishing mark of the Mahometans, and prevails in all those countries which have embraced their faith. It is difficult to believe that the Egyptians adopted this rite from their own slaves, the Israelites; and it is obvious to infer that the Israelites borrowed it from the Egyptians. It was, indeed, adopted by Abraham, at the command of God; and yet, as Abraham is known to have passed some time in Egypt, the inference

---

* It would be a lawful subject of enquiry, if we possessed more historical data, how far the idea of the scape-goat may have lingered among the Jewish people, at the time when they asked Pilate to crucify Jesus, but to release Barabbas.

seems still to be admissible that he adopted it by imitation from the people among whom he sojourned.

These four points of similarity between the Egyptian and Israelitish modes of worship are all that I propose to bring forwards; but a treatise might be written on the subject, founded in part on the account which Herodotus gives of the Egyptian sacred rites, and partly drawn from other sources. The view here taken has, it appears, forced itself upon the mind of a living writer, Mr Sharpe, who has written a History of Egypt, displaying great learning and research. The observations which here follow, taken from his work, are suitable to our present subject:

How much the Jews were indebted to the Egyptians for their learning, philosophy, and letters, is one of the most interesting inquiries in ancient history. Moses had been brought up in the neighbourhood of Heliopolis, the chief seat of Egyptian philosophy, and carefully educated in all the learning of the Egyptians, under the tutorship, as tradition says, of Jannes and Jambres, while too many of the Israelites were given up to the idolatry and superstitions of the country. Hence many of the Egyptian customs, as seen by the historian Manetho, are clearly pointed at and forbidden by the laws of Moses, while others, which were free from blame, are even copied in the same laws; and much light may be thrown on the manners of each nation by comparing them together. The chief purpose for which the Jews were set apart from the other nations seems to have been to keep alive the great truth, that the Creator and Governor of the world is one—a truth, assailed by the superstitious in all ages; and Moses proclaimed, that all the gods which the Egyptian priests wished the ignorant multitude to worship, were false. The Egyptians worshipped the stars as emblems of the gods, the sun under the name of Rea, and the moon as Joh or Isis; but among the Jews, whoever worshipped any one of the heavenly bodies was to be stoned to death. The Egyptians worshipped statues of men, beasts, birds, and fishes; but the Jews were forbidden to bow down before any carved image. The Egyptian priests kept their heads shaved; while the Jewish priest was forbidden to make himself bald, or even to cut the corner of his beard. The people of Lower Egypt marked their bodies with pricks, in honour of their gods; but the Jews were forbidden to cut their flesh or make any mark upon it. The Egyptians buried food in the tombs with the bodies of their friends, and sent gifts of food to the temples for their use; but the Jews were forbidden to set apart any food for the dead. The Egyptians planted groves of trees within the court-yard of their temple, as the Alexandrian Jews did in later times: but the laws of Moses forbade the Jews to plant any trees near the altar of the Lord. The sacred bull Apis was chosen by the priests of Memphis for its black and white spots, and Mnevis, the sacred bull of Heliopolis, had nearly the same marks; but the Jews, in preparing their water of purification, were ordered to kill a red heifer without a spot. HISTORY OF EGYPT, pp. 33—35.

The return of the Israelites into the land of Canaan opens to our view a third period of their history, and a third state of their religion. The priests and Levites play a conspicuous part everywhere among them, deriving their institution from Moses, but, singularly enough, not practising his precepts, or preserving the purity of worship which he had taught them.

It would extend this work indefinitely to enter here into a full examination of this subject. I shall therefore name only a few facts which imply that the people, returning to the country of their ancestors, resumed at least one custom which had existed in the times of the patriarchs, and also that the people, or at least some portion of them, were still idolaters down to the latest period of the Hebrew monarchy. In the first place, the practice of having household gods was resumed, or perhaps had never been broken off, exemplified in the history of Micah:

And the man Micah had an house of gods, and made an ephod, and teraphim, and consecrated one of his sons who became his priest. JUDGES, xvii, 5.

This reminds us of the flight of Jacob from Padan-aram when Rachel stole the images, teraphim in the Hebrew, belonging to her father:

And Laban went to shear his sheep: and Rachel had stolen the images that were her father's. GENESIS, xxxi, 19.

Laban pursues Jacob in his flight towards Canaan, and in his expostulation, when he comes up with him, he uses these words:

And now, though thou wouldest needs be gone, because thou sore longedst after thy father's house; yet wherefore hast thou stolen my gods?

Bishop Patrick and Dr Stackhouse explain the teraphim by an imaginary train of thought, which may amuse the reader by its originality, but cannot produce the conviction that it is based upon either probability or truth:

They were objects of worship or instruments of divination. It is supposed that Rachel stole them; either because, having still a tincture of superstition, she feared Laban should enquire of them which way Jacob was gone; or because, having been brought off by Jacob from the false notions and bad customs of her country, she desired to convince her father of his superstition, by letting him see, that his gods (as he called them) could not preserve themselves, much less be of any service to him: or because she intended to give herself some portion of his goods which she thought justly belonged to her, and of which he had deprived her. It is supposed the images were made of gold or silver, or some other valuable substance.

Dr Lightfoot represents the teraphim in a different point of view, equally imaginative as the foregoing:

The teraphim were probably the pictures or statues of some of Rachel's ancestors, and taken by her for the preservation of their memory, when she was about never to see her father's house again.

In the next place, we find a narrative in the Second Book of Kings (xxiii, 11—14) which shows that the injunctions of Moses and others against idolatry, and to support the worship of the true and only God, Jehovah, were by no means too severe or needless, but were, however, far from successful in exterminating idol-worship. The dedication of horses to the service of the sun, a very general Eastern superstition, from which the Greeks received the mythological history of Phaeton; the worship of Ashtaroth, introduced in the earliest ages by the Sidonian merchants, under the name of Astarte, into Greece; the worship of Chemosh, the Moabitish deity, whose name occurs with that of Omri on the lately discovered Moabitish stone—all these are comprised within three verses in the following passage concerning the reform of religion in the reign of King Josiah:

He took away the HORSES that the kings of Judah had given TO THE SUN, at the entering in of the house of the Lord, by the chamber of Nathan-melech, which was in the suburbs, and burned the chariots of the sun with fire... And the HIGH PLACES that were before Jerusalem, which were on the right hand of the mount of corruption, which Solomon the king of Israel had builded for ASHTORETH the abomination of the Moabites, and for MILCOM the abomination of the children of Ammon, did the king defile. And he brake in pieces the images, and cut down the groves, and filled their places with the bones of men.

It is in vain, therefore, that the commentators seek to evade a fact which plainly shows that idolatry was the religion of those times, not, perhaps, such primary idolatry as the statue of Olympian Jove indicated among the Greeks, but an inferior species, by which even men, who recognize the power and majesty of God, as they are shown in the magnificent works of Nature, are yet prone to deal in secondary agencies, spirits, wizards, ghosts, charms, and amulets—anything, in short, which brings down the great idea of God to the low level of their own weak understandings.

A striking contrast to this image-worship is presented by the same people, when they came back from Babylon—no more teraphim or household deities—nothing more is said of a plurality of deities—the gods of the mountain and the gods of the plains merge into the omnipotence of the one God, surrounded by the angels, archangels, and the whole army of Heaven. Conspicuous, however, above all his satellites is the Almighty Jehovah. His attributes are those which, in the present day, are held in reverence by half the world, and his religion assumes that shape which we find impressed upon the Gospel-histories of the New Covenant.

The appearance of angels, however, in this stage of the Israelitish religion, demands to be noticed. Whilst these by some are divided into two classes—the good, who minister to the welfare of mankind, and the bad, who are ever lying in wait to do us harm—others have interpreted their existence as an imaginary but needful addition to that personification of good and evil which is so characteristic of the Oriental mind. For the majestic scheme of an Almighty Creator and Preserver of the Universe surrounded by the Heavenly Host above described, was contrasted, in the later theology of the Hebrews, with a corresponding picture of a rival agency, always engaged in counteracting the benevolent purposes of Jehovah. Satan was the name of this demon or hostile spirit; and under his commands were a legion of evil spirits, ever abiding his bidding, and ready to do his will. This particular phase of the religious belief of the Jews is not recognised in their history before the return from the Babylonish Captivity: for the older religion of the Jews recognised only one ruler of the world, to whose providence all events whether good or evil were ascribed; nor do the very obscure accounts of supernatural beings appearing to Lot and Abraham possess sufficient reality to remove this inference; and as the religion of the Persians is known to have turned upon the same opposing principles of good and evil, it is a reasonable inference that the Jews first acquired these views during the seventy years which the principal men of their nation passed among the Chaldean, Babylonian, and Persian philosophers, who followed the doctrines of Zoroaster.*

From the time that this new element entered into the religion of the Jews, a corresponding meaning is found attached to the word Satan, which formerly signified nothing more than an enemy, or adversary, but now began to be the designation of the power of evil. Used in this sense for the Devil, the word Satan occurs in only four passages of the Old Testament; and even in one of these it is inaccurately so rendered in our English Bible, for the word in that verse also means nothing more than an adversary. The place where it is inaccurately rendered by the English word Satan, meaning the Devil, is in Psalm cix, verse 6 :

* "Hyde and Prideaux, working up the Persian legends and their own conjectures into a very agreeable story, represent Zoroaster as a contemporary of Darius Hystaspes. But it is sufficient to observe, that the Greek writers, who lived almost in the age of Darius, agree in placing the era of Zoroaster many hundred, or even thousand, years before their own time. The judicious criticism of Mr Moyle perceived, and maintained against his uncle, Dr Prideaux, the antiquity of the Persian prophet. See his work, vol. ii. . . . . That ancient idiom [IN WHICH THE ZENDAVESTA WAS COMPOSED] was called the Zend. The language of the commentary, the Pehlvi, though much more modern, has ceased many ages ago to be a living tongue. This fact alone (if it is allowed as authentic) sufficiently warrants the antiquity of those writings, which d'Anquetil has brought into Europe, and translated into French."—GIBBON, chap. viii.

Set thou a wicked man over him; and let Satan stand at his right hand.

Here there seems to be no necessity for understanding the word to have any other meaning than that of adversary, by which a satisfactory sense for the passage is obtained.

But the other passages in which the word Satan is found in its new sense, occur in books which were, without doubt, wholly written after the return of the Jews from Babylon, and not compiled out of ancient originals like some earlier parts of the Bible, where many passages have probably been preserved entire. They are the following:

I Chronicles, xxi, 1. And Satan stood up against Israel, and provoked David to number Israel.

Job, i, 6. Now there was a day when the sons of God came to present themselves before the Lord, and Satan came also among them. And the Lord said unto Satan, &c. &c.

Zechariah, iii, 1, 2.—And he showed me Joshua the high priest standing before the angel of the Lord, and Satan standing at his right hand to resist him. And the Lord said unto Satan, "The Lord rebuke thee."

The books of Chronicles are universally allowed to belong to the latest period of the Jewish Commonwealth. Zechariah also is admitted to have written about the same time, and those who still look upon the book of Job as a work of remote antiquity, have to encounter and explain the difficulties which militate against its antiquity, and have been already noticed in this work.

But the passage in Chronicles where the name of Satan occurs may be compared with the corresponding narrative in II Samuel, xxiv, 1, where David's sin in numbering the people is described:

And again the anger of the Lord was kindled against Israel, and he moved David against them to say, Go, number Israel and Judah.

Here it is the anger of the Lord against Israel, which prompts David to commit an act that was disagreeable to God: but in Chronicles it is the enmity of the Devil, or Evil Spirit, which impels the King to sin. The former account flowed naturally from the opinions which the ancient Israelites held concerning the anthropomorphism, and consequently, the human feelings of anger, friendship, and revenge, which they ascribed to the Almighty. This view of the subject is beautifully expressed in the latter part of the prophecies of Isaiah—if, at least, this part also is to be considered as written by him, and not, as some think, by one who wrote in a later age. In the forty-fifth chapter, the Almighty is represented as addressing Cyrus in these words:

I am the Lord, and there is none else, there is no God beside me. I girded thee, though thou hast not known me: that they may know from the rising of the sun, and from the west, that there is none beside me. I am the Lord and there is none else. I form the light and create darkness: I make peace and CREATE EVIL: I the Lord do all these things.

That God is the author of evil as well as good was no doubt the belief of the early Jews, but their connection with Babylon brought new elements into their belief; and perhaps the assertion that God created evil as well as good was aimed against the first appearance of the dualistic system, which ranged the powers of evil under a banner hostile to Jehovah and the powers of good. Thus the latter of the two narratives which have been quoted, exhibiting the name and influence of Satan over David, was written when the Jews had imbibed other notions of evil, which they were probably the more ready to adopt, because the character of the Deity was thereby relieved from the imputation of sometimes being the cause which impelled mankind to sin. The two antagonistic principles of the Persian or Chaldean theology easily caught the warm imaginations of the Jewish people, who did not perceive that the belief in a God of evil narrowed the dominion of the God of Good, in the same proportion as it exalted by contrast his moral perfections.

The existence of evil has always been a greater difficulty to the philosopher than to the theologian; and has by neither of the two been very satisfactorily explained. That there was once a race of heavenly beings who, by rebellion, fell from their first estate, long before the creation and the fall of man, has always been a prominent feature in Oriental mythology, and been made the subject of some of the highest flights of poetry, even among the nations of the West. It has indeed been thought that some obscure passages in the Bible have refer-once to the fallen angels, and that Satan, the Adversary or calumniator, called by us the Devil, from the Latin word diabolus, which means calumniator, was, in fact, the chief of the angels which fell from Heaven. The human race, at a later period, were created perfect and without sin; but they also disappointing the expectations of their Creator, through disobedience to God's commands, were expelled from the happy garden in which they first were placed. The evil spirit who thus succeeded in frustrating the designs of God, and tempted our first parents to disobey, was Satan, who, having been punished for his own sin, became from that time the enemy of God, and has ever since sought to hinder mankind in their aspirations after good, and to prevent them from regaining God's favour, which they had forfeited, and the state of happiness from which they had fallen.

The destruction of all our race, except eight persons, by a flood, was a later punishment which God inflicted on mankind for disobedience; but the sinful element still remained, until the Mediator, our Saviour, came for the purpose not so much of eradicating evil practices from the acts and conduct of mankind, as of instilling a new principle of action, which should save them from future sin, and from a further infliction of punishment on the whole race at the hands of God. This, then, was the state of things at the beginning of our era; and from this time to the present the rival sects of Christians and Jews have been at variance, the latter thinking that the Mediator, who shall restore them to happiness, and perhaps to their former temporal prosperity, is still to come; while the former believe that he is come already, in our Lord and Saviour Christ. Let this, then, suffice for the present on the subject of the word Satan, as entering into the national religion of the Jews.

Another word which throws some light upon our present subject is *Nabi*, "prophet," which, as already stated in page 118, was a new word, acquired by the Jews at Babylon, and afterwards used in an altered sense in consequence of the arts of astrology, prophecy, and divination, for which the Chaldees were famous, not only in the time of Cyrus, Ezra and Nehemiah, but five hundred years afterwards, at Rome, Alexandria, and in almost every country of the known world.

The notices which the Greek and Roman writers have left concerning these peculiarities of the Israelitish people, are in general very slight. This arises, no doubt, from the reserve which the Jews always showed towards other nations, amounting, in fact, to moroseness and animosity towards all foreigners. Yet Diogenes Laertius has described the theology of the Jewish nation as an off-shoot from that of the Chaldees, to whom he attributes the power of divination or prophesy, and the belief in two opposite principles, the one of evil and the other of good. The whole section is curious, and bears so close a relation to the present subject that no excuse is needed for quoting it here at length:

They say that the Chaldees occupied themselves with astronomy and foretelling: and the Magi with the worship of the gods, and sacrifices and prayers, as being the only persons whom the gods listened to. And that they make declarations concerning the being and origin of the gods, whom they state to be Fire, Earth, and Water. That they condemn images, and especially those persons who say that the gods are male and female.

7. That they deliver discourses on justice, and think it unholy to dispose of the dead by burning them. That they approve of a union with one's mother or daughter, as Sotion observes in his 23rd book. That they study divination and prophesy, and say that the gods appear to them. That the air is full of forms, which by emanation from the burning of incense are admitted to the sight of those who have sharp eyes. That they forbid the wearing of artificial and golden ornaments. Their clothing is white; their bed a pallet: their food is herbs, and cheese, and a cheap kind of bread; their staff is a cane, with which, it is said, they pierce their cheese, and so divide and eat it.

8. But they are not acquainted with magical divination, as Aristotle observes in his Treatise on Magic, and Dinon in the fifth book of his History. The latter also says that Zoroaster, interpreted means 'the star-worshipper,' and Hermodorus says the same. Aristotle, in the fifth book of his Philosophy, says that they are more ancient than the Egyptians, and that they hold two principles, a good genius, and an evil genius, the former named Zeus [Jupiter] or Oromasdes, the latter Hades [Pluto] or Arimanius. Hermippus also mentions this in his first book on the Magi, and Eudoxus in his Period, and Theopompus in the eighth book of his Philippics.

9. He says also that, according to the Magi, men will rise from the dead, and become immortal, and that things will remain by

their appellations. The same is related by Eudoxus of Rhodes. But Hecataeus says that, according to the Magi, the gods are also born: and Clearchus of Soli, in his book on Education, says that the Gymnosophists are descended from the Magi. Some say that the Jews also are an offshoot from them. Moreover those who have written about the Magi, condemn Herodotus, observing that Xerxes did not throw his javelin up at the sun, nor cast chains upon the sea, because these have been declared by the Magi to be gods: but that his removing statues was a very likely thing for him to do. DIOGENES LAERTIUS, *Proem.*, § 6.

Even the Jewish writings themselves bear testimony to the Oriental origin of their celestial hierarchy: for the Jerusalem Talmud says that the names of the angels, as well as those of the months, came from Babylon with the Jews who were returning from captivity.

CHAPTER XXXVIII.

ON THE ART OF WRITING — ITS GRADUAL DEVELOPMENT THROUGH FIVE STAGES — 1. MEXICAN PICTURE-WRITING: 2. EGYPTIAN HIEROGLYPHICS: 3. CHINESE WORD-WRITING: 4. HEBREW SYLLABIC OR CONSONANTAL WRITING: 5. ALPHABETIC WRITING.

The changes which are effected by lapse of time in the language of a nation, though partly influenced by external causes, are, nevertheless, partly independent of those causes. Motion is one of the principles of the universe and not merely of human things. Nothing is stationary: the very outlines of the material globe, on which we live, are always changing; the ocean, which washes the coasts of the solid continents of the earth, is ever fretting and chafing, as if eager to extend its dominion; and, while in some parts it has made large encroachments upon the land, it has in other places receded before its enemy: so that, whilst ships now sail over water where the husbandman formerly drove his plough, we may elsewhere gather fruit and flowers where once the sailor steered his ship.

Man is subject to the same physical laws as the creation which surrounds him. Through the long period of authentic history, no nation has retained for two hundred years all the original elements of its constitution. Its language, as well as almost all other features, has submitted to the law of change. The life of even one man is long enough to furnish instances of this law. New fashions arise, whether of dress, gait, speech, pronunciation, or writing, which draw after them the imitation of the young, whilst they, as surely, bring down the reprobation of the old, who think nothing right or good, but what themselves did in the earlier period of their lives.

Novelty is in fact a constant charm; to the love of change may be ascribed the disappearance of many things in no wise inferior to others, which have occupied their places; but those also have had their day, and been again succeeded by others, to which a similar period of existence followed by a similar decay has been assigned. It is related by Horace, that his predecessors in the poetical art, Ennius and Lucilius, had enriched the native tongue of Latium by the introduction of new words to express thoughts and ideas, which perhaps only wanted names, because the ideas were themselves new to the ruder intellects of the Roman people; and it was the claim of him who tells us this, that he should himself be allowed to coin a few fresh words, which before his time were unused or unknown. The law of finality must be abandoned in every branch of human learning and science, and indeed in every department of human life. It must be abandoned by the historian and by the student of history also; Time, the destroyer of all human works, is found to spare germs of truth, which often reproduce in a more perfect and real form what has been thought to have gone from us for ever.

In reviewing the history of the world, we find it necessary to be guided by principles which derive their force chiefly from the law by which everything is continually moving forward; and yet this very law has often in its course deposited grains of truth, which have enabled us, even when ages have passed away, to discover however faintly the character of events, however enshrined in the legendary tales, in which the imagination of rude and even of civilized nations has delighted. These observations can hardly too often be repeated, and their truth is indeed beginning to be more readily acknowledged in the present age, when every record of the past is examined with the utmost accuracy, in order that we may arrive as nearly as possible to the full appreciation of its truth.

In accordance then with the inference, that the language of the Israelites changed with the outward circumstances in which they were placed, it will not be out of place to examine minutely the style of writing in which that language first appeared in the world; and in which it has come down to our times. For, if we can suppose any people in the world to have retained the use of the same language so completely that a book, written nearly a thousand years ago, could be still read to the people by their priests and teachers, so as to be understood by the audience, the people selected to illustrate this permanence of language could not be the Israelites, who, as we have seen in former chapters, went through most remarkable and continual vicissitudes. And if the language, so also the vehicle in which that language has flowed down from early times, may with great probability, approaching almost to certainty, be supposed to have varied according as different modes of writing were devised by the ever-varying and progressive intellect of mankind.

I shall therefore devote the present chapter to an inquiry into the origin of the Art of Writing, and especially of Alphabetic Writing, by the help of which alone we have obtained almost all the knowledge that we possess both of former times and of our own species.

The art of writing is the most noble that mankind have yet acquired. It enables persons residing in remote quarters of the world, to communicate their thoughts to one another with no more delay than the time necessary for transmitting the vehicle to which those thoughts are consigned: and it furnishes the means of handing down the history of past ages to the most distant posterity, and so of accumulating, for the benefit of each succeeding generation, all the wisdom which their predecessors have laid up.

Yet the origin of this art, so wonderful for its results, and so useful to mankind in the daily business of life, is lost in obscurity, though it has been often investigated with all that profound sagacity of which men are capable, when they apply the powers of their intellect to a specific subject of enquiry.

We shall in vain hope that it will ever be discovered to whom mankind is indebted for the invention of this wonderful art: for, as the name of the inventor has not been recorded, no stretch of intellect can supply the absence of what is evidently a matter of fact, until some fresh documents shall be discovered, which may help us to elucidate the difficulty.

It has been maintained by some authors that the art of alphabetic writing was first given to mankind by an immediate revelation from God. Among those who hold this theory may be mentioned Dr Wall, formerly professor of Hebrew at the University of Dublin. In a work * published on this subject some years ago, he has propounded an opinion that the knowledge of Alphabetical Characters was first communicated by God, through Moses, to the Israelites at the time of the promulgation of the Hebrew Law. And the learned author states as the basis of this conclusion that the inhabitants of Egypt, where alone the Israelites could, by human means, have previously learnt the art of alphabetic writing, did not possess that art, until long after the time of Moses and the delivery of the Law. I accept the premises which the learned professor has laid down and established with much learning, but I deny his conclusion, because a better and more rational inference seems to follow, namely that the Hebrew law was not given by Moses, in alphabetic writing, at all.

If then we reject the theory, that this art came by im-

* An examination of the ancient orthography of the Jews, and of the original state of the text of the Hebrew Bible. Part the First, containing an Inquiry into the origin of Alphabetic Writing; with which is incorporated an essay on the Egyptian Hieroglyphics. By C. W. Wall, D.D. senior fellow of Trinity College, and professor of Hebrew in the University of Dublin. Royal 8vo, London, 1835. Two other volumes followed at a later date.

mediate revelation to mankind, it must be supposed to have proceeded from the natural talents of the human race, gradually from small beginnings elaborating the invention until it has at length attained to its present state of perfection. It remains to be shown that existing facts strongly corroborate this view, and that no other view is compatible with these facts. "There can be little doubt," says an author who has been previously quoted, "that the primitive ages possessed some means, besides oral tradition, of recording and perpetuating their several branches of knowledge, but respecting the nature of these means we are left somewhat in the dark. It is universally allowed that no human device could have answered this purpose better than alphabetic writing." But it is not necessary that this art should have existed in several of the ancient nations; for we find that in several nations both ancient and modern, the absence of this art has been no impediment to the happiness of the people, or to the existence among them of wise and intellectual men; for even in the back settlements of America we find men accommodated like savages, but informed as members of civil society; and in ancient authors we read of sages, of no mean fame, residing amongst rude and barbarous nations.

The art of writing, however excellent, is no more than one of the numerous arts by which the life of man is embellished and improved, and it is possible for a people to attain to a high state of advancement in many respects, whilst its individuals may be able neither to read nor write. We are too apt to attach the idea of barbarism to those who are ignorant of the art of reading and writing, forgetting that some of our own kings, and almost all our nobility in former times, knew nothing of either the one or the other. Perhaps a just idea of this subject may be formed by saying that a nation ignorant of the use of letters, can progress in civilization only to that point which the life of one man can attain to, because the use of letters alone can enable a nation to store up the successive and accumulated wisdom of several lives.*

* "The Germans, in the age of Tacitus, were unacquainted with the use of letters, and the use of letters is the principal circumstance that distinguishes a civilized people from a herd of savages incapable of knowledge or reflec-

Yet if we take the most simple and untutored people that History has made us acquainted with, we shall find that they have some mode of conveying their thoughts, analogous, though infinitely inferior, to alphabetic writing.

§ 1. *Mexican Picture-writing.*

The first attempts of a people to convey to a distance, or to deliver down to a future age, the knowledge of an event, would obviously be to draw a picture of that event with all its circumstances delineated, as they presented themselves to the eyes of the narrator; and this mode has, no doubt, been practised in every nation of the earth. It is indeed practised at present in every country, where books are printed, as being the only mode in which many subjects, treated of in those books, can be faithfully and satisfactorily described. Pictures are still used for such purposes, where written language would fail, though they are now used only as subordinate to letters, whereas in certain nations, that have come to our knowledge, picture-writing has been the only mode of conveying the information which now is transmitted by means of alphabetical characters. That this is not a mere theory may be shown by the instance of the Mexicans, who, when invaded by Cortes in the sixteenth

---

tion. Without that artificial help, the human memory soon dissipates or corrupts the ideas intrusted to her charge; and the nobler faculties of the mind, no longer supplied with models or with materials, gradually forget their powers; the judgment becomes languid and lethargic, the imagination languid or irregular. Fully to apprehend this important truth, let us attempt, in an improved society, to calculate the immense distance between the man of learning and the illiterate peasant. The former, by reading and reflection, multiplies his own experience and lives in distant ages and remote countries, whilst the latter, rooted to a single spot and confined to a few years of existence, surpasses, but very little, his fellow-labourer the ox in the exercise of his mental faculties. The same, and even a greater, difference will be found between nations than between individuals, and we may safely pronounce, that without some species of writing, no people has ever preserved the faithful annals of their history, ever made any considerable progress in the abstract sciences, or ever possessed, in any tolerable degree of perfection, the useful and agreeable arts of life."—GIBBON, chap. ix, vol. i. p. 352 of the 12 vol. edit. London, 1832.

We may add, that the oldest Runic inscriptions are supposed to be of the third century, and the most ancient writer who mentions the Runic characters is Venantius Fortunatus (CARMEN vii, 18), who lived towards the end of the sixth century.

century, possessed no alphabetic writing at all, but made use of pictures taken on the spot, to describe to their king in his capital city the nature of the foreigners who had landed on his coasts, their ships, their arms, accoutrements and general appearance. The effect which these pictures produced on the minds of those who had not seen the Spanish invaders, was no doubt the same as that which would be conveyed to the mind of a Frenchman, on entering the Gallery of Battles at Versailles, by the large pictures of the battles of Wagram, Austerlitz, and others, which are there suspended. If all historical records of Mexico on the one hand, or of France on the other, were destroyed, and these pictures alone were preserved, they would still tell the story of those events, though without that vividness of detail, or identification of nation, which could only be obtained from collateral sources.

§ 2. *Hieroglyphics.*

The incompleteness of such Picture-writing would suggest itself sooner or later to those who practised it, according to their capacity for carrying arts to perfection. The Mexicans do not appear to have ever advanced beyond this first stage in what may be termed the literary art, and this is a strong argument against the supposed antiquity of the Mexican nation. There are certain stages, through which, more or less, all nations must pass, and a people, that have not advanced beyond picture-writing, have made but one step at all in the road of improvement. We must turn to Egypt for the next step, and there we find traces of the more advanced species of writing which is generally denominated HIEROGLYPHICS.

To understand aright the peculiar characters which pass under this name, we must not lose sight of the antecedent Picture-writing, from which Hieroglyphics sprang. The original delineation of an event would, as we have seen, be but imperfectly understood by the next generation, and the picture would in process of time require the aid of an interpreter to explain all its various circumstances and details. The question then was, in what manner could certain symbols be placed in connection, one with another, so as to represent a train of ideas, descriptive of certain subjects, which those who possessed the key to this system, could understand? This question occurred to the ancient Egyptians, and they solved it by choosing a series of emblems, mostly objects of common occurrence in their country, and attaching to these objects a certain meaning which should always be the same under the same circumstances; and so was formed the celebrated Hieroglyphical system of that nation. The long duration of the Egyptian culture has furnished us with satisfactory proof that this statement of the origin of Hieroglyphics is correct: for in Egypt are preserved not only immense numbers of such inscriptions; but also of fresco paintings, evidently wrought for the purpose of handing down to posterity the knowledge of certain great events. Thus we have, in the same country, instances of both the earliest kinds of writing, namely the Hieroglyphical, and the Pictorial from which the former is an offshoot.

But it must be admitted after all with regret, that the Hieroglyphics, however they may be an improvement on Picture-writing to those who possess the key of the system, yet to those who have no clue or a weak one to the interpretation of them, they are as obscure as the Picture-writing from which they first arose.

It must not, however, be inferred that modern ingenuity has been altogether baffled in its attempt to decipher the Egyptian Hieroglyphics. The key has not been altogether lost, for the meaning of some of their symbols has been preserved by ancient authors. One instance of this may suffice; it is from a passage of Clemens Alexandrinus who lived at the beginning of the third century of the Christian æra.

At Diospolis in Egypt, on the temple called Pylon, is sculptured, a boy, the emblem of birth; an old man, the emblem of death; the hawk, an emblem of God; and a fish, that of hatred; and a crocodile (having here a different meaning from that which I before named for it), the emblem of impudence. The whole then put together symbolically seems to me to mean, "O you who are born, and you who die, God hates impudence."—*Strom. v.* 413, *ed. Heinsii.*

It has been properly observed of such hieroglyphical inscriptions, that the want of connecting particles makes it difficult to ascertain their exact meaning. Thus the five figures, a boy, an old man, a hawk, a fish, and a crocodile, may have other meanings, besides that which Clemens Alexandrinus has assigned to them, though the five prevailing ideas would be repeated in all. For example, they may mean, " Young and old may become Gods by hating impudence." This, it must be admitted, is a serious defect in the system of Hieroglyphics, though it is equally evident that they show a great advance from the more ancient and simple mode of Picture-writing.

§ 3. *Word-writing.*

I proceed to speak of the third distinct species of writing, which, though emanating from the former, has certain marks peculiar to itself, or at least common to those other kinds of writing which have sprung out of it. According to this mode, every word, representing a separate idea, is expressed by a single character. This kind of writing exists still, though much modified and improved, among the Chinese. In all the languages of China Proper the word for *man* is represented in writing by a certain character, which all the inhabitants of the country recognise to mean the same thing, though in the different dialects, the words, when uttered by the mouth, sound decidedly and essentially different. The nature of this system may be easily illustrated by a similar mode which prevails among ourselves. The Arabic numerals 1, 2, 3, 4, 5, 6, 7, 8, 9, 0, and the Roman numerals I, II, III, IV, &c., as well as the Greek, A, B, &c., &c., are well known in all the nations of the world; though in every different country, the word or name by which each of these is pronounced, is entirely different, yet the idea which these signs convey to the mind is essentially the same.

There are evidently great advantages in this mode, over the Hieroglyphical which preceded; for in Hieroglyphics, as far as we yet understand them, there were fewer means of denoting many particles and minor words of a sentence, which are yet necessary to make the meaning pointed and definite. But in word-writing, according to which it is not necessary that there should be any symbolical analogy between the word, or idea, and the character expressing it, there is no reason why prepositions, conjunctions, and all the inflections of noun or verb may not have their representatives in the written sentence. I do not mean to deny that the written characters were first chosen from some fancied similarity to the object represented by them. It is most probable that they *were* chosen for this reason, and thus they show the third stage in the art of writing, rising as naturally out of the second, as that had before arisen from the first. There is also another peculiarity in this system of word-writing, which in certain cases might be particularly advantageous. It has been shown that persons speaking different languages might use the same books, in the same way as Englishmen and Frenchmen use the same arithmetical tables, containing nothing but figures, which, though pronounced differently, are understood by all alike. It is evident, however, that this advantage would not result in the case of languages, where the words of a sentence are placed in a different order, or where a larger number of words go to make up the same idea in one than another, or where the ideas are differently divided between the words.

The Chinese* are the only people among whom this kind of writing is known, and the general disadvantages of it are signal. As every word has a separate character, a person who has never before seen any particular word written, is unable to complete the sentence until he has obtained the sense of that word. As the nature of the Chinese language is perhaps known to few persons in this country, except those who have been resident in China itself, an analysis of its principles may not be without interest to the reader.

* The antiquity of the Chinese monarchy may be admitted: but it may be doubted whether literature presents any contrast to that of other nations. Gibbon, that most profound of all modern historians, probably thought the same, when he wrote as follows:—

"The æra of the Chinese monarchy has been variously fixed, from 2952 to 2132 before Christ; and the year 2637 has been chosen for the lawful epoch, by the authority of the present emperor. The difference arises from the uncertain duration of the first two dynasties; and the vacant space that lies beyond them, as far as the real or fabulous times of Fohi or Hoangti. Sematsien dates his authentic chronology from the year 841: the thirty-six eclipses of Confucius (thirty-one of which have been verified) were observed between the years 722 and 480 before Christ. The *historical period* of China does not ascend above the Greek Olympiads."—GIBBON, iii, 328; Lond., 1823.

In the first place, there are in the Chinese language about 44,000 words all monosyllabic, and each having its own character, either simple or compound, to express it in writing. Thus *ma*, a 'horse,' has a simple character, whereas *hsin*, 'faith,' is expressed by a character made up of two others, *jen*, 'a man,' and *yen*, 'words'; and this compound character, which, according to its elements, would be pronounced *jen-yen*, suggests to a Chinaman the simple sound or expression of the word *hsin*. But, although there are 44,000 separate characters expressive of 44,000 words, denoting so many ideas or things, European students have discovered only about 400 separate monosyllabic sounds in the language, so that each of these 400 sounds or spoken words, modified it is true by tones and other devices, has a large number of meanings, and is represented by a large number out of the 44,000 characters before described. Indeed one of the 400 sounds, *ee* or the vowel *i*, pronounced as in French and Italian, has 1,500 meanings, each represented by one of the 44,000 characters. The best illustration of this is the English word *club*, which means a *society*, or a *cudgel*; or the words *vale*, *veil*, and *vail*, which are pronounced alike, but have different letters to express them. If every one of the 400 Chinese elementary monosyllabic sounds expressed an equal number of ideas, each sound would be represented by 110 characters, and would denote 110 different things, but whilst the sound *ee* has 1,500 characters, some sounds have only one meaning, which is expressed by one character only. But there is also another class of characters, 214 in number, called radicals, and these are the elements out of which the 44,000 significant characters are formed in writing. Some of these radicals have in themselves no meaning at all, but only serve to make up with others the significant 44,000 characters. We have in English many such monosyllables, which have no meaning except in combination with other syllables. Thus the word *vir-gin* is made up of *vir*, having no meaning, and *gin* which has a meaning, although wholly unconnected with the meaning of the compound *virgin*. There is, however, this difference between the English and the Chinese: the compound word in the former language is expressed by the same sound combined, which its parts yield separately; but in Chinese two characters, having each a separate sound and representing each a separate thing, denote only one particular thing when they are compounded, and are expressed by a word wholly different in meaning and sound from the two words in their former uncompounded state. Thus, in order to speak and properly pronounce the 44,000 Chinese words, the learner must study the 400 sounds to which those words are limited, but in order to read and write the language, he must study the 214 radicals, out of which the 44,000 characters representing the words, are all more or less compounded in writing. It must, however, be understood that the Chinese themselves generally know nothing about the number 400, which the Europeans have ascertained by their analysis of the language: nor indeed are there many Englishmen who have ever attempted to count the number of separate monosyllabic sounds which are found in pronouncing the 40,000 words of which the English language consists.

From this slight sketch, which has received the approbation of the best English students of Chinese, it must be apparent that the difficulty of learning to read and write that language is a sufficient reason why our knowledge of it is so confined. To speak it indeed is a matter of much less difficulty: for the absence of inflections, both of nouns and verbs, gives great facility to the learner, more than enough to compensate for the system of tones which otherwise are a great impediment to its acquisition.

§ 4. *Syllabic or Consonantal writing in use among the Hebrews.*

At the point which we have now reached, a new and important principle has been introduced into the art, whose progress is here delineated. The original similarity between the symbol and the object represented, either no longer exists or is at all events no longer essential. In the two systems of Picture-writing and Hieroglyphics, the characters employed were ideagraphic, *i.e.* descriptive of the ideas which the words themselves would have represented, and consequently could not be chosen at discretion; but in the third stage of the art, *word-writing*, the symbols, though partly still, and especially in their origin, ideagraphic, yet in process of time had partly lost this character, for they no longer presented an appearance analogous to the objects and ideas represented. According to this system every sound, which the human voice could express, had now its peculiar emblem, and those who were acquainted with a given number of these characters, could make use of them in writing, as far as the arithmetic combination of those characters will allow.

These three methods of writing seem to have sprung naturally, the third from the second, and the second from the first. But the next improvement which was made in this art, was far more important. The necessity of learning new characters for every new word was still an impediment and a burden. By a happy thought it was successfully overcome. Words were resolved into their first elements, and SYLLABIC or CONSONANTAL WRITING was invented. It was found that about twenty characters denote all the consonantal sounds which the human voice can ordinarily express. The number naturally varied in different countries, but the principle was gained, and its development was simple and easy. It is universally admitted that the old Hebrews used this mode of writing, consisting wholly of consonants, which were pronounced by inserting a vowel sound between them. It is true that it might be difficult to know what vowel sound should in every case be inserted between the written consonants: this was left for the reader to supply by his knowledge of the language. Thus the first word in the Hebrew Bible being composed of the consonants B, R, S, T, might be pronounced *Barasat, bereset, birisit, borosot, burusut,* and in twenty other ways, according to the combinations of the letters a, e, i, o and u. Still the sounds do not greatly differ from one another, and a person who understood the Hebrew language well would have no difficulty, arising from this cause, in reading any book that might be placed before him. When however the Jews, in later ages, came into contact with other nations, and their language became corrupted from its purity, they seem to have been sensible of some inconvenience from their old mode of writing: hence arose those diacritical points and other contrivances, which, like the accents and breathings of the Greek grammarians, have for ever puzzled and rendered intricate—

now that the Greek and Hebrew have become dead languages—that which they were at first intended to explain.

§ 5. *Alphabetical Writing, as used by the Greeks and other ancient and modern nations.*

The last step in this progressive art was now to be made; to insert vowels between the consonants of which the Hebrew tongue consisted. When this was done, the art of ALPHABETIC WRITING was attained: the gulf which writers are pleased to describe between the literate and illiterate state was now for ever closed. Not, however, until the seventh or eighth century before Christ, can we discover any indications that Alphabetic Writing was at all in general use among mankind, or at least amongst those nations where the literature of the west had prevailed. First the Greeks, afterwards the Romans, and, imitating them, almost all the modern nations, have adopted this art. The Chinese alone retain their ancient mode, according to which every word has its ideagraphic character; and yet even the Chinese have, in writing foreign names, been obliged to conform in part to a system which prevails over all the rest of the world.

Nearly three thousand years may have passed since that art began to be of much esteem among men, and two thousand since the present style of writing arrived at its present maturity. In the busy age in which we live, the mind of man has suggested many improvements of its numerous details, but many ages will probably pass before mankind will make any fresh advance at all commensurate with the progress that has already been attained in this noble art.

CHAPTER XXXIX.

ALPHABETIC WRITING UNKNOWN TO THE EGYPTIANS, AND CONSEQUENTLY TO MOSES.

In tracing the gradual formation of our present system of writing through the five stages mentioned in the last chapter, I have rather followed an ideal than a real connection between those stages; for it would be difficult to point out any nation in the world where they have all existed in succession. Great improvements are generally slow of growth, unless those who experience them are acted upon by causes from without.

The change from Picture-writing to Hieroglyphics would probably be easy to an intelligent and improving people; and from Hieroglyphics to the Word-writing of the Chinese, the transition would perhaps be scarcely less obvious. But from these ideagraphic modes to the purely arbitrary phonetic system which we call alphabetic writing, the interval is wide, and it cannot be proved that any nation has ever, by its own internal impulses, been able to pass it.* The case of the Chinese is a living proof of the truth of this principle: until they abandon the system of inventing or combining a fresh character for every new word—which is the plan they now follow—and reduce all their vocabulary to a limited number of arbitrary elements similar to our letters, we may assert with confidence that their literature, whilst it increases in extent, will not equally increase in usefulness; and this opinion loses little of its weight from the fact that the language itself is most peculiar, and that none of those who study it have yet been able to suggest any mode of adapting it to the Roman alphabetic system.

But I have asserted that there is a wide chasm between the last stage of ideagraphic writing, and the nearest form of a written language that has arbitrary symbols. Let us then see what is the case with the Egyptians—for they alone of the three ideagraphic nations, by their connection with the Hebrews, concern the present enquiry. In this part of the subject, I find my views confirmed by Dr Wall; and shall therefore make an extract from his work concerning the difficulty which attends the later stages, as I have before described, in carrying the art of writing to perfection.

The ideagraphic system of the Chinese has been now, and that of the Egyptians was formerly, such a length of time in use, that it

* This chapter on the Egyptian Hieroglyphics is here left without much alteration, the same as it was written nearly thirty years ago. Those who have investigated the subject since, have arrived at a partial interpretation of the Hieroglyphics, but I think the principles and line of argument pursued in this chapter will still be found safe and correct as regards the general nature of the hieroglyphical form of writing.

can be hardly expected that any specimens of the primitive [*i.e.* pictural] writing of either nation should be still extant; though, from the extreme durability of the materials employed in Egypt, it is possible that some of her earlier records may have survived the ravages of time. In America, however, at the time of its discovery by the Spaniards, all the writing was of the first grade, so that no species of it could have been of very ancient origin. That of the Mexicans was decidedly the best, though the Peruvians had made a greater progress in arbitrary signs. To register events they employed *Quipos*, or branches of trees with strings tied to them, which were variously coloured and knotted; and Acosta maintained, that by the different combinations of colours or knots they could express their thoughts as fully and accurately as we can by means of letters. But there is strong reason to think, as Robertson, in his History of America, has justly remarked, that the Spanish Jesuit was mistaken in the estimate he had formed of the utility and perfection of these Quipos, and that they were little better than numerical scores, the knots indicating numbers; and the colours, the subjects to which the reckoning was applied. Besides, the signs under consideration not being drawn or insculped upon any surface, the registers formed of them could not, except in a very loose sense of the word, be called *writing*. The pictural characters of the Peruvians were better entitled to that denomination, but they were very gross and imperfect. In such characters the Mexicans had greatly the superiority, and interspersed among these they employed other graphic figures of an arbitrary kind to represent objects of thought not perceptible to the sight. Still their writing could only be considered as an improved species of the first grade, for the prominent feature of it was picture representation of events.*

Where men have not advanced beyond the first stage of the art, they readily exchange it for alphabetic writing, when they come within reach of that very superior method of communication; what they have had no great difficulty in acquiring, they do not particularly prize, and it is at once given up for a better system. But the case is very different with respect to those nations, which had proceeded through the different grades of ideagraphy to its final state, before they got an opportunity of making the exchange in question: the more cumbrous and difficult of acquirement their several systems have proved to be, with so much the greater obstinacy will they be found to have clung to them. In fact, it is a very general

---

* A splendid collection of the Mexican hieroglyphs was published in London, 1830, in seven folio volumes, at the expense of Lord Viscount Kingsborough.

principle of our nature to value things, not so much by their intrinsic worth, as by the difficulty of acquirement, even when that difficulty is in itself a proof of imperfection. National pride and prejudice also enlist themselves in favour of an old established practice associated with the earliest recollections of a people, and render the mind averse to instituting a fair inquiry into the merits of a foreign system. But besides the common cause of undue bias, which must have equally affected the Egyptians and Chinese, separate ones may also be assigned. That which peculiarly operated on the former people was superstition; and how powerful an influence it exerted in the continuation of their unwieldy method, is evident from this consideration—that they could not have been entirely ignorant of the great superiority of alphabetic writing: as a conquered people they must have become acquainted with much of its nature, and of the advantage of adopting it, at all events from the commencement of the Ptolemean Dynasty; and yet five hundred years after this knowledge had been forced upon them, Clemens Alexandrinus speaks of the different species of Egyptian ideagraphy, intermixed indeed with a phonetic use of signs, as still practised in his day. The characters of their principal kind of writing they connected in some way with religion, and called them sacred; in consequence of which they never gave up the use of them, or adopted a mode of writing purely alphabetical, until they changed their creed.* It was on account of these characters having been originally confined to religious uses, and insculped in stone, that the Greeks distinguished them by a name implying both particulars, and called them *hieroglyphs;* but the word is now taken in a more general sense, and applied to ideagraphs of every kind, without reference to either the use made, the surface on which they are drawn, or the country they are found in.

Of the natural tendency of the mind to the first species of writing, some proofs have been already given; and an additional one is, I conceive, supplied by man's frequent recurrence to it after all necessity for the expedient had ceased :—" Naturam expellas furca, tamen usque recurret."

Thus, at the present day, there are primers filled with prints or imperfect delineations of the transactions described in their texts; the imagination being thereby called in to the assistance of the

* "Although Clemens includes the employment of hieroglyphs as letters in his account of the different kinds of Egyptian writing, yet he does not make mention of any kind purely alphabetic. The Egyptians, therefore, had no such writing till after his age, and the oldest they could have had was the Græco-Coptic. But all the remains of this writing which have come down to our times, were evidently the productions of Christians."

judgment to help the young and illiterate to understand writing of a more artificial construction. And in former times, when reading was a far more difficult operation than it now is, there was a still more general application of pictural characters to this purpose. In order, therefore, to judge of the antiquity of an Egyptian record by the appearance in it of such characters, there is a caution to be observed. Should they be found, in a large proportion, in the body of an insculpture, the hieroglyphs would be of the very oldest kind; but when they occur, not in the text, but in accompanying tablets, that is, when they are introduced, not from necessity, but merely for illustration, they are then compatible with writing of a much more recent date. Accordingly, they appear in this way in great numbers of rolls of papyrus, which, though probably the very oldest MSS. now extant, were yet written at a time when Egyptian ideagraphy had arrived at the most advanced stage of its improvement.

It was a reasonable inference that the ancient Egyptians had not advanced beyond the ideagraphic system of writing, which we call Hieroglyphics, until a late period in their history. If so, the Israelites, at the Exode, had no knowledge of what we now term written characters, but only of hieroglyphics, such as they had seen in Egypt. Whatever therefore Moses wrote, must have been written in hieroglyphics; the two tables of stone were written in hieroglyphics, and consequently the Book of the Law, or the Pentateuch, must have been compiled in a later age. The truth of these deductions will of course depend on the soundness of the premises, that the writing of the ancient Egyptians was not alphabetic, but consisted of hieroglyphics only.

To investigate this subject fully, would require more time and space than the limits of this work allow; and yet the conclusion to which the premises lead is so important, that the subject cannot altogether be dismissed without consideration. I shall therefore endeavour to arrange as intelligibly as possible, the reasons which lead to the inference that the art of alphabetic writing was unknown to the ancient Egyptians until many centuries had passed after the time of Moses.

§ 1. *Positive testimony of ancient authors to a peculiar character of writing among the Egyptians.*

The most early historian who has written about the

ancient Egyptians is Herodotus; but it unfortunately happens that his notice of their system of writing is remarkably brief. In the 36th chapter of the second book of his History is the following passage:

> The Greeks write letters and calculate with balls, guiding the hand from left to right, but the Egyptians from right to left: and, doing this, they argue that it is they who do it to the right, and the Greeks to the left. They use two kinds of characters, one of which is called the sacred, the other the common character.

Nothing can be gathered from these words, to decide the question whether the Egyptians used ideagraphic or alphabetic writing. We learn no more than that they wrote from right to left, and had two kinds of writing, but it is not said that these kinds differed in principle, the one from the other.

In the Historical Library of Diodorus Siculus, who lived 400 years after Herodotus, is the following passage:

> The Egyptians teach their children two kinds of letters, those called sacred, and those of a more popular nature.—D.S., i, 21.

The Latin historian Tacitus lived about 80 years after Diodorus. A passage which occurs in his Annals, book ix, chap. 14, certainly seems to show that the writer considered the Egyptian writing to be ideagraphic.

> "Primi per figuras animalium Ægyptii sensus mentis effingebant (ea antiquissima monumenta memoriæ humanæ impressa saxis cernuntur); et literarum semet inventores perhibent."

The Egyptians, first of mankind, represented the thoughts of the mind by means of the figures of animals (those most ancient monuments of man's remembrance, which may still be seen, engraven on the rocks); and they give out that they were the inventors of letters.

Of what letters? it may be asked. Of the letters which the historian had mentioned, namely, the figures of animals which in Egypt were made to discharge the office of letters. The latter part of the sentence explains the former, unless it is supposed to describe a further invention, namely that of alphabetic writing also, in addition to Hieroglyphics. In whichever sense we take it, the sentence is equally applicable to our purpose. Tacitus attributes to the Egyptians the invention of hieroglyphics, and considers these to have been the precursors of alphabetic characters.

About a hundred years after the time of Tacitus, i.e. about A.D. 200, lived Clement of Alexandria, who has already been referred to, see at p. 374. It appears, from a famous passage in his works, that the Egyptians still practised the art of hieroglyphical writing; and it is remarkable that though Clement gives us a tolerably minute description of its different kinds, he describes no purely alphabetical system at all, as current in Egypt at that time.

The educated amongst the Egyptians immediately learn, first of all, the system of Egyptian letters called *Epistolographic*, secondly the *Hieratic*, which the sacred scribes make use of, and lastly, the perfect kind, the *Hieroglyphic*. One species of the last is that which speaks directly by means of the first elements; another kind is symbolic. Of the symbolic, one kind speaks directly by means of imitation, a second kind is written as if metaphorically, and a third, on the contrary, allegorizes by means of certain enigmas.

Thus, when they wish to describe the sun, they make a circle, and for the moon a lunar figure; these are instances of the direct kind.

In the metaphoric species they transfer and change according to peculiarities; or they alter them, or change their forms in many ways and so engrave them. Thus they consign the praises of their kings to theologic descriptions, and carve them in anaglyphs.

Of the enigmatic kind let this be an instance: They represent the other stars, on account of their oblique courses, by the bodies of serpents, but the sun by that of the beetle, because it makes a round-ball of cow-dung and rolls it up with an opposite aspect.

Although this description appears at first sight to be almost as obscure as the original subject, which it is adduced to explain, yet its mazes may be threaded, and a tolerably good idea formed of the various kinds of writing which, according to Clement of Alexandria, were in use among the Egyptians.

In the first place there were three principal divisions, the Epistolographic, the Hieratic or Sacerdotal, and the Hieroglyphic, which have all been recognised by those who in our own times have explored the ruins in Egypt, with a view to elucidating this very matter. It is admitted by almost all who have written on the subject, that these three kinds of Egyptian writing are based on the same principles, and differ only in the greater or less perfection with which the characters are delineated. In the Hieroglyphic style, the figures retain their natural shape with tolerable accuracy, whilst the Sacerdotal writing is more cursive, and the Epistolographic or common writing of the country is loosely delineated and very far removed from the original symbols. A ready instance of the difference between the three kinds may be found in our own handwriting. We have the old Gothic character, the Roman letters, in which books are generally printed, and the cursive letters found in manuscripts.

The identity of the three kinds of Egyptian characters, —I mean identity of principle,—has been generally admitted by the best authorities. Dr Young's remarks upon the subject are as follows:

The question, however, respecting the nature of the Enchorial character, appears to be satisfactorily decided by a comparison of various manuscripts on papyrus, still extant, with each other. Several of these published in the great *Description de l'Egypte*, have always been considered as specimens of the alphabetical writing of the Egyptians, and certainly have as little appearance of being imitations of visible objects, as any of the characters of this inscription [*the Rosetta inscription*], or as the old Arabic or Syriac characters, to which they bear, at first sight, a considerable resemblance. But they are generally accompanied by tablets, or delineations of certain scenes, consisting of a few visible objects, either detached or placed in certain intelligible relations to each other; and we may generally discover traces of some of these objects, among the characters of the text that accompanies them. A similar correspondence between the text and the tablets is still more readily observed in other manuscripts, written in distinct hieroglyphics, slightly yet not inelegantly traced, in a hand which appears to have been denoted by the term Hieratic; and by comparing with each other such parts of the text of these manuscripts as stand under tablets of the same kind, we discover, upon a very minute examination, that every character of the distinct hieroglyphics has its corresponding trace in the running hand: sometimes a mere dash or line, but often perfectly distinguishable, as a coarse copy of the original delineation, and always alike when it answers to the same character. The particular passages, which establish this identity, extending to a series of above ten thousand characters, have been enumerated in the *Museum Criticum*, they have been copied in adjoining lines, and carefully collated with each other; and their number has been increased by a comparison with some yet unpublished rolls of papyrus lately brought from Egypt. A few specimens from different MSS. will be sufficient to show the forms through which the original representation has passed, in its degradation from the *sacred* character, through the *hieratic*, into the *epistolographic* or common running hand of the country. SUPPL. OF ENC. BRIT. article Egypt, p. 54.

A question here occurs, which can be answered without much difficulty. How has it arisen that Herodotus and Diodorus Siculus mention only two kinds of Egyptian writing, whilst Clement says that in his time there were three? It may be replied that Herodotus perhaps considered the Sacerdotal and Common characters to be the same; for they are not very different in form, having both a strong tendency to a cursive form. Or, it is very likely that the third species may have been a further development of the other two during the three hundred years that intervened between the age of Clement and of Diodorus.

Returning then to the description, before quoted from Clement, we find that he says nothing of the Epistolographic and Hieratic modes, but confines himself to the Hieroglyphic as being the most important, and in fact, if our former remarks are correct, the parent of the other two.

Clement, then, tells us that of the Hieroglyphic writing there are two subdivisions; 1. that which is significant by means of the first elements: and 2. the symbolic. Of these two kinds, he unfortunately omits to describe the former, and confines all his attention to a description of the latter, the symbolic style. As the name *symbolic* gives a tolerably accurate idea of what is intended to be signified, namely Hieroglyphics specifically so called, and as its subdivisions, the direct, the metaphoric, and the enigmatic, are mere modes of the symbolic, it can answer no good purpose to occupy our time in further illustrating them. The whole of the question turns on the meaning of that subdivision of hieroglyphical writing, *which speaks by means of the first elements*. After many years of doubt, during which different authors have expressed opposite opinions concerning the meaning which Clement of Alexandria intended to convey by this phrase, it is now generally admitted, that the *first elements* are the *first letters of the words:* and that this mode is, in fact, the link by which Hieroglyphics are connected with the alphabetic system. It is a remarkable confirmation of this opinion that a rude sort of alphabetic writing, founded on the first letter of each word, has actually been discovered among the hieroglyphics of Egypt: but every instance of this sort is so recent as to confirm, without a doubt, the theory that the alphabetic principle was first introduced into Egypt in consequence of its intercourse with Greece, and did not exist even in the tenth century before Christ, much less at the far earlier period when Moses led the Israelites through the deserts of Arabia.

According to this rude alphabetic mode, a word might be expressed by a series of objects, the first letters of whose names spelled the word required. Thus the word 'house' might be represented by five pictured images, Hen, Owl, Urn, Stork, Egg, because the first letters of these names, *h, o, u, s, e,* make up the word required. This mode will readily occur to the mind of the reader as the basis of those spelling books for children, in which each letter of the alphabet is connected with the name of some natural object, as C for cat, D for dog, H for horse, and many others.

The cumbersome nature of this mode of writing is apparent: it has little in common with the modern alphabets, by which thought may be transferred to paper almost as soon as it arises in the mind, and as quickly as it can be expressed in words. There are, moreover, other features of this system, as it prevailed among the Egyptians, which show plainly that it was confined in its use, and only applied where other modes, then known, failed to be applicable at all. It appears, by an inspection of the Egyptian monuments, that proper names alone are expressed by these picture letters, and that each name so written is surrounded by an oval line, as a guide to the reader that the figures enclosed within the line must be read not hieroglyphically, but according to the first letter of each object's name. Again, as the same letter may be represented by a variety of objects, all of which have that letter standing the first in the name which expresses it, the result is that the same word may be expressed by a variety of pictured objects, each different from the others, and this would cause much distraction to the reader's mind, and much uncertainty in the subject represented. This difficulty may be illustrated by a plain example in English. Whilst one writer might represent the word *house* by the five objects before described, *hen* for *h*, *owl* for *o*, *urn* for *u*, *stork* for *s*, and *egg* for *e*, another might represent the same word by a different combination, as for example; *Hippopotamus, Ostrich, Unicorn, Sheep, Elephant.* Neither is this an imaginary theory; for such various modes actually occur on the monuments of Egypt, where the names of Psammitichus, Cleopatra, Berenice, Ptolemy, and other princes, are written with various pictured objects, and it is discovered by a patient investigation and comparison of these, that many of the letters have three, four, six, and even a dozen corresponding objects by which they may be represented. Whether the Egyptians possessed any orthographical rules by which the use of these figures was regulated, has not yet been discovered.

Still, this difficulty being removed, so many remain to impede the general use of this system of writing, that it must ever be limited, as it was in Egypt, to a very narrow sphere of use, and furnishes no argument against the principle for which we are now contending, that a hieroglyphical, and not an alphabetical, mode of writing, prevailed in Egypt, long after the time of Moses and the Exodus.

§ 2. *Absence of all mention of phonetic or alphabetic legends in the writings of the ancients.*

The cursory manner in which Clement of Alexandria dismisses in a few words his account of that kind of Egyptian writing which is acknowledged to have been phonetic, is a circumstance much to be regretted. Still this very omission is not without its significancy, and it strongly militates against the supposition which has within the last few years been advanced, that the greater part, or certainly a considerable part, of Egyptian writing was alphabetic.

The supporters of the theory now in vogue, says Dr Wall (in p. 20 of his work), endeavour to account for the ancients not having transmitted to us a single phonetic legend, by the remark, that alphabetic writers would be more struck with ideagraphic ones, and, therefore, more likely to record such. This explanation very imperfectly accounts for their *total* omission of phonetic examples, and it does not at all account for their giving the writing the general character of being symbolic or ideagraphic, if the greater part of it really was, as is now supposed, of quite a different nature.

§ 3. *Present appearance of the Egyptian monuments and various opinions about them.*

Under this head might be comprised a full and complete investigation of every inscription which now exists; but we must be content to limit our observations to the inferences which have been drawn by others, who have made the Egyptian remains an especial subject of their study. An antecedent argument that the Egyptian hieroglyphics describe ideas and not words, may clearly be derived from the general opinion of mankind, prevalent over the whole world, concerning their nature. This opinion is certainly vague, because it cannot be traced to any better source than the general appearance which the Egyptian hieroglyphics present to the eye of the beholder. In order to appreciate this kind of internal evidence, it is necessary to visit the soil of Egypt, or at least to inspect the large collections of Egyptian remains which enrich the museums of different cities. The impression left on the mind by such a process is certainly to the effect that those sculptures denote pictural ideas and not words or letters. And every attempt to maintain the contrary proposition has hitherto ended in a confirmation of the original opinion, always excepting the foreign words before mentioned. The opinions of different writers may here with propriety be introduced.

The first of these is Dr Young, who started the theory *that perhaps the Egyptian hieroglyphical characters may have the force of letters, and designate words not ideas.* The early death of this talented man cut short his investigations almost immediately after he had pointed out the way in which he intended to pursue them, and left the field open for Mr Champollion: as the inquiries of this latter gentleman have at two different periods led him to put forth views rather conflicting with each other, it does not appear that much real progress was made by him in this difficult subject. In 1812, he published an essay at Grenoble, entitled 'De L'Ecriture Hieratique des anciens Egyptiens," in which he expressed certain opinions, which, not having an opportunity of consulting the original essay, I quote from the little volumes, "Egyptian Antiquities," vol. ii, p. 348, published by the Society for Diffusing Useful Knowledge.

1. That the writing of Egyptian MSS. of the second kind (the hieratic) is not *alphabetic*.
2. That this second system (of writing) is only a simple modification of the hieroglyphic system, and differs from it only in the form of the signs.
3. That the second kind (of writing) is the *hieratic* of the Greek authors, and must be considered as an *hieroglyphical tachygraphy*.
4. Lastly, that the hieratic characters (and consequently those from which they are derived) are *signs of things and not of sounds*.

There is little doubt, we think we may say none, that to the time of Dr Young's discovery, M. Champollion was convinced, as he expresses himself, that the " hieroglyphics are signs of things and not of words." In his letter to M. Dacier of September 22, 1822, on the contrary, he expressed himself in the commencement of his letter in the following manner:—" I may venture to hope that I have succeeded in showing that both the *hieratic* and *demotic* (enchorial) writing are not entirely alphabetical, as had been generally supposed, but often also *ideagraphic*, like the hieroglyphics themselves, that is to say, that they represent sometimes the *ideas*, and sometimes the *sounds* of a language. I think I have at last succeeded, after ten years of assiduous research, in bringing together data almost complete on the general theory of these two kinds of writing, on the origin, the nature, the form, and the number of their signs, the rules of their combinations by means of those among these signs which have functions purely logical or grammatical, and in having thus laid the first foundation of what we may call the grammar and dictionary of these two modes of writing which are employed in the great number of monuments whose interpretation will throw so much light on the general history of Egypt." Not a word is here said of the Grenoble publication; nor does the author any where else in this letter make the slightest allusion, that we can find, to his former opinion on the nature of the hieroglyphics. The author goes on to state, that the subject of this letter is the pure hieroglyphics, " which, forming an exception to the general nature of the signs of this kind of writing, were endowed with the power of *expressing the sounds* of words, and have been employed on the public monuments of Egypt in recording the *titles, names, and surnames of the Greek and Roman sovereigns*, who successively governed it.

Two years after the last date, namely in 1824, M. Champollion published his great work "Précis du système hiéroglyphique, &c.," in which he reviews the whole subject which for so many years had occupied his attention.

The author's conclusion (continues the writer of the "Egyptian Antiquities"), as to the nature of what is called hieroglyphical writing, is this:—"The Egyptians, possessing three different modes of expressing their ideas, employed in the same text that mode which seemed best adapted to the representation of a given idea. If the object of an idea could not be clearly indicated either by the direct mode of a *figurative* (pictorial) character, or tropically (indirectly) by a *symbolical* character, the writer had recourse to *phonetic* characters, which readily accomplished either the direct or indirect representation of the idea, by the conventional mode of exhibiting the word which is the sign of this idea. Consequently the series of phonetic characters, was the most efficient and the most common part of the Egyptian system of writing; by them particularly the most metaphysical ideas, the most delicate shades of language, the inflexions, and, finally, all grammatical forms, could be represented with almost as much perspicuity as they are by means of the simple alphabet of the Phœnicians or Arabs.

It follows from all that has been said, and is indubitably proved,—

1. That there was no Egyptian writing altogether *representative* (pictorial), as the Mexican has been supposed to be.
2. That there does not exist on the monuments of Egypt any regular writing altogether *ideagraphic*, that is, composed altogether of figurative and symbolical characters.
3. That primitive Egypt did not employ a mode of writing altogether *phonetic*.
4. But that the *hieroglyphic* mode of writing is a complex system —a system, *figurative, symbolical,* and *phonetic,* in the same text, in the same phrase, I would almost say in the same word."

This conclusion is certainly not very flattering to those who may hereafter enter upon the investigation of the Egyptian hieroglyphics. But it is sufficient to show that, according to both the theories which M. Champollion has adopted, the Egyptian writing was either very partially alphabetic, or even not alphabetic at all.

The same inference has been drawn by others, who, since the time of Champollion, have examined the Egyptian monuments.

Zoëga, a learned Italian, by studying the obelisks and

other Egyptian remains in Italy, made out a list of 958 different hieroglyphical characters. To suppose that these represented letters is an absurdity; for no known language ever yet contained so many as 958 elementary characters such as we call letters, and, if they represented words— even monosyllables—or simple ideas, which are represented by words, the language was clearly not alphabetic.

Even in the short compass of the Rosetta stone, in fourteen lines, M. Champollion detected no less than 166 different characters to which the same observation applies, that they are too many to be letters, and if they represent words, the language is not alphabetic.

Again, in all the twenty lines, of which the hieroglyphical part of the Rosetta stone consisted, when unmutilated, there were about 2218 characters; and in the portion of the stone, giving the same meaning in the Greek language, the number of letters altogether was 7290. It appears then, that if the hieroglyphical characters were letters, the Egyptian language could express as much as the Greek in less than one-third of the number of the characters. This is surely a strong reason for believing that the hieroglyphics denote ideas or words, and not letters, and it is strengthened by an observation made by M. Champollion himself, that many of the characters in the hieroglyphic text of the Rosetta stone are purely figurative or pictorial, as is manifest even by their shape. Thus he recognized, in the Greek, the following words, *temple, image, statue, child, asp,* and *column*, all of which, in the hieroglyphical part of the Rosetta inscription, were represented by their corresponding figures, and not by words formed out of letters.

§ 4. *Sameness of the written but difference of the spoken language in the various parts of ancient Egypt.*

It has been observed, in our notice of the Chinese language, that its written characters can be understood by all the tribes and nations, notwithstanding the great difference of dialect which prevails in that vast empire. But it appears, from the sameness of the hieroglyphical inscriptions in Egypt, even in provinces many hundred miles apart, that the state of things was precisely similar. The hieroglyphics found on the borders of Ethiopia are identical with those which occur in the Delta near the sea; yet it is certain that the dialects must have been numerous, and differed much from one another in so large a tract of territory. As the inscriptions were of course intended to be read, it is a natural inference that those who spoke different dialects could all read these common inscriptions; but this can only happen when the characters are ideagraphic; *i.e.* when they suggest the same ideas to the minds of persons speaking different languages, for, if the emblems suggested words only and not ideas, they would be intelligible to those only who spoke the language in which those words are found. An instance of this may easily be given. If the following inscription were placed in some conspicuous place

$$30 - 10 = 20,$$

it would be intelligible to Englishmen, Frenchmen, Germans, &c., without the least difficulty; but each of these nations would read it in a very different manner; and the words which each employed would be unintelligible to all the others. Thus the Englishman would read it,—

"Thirty minus ten is equal to twenty."

The Frenchman would say,—

"Trente moins dix égale vingt." &c.

If therefore inscriptions of this kind should hereafter be found in every part of Europe where it was known that the languages varied much, it would be a proof that the mode of writing arithmetical subjects was nevertheless the same, and consequently ideagraphic. This is the case with all the Egyptian hieroglyphics, from one end of Egypt to the other, even where it is known that the dialects differed most, and so identical is the style of the hieroglyphics that it is difficult to determine the age of any of them, for they are the same whether they belong to the 200th or the 2000th year before Christ.* The writing, therefore, of the Egyptians was ideagraphic, and continued so for many centuries, with, apparently, no improvement in its perspicuity, or alteration of its style, beyond the introduction of a phonetic system as we have before described it, to express foreign names, the ideas of which would not of course form part of

* The zodiac of Dendera was supposed to belong to the times of the Pharaohs, until an inscription was deciphered which proved it to be of the age of Tiberius, and many other inscriptions are found of the Roman period, whilst it is difficult to say whether the temples on which they are carved, are of the same date or of remote antiquity.

their usual train of thought, and would therefore have no representative emblems among their usual ideagraphic characters.

§ 5. *The introduction of the Greek alphabet into the Coptic or later Egyptian language, shows that there was no previous Egyptian alphabet.*

Egypt, though intimately connected by commerce with Judæa, and separated from it by a very narrow strip of sandy desert, was later than some of the other ancient kingdoms in receiving the doctrines of Christianity. But it was comparatively late, when we consider its supposed antiquity, that Egypt received the rudiments of learning, such as now pass under that name.

We are informed by Herodotus that the first intercourse between the Egyptians and foreigners took place in the reign of Psammetichus, about the year B. C. 670.

But to the Ionians and the Carians who had done it with him, Psammetichus gives places to live in opposite one another, with the Nile between them, to which *places* the name Camps was given. These places then he gives to them, and he gave them all the other things which he had promised, and he also placed with them Egyptian children to learn from them the Grecian tongue and from those when they had learnt it, the present interpreters in Egypt have sprung.—HEROD. ii, 154.

This account of Herodotus is confirmed by Diodorus Siculus (B. C. 20), both as to the reign in which the intercourse with Greeks began; and as to the immediate consequence of that intercourse. But the latter historian uses a more general term, and apparently tells us that the Egyptian children were instructed, not merely in the Greek tongue, but in Greek learning generally.

And [Psammetichus] being singularly fond of the Greeks, taught the children the Greek education. And in general, he first of the kings in Egypt opened to other nations the ports throughout the rest of the country, and afforded much security to strangers who sailed thither. For those who ruled before him made Egypt inaccessible to strangers, slaying some, and enslaving others of those who sailed thither.—DIOD. SIC. i, 67.

Still later than Diodorus, we find that, even in the days

of Clemens Alexandrinus, who died in the beginning of the third century after Christ, the Egyptian priests continued to maintain their empire over the minds of the people, and still practised their mystic ceremonies in every part of Egypt. But there had been two powerful principles brought into action, which sooner or later were certain to destroy effectually the ancient system. The dynasty of the Ptolemies, beginning 280 years B.C., had introduced into Egypt so large a number of Greek settlers that a sensible effect was produced on the language and habits of the people. It is also said that there were at least a hundred thousand Jews dwelling in Alexandria or the neighbouring provinces. The foreign element was therefore remarkably powerful, and, as we have seen, the ancient hieroglyphical system had been modified by the introduction of initial letters used phonetically and no longer ideagraphically. But it was reserved for Christianity to effect the total overthrow of the hieroglyphics, and to assimilate the literature of Egypt to that of Greece and of other nations. The result of this change was the appearance of a new language, expressed in writing by Grecian characters. The Coptic language first appears soon after the introduction of Christianity into Egypt; and no books exist in the Coptic language, except rituals, books of devotion, and translations of the Scriptures.

There are strong grounds for believing that numerous words, remaining from the old Egyptian, entered into the composition of this dialect; but it is equally certain that the Greek language contributed its share, and perhaps also Arabia, which has so often been mixed up with the revolutions of Egypt, may have furnished a considerable number of words and idioms. All this was the natural course of events, as similar cases may be cited from almost every nation in the world. But why was the Greek alphabet selected as the vehicle in which this new language was to be conveyed? If the Egyptian language possessed an alphabet of its own, there would be no necessity for the adoption of any other. For the same reason, also, the older inscriptions of the country could scarcely have become unintelligible, as they now are. The gradual change of the idiom would have shown itself, no doubt, as it has done in the English language, but the letters, those fixed elements of words, would have been still the same. This, however, was not the fact: for the character in which all Coptic books were written, is essentially Greek, and as different as can be conceived from all the older Egyptian writing, whether inscribed on the public buildings, or preserved in the numerous rolls of papyrus, which are continually found among the ruins. This is a remarkable circumstance; for there is no gradation between the hieroglyphics and the Coptic Manuscripts. It appears, also, by the discoveries of Champollion, Dr Young, and others, that the hieroglyphical system comes much later down than the beginning of the Christian era. It therefore existed contemporaneously with the transcription of Coptic manuscripts, each decidedly different from the other. It was this difference which prevented a fusion of the two. The hieroglyphics were essentially ideagraphic, like the present writing of the Chinese. All attempts to combine them with an alphabetical system are clumsy and unsuccessful. It is possible to express, as the Chinese have done, names by the characters which come nearest to the sounds of those names; or, as the Egyptians did, to use initial letters to express phonetically those words which they derived from their connection with other nations; but the fate which befel the Egyptian hieroglyphics, might probably some day or other fall upon the literature of the Chinese. The result would possibly be that an alphabet would be adopted, in which all new books would be written, whilst their 214 simple characters, with the 44,000 more complex ones which seem to have been formed out of them, would, in seventy years after the change takes place, become as unintelligible as the hieroglyphics. If such a revolution ever should be made, the argument on which I am now insisting will be as applicable to the case of the Chinese as it now is to that of the Egyptians. Their language previously to the change had no alphabet of its own but was ideagraphic, for when at a later date it appears as decidedly alphabetic, it was obliged to borrow from a foreign language the characters which were to form its alphabet.

CHAPTER XL.

MARKS OF HIEROGLYPHICS IN THE BIBLE.

CONSISTENTLY with the theory that the original laws of Moses were written in Hieroglyphics, and not in Alphabetic characters, we may proceed to enquire whether the existing Hebrew Bible furnishes any marks of having been derived from former ideagraphic writings. Such marks would, by the nature of the case, be few and far between; for when the Hebrew Scriptures had once been brought into their present form, the advantage of the alphabetic system would cause the former mode to be practically cast aside for ever, and it is therefore only in the references to other writings, or to facts extraneous to the Old Testament itself, that any indication of hieroglyphics would be found.

The Hebrew has been shown to be the language of Canaan, not only by the testimony of Isaiah, by the Phœnician inscriptions, especially the Moabite stone lately discovered, and by other monuments, but also by the impossibility that the tribes of Israel, settling among the people of Canaan, should talk any other language than that of the country in which they have settled. The language itself may betray marks of an hieroglyphical origin, as it in fact does, in the imperfect manner in which the letters, out of which every Hebrew word is formed, express the meaning which the word is meant to convey. Referring to the five stages through which the art of writing has passed, we cannot fail to see the abruptness with which the arbitrary character of the earlier stage has been changed into its new mode of expression. But irrespectively of this, there may be facts in the history which point to an ideagraphic style of writing. Three examples shall here be brought forward; and possibly, by a minute examination, other instances, though not so forcible, may be found.

1. The first instance of a reference to hieroglyphics occurs in Exodus, xxxix, 30.

And they made the plate of the holy crown of pure gold, and wrote upon it a writing, like to the engravings of a signet, " Holiness to the Lord." And they tied unto it a lace of blue, to fasten it on high upon the mitre, as the Lord commanded Moses.

Whether the words "Holiness to the Lord" are correctly translated, or whether they mean Consecrated to the Lord's service, the passage would have been in no wise remarkable, or at all applicable to our present subject, if its import had been that a stag's head or any other figure of man or beast had been engraved on the plate of gold, but we find that an abstract idea was thereon expressed, and it seems to be plainly shown that the writing was not in alphabetic, but in emblematic, that is, ideagraphic characters; for otherwise the writing would not have been like that of a signet. It is even now less common to see words than emblems and devices engraved on seals. Such devices have a conventional meaning; for instance, a Cupid depicted on the seal of a letter is a significant mark that the object of the missive is Love: two hands clasped designates two persons joined in a league of friendship, and many other such devices are used to express the passions of the mind, and qualities of various kinds. This emblematic kind of writing is, however, now used only for particular subjects, especially those in which brevity is needful, as in the case of seals before mentioned. But the Egyptians used this mode to represent every word which occurred in their language, and every sentiment that found a place in their minds. Thus a picture of the ship Argo had reference to navigation and safety from floods or shipwreck; a bird's wing stood for the wind; the season of the year, or any particular month of the year, was indicated by the figure of some animal or bird of passage, which showed itself at that time. It is indeed true that the number of words, and modifications of thought that required separate words to express them, would soon exceed the number of such emblems, however numerous these might be; several ideas would come to be expressed by the same signs, and so endless obscurity would arise. This would lead to the abandonment of such a system, when the more accurate alphabetic mode was invented. But as regards the case now under consideration, when we find the sentiment "Holiness to the Lord" engraved like the writing of a signet on a plate of gold, the inference obviously suggests itself that a people so recently escaped out of Egypt carried with them a knowledge of the hieroglyphical or emblematic kind of writing, for which the Egyptians were famous.

2. A similar case of hieroglyphics might be adduced in the Urim and Thummim, noticed in Exodus, Leviticus, Numbers, Deuteronomy, I Samuel, Ezra, and Nehemiah. The Greek translators have translated the words *Manifestation* and *Truth;* but the Authorized Version retains the original Hebrew words. Volumes have been written on the subject, which is still as obscure as it was in the time of Josephus.

3. But the third instance to be here noticed belongs to a later age and country, and nevertheless has peculiarities which speak still more strongly in favour of our present argument—the mysterious writing seen on the wall during the feast in the palace of King Belshazzar. A hand was seen suddenly to trace characters, which alarmed both Belshazzar and all his guests. We must take the sequel from the account which the book of Daniel gives of it:—

> The king cried aloud to bring in the astrologers, the Chaldæans and the soothsayers; and the king spake and said unto the wise men of Babylon, "Whosoever shall read this writing and show me the interpretation thereof shall be clothed with scarlet, and have a chain of gold about his neck, and shall be the third ruler in the kingdom." Then came in all the king's wise men, but they could not read the writing nor make known the interpretation.—DANIEL, v, 7, 8.

The wise men of Babylon, it seems, were unable even to decipher the characters, much less to find out their meaning. The writing, therefore, could not have been expressed in the Chaldee, Hebrew, or Syriac alphabet, nor in that of any other known Asiatic language.

In this emergency, the queen recommends that they should send for Daniel, whom Nebuchadnezzar, the king's father, had made "master of the magicians, astrologers, Chaldæans, and soothsayers." The rest of the history is well known: Daniel's reading and interpretation of the writing are thus described:—

And this is the writing that was written, MENE, MENE, TEKEL, UPHARSIN. This is the interpretation of the thing:—MENE, God hath numbered thy kingdom, and hath finished it; TEKEL, thou art weighed in the balance, and art found wanting; PERES, thy kingdom is divided and given to the Medes and Persians.—DAN. v, 25-28.

It is difficult to explain the whole narrative on any other supposition than that the writing was hieroglyphical. If the four groups of letters which form the *mene, mene, tekel upharsin*, had been composed of alphabetic characters, there surely would have been some one among the learned Chaldæans who, even if they could not explain the meaning, could at all events have read the words, seeing that they are in that dialect of Hebrew which we call Chaldee; and as the words have a very intelligible meaning in that tongue, it is hard to suppose that some one or other would not have the acuteness to explain their application. The words have the following meanings:—"*Mene*, he hath numbered" (repeated by way of emphasis); "*Tekel*, he hath weighed;" "*Upharsin*, and they divide." But the word *Peres*, which in Daniel's interpretation is substituted for *upharsin*, and which is a correlative of that word (both being derived from *paras*, to divide), is also the proper name for the Persians, who, according to some chronologers were at that very time in conjunction with the Medes, besieging Babylon. These facts seem to show that there would be no difficulty in finding out the application of the miraculous handwriting on the wall, if only the words themselves could be read. The whole legend is far from obscure:—" He hath numbered [thy days]; he hath weighed thee; and they divide thee [the Persians!]." We are necessarily then driven to the conclusion that the writing was hieroglyphical, or at all events not in the usual alphabetical character as known to the Asiatics in general. But the Chaldees were, for aught we know to the contrary, wholly ignorant of the hieroglyphical system, for the Egyptians and Assyrians, according to all that we know about them, never met but in battle: they were rivals for the sovereignty of the eastern world, and were separated by the smaller states of Palestine and Syria, which often owed their safety to the jealousy of these two rival empires, and sided at different times with the one or the other of the two. Now, we know that Daniel was an adept in the occult sciences, even among the Chaldæans, and was made by Nebuchadnezzar " master of the magicians, astrologers, Chaldæans, and soothsayers." He was no doubt well acquainted with the old traditions and records of his countrymen, the Israelites. We are told that only an hundred years before his time the Law of Moses was found in the Temple of Jerusalem, still, perhaps, written in the old hieroglyphical characters. The intercourse between Canaan and Egypt had been closer than ever under the later kings of Judah; a knowledge of the Egyptian hieroglyphics was very probably kept up, and Daniel can hardly be supposed to have been ignorant of them. It was this circumstance which enabled him to surpass the wise men of Babylon, and to read the miraculous handwriting on the wall of King Belshazzar's palace.

CHAPTER XLI.

STYLE OF THE OLD TESTAMENT THE SAME THROUGHOUT, BECAUSE ALL WRITTEN OR COMPILED AT THE SAME TIME—CHALDAISMS IN THE EARLY PARTS OF THE BIBLE, THOUGH NOT SO MANY AS IN THE LATER BOOKS—REASON OF THIS—CHALDEE AND HEBREW VERY SIMILAR.

IT may, not without justice, be demanded, that I should now reply to an objection which might be made referring to the language or style observable in different parts of the Old Testament. If that volume was compiled and put into its present form all at once after the Babylonish captivity, its style will certainly exhibit marks of uniformity, and also of the corruption, which it necessarily underwent by the mixture of Chaldee words and idioms. This is a reasonable inference, and I believe that facts will both warrant the inference, and confirm the supposition upon which it is grounded.

It has been observed by more than one writer that those who are best acquainted with the original writings of the Old Testament, agree that there is a marked difference in the style and language of its several authors; and one of these in particular concludes from that difference, that it is certain the five books, which are ascribed to Moses, were not written in the time of David, the psalms of David in the age of Josiah, nor the prophesies of Isaiah in the time of Malachi.

But as some of those who have said this, are known to have had little acquaintance with the language in which the Old Testament is written, the opinion before mentioned loses much of the value which might otherwise be attached to it; and the small value which it possesses is entirely set aside by more decisive evidence to the contrary, coming both from those who have always been well acquainted with the original Hebrew, and also from others who have written at a later period, since the knowledge of this language has been more generally cultivated, and received additional illustration concurrently with every other branch of literature and science. Let us then hear the testimony of Dr Wall on this subject:

It is to be observed that never was a human being more venerated by his countrymen than this prophet [*Moses*] was, and that in consequence the style introduced by him was closely imitated by all the succeeding Hebrew writers. This is very decidedly proved by the fact, that although Hebrew continued a living language for nine hundred years after his time, yet there is scarcely more variation of orthography in the different parts of the Hebrew Scriptures than if they had been written by different authors in the same year. Part of this wonderful identity is indeed to be attributed to a cause (of which the remotest suspicion has not been hitherto entertained) which shall be explained in my next publication: but the remaining part is quite sufficient to establish the reality of the imitation in question, and thereby to account for the continuation, through the subsequent Hebrew compositions, of the peculiarities which are found in the Pentateuch. (p. 344.)

Here is clearly stated the fact that the books of the Old Testament are all written in the same style, and the reason of this identity is said to be the veneration which the Israelites paid to the memory of their great lawgiver. But, surely, we must not believe that divine teachers, such as the Hebrew writers are supposed to have been, would write in a style that was in use 900 years before, to the manifest detriment of all the existing generation then alive, out of regard to a single man, who had been dead for so many centuries. I think those who have gone through the preceding chapters of this work, will doubt whether the later writers had any opportunity of imitating the style of the Pentateuch; for if it was in existence at all, it was certainly mislaid and lost, until found by Hilkiah the priest and Shebna the scribe in the reign of king Josiah. But, granting that it was in public use, it may be doubted whether all succeeding writers would copy its style. Dr Wall himself was not convinced of it, when he wrote what has been quoted above, for, at page 362, we find another reference to the same subject.

I have already noticed how very little change took place in Hebrew during the 900 years that it continued a living language after the time of Moses. This undoubtedly is to be attributed principally to the veneration in which the Jewish legislator was held by his countrymen; but part of the effect must be laid to the account of the great fixedness and stability of the Shemitic languages. One of them, the Arabic, is yet spoken through extensive regions of the world, and now at a distance of near 4000 years from Abraham, it still retains a great number of words and also the grammatical inflexion of the verbs, the same as they are found in Hebrew.

Here we have a second reason given why the style of Malachi is identical with that of Genesis, and though it should be admitted that the two reasons are not opposed, the one to the other, yet it must be evident that, if the second reason be the true one, the first loses all its force, and becomes unnecessary; for if the language of the Hebrews was permanent, the later writers could not have imitated the idiom of Moses out of reverence for his character, but as a matter of necessity, whether they would or not. It has indeed been asserted that the Shemitic languages and especially the Arabic, have all this permanent character: but here again a contrary view has been successfully maintained. For all students of Arabic have found as great a difference between the present dialect, and that in which the Koran was written twelve hundred years ago, as exists between modern English and Anglo-Saxon, which prevailed in this country at the time of the Norman conquest. I therefore set aside both the reasons given above, to account for the fixity of language of the Bible, because they are mere suppositions, and substitute a third reason **why** the style of all the Old Testament is the same throughout: namely, because it was all written at or about the same time.

We may now proceed to notice the second objection which might be made to the supposition that the whole of the Old Testament was written after the Babylonish captivity, that not only should its style be proved to be similar throughout, but also the whole of it, and not merely the later books, ought to bear traces of the corruption which it suffered in consequence of that great national calamity; in short, we should expect to find Chaldaisms, i.e. Chaldee words and forms of speech, occurring not only in the books which are admitted by all to have been written since the Babylonish Captivity, but in all the earlier books as well. To this observation it is replied that Chaldaisms do actually occur, not only in the later books, but even in the books of Moses, though for reasons, which will presently be assigned, instances of Chaldee idioms are brief and few.

The only instance which we will notice is in connection with the name of the Almighty in Genesis i, 1, which, as is well known, is *Elohim*, a word in the plural number. Dr Gesenius says, in his "Thesaurus," that the singular of this word never occurs except in poetic language, in imitation of the Aramæan [Syrian] languages, or in later Hebrew.

To this Dr Lee, in his Hebrew Lexicon, under the word Elohim, makes the following objection:

It [*i.e.* the singular] occurs, however, in Deuteronomy xxxii, 15, 17. Are we to suppose that Moses had *imitated the Syrians* here, or that this exhibits a specimen of *modern Hebrew?* The word occurs, moreover, again and again in Job, who must have lived as early as the sons of Israel.

The writer points out truly that in Daniel xi, 37—39 we have the singular form, *Eloha* or *Aloha*, in the mention of a strange god, occurring twice; and it may be added that in the same thirty-second chapter of Deuteronomy we find a still more simple form of the name *Al* or *El* occurring, and that the true interpretation and distinction of these words has always caused much embarrassment to interpreters and lexicographers. The mind of the reader reverts naturally to the Arabic *Allah*, by which name the Almighty Creator is known throughout all those nations which have embraced the Mahometan religion.

If it had occurred to Professor Lee that the Old Testament is a continuous compilation, put together in more modern times out of original documents, he would not have asked the question whether it was Moses, but whether it was the compiler of the Old Testament who imitated the Syrians. If the whole of the Old Testament was compiled long after the Babylonish captivity, we must not infer that Chaldaisms would be found in the earlier books: for the pure Hebrew language, such as we have it, was the language which the Jews spoke immediately after the captivity, and the Chaldaic Hebrew was the dialect into which the pure language had degenerated in the course of the first hundred or two hundred years, after the Jews had returned back to Judæa. But even if the Chaldaic idiom was introduced into Judæa with the Babylonian captivity, we might certainly expect to find Chaldee, *i.e.* Syriac expressions in every part of it, though rarely of course in the early part of the Old Testament, because, as the original documents for the preceding history, had been written before the Israelites had come much into contact with the Chaldees, it is probable that they would contain no Chaldaisms at all, and yet the compiler might be very likely to introduce a few in the course of his labour of uniting so many fragments into one narrative.

The occurrence of the singular name of God in Deuteronomy xxxii, 15, 17, may therefore be both a Chaldaism and a specimen of modern Hebrew, notwithstanding that some writers seem to have thought this impossible, because they considered Moses to have written the Pentateuch as we now have it.

The true difficulty is, not to explain why the name of God in the singular number occurs in the Scriptures of a nation that so rigidly believed in only one God as the Jews, but how it is possible that a word expressive of a variety of gods could find its way into those books. Professor Lee gives us an account, but not an explanation, of this matter:

The plural *Elohim*, used for the *True God*, has given rise to various speculations; some supposing, particularly the elder divines and Hutchinsonians, that the notion of a Trinity in Unity lay concealed in this word; others, again, particularly the Rationalists of modern Germany, have thought that vestiges of a very ancient polytheism were discoverable in it. Both seem, in this case, to have taken too much for granted, viz., that the ancients were guided in their writings by the technical rules of modern grammarians; and also that they were complete metaphysicians: neither of which can be maintained; hence both are probably false. .... The Rationalists, too, suppose that from the occurrence of this word in conjunction with, or separated from, that of Jehovah, they can ascertain the fact that the book of Genesis was originally composed out of two or more documents: one containing the one word, another the other, &c. Gesenius has applied this theory to the book of Psalms also; and has actually ascertained that, in some instances, the one word occurs more frequently than the other. This theory, as applied to Genesis, must necessarily be false, for we are expressly informed, Exod. vi, 2, 3, that the word Jehovah was unknown to the patriarchs: and the probability is, that, if this book is really patriarchal, which I believe to be the case, the introduction of this word must have been the work of Moses, its authorised editor. In all the other cases, the inquiry can afford no useful result.

To these remarks I have only to reply that every inquiry, which leads to fixing an historical fact or removing a popular error, is both useful and important. Let it be granted that the name of Iao or Jehovah was first introduced by the revelation of God to Moses. The difficulty still remains to account for its being coupled with the plural Elohim, as if we should say in English the "Gods Jehovah." This would be a remarkable expression, if it occurred in the Greek or Latin language; and yet the Greeks and Latins actually believed in a plurality of gods. How then is it to be explained? It may be admitted that Jehovah, the specific name of the Israelitish God, was a new term, unknown to preceding generations and even to Abraham, Isaac, and Jacob: but the generic term Elohim—"gods"—could not be a new term, even to a nation who admitted one God only. It may be explained by supposing that the Canaanitish nations, among whom the Israelites settled, and whose language they gradually learnt in the place of the Egyptian language which they gradually forgot, worshipped a variety of gods, whom

they expressed collectively under the name of Elohim—
"the gods." According to this view, the word *Elohim* was
adopted by the Hebrew strangers, when they entered the
land of Canaan and learnt its language—possibly, before
they knew that it had originally a plural signification—and
so the original documents of the early part of the Hebrew
Scriptures contained the expression Jehovah Elohim, "the
Gods Jehovah," which was accurately copied by the later
compiler, though it was sometimes, and particularly in more
modern times, modified into the singular number, which was
far more consistent with the peculiar monotheism of the
Israelites.

Thus then the occurrence of the name of God in the singular number, at Deuteronomy xxxii, 15, 17, and elsewhere, may be, as Gesenius supposes, a Chaldaism, adopted or introduced, unwittingly, by the compiler. But Dr Lee himself shows that it is in many cases difficult to say whether the expression is a Chaldaism or a genuine Hebraism. In his Hebrew Grammar, art. 223, 6 [page 264, ed. 1827], he says of the expressions *he hath called thee*, Isaiah liv, 6, and *thy being created*, Ezek. xxviii, 15, that they are "generally thought to be Chaldaisms. In this case, however, the pause-accent will be sufficient to account for the anomaly."

It is difficult, it would seem, to distinguish the Chaldee and Hebrew dialects. They are so similar that the Hebrew grammar, by the addition of a few pages, becomes adapted to the Chaldee also, and one Dictionary does for both. Vitringa passes the same judgment in his *Observationes Sacræ*, i, 4:

"Sane Chaldæam aut Syriacam linguam etiam nunc experimur omnium minime ab Hebræa lingua differre, ita ut dialectus potius et varia eloquutio, quam lingua ab Hebræa diversa, habenda sit."	In truth we even now find that of all languages the Chaldee or Syrian differs the least from the Hebrew, so that it is rather to be esteemed a dialect or varied pronunciation than a different language.

This will also account for the remarkable fact that the language in which the Old Testament is written, and which we term Hebrew, is actually termed Chaldee by Philo Judæus, *lib.* II, *de vita Mosis, vol.* ii, *pag.* 138, *edit. Lond.* 1742.

The Laws were written formerly in the Chaldee tongue [γλώσσῃ χαλδαϊκῇ] and remained for a long time in the same state, not changing the dialect, so long as they did not reveal their beauty to other nations.

The inference which I would draw from these observations is this—that the common Hebrew is the language spoken by the Israelites between the Captivity and the Christian era, changing gradually, without doubt, as all languages change with time,—that we know nothing of the earlier dialect, beyond what has been preserved by those who have compiled out of it the books which we still have, because no writings in which it occurs have come down to us in their original state—and lastly, that the Chaldee as it is called, is no more than a modified dialect of the Hebrew, existing first concurrently with it, and afterwards, when the Jewish state was broken up by the Romans, superseding for a time the purer Hebrew; and then, like all other human dialects, perishing in due course of time, like the Hebrew which it had superseded.

CHAPTER XLII.

ALPHABET OF CADMUS—PHŒNICIAN ORIGIN OF LETTERS—CONCLUSION.

If it should then appear certain that the Egyptians did not possess an alphabetic mode of writing when the Israelites escaped from captivity, it is an obvious inference that the fugitives, who had all been born and bred in Egypt, could not convey with them into the desert the knowledge of an art, which was still, for many centuries, unknown in the country where they had so long sojourned. The only writing with which even Moses himself was at this time acquainted, was the hieroglyphical, such as prevailed in Egypt. But between the hieroglyphical style of writing and the Hebrew mode, found in the books ascribed to Moses and to other authors of the Old Testament there is a wide interval, which hardly could have expired until more than one generation had passed away. There is, in fact, as we have seen in Chapter xxix, an intermediate stage—the symbolic mode, as still practised in China—between the Egyptian hieroglyphics and the Hebrew consonants. Here then is the most important question connected with our subject. Where and by what means did the Hebrews acquire the art of writing, as exemplified by the particular letters or characters in which the books of Moses and their other Scriptures are composed? A few words on this subject will be sufficient.

The common letters of the alphabet are said to have been introduced into Greece by Cadmus, as some say about 1300, but according to Sir Isaac Newton and Mr Fynes Clinton, not more than 1000 years before the Christian era.

That letters were at that time unknown to every other European nation, is a point which has always been considered as certain, until the opposite opinion was taken up by the Celtic antiquaries, some of whom advanced the plausible conjecture that the Phœnicians, with their merchandize, may have introduced their letters also into Ireland and the other north-western countries of Europe to which they traded. Other Celtic scholars have contended for the antiquity of the northern Runic characters; others again for an early Pelasgic alphabet in Greece; but neither of these systems has yet acquired so much stability as to supersede the current opinion that Greece first, and through her the rest of Europe, owe letters, as well as civilization generally, to Phœnicia. We need not now inquire from what other, more easterly, people the Phœnicians themselves acquired their alphabet; for it is sufficient to show that letters were transmitted by them to Greece, 200, if not 500, years, according as an earlier or later date is assigned to Cadmus, after the time of Moses. Pursuing the train of Grecian history downwards from the time of their introduction, we find that even then four hundred years passed away before Homer lived and composed his poems on the Trojan war. It is also said that these poems were preserved by oral tradition alone two hundred years longer, until Pisistratus, or as some say Solon, and others Lycurgus, collected them in writing and introduced them into Greece. Whatever may be the age at which Homer lived, and composed those celebrated poems, it is admitted by all that they did not come to the knowledge of the

Greeks until about the year 600 before Christ, and were not, in fact, until that time, reduced into the form of separate and perfect poems.

It is well known that the alphabet of Cadmus consisted of sixteen or seventeen letters only : but the Hebrew alphabet has two and twenty. This seems to show that the alphabet of Cadmus is the more ancient of the two. Languages become more varied, and their alphabets more extensive, as time advances. The English language contained 24 letters only until a very recent period, when I and J, U and V, from having been originally identical, have become distinct letters. If Cadmus * migrated from Palestine, as is said, so long after the time of Moses, why did he take only 16 or 17 letters with him, and not all the 22 that had been so long used, according to received opinions, in the country which he left behind him? The natural inference from this fact is that the 22 Hebrew letters were *not all* used in Palestine until after the time of Cadmus; and if the Hebrews copied their letters from those of Cadmus, they would at first have taken 16 only, and afterwards, as the necessity for more arose, they would have increased that number to two and twenty. I believe that this process actually took place— that the Hebrews learnt their alphabet and most of their civilization from the Phœnicians and other inhabitants of Canaan, and that in the age of Cadmus they used only 16 or

---

* I am not ignorant that opinions are divided concerning the age of Cadmus: some chronologers make him contemporary or almost contemporary with Moses; others make him to have lived more than 200 years later. I prefer the latter opinion, on the general principle of not taking everything for truth which is told us by historians, whose aim is to exalt the antiquity of their nation. No books existed in Greece until many hundred years after the time of Cadmus, and I look with extreme suspicion on all narratives, handed down by tradition before books were invented. Mr Fynes Clinton, in his Fasti Hellenici, vol. i, page 86, observes : " We cannot assign more than a century to the period which elapsed from the coming of Cadmus to the death of Eteocles ; which will place Cadmus at about 130 years before the fall of Troy." But the war of Troy is placed by the common chronology in 1180, and by Sir Isaac Newton as late as 900 years before Christ. This calculation makes the age of Cadmus vary from B.C. 1310 down to B.C. 1030, consequently from two to five hundred years after the time of Moses. It is the opinion of Deutsch (*Literary Remains*, p. 181) that Cadmus is the Phœnician name of Hermes Trismegistus, and that these two and also Taaut are names of the same mythological personage.

17 letters, because at that time the Canaanites possessed no more.

Josephus, in his treatise against Apion, chapter vii, says that letters were not known in Greece till Homer's time.

Marius Victorinus in his Grammar, i, 1, on Orthography, says that—"The inventors of letters, Cadmus and Evander, brought letters, sixteen in number, the former from Phœnicia into Greece, the latter among us [the Latins.]

Priscian, the celebrated grammarian, in his chapter on the number of letters in the alphabet, says that "among the most ancient of the Greeks there were not more than sixteen letters, which the Latins received from them and preserved their antiquity uninterrupted."

Isidore, of Seville, in his *Origines*, i, 4, says—"That ancient writing was composed of seventeen Latin letters."

In Cyril, of Alexandria, who wrote in the fifth century, is the following passage on the same subject:—

Eupolemus, the historian, putting together the accounts on that subject, says plainly in the book about the kings in Judea, that Moses was their first wise man, and that he gave the Jews grammar, such, I suppose, as was in use at that time; and that the Phœnicians from them established that science, being neighbours of the Jews, and delivered it to the children of the Greeks, Cadmus having been born among them, and having taught the first elements [letters]. This history is mentioned severally in the Stromateis by Clement of Alexandria, a man of repute and fond of learning, and well read in Grecian literature, beyond most of those who went before. Thus the knowledge of the first elements came from the Hebrews to the Greeks through the medium of Cadmus. (*In Jul.* vii.)

"There is no reason," says Shuckford,* "to think the first and most ancient Hebrew alphabet had thus many letters. Irenæus says expressly that the ancient and primitive letters of the Hebrews, also denominated *Sacerdotal*, are ten in number."

It is commonly said that sixteen letters formed the alphabet of Cadmus; these were $a, \beta, \gamma, \delta, \epsilon, \iota, \kappa, \lambda, \mu, \nu, o, \pi, \rho, \sigma, \tau, \upsilon$. But it appears from old inscriptions that the letter U was not used, its place being supplied by O: if this be so, we must fill up the number of the sixteen letters by

* "Connection of Sacred and Profane History," vol. i, p. 255, 3d edit. note.

inserting F the digamma, which certainly occurs in inscriptions, and had a power kindred to that of U, V or W. As the Hebrew has no U, but a *vau* or *waw*, sounding something like V, W, or F, the likeness between the Greek and Hebrew alphabets is rendered remarkably striking.

Some ancient writers tell us that the Grecian alphabet was increased from its original sixteen letters by Palamedes, who added θ, ξ, ϕ, χ, and by Simonides, who added ζ, η, ψ, ω. But several of these letters occur also in the modern Hebrew alphabet; yet it is almost certain that neither Palamedes nor Simonides ever was in Phœnicia or the land of Canaan, they therefore did not borrow these letters from the Israelites, as is proved also by the nature of these letters, which either are double letters, combined of two others, as *zeta* or *zed* which is a combination of *d* and *s*, or bear a certain relation to other letters for prosodial purposes, as *eta* and *omega*, which are merely long forms of *epsilon* and *omicron*.

If then the supplementary letters were invented in Greece they must evidently have been borrowed from the Greeks by the Hebrews: nor is this supposition so improbable as it may seem; for in the age of Alexander there was a great influx of Greeks into Palestine: Grecian arts and Grecian literature were introduced, and in the days of the Syrian kings, who bore the name of Antiochus, Judæa narrowly escaped from becoming altogether a Grecian province. Here then is to be found the channel through which the Hebrew alphabet, originally consisting of ten, and afterwards of sixteen letters, was finally increased to the number of two and twenty. At the same period also, the limited means which the ancients possessed for multiplying books were wonderfully increased by Eumenes king of Pergamus, who, in imitation of the Egyptian papyrus, and in rivalry of Ptolemy's famous Alexandrian library, caused the material called *Pergament* or *parchment*, to be fabricated from the skins of goats, and on this new substance all the most famous Grecian writings were copied out to enrich the newly formed library of Pergamus.

These facts seem to show that books were first brought into general use and their use finally extended, between the sixth and third centuries before the Christian era. The same inference, too, seems to follow from the prevalent use of inscriptions anterior to that date. Herodotus relates that he saw an ancient hexameter verse—the most ancient then known—sculptured in Cadmean letters by Amphitryon on a tripod at Delphi. It appears, indeed, that before the date so often already mentioned books, as we now have them, were absolutely unknown: everything was carved in stone; laws were promulgated and proclamations issued by means of inscriptions. The two tables of stone given by God through Moses, have nothing to distinguish them from other similar tablets, which have been used by all nations for the same purpose. The Decemviri, at Rome, followed the same mode, which continued to be practised in Athens, and over all Greece, for many hundred years, and within the last few years the Moabite stone commemorative of genuine events that occurred about 800 years before Christ, leads to the same inference, which is not weakened by the discovery of papyrus books written still earlier in Egypt, for they are written in Hieroglyphics and not in Alphabetic characters. These facts lead to the belief that it was not different with the Israelites, a nation chosen indeed by the Almighty to play a signal part in the religious history of the world, but endowed with no peculiar development of intellectual genius, that might enable them to outstrip the rest of the world, in arts, letters, or general civilization.

INDEX

TO THE PRINCIPAL MATTERS CONTAINED IN THIS VOLUME.

N.B.—The Arabic numerals denote the pages of the work: the small letters, i, ii, iii, iv, &c., denote the Chapters of the Bible.

ABRAHAM and Sarah, 231; nature of his religion, 351.
Acts of the Apostles quoted, i, 345; vii, 238, 303; xxi, 344.
Agag named before his time, 138.
Alexander the Great, 60.
Amos; his book quoted, i, 184; viii, 255.
Anachronisms, &c., generally in the historical parts of the Old Testament, 228.
Anthropomorphism, natural to man, 351.
Apocryphal books; their names, 20.
Ausonius; grammatical fancies in his poems, 306.
BABYLONISH Captivity, seventy years, 51; named in the Pentateuch, 268; political, and not so extensive as generally supposed, 294; three captivities of Judah, and three of Israel, 283, &c.
Babylonish mode of building alluded to in Genesis, 270.
Baruch, an apocryphal book, 24.
Bedan, name of judge unknown, 299.
Bede; his elegy quoted, 306.
Bel and the Dragon, 24.
Belshazzar's feast, and writing on the wall, 401.
Books, earlier, quoted in the Pentateuch, 113, 114.
CADMUS; his alphabet of sixteen letters only, 410.
Canaanites; of their expulsion from Palestine, 130.

Canon; variation in the number of its books, 26; its original threefold division, and dates of origin, 194.
Canticles, or Song of Solomon, 23; of dubious authorship and of dubious morality in parts, 205; quoted, i, 207; iii, 208; vii, 206; viii, 207.
Carpenter's Apostolical Harmony of the Gospels quoted, 347.
Chaldees; account of them from Diogenes Laertius, 366; their language; only 283 verses of it in all the Bible, 328, 332.
Champollion; his works on the Egyptian Hieroglyphics, 391, &c.
Cherubim, probably imitated from the Egyptians, 356.
Chinese; their system of wordwriting described, 375; their literature cumbersome, 398.
Chronicles; contents of the books, 22; examination of them, 168; verbal coincidences with other books, 169; FIRST BOOK quoted; i, 36, 168; ii, 159; iii, 274; vii, 150, 235; viii, 235; x, 37; xxi, 267; xxii, 81; xxvi, 243, 363; xxvii, 39; xxix, 39: SECOND BOOK quoted; iv, 86; viii, 264; ix, 39; xii, 15, 272, 279; xiii, 39; xiv, 193; xvii, 86; xx, 39, 266; xxiv, 82; xxv, 82; xxvi, 40; xxviii, 283, 291, 292; xxix, 40; xxx, 82; xxxii, 40; xxxv, 40, 88, 209, 281; xxxvi, 272, 275, 288, 289.
Circumcision named by Herodotus,

249; copied from the Egyptians, 250; common to Egyptians, Jews, and Mahometans generally, 357.

Clement of Alexandria; his account of the hieroglyphics, 386, 397.

Clinton's Fasti Hellenici quoted, 73.

Commandments; two versions of them, 258.

Connection of narrative between the Historical Books, 229.

Contemporary History; its value, 61.

Coptic letters copied from the Greek, 397.

Cyril of Alexandria quoted, 413.

DANIEL; his book thought by some to be an historical tale or fiction, 222; named in the New Testament, 224; in the Apocrypha, 225; his book quoted, i, ii, 188; v, 401; viii, ix, x, xi, xii, 189.

David and Saul; their first introduction to one another, 261.

Davies; his Celtic Researches quoted, 315.

Deuteronomy; contents of the book, 21; book quoted; i, 241; iii, 126, 136, 137, 143; iv, 102, 119; v, 36, 102, 258; ix, x, 102; xii, 143; xvii, 267; xxvii, 102, 109; xxviii, 102; xxix, 269; xxxi, 102, 103; xxxii, 141, 407, 409; xxxiii, 113; xxxiv, 29, 132, 301.

Deutsch's Remains quoted for Hebrew writing, 311.

Diodorus Siculus quoted, 385, 396.

Diogenes Laertius; his account of the Chaldees, 366.

Dion Cassius; his notice of the Jews and of the Sabbath, 257.

Dordrecht; epigram on the synod held there, 307.

ECCLESIASTES, 22; opinions about it, 203; its authorship not consistent with the history of Solomon, 205; book quoted, i, 203.

Ecclesiasticus, or wisdom of Jesus son of Sirach, 24.

Eden; the garden with its four rivers, 133.

Egyptians; anachronism about their enmity to shepherds, 114; their hieroglyphics described,

373; ignorant of an alphabet until a late date, 381; their writing described, 385.

Elohim; plural name of God, analogous to Ali and Allah of the Mahometans, 351; its singular form Eloha, and various explanations of the names, 406, &c.

Enoch; book discovered in modern times, 25.

Esdras (or Ezra); Apocryphal works, under his name, 23, 174; SECOND BOOK quoted, xiv, 175.

Esther; the book of her history, 22, 24; summary of the narrative, 216; irreconcilable with profane history, 218; Book quoted, ii, 219; iii, 217; ix, 217, 221.

Eupolemus, quoted by Cyril, 413.

Exodus, 21, Book quoted; i, 318; ii, 139, 319; vi, 113; vii, 302; xi, 113; xii, 236; xv, 138; xvi, 132, 253; xvii, 100, 321; xviii, 140, 321; xix, 35; xx, 35, 258; xxiii, 254; xxiv, 100, 141; xxv, 101; xxxi, 101, 254; xxxii, 101; xxxiv, 101; xxxv, 254; xl, 101.

Ezra, 22; rewrote the Law of Moses, which had been burnt, 177. His book quoted, ii, 275, 295; iii, 92; iv, 332; vii, 93, 172; viii, 243; ix, 174.

Ezekiel, 184. Book quoted, xiv, 215.

FABRICIUS; his Codex Pseudepigraphus Novi Testamenti, 25.

Farrar's Life of Christ quoted, 327.

GALATIANS, Epistle quoted, iii. 239.

Genesis, 20; Book quoted, i, 242, 406; ii, 33, 133; ix, 135; xi, 270, 298; xii, 123, 128, 130, 139, 298; xiii, 119, 129, 130, 139; xiv, 120, 134; xv, 237; xvii, 231, 250; xviii, 231; xix, 142; xxi, 123, 231; xxii, 142; xxiii, 119, 120, 232; xxv, 232; xxviii, 123; xxxi, 125, 359; xxxii, 132, 142; xxxiii, 121; xxxv, 120, 122, 233; xxxvi, 36, 130; xxxvii, 135; xl, 125; xli, 317; xlvi, 233, 234, 315; xlvii. 315; xlviii, 122, 316; xlix, 120.

Gibbon quoted, 362.

INDEX.

God; his different names, 41; *see* Elohim.
Grammatical Subtleties, especially in the Hagiographa, 305.
Groves and High Places common to the Canaanitish nations, 354.
HABAKKUK, Book quoted; i, 184.
Haggai, Book quoted; i, 184.
Hebrews; name given not from Heber, but because they were foreigners, 311; their writing described, 378; their language still spoken in the time of Christ, 341. Epistle to the Hebrews quoted, ix, 301; xi, 298, 303.
Herodotus quoted, 385, 396, 415.
Hieroglyphics; traces of them to be found in the Bible history, 399.
Historical Books of the Old Testament; a continuous narrative, 28, &c.; chronological summary of them, 43.
Hosea; his book quoted; i, 184; vi, 183.
ISHMAELITES named as same with the Midianites, 135.
Isidore of Seville quoted, 413.
Israelites; different accounts of their sojourn in Egypt, 235; chronological table of the years, 239; spoke Egyptian in Egypt, and learnt the Hebrew or Canaanitish language in Canaan, 309.
Isaiah quoted; i, 183, 184; viii, 243; xxxvi, 36; xlv, 364.
JACOB; errors about his children, 233; his connection with Laban, and the different languages spoken by them, 313; language spoken by his children, 32.
Jannes and Jambres, Egyptian magicians, 302; named by Pliny, 303.
Jehovah, the same name as Jove, 351.
Jeremiah; his book quoted; i, 184; vii, 247; ix, 250; xi, xv, 80; xvii, 256.
Jerusalem; its restoration by Cyrus in harmony with the designs of Providence, 173; its final destruction, 289.
Jethro, father-in law of Moses; variation in his name, 140.

Job, 22, 210; a poem, not a history, 210, &c.; addition to it from the Septuagint, 211; reasons why it might be thought a religious or moral tale, 212; book quoted, i, 363; xlii, 213.
Joël; his book quoted, i, 184.
John's Gospel quoted; i, 345, 347; v, xix, 342, 343; xx, 347.
Jordan; error in the expressions *on this side* and *beyond Jordan*, 240.
Jonah; his book; i, 184.
Josephus; sketch of his life and works, 54, 413.
Joshua, 21; not author of the book, 144; error of *we* for *they* in chap. v, verse 1, 145. His book quoted, i, 29, 76; v, 132, 144, 148; vi, 146; viii. 76, 109; ix. 148; x. 38, 148, 150, 151; xii. 124; xiii. 151; xiv, 120, 151, 243; xv, 148, 152; xvi, xvii, 152; xviii, 123; xix, 152; xxiii, 76; xxiv, 29, 153, 243.
Judæa; excessive accounts of its population, 266.
Jude's book quoted, 301.
Judges, 21; chronology of the book, 47; Book quoted, i, 29, 125, 147, 148, 152, 156, 157, 324; iii, 334; iv, vi, 147; vii, viii, 148; ix, 164; xvii, 157, 359; xviii, 157; xix, 30, 157.
Judith, 24; Book quoted, 299.
KHETUBIM or Hagiographa analysed, 191; its historical books, 194; its poetical books, 197.
Kings; Books of Kings examined, 22, 165; FIRST BOOK quoted, i, 31, 166; ii, 82; iii, 279; iv, 166; 204, 243, 244, 268; vii, 85; viii, 81, 83, 85; ix, 156, 166, 264, 265, 325; x, 265; xi, 38, 204, 268; xii, xiii, 166; xiv, 40, 167, 279; xxii, 31, 265; xxiv, 275; SECOND BOOK quoted, i, 31; viii, x, xiii, 167; xiv, 82, 167; xv, 282, 283; xvi, 283; xvii. 167, 168, 284; xviii, 36, 284; xix, 285; xxi, 287; xxii, 87; xxiii, 88, 281, 360; xxiv, 274, 288, 293; xxv, 168.
Kings of Judah and Israel; chronological tables of them, 48—51.
LABAN and Jacob, 312.
Lamentations, of uncertain date and authorship, 209.

Law; passages of the Pentateuch where the Book of the Law is named, 100; the book sprinkled by Moses, 301.
Lee, professor of Hebrew; his Hebrew Lexicon quoted, 339.
Leviticus; contents of the book, 21; Book quoted, xvi, 247; xxvi, 255.
Lightfoot, Dr.; his note on Eli, Eli, 347.
Luke's Gospel quoted, iv, 349; xxiii, 343.
MACCABEES, 24; FIRST BOOK quoted, ii, 225.
Malachi; his date, 32; book quoted, i, 184; ii, 187; iii, 186; iv, 80.
Manasseh; his prayer, 24.
Marius Victorinus, 413.
Mark's Gospel quoted, iii, v, xiv, xv, 345, 346, 347.
Marriage-law harsh in time of Ezra, 174.
Matthew's Gospel quoted, xiv, 346; xviii, 347; xxi, 345.
Meribah; description of its water, 137.
Mexican picture-writing described, 372.
Micah; his book quoted, i, 184; vi, 183.
Michael and the Devil; contest between them, 301.
Milman; his account of Ezra, 273.
Moabite Stone lately discovered, 399.
Monoliths common to many nations, 354.
Moses, manner in which he is named in the Pentateuch, 111; his own death recorded in it, 116; called a king: meaning of the phrase, 131; his law not observed, 267; its preservation doubtful during the captivity, 271; his law exists only as set forth by Ezra, Nehemiah, and others, 173; called the son of Pharaoh's daughter, 303; name doubtful, whether Hebrew or Egyptian, 319.
NABI or Nebbi, "prophet," an old name among the Hebrews, 365.
Nahum; his book quoted, i, 184.
Names in the Pentateuch, about which anachronisms exist, 118; Hebron, 119; Dan, 120; Succoth, 121; Eshcol, 122; Bethlehem, 122; Bethel, 123; Beersheba, 123; Hormah, 124; Gilead, 125; Land of the Hebrews, 125; Beer, 127.
Nebuchadnezzar; his invasion of Palestine, 272.
Negroes in the West Indies, 318.
Nehemiah, 22; his book quoted, i, 93; ii, iii, 243; iv, 296; viii, 93, 314; ix, 300; x, 256; xiii, 186, 256, 263, 315.
Numbers; contents of the book, 21. Book quoted, x, 321; xi, 140; xii, 113, 321; xiii, 122, 141; xiv, 124, 300; xv, 255; xx, 137, 322; xxi, 38, 113, 124, 127, 137, 242, 322; xxii, 137; xxiv, 138, 268; xxv, xxxi, 323; xxxii, 126; xxxiii, 102.
OG; his bedstead described, 137.
Obadiah; book quoted, i, 184.
Onkelos, his Targum, 60.
Ophir; Solomon's trade with it, his ships, and uncertainty of its position, 265.
PARCHMENT used first by Eumenes, king of Pergamos, 414.
Patriarchs; chronological tables of them, 45, 46.
Pentateuch; Internal Evidence in favour of Moses, 97; against the claims of Moses, 108.
Pharaoh Necho slays Josiah at Megiddo, 281.
Pharaoh's daughter, 319.
Philo the Jew; his allegorical interpretation of the Pentateuch, 277, 409.
Phœnicians introduce letters into Europe, 412; their inscriptions all in the Hebrew language, 312, 399.
Pliny names the Jewish magicians, 303.
Pre-historic records and allegorical narratives, 275.
Prideaux; his connection of the Old and New Testament, 329, 335.
Priscian the Grammarian quoted, 413.
Prophets; their dates and order, 23; form one of the three original Divisions of the Hebrew Scriptures, 181—191; how they dif-

fered from the Priests, 181; formerly called Seers, 161; how their teaching differed from the Mosaical Law, 182; the several prophetical books analysed, 184—190.
Proverbs, 20; divided into five books or chapters, 201; quoted, 201, 202.
Psalms, 22; its extent of meaning, 197; an additional psalm from the Septuagint, 199; five books of Psalms, 200; quoted, xv, 182; lvii, xcix, cv, cvi, cix, 79.
Ptolemy king of Egypt, 601.
Pul king of Assyria invades Palestine, 282.
Purim; Feast so called, 220.
REHOBOAM; his connection with Egypt, 279.
Ruth; the Book examined, 211, 158; book quoted, i, 30, 158; iv, 158.
Rosetta Stone; number of characters on it, 394.
SABBATH, 252; punishment for breach of it, 254.
Samaritan Pentateuch; copies of it lately brought to Europe, 103; its supposed antiquity uncertain, 105; furnishes no argument about the Hebrew text, 107.
Samuel, his prospective description of a king, 260; FIRST BOOK examined, 159; quoted, i, 30; v, vi, vii, 160; viii, 260; ix, 118, 161; xii, 162, 300; xvi, 261; xvii, 261, 262; xviii, 163; xxv, 162; xxvii, xxviii, xxx, 163; xxxi, 30, 361. SECOND BOOK examined, 163; quoted, i, 30, 150; ii, iv, v, 163; viii, 333; x, 243; xv, 161; xvi, xviii, 164; xxiii, 165; xxiv, 31, 165, 170, 266, 363.
Scapegoat; ordinance borrowed from the Egyptians, 248, 357.
Septuagint, 58; its date, 212.
Sharpe; his history of Egypt quoted, 358.
Shishak; his invasion of Palestine, 272; same as Sesostris, 279.
Shuckford; his connection of Sacred and Profane history quoted, 413.
Simmias, 306.

Sinew that was not eaten, 132.
Slavery; its nature and practice in Syria, Palestine, Assyria, 290; its effects on language, 318.
Song of Solomon (see Canticles).
Solomon; extent of his dominions, 244; error in the number of his officers, 264.
Song of the Three Children, 24.
Stuart, Professor of Hebrew, quoted, 338.
Susanna; Book quoted, 24.
TALMUD of Jerusalem, 367.
Tacitus quoted, 385.
Targums, 59; later than the time of Christ, 336.
Tarshish; its doubtful position, 265.
Temple of Jerusalem, obscurely prefigured, 138.
Teraphin stolen by Rachel, 354.
Testament; Books of the Old Testament; their names, 19; their history continuous, 28; division into three classes, 27; compiled from more ancient books, 33; narrative broken and interrupted here and there, 33; repetitions in the narrative, 35; first appearance of the book in Europe, 52; sameness of style throughout, 403; quotes earlier books, 38; its reputed authors, 64; number of books, chapters, and verses in it, 309.
Theodotion; his version of the Hebrew text, 59.
"This day" denotes a long interval, and a later date, 111.
Timothy; Second Epistle quoted, iii. 302.
Tobit, an apocryphal book, 24.
Tradition, always either fabulous or mixed with fables, 71, 75.
URIM and Thummim; meaning unknown, 401.
VOWEL-POINTS later than the Christian era, 338.
Vulgate or Latin translation of the Bible differently arranged, 20.
WALL (Dr) on the Egyptian hieroglyphics, 390, 404, 405.
Wisdom of Solomon, 24.
XENOPHON; his Cyropædia a moral tale, 222.

YOUNG (Dr) on the Hieroglyphics, 387, 391.

ZACHARIAH, son of Jehoiada; his father described under different names, 193.

Zechariah the prophet; his book quoted; i, 184; iii, 363.

Zephaniah, i, 184.

Zodiac of Dendera, 397.

Zoega on the Egyptian Hieroglyphics, 393, &c.

THE END.

www.ingramcontent.com/pod-product-compliance
Lightning Source LLC
Chambersburg PA
CBHW030544300426
44111CB00009B/853